COMPUTER LANGUAGES

COMPUTER LANGUAGES.
A GUIDE FOR THE PERPLEXED

NAOMI S. BARON
Southwestern University

ANCHOR BOOKS
ANCHOR PRESS/DOUBLEDAY
GARDEN CITY, NEW YORK

LIBRARY OF CONGRESS CATALOGING-IN-PUBLICATION DATA

Baron, Naomi S.
Computer languages.

Includes index.
1. Programming languages (Electronic computers)
I. Title.
QA76.7.B366   1986   005.13   85-24542
ISBN 0-385-23214-4
ISBN 0-385-23213-6 (PBK)

To Ma-Baba
Across the World

ACKNOWLEDGMENTS

My indebtedness and gratitude is equally divided between institutions and individuals. The Graduate Institute of Liberal Arts at Emory University provided an especially congenial academic home during the 1983–84 academic year, when the book was conceived. A fellowship from the John Simon Guggenheim Memorial Foundation enabled me to spend the 1984–85 academic year ensconced in the Perry-Casteñada Library at the University of Texas at Austin, where most of the book was written. My special thanks to the Department of Linguistics at UT (where I was a visiting scholar) and to Jo Anne Hawkins, Director of Circulation at the PCL, for most generous library privileges. And finally, my continuing appreciation to Southwestern University, which has extended warm collegial support during the completion of the book.

Robert Horick, Jean Rogers, and Winfred Lehmann have graciously read portions of the manuscript and helped avert some professional faux pas. (I assume responsibility for the rest.) Moshé Zloof provided useful comments on my discussion of the language QBE. My thanks also to Joan Hall (of Plum Hall) and INMOS Corp. for their assistance. Paul Aron and especially Whitney Bolton have saved me from much stylistic embarrassment by their painstaking editing. Felicia Eth has admirably steered the book along the enigmatic shores of the publishing world. But my biggest debt is to Nikhil Bhattacharya, who suggested the project in the first place, weathered all of its triumphs and tragedies, and refused to let me quit until it was done.

CONTENTS

CONTENTS

FIGURES

PART I

THE LANGUAGE METAPHOR

CHAPTER 1

Prologue

To be human is to be linguistic. In every society, people share experiences, express emotions, coordinate efforts, and communicate with one another through language. We all grow up speaking at least one language. Many of us go on to learn additional languages, enabling us to interact with other societies that are now ongoing (e.g. Navaho), preserved in writing (e.g. Sanskrit or Attic Greek), or both (e.g. Russian, Portuguese, or Italian).

But recently a new set of languages has arrived on the scene. These languages are used to communicate with machines, not people. The machines, of course, are computers.

The study of computer languages has become an international phenomenon. "Speakers" of BASIC number in the millions. Pascal recently joined French, German, Spanish, and Latin as languages in which enterprising American high school students may officially demonstrate proficiency before entering college. The newsstands and bookstore shelves are laden with thousands of pages extolling the virtues of one computer language or another. At the same time, computer programming—that is, using a computer to solve problems—has become an established profession. Like economics or medicine, computer programming is replete with specialists and subspecialists, disciplinary gurus, and annual meetings.

For the non-initiate, the world of computer languages can be bewildering and even intimidating. Given the welter of languages, it's hard to know where to begin. Many people question *whether* to begin at all.

For the casual or even seasoned programmer, intimidation is often replaced by rank conservatism. People who have learned one language tend to assume it must be the best language available.

Yet learning to program in a particular language guarantees nothing about the programmer's knowledge of what a computer language really is, how it differs from natural languages like English or Korean, how computer languages differ from one another, and how to decide which language or languages to learn. Most programmers learn the first language they encounter—like marrying the first person who asks. When it comes to knowing *about* computer languages, the average "monolingual" hobbyist (or even professional) has little advantage over the total novice.

PRAGMATISM OR PRIESTHOOD?

In the early days of computing (i.e. the 1950s and 1960s), there was no question of the average person knowing very much about computers. The computer lived in a noisy, over-air-conditioned temple, where it was serviced and guarded by its priests. Natural scientists, and occasional psychologists or sociologists, learned the basics of FORTRAN, but it was the computer operator—not the end user—who actually fed the punched cards containing the program into the machine.

With the development of the microchip, the entire scenario changed. Instead of costing a million dollars, a computer could be had for several hundred. Admittedly, the early microcomputers were primitive by today's standards (no keyboard, no display screen), and you had to build the thing yourself. Even with the appearance of the first preassembled microcomputers in the mid-1970s, there was almost no off-the-shelf software. If you wanted the computer to do anything, you had to program it.

Amazingly, thousands of "laymen"—dentists, teenagers, firefighters—did just that. People taught themselves assembly language or BASIC, and wrote programs to deal with problems they cared about solving (including managing patient records, turning a light bulb on or off, and making the starship *Zennia* blast the forces of the Great Plutonia out of the galaxy). Like the development of public libraries, the emergence of the microcomputer afforded the opportunity (at least in principle) for anyone to learn and create. Gradually, educators began to see the potential of the microcomputer not merely as a way of automating arithmetic drills or simulating chemistry experiments but as a means of teaching children how to formulate and solve problems. Programming became an end in itself, and children around the world began learning BASIC or COMAL or Logo.

New generations of microcomputers have become exponentially more powerful than their predecessors. In hardware, we have moved from 4-bit to 8-bit to 16-bit and now 32-bit machines. A subculture of programmers has emerged that is producing a widening stream of software before which most homegrown efforts pale. Some novices are beginning to question whether learning programming is worth the effort. School administrators who, but a few years ago, insisted that "computer literacy" necessarily include the ability to program in at least one language are now having second thoughts. A new computer priesthood—one created and sanctioned by users—is beginning to emerge.

At the same time, changes are coming about on the professional side. Until a few years ago, "learning to program" meant learning one of a small handful of languages created in the 1950s or 1960s. Today, there are dozens of languages to choose from.

What language does the would-be serious programmer learn? Decision making is typically left in the hands of another priesthood. Students can only study the languages that happen to be taught, and most institutions don't yet teach the most modern languages. Even worse, books or courses that talk about programming languages (e.g. examining what all languages have in common, or contrasting different computer language families) typically can be understood only by computer science majors who have already had three or four computer courses. Students who study only Pascal rarely have the opportunity to learn about computer languages more generally. And people who take no formal programming courses typically end up learning nothing *about* computer languages.

Some vocal computer scientists (who are also members of the priesthood) are satisfied with this state of affairs. Why, they ask, should the average person learn to program—or even learn *about* programming languages—when the chances of writing programs as good as those available off the shelf are practically nil? Why not let the user be a good consumer who utilizes the programs available and prods the industry to create new programs when there is a perceived need?

The critical reason for not relegating control of computers to a priesthood is that the computer is a general-purpose machine. Like combustion engines and electric motors, which produce power for a potentially limitless number of machines, the computer can, in principle, be used for any operation in which information must be stored, manipulated, and retrieved. The computer is so new that we are just beginning to figure out what those functions might be. We have little idea what kinds of computer languages are even possible, and which of that untapped reservoir of programming functions they might be used for.

BEYOND WORD PROCESSING

In the 1950s, '60s, and '70s, many people confused the computer with a number-cruncher, since the overwhelming majority of programs dealt with numerical analysis. (Hence, the name ''computer.'') Today, a sizable portion of users confuse computers with word processors. Many people buy a computer to simplify the preparation of documents and occasionally balance a budget or play a game. To go any further you have to learn to program, and to program well takes sustained effort and training.

But writing your own programs isn't the only—or even the most relevant—reason for learning about computer languages. Then why learn about computer languages? To participate in contemporary culture. To become a discriminating consumer. To prepare for the future.

Participating in Contemporary Culture

Being part of a social group means speaking its language, understanding its suppositions, sharing its folkways. As societies change, so must their citizens' knowledge.

Consider the emerging need for ''scientific literacy'' over the past two decades. With exploding developments in science and technology, especially after World War II, our cultural and linguistic repertoire also expanded. The daily newspapers spoke of *lunar landing modules* and *lasers* and *quarks* and *DNA*, terms with which we needed to become familiar. Average citizens had to start making decisions on the development and use of things scientific: Should we vote more taxes for studying acid rain? Should we declare our city a nuclear-free zone?

Talk of "computer literacy" has joined the ranks of "scientific literacy." Whatever is meant by "computer literacy," it entails the ability to understand the basic terms of computer discussion. Admittedly, we don't go to the polls to vote on computer languages. And unlike herbicides and chemical waste, neither FORTRAN not BASIC is actually hazardous to our health. Yet what you don't know about computers and computer languages can hurt you. Obviously you can waste time and money by learning a computer language that doesn't fit your needs. But more importantly here, you can be intimidated by what you don't understand. You can mistake your own ignorance ("I thought GOTO was Shakespearean English" or "How can computers do garbage collection?") for incompetence. You can invest authority in people who neither understand nor care about your interests. Software producers don't always develop the best programs any more than Detroit always builds the safest possible cars.

Becoming a Discriminating Consumer

Americans are fond of buying new toys and soon relegating them to the closet. Video cameras, scuba-diving equipment, and now computers. Why are so many yet-unpaid-for computer systems gathering dust? People don't understand what to do with them. And it's not their fault.

If you want to learn about using computers, where do you start? If you are in school, you may be told to sign up for Computer Science 1, which teaches, say, FORTRAN. But how many people really have a need to learn FORTRAN? For your purposes, LISP or PROLOG or FORTH may be more appropriate. However, if you don't know the possibilities, you may judge your frustration to be with computers when the discomfort really comes from learning an inappropriate language.

For independent consumers, the situation is equally chaotic. Should you start learning BASIC because it's built into your machine? Many people are talking about Ada and C. Should you learn one of these languages instead?

Learning about computer languages makes you a discriminating computer user. You understand what you want to learn—and why. You appreciate the widely diverse approaches that can be taken to programming the same problem, using different languages. You are in a position to evaluate the claims made about individual languages—claims often made by people who know little if anything of the alternatives.

Preparing for the Future

The greatest fear many people have of computers is fear of obsolescence. What if I buy a computer that becomes outdated within a few months? What if I spend years learning a computer language that goes the way of 78 rpm records? Many users of BASIC and even Pascal have expressed such sentiments.

The simplest way to prepare for the future of computer languages is to learn about newly emerging languages (like Smalltalk and Modula-2 and micro-PROLOG). We must learn to discriminate between professional dogmatism ("There'll always be a FORTRAN!") and down-to-earth pragmatism (e.g. most people using computers aren't doing number-crunching; language software doesn't have to be expensive to be powerful; some of the especially interesting languages aren't widely taught—or used).

No one can accurately predict the future—especially the future of computing. But much of what will be common knowledge in the next decade is already in prototype or being used by a small cadre of programmers. The problem is that average computer users or even many professors of computer science have little grasp of the diversity in the world of contemporary computer languages, much less the prognosis for individual languages.

WHY THIS BOOK?

This is a book about the conceptual underpinnings and empirical diversity of computer languages. It is written for the generally educated reader, including computer novice and programmer alike.

If we are to make sense of computer languages, we need to understand how we can talk about inanimate machines using symbol systems (an activity we typically identify with human beings). And so we'll start (Chapters 2 and 3) by looking at the differences between human language and computer language. Developing the language metaphor, we'll see how computer languages work, how they evolved, what shapes and functions computer languages have, and how (and why) they differ from one another. Part II systematically introduces the spectrum of computer languages you are likely to encounter, at least in the next few years. Over twenty languages are discussed in some detail (a number of others are described more briefly in the Appendix). The book concludes (Part III) with a look at the future of computers and computer languages.

The book has several biases that need to be declared at the outset. There is a decided emphasis on computer developments in the United States. (This emphasis reflects the author's own area of expertise, not any value judgment on developments elsewhere.) You will also find that more attention is paid to the use of computer languages on microcomputers than on larger systems.

And finally, before we begin, a few words about style. The first concerns orthography—the spelling of computer language names. Why do some computer language names appear all in capital letters while others have only the first letter capitalized? In principle, those names that are all capitalized represent acronyms for descriptive titles (e.g. COBOL = COmmon Business Oriented Language). Similarly, names in which only the first letter is capitalized are names in their own right (e.g. Ada is named after Augusta Ada Byron, Countess of Lovelace).

In practice, the computer literature is full of inconsistencies. You will find the same language spelled more than one way (e.g. LISP and Lisp, Logo and LOGO). While there is a growing trend to shift to a uniform format in which only the first letter is capitalized, we will stick to the traditional spellings.

Second, there is the problem of jargon. Like many areas of specialization, the computer world is full of terminology that seems to do violence to the English language. Computer people speak of *inputting* and *outputting, formatting* and *debugging*. In this book we will follow the linguistic conventions of "computerese," recognizing that language purists may justifiably balk at some of the locutions.

And third, this book is full of metaphors. An operating system is like a traffic cop. The structure of Pascal is like the structure of a small town. Organizing the components of a program in C is like putting together components of a stereo system. The decision to use so many metaphors reflects the pedagogical assumption that it is often easier to learn a strange concept through analogy than to approach it head-on.

CHAPTER 2

Languages and Computer Languages

Do Computers Really Use Language?

What does it mean to couple the idea of language with a machine? Normally, we associate language with human beings. People communicate with each other through language. We know that animals all have rudimentary means of communication, and we occasionally talk of the "language" of dolphins or bees or baboons. But here we are being metaphoric. We don't confuse the sniffing of dogs or the screeching of cats with "real" languages like Polish and Potawatomi.

Unlike systems of animal communication, computer languages look surprisingly like the languages that people use with one another. There is a wide variety of human languages and of computer languages. Both language types have precise—and elaborate—content that must be learned. The level of complexity of bird mating calls seems trivial before the subtleties of Arabic or Ada. Human and computer languages both evolve (though in different ways) as the needs of their users change. And unlike adaptation in animal communication, this evolution is often swift and even conscious.

If human beings are the designers of computer languages, it would seem reasonable to expect computer languages to be created in the image of natural languages, and for both kinds of language to work in much the same way. Of course, it's not as simple as that. To begin with, we don't understand enough about the structure of natural language to be *able* to replicate it. More to the point, computer languages weren't originally designed by people who knew or thought very much about the workings of human language. Their purposes had nothing to do with emulating what people do in communicating with each other. The phrase "computer language" began as a convenient metaphoric hook upon which to hang instructions for manipulating the insides of a machine.

But like Dr. Frankenstein's monster, the creature has taken on a life of its own. As computer languages grew and multiplied, as they attracted more users, as computer professionals consciously sought ways of making computer languages more intelligible to the rest of us, the edifice of computer languages increasingly came to resemble that of our own languages.

NATURAL LANGUAGE

Language isn't so much a *thing* as it is a *relationship*. It makes no sense to talk about words or sentences unless the words and sentences mean something. For sentences to mean something, their components must be linked together in an orderly way. A linguistic expression must be encoded in some medium—such as speech or writing—for us to know it is there. And there must be people involved in all this to produce and receive linguistic messages.

Thus there are five interrelated components that go to make up human language: *meaning* (or semantics), *linkage* (or syntax), *medium, expression*, and *participants*.

Meaning

We use natural language to talk about or *represent* things. Objects (like trees), activities (like running), or characteristics (like blue) in the physical world. We also use language to represent more abstract things (like confusion or the special theory of relativity). And finally, we use language to represent things in our imagination: unicorns, Martians, World War III. We do all this by associating words and sentences with objects or experiences (real or imagined) that we want to talk about. The study of language meaning is formally called *semantics*.

Linkage

Languages contain precise (and typically complex) sets of "rules" that dictate which linguistic units can be linked with which other ones, and in what order. The study of such linkage is called *syntax* (or sometimes *grammar*). Even if you learn all the words in the Oxford English Dictionary, you don't know the English language if you don't know its syntax. Syntax determines the order of words in a sentence. It modifies meanings, changing singulars to plurals or present to future tense. And syntax can add variety to language, letting us choose between "I want to ask you something" and "There is something I want to ask you."

Medium

The medium through which we express language is something we tend to take for granted. As linguistic animals, our primary medium of communication is speech (and sometimes sign languages), but as civilized animals, most of us can also communicate with one another through writing.

Our medium of expression may affect the sorts of things we choose to express, or the way in which we express them. We "say" things differently when we speak face to face than when we use the telephone, write to one another, or use computers to send electronic mail or to engage in computer conferencing.

Expression

Among the parts of the linguistic pentangle, expression is the easiest to describe. It's what comes out—the spoken phrase, the written paragraph, the American

Sign Language hand sign indicating "home." Expression is the tip of the linguistic iceberg, the part we actually see or hear.

Participants

Language exists because people need efficient and reliable means of communicating with each other. Yet the relationship between a language and its participants works two ways. The cast of participants in a linguistic exchange ends up influencing the very shape of the language itself. Nursery school teachers don't speak the same way to their pupils as they do to their supervisors. We write letters differently to our close friends than to the nameless "To Whom It May Concern" at the Internal Revenue Service. As we'll see, the nature of participants is one of the most important distinctions between natural languages and computer languages.

NATURAL LANGUAGES VS. COMPUTER LANGUAGES

Meaning

Like natural languages, computer languages serve to represent something. However, that something isn't experience. In fact, depending upon the perspective you take, computer languages represent three altogether different states of affairs. There is the *user's perspective*, the *software perspective*, and the *hardware perspective*.

From the user's (i.e. programmer's) perspective, a programming language is a medium for writing a program that represents a problem to be solved. This program becomes, in turn, the object that the computer language software must represent to the machine. This representation takes the form of binary instructions (i.e. 0's and 1's). From the hardware perspective, these 0's and 1's are the objects to be represented to the internal workings of the computer itself. By using the instructions from a system called microcoding, these 0's and 1's are represented to the hardware as high or low electrical voltage (see Figure 2.1). Representation in computer languages from the user's perspective most nearly approximates representation in natural language. Yet representing an object or an idea isn't the same thing as representing a problem.

In the case of natural language, the real-world object being represented might be a tree; the means of representation, written language; and the representation itself, the letters *t-r-e-e*. While the word *tree* indeed can be represented on a computer (e.g. as the name of a variable or as text to be handled by a word processing program), it's easier to illustrate computer representation by considering the kinds of commands common to all computer languages.

Consider the activity of addition. The problem to be solved is how to add two numbers together. To make the computer represent the process of addition, we need to write a line of programming code in a particular language. In Figure 2.2, we have used a language called Motorola 6800 Assembly Language (the

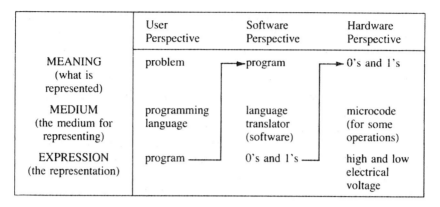

	User Perspective	Software Perspective	Hardware Perspective
MEANING (what is represented)	problem	┌─►program	┌─► 0's and 1's
MEDIUM (the medium for representing)	programming language	language translator (software)	microcode (for some operations)
EXPRESSION (the representation)	program ─────┘	0's and 1's ──┘	high and low electrical voltage

Figure 2.1   Representation in Computer Languages

Motorola 6800 is a microprocessor) to illustrate the process of addition from the perspective of the user, the software, and the hardware.

Even without explaining all of our terminology just yet (we'll do that later in the chapter), we can get an idea of how addition works. The user writes the instruction for addition (ADDA—that literally means to *add* a number to the contents of hardware register A) using the correct vocabulary and syntax of 6800 Assembly Language. This instruction must then be translated either by using a software assembly program or by looking up the binary code in a table. The resulting series of 0's and 1's are then translated once again into electrical impulses. (See the entry on assembly language in Chapter 5 for a more detailed discussion of how a computer does addition.)

Linkage

Both natural languages and computer languages use syntax to join together smaller pieces of language. Yet there is a difference in the *kinds* of rules that

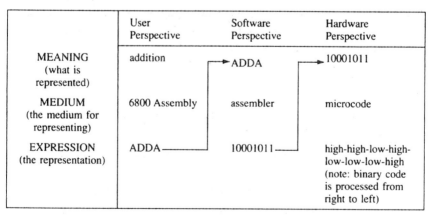

	User Perspective	Software Perspective	Hardware Perspective
MEANING (what is represented)	addition	┌─► ADDA	┌─► 10001011
MEDIUM (the medium for representing)	6800 Assembly	assembler	microcode
EXPRESSION (the representation)	ADDA ─────┘	10001011 ──┘	high-high-low-high- low-low-low-high (note: binary code is processed from right to left)

Figure 2.2   Computer Representation of Addition

computer languages use. Instead of rules for, say, pluralization or word order, we might find computer languages having rules through which to instruct computers to add four numbers, to alphabetize lists, or to have robots weld together two pieces of metal.

Another difference is the sheer number of rules involved. While natural languages have many thousands of rules (and exceptions), the most sophisticated computer languages have only a fraction of that many.

There is also enormous freedom in *how* people can use natural language. We can say the same thing in five different ways. We can intentionally use words ambiguously. We can create sentences no one has ever said before, make up words, or use words metaphorically. And we can even say things that are not quite grammatically correct and still safely assume that our listener will probably manage to understand our intent.

Computer languages have little of the leeway and richness of natural language. If you type into a computer "Slowly the man made his way up the hill" and "The man made his way up the hill slowly," today's average computer program can't recognize the two lines as meaning the same thing. As any programmer knows, most programming languages won't even allow you to forget a period or misplace a comma, much less make a simple grammatical mistake. Generally speaking, ambiguity is intolerable, metaphor is incomprehensible, and novelty an invitation to misunderstanding.

Admittedly, the newest generation of software is slightly more flexible. Spelling and grammar correction programs are beginning to appear that make amends for our failures in basic literacy. So-called natural language front end systems can now recognize phrases as synonymous or detect a limited number of ambiguities (see the entry on Intellect in Chapter 5). All in all, though, the amount of variation or novelty that computer languages allow is trivial compared with natural languages.

Similarly, while natural languages have many functions, the only thing you can do with a computer is give instructions. Specifically, instructions on what switches to turn on or off. User-friendly languages that print "Hello" when we sign on or congratulate us when we do a calculation correctly lull us into believing that computer languages have the flexibility of natural languages. They don't. Instead, they are very much like the player piano that can be loaded to perform anything from Brahms to boogie. Yet the piano itself is no pianist. It is only registering perforations on a paper tape.

Medium

The basic context in which people use natural language is in speaking with one another face to face. Yet an enormous amount of what people "say" isn't contained in the words themselves. It is woven into the physical scenario between the two people conversing: facial expression, body posture, intonation, signs of ease or restlessness.

Besides letting us use non-verbal communication to fill in linguistic gaps, face-to-face language has another important advantage. It allows us to interrupt. We can complain to speakers that we don't understand what they are talking about. We can even protest that we *do* understand, are getting bored, and want to go on to something else.

The rules of the game in writing are quite different. There's no audience present to provide feedback: no puzzled look, no yawn of boredom, no demand for clarification. Authors have no simple way of knowing whether they are being understood. Their only recourse is to be more cautious (that is, more formal and more grammatical) in writing than they would ordinarily be in speaking.

As written languages, computer languages demand the same kind of caution. No friendly listener is sitting by asking for clarification or forgiving our malapropisms. Instead, if we make a mistake on the computer, we are told merely to try again. Sometimes we can figure out what went wrong. Other times we simply stare at the error message, having no idea where to begin. Users sometimes feel like policemen presented with an unidentified body, having no clue who the person was, who killed him, or why.

We have said that computer language is always written language. But what about voice recognition and speech synthesis? Aren't those forms of spoken language? Not really. The computer doesn't actually understand language or speak any more than a dog or mynah bird. At its basic level of operation, the machine only responds to 0's and 1's.

Expression

Both natural languages and computer languages have means of expression. The significant distinctions between the two lie elsewhere.

Participants

Beyond all the differences we have looked at so far, it is the participants that most distinguish between natural languages and computer languages. Empirically, we all know that natural languages are used by human beings, while computer languages are only used *by* people *in order to* communicate with machines.

Spoken conversation allows us to accommodate our language to the needs of our interlocutor (i.e. listener) or the demands of the situation (e.g. expressing condolences at a funeral, being heard while a plane is flying overhead). We learn such "adaptation" skills as children in the very process of acquiring grammar and vocabulary.

Computer languages make no such allowances. Ada is Ada, whether you like it or not.

But the ramifications of having a human being versus a machine for an interlocutor go much further. They define the kinds of messages that can be exchanged, the ways in which languages develop and change, and the kinds of diversity we can expect languages to have.

Take first the issue of message exchange. While students of cognition and language don't yet understand how people actually comprehend human language, some things are clear. To "comprehend" language is to make direct sense of what is being said. If I tell you a tidal wave is coming, you don't translate the sentence into Morse code before trying to interpret it. Your response may be directly linguistic ("Let's get out of here"), or you may just start running. You also have the option of ignoring my comment altogether.

We know precisely how computers understand language because we build them ourselves. And paradoxical as it sounds, computers don't understand the lines of computer language code that we type into them.

Before the computer can "comprehend" a message we input, a lot of translating has to go on. The *kind* of response that computers can give to us humans is also quite different from what happens in natural language exchange. After our message has been translated into "language" the computer understands, the computer *processes* our statement, produces a result, converts the result into language we the human user will understand, and then ships it back to us. The computer-as-interlocutor has only two options: respond to our query or indicate that it doesn't understand the request. There is no third possibility. If the results of a meteorological computer program indicate that a tidal wave is imminent, the ordinary computer can't dash out of the building to seek higher ground.

The asymmetric relationship between human languages and computer languages has some important linguistic consequences. Because human languages involve cooperation *between people*, a new language can only arise (and change in a language can only take place) when a large number of people agree to share the same linguistic conventions. The case of a computer language, consciously designed by at most a handful of people, is quite different. The only requirement is that the *computer*—not people—can respond appropriately to the language. If only one person creates and uses a computer language, it is still a language. However, if I design a language for human beings to use (like Ludwik Zamenhof designing Esperanto a century ago), but no one else decides to use it, it isn't a language in any practical sense.

As a result, while the number of human languages is comparatively small, the number of computer languages is potentially infinite. There are several billion people alive today, but together they speak at most a few thousand languages. In the case of computer languages, it is possible for there to be a different computer language (or even several languages) for every person on earth who uses computers. Already, then, there could be several million computer languages.

How Does a Computer Language Work?

We now have a better sense of what we mean by a computer language. But how do such languages actually work? We know that computer languages give the illusion of letting us carry on a dialog with a machine. To understand how that dialog is possible, we need some basic familiarity with the inner workings of the machine itself.

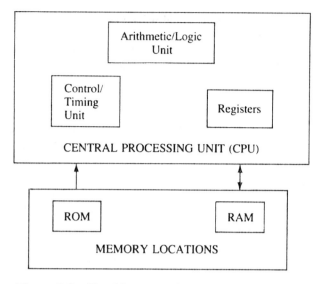

Figure 2.3   Von Neumann Computer Architecture

COMPUTER ORGANIZATION

All modern computers—from mainframes to micros—are constructed essentially the same way. The original design was worked out by John von Neumann at Princeton in the mid-1940s. Figure 2.3 illustrates the von Neumann design.

The computer is a device that stores and manipulates pieces of information. Ignoring for the moment the question of what the information looks like, consider what the computer does with the information once it arrives.

Each piece of information must be stored in a memory location. Some memory locations are filled up when the computer is originally assembled at the factory. The computer is able to read what is in these locations and manipulate the information, but it can't put different information into these locations. Preset memory locations are called ROM, for *Read Only Memory*.

Other memory locations can accept new information each time the computer is used. This information may come from the keyboard input or from files stored on a disk. In either event, the information is "written" into the second type of memory location, called RAM. RAM literally means *Random Access Memory*, indicating that you can access the memory locations in any order. (NOTE: Herein lies a confusing piece of computer terminology. You can randomly access *both* ROM and RAM. Therefore, a more appropriate name for RAM is Read/Write Memory—contrasting with Read Only Memory—because you can both read information from these memory locations as well as write information to them. By long-standing convention, we speak of RAM but think of it as Read/Write Memory.)

The memory locations are nothing more than information warehouses. The information itself doesn't become useful until you do something with it. The central processing unit (CPU) is the place where the transformation from raw materials to finished product takes place. In broad outline, the operation goes like this:

A piece of information is summoned from its location in memory to the CPU. This information is temporarily stored in a register (of which there are several). Other pieces of information are then summoned and placed in other registers in the CPU. Once all the players have been assembled, we can do something with them. It is the job of the arithmetic/logic unit to manipulate the information that is waiting in the registers. There are only a handful of manipulations that can take place. For example, the contents of two registers can be added together; they can be subtracted one from the other; or they can be compared. Once the manipulation has been done, the result is shipped back down to the memory locations, where it is written into one of the RAM memory slots, replacing whatever had been written there before.

Directing all this activity—moving from memory locations up to the registers and then into the arithmetic/logic unit and back to the memory locations—is the job of the control/timing unit. With the von Neumann architecture, only one piece of information can be processed at a time.

The "brain" of the computer is this central processing unit (also known as a microprocessor). The CPU is typically contained in a microchip, a small oblong unit about two inches long and made up of silicon, wires, and plastic casing. The computer itself is full of many such chips (e.g. memory locations are simply sets of chips). However, the CPU is the most complex and powerful chip in the computer. The strengths and weaknesses of a computer are heavily dependent upon the chip selected for its CPU.

Contemporary microcomputers are often classified in terms of the kind of chip they use for their CPU. These chips, in turn, are sometimes labeled by the name of the company that manufactures them. The Intel 8088, for example, is used in the IBM PC, while the Motorola 68000 is used in the Apple Macintosh. The actual names of these chips are important to know, because individual assembly languages are tailored to specific microchips (see the entry on assembly language in Chapter 5).

What determines the actual information to be stored in the memory locations or the kinds of manipulations that will be made upon these pieces of information in the CPU? The answer is, computer programs.

PROGRAMS AND LANGUAGES

A computer program is nothing more than a set of instructions to the computer hardware. Sometimes these instructions are quite specific, telling the computer how to manipulate information and produce a result. Other times, the program states the result that the user wants ("What city has the largest population in the United States?"), and a program within the computer figures out how to solve the problem.

Computer languages are actually special kinds of computer programs. The relationship between programs and languages is a relationship between content and form. Computer programs (content) are written *in* computer languages (form), much as Shakespeare wrote *in* English. The same programming task can be written in more than one language, just as the writings of Shakespeare can be translated into Bengali or Russian. You end up with another program, but one that solves the same problem as the original.

When you buy a computer language, what you purchase is a program that translates the lines of code that you write (according to a particular set of conventions) into a form that the computer hardware can understand. When you buy a book on BASIC or Pascal or C, you are buying a *primer* on those lexical and syntactic conventions. The computer hardware doesn't understand those conventions. And so, when you write a program in, say, BASIC, that program has no obvious relationship to the information the computer hardware eventually receives. It is the job of the language translation program to make this conversion.

If computer languages are actually programs, how do you know whether a given sequence of lines of computer code is just a program (written in a language) or whether it is a language in its own right? Many "applications programs" on the market today (such as Visicalc, WordStar, or Lotus 1-2-3) are sometimes called programming languages.

If we define a computer language as a set of rules that allow its users to provide instructions to a computer for the solution of any problem, then all-purpose programs like BASIC and Pascal qualify as languages, while Visicalc and WordStar don't. However, if a language is any set of rules for instructing a computer (with no restrictions on the range of tasks it can undertake), then the door is left open for the likes of spreadsheets and word processing programs. Anyone who has tackled the more elaborate applications programs knows they rival traditional languages in complexity.

Besides computer language programs, there is another set of programs that are used *alongside* the traditional programming languages. Some of these programs are absolutely necessary for doing anything with the computer, while others make the job of programming easier. In the first category are operating systems, while in the second are editors, subroutines, macros, toolkits, assemblers, linkers, and debuggers.

Operating Systems

Operating systems are programs that orchestrate the inputting of data (from the keyboard or disk drive), the hardware's actions upon these data, and the outputting of results (to the CRT display, to a printer, or back to the disk). Much like the control/timing device in the CPU, the operating system is a traffic cop. The difference between the CPU and the operating system is the type of traffic that has to be directed.

On microcomputers, the operating system is typically divided up into several pieces. Many of these pieces are built into ROM chips directly. The program for starting up the machine may be on one ROM chip; the program for receiving input from the keyboard and displaying it on the monitor, on another chip; and the program for outputting data from RAM memory chips to a printer may be on yet a third ROM chip.

The part of the operating system that transfers information from the disk drive into RAM memory chips, and later reads that information back to the disk, is called a *disk operating system* (or DOS). Disk operating system programs must be specially written for the CPU being used. Any computer using a disk drive must have at least one disk operating system program.

Since disk operating systems are tailored to CPUs, it is in principle possible to run the same operating system on any computer using a given CPU. This has happened with MS DOS (*M*icrosoft *D*isk *O*perating *S*ystem), which is now widely used on microcomputers running on an Intel 8088 chip (or a compatible chip). Previously, the most famous of the portable operating systems was CP/M (*C*ontrol *P*rogram for *M*icrocomputers), which was written by Digital Research and runs on the Z80 microprocessor.

Some operating systems programs which were originally designed for minicomputers and now are used on microcomputers combine a number of separate functions within one large program. Besides managing communication between the disk and the hardware, they may incorporate programs that help you edit your text, locate errors in the program, or even share files with other users with whom your computer can communicate. The best known of these multifunction operating systems is UNIX, a system developed in 1969 at Bell Laboratories. There are also now many UNIX derivatives, such as VENIX, XENIX, and ULTRIX. Another multipurpose operating system program that has become popular with microcomputers is the p-system, developed by Kenneth Bowles at the University of California at San Diego (see the entry on Pascal in Chapter 5).

On microcomputers, basic disk operating systems (like MS DOS) or more elaborate systems (like UNIX or the p-system) are not built into the hardware. Instead, either they are supplied as one of the programs on the "system disk" that you receive when you buy your computer, or you must purchase them separately. A copy of the disk operating system must be loaded from the disk drive into Read/Write Memory (RAM) every time you want to load information from a disk, write information to a disk, or run an applications package. A copy of the operating system program is sometimes already included on commercial applications program disks, and is automatically loaded when you load the contents of the applications disk into RAM. (Other times you must load the disk operating system separately, or place your own copy of the disk operating system on the applications disk.) When you format a new, blank disk, you sometimes put the disk operating system program onto your blank disk at the same time you divide it into sectors and tracks.

It is important to know about operating systems because the computer language that you buy (that is designed to run on your particular computer) is also designed to run on a particular operating system. If you are using an operating system other than the one your computer normally comes with (e.g. using CP/M rather than DOS 3.3 on an Apple IIe to which a Z80 microprocessor has been added), you must match your language disk both to your hardware and to your operating system.

Editors

An editor is a program for letting you input and modify text. This text may be the lines of a computer program (e.g. written in Pascal or C), or it may be natural language text for which the computer is serving as a word processor.

Subroutines

A subroutine is a set of lines of programming code that is used more than once. The set might appear several times in the same program, or in different programs. Subroutines might be written to take the average of a group of numbers or to arrange a list of names alphabetically. Any time you want to carry out one of these common tasks, you invoke a subroutine rather than having to write the program all over again. Programmers may write their own subroutines or draw upon subroutine ''libraries'' that have been developed for popular languages like BASIC, FORTRAN, and C.

Macros

Like a subroutine, a macro is a set of lines of programming code that tend to be used repetitively. Macros are used to simplify the number of lines of code (or even the number of keystrokes) required for the everyday tasks that must be carried out when using a computer. These include logging onto a large computer system, connecting up with a telephone access code, or saving a program and logging off. Macros are invoked by whatever command the user predefines (e.g. a single word or a single mark of punctuation).

Unlike subroutines, where only one function is being performed (e.g. averaging numbers), a single macro can encompass any number of conceptually unrelated tasks (e.g. logging onto a computer *and* calling up an on-line information service *and* giving your user identification number). Macros are especially common in using applications programs, while subroutines are generally used when working with a traditional programming language.

Toolkits

Toolkit is a generic term for several kinds of programming aids. Toolkits generally include macros, but may also include ways of making your programs run faster.

Assemblers

An assembler is a program that automatically translates lines of code in assembly language programs into the 0's and 1's that the computer hardware can understand. All assembly languages make use of assembler programs. However, assemblers are also used to do intermediate translations for some higher-level languages as well.

Linkers

A linker is a special program joining together separate programs and allowing them to run as a single program. Linkers differ from subroutines or macros in that subroutines or macros are placed directly *into* the program you are writing, while linkers allow you to connect several independent programs that come together only when you are actually running (rather than writing) the program.

Debuggers

A debugger is again a program, but this time one that you invoke *after* you have written your program. The debugger is used when your program won't compile or won't run. The job of the debugger is to help you find where you made a mistake and what that mistake is.

PROGRAMMING ENVIRONMENTS

As the use of computers becomes at once more sophisticated and democratic, there is a growing tendency to combine together many of the programs that we have been talking about into unified *programming environments*. A programming environment is a set of tools to help create, edit, test, debug, display, and understand programs. By having available different programs under one umbrella, users are able to integrate their programming activities (e.g. easily shifting between the editor and the debugger). Integrated programming environments enable experienced programmers to use a computer language more efficiently and powerfully than if dealing with individual program components. They also help novices understand how the act of programming is not one but an integrated network of tasks.

Programming environments are sometimes labeled by the name of an operating system and sometimes by the name of a language. Among the programming environments that are also operating systems, the best known are UNIX and the p-system. Since programming environments (and operating systems) are themselves programs, they must be written in a programming language. UNIX, for example, is written almost entirely in C.

The other group of programming environments is defined with reference to particular languages. In fact, the components of the environments are often parts of the languages themselves. The language FORTH, for example, is composed of an interpreter *and* an editor *and* an operating system, all of which are written in FORTH. The newer implementations of LISP tend to function within rich programming environments. The Smalltalk environment has become much better known than the traditional components of the Smalltalk language itself. And even humble BASIC, in most of its microcomputer implementations, is embedded within an environment containing an editor and debugger.

DOING PROGRAMMING: FROM PROBLEM TO PROGRAM TO RESULT

Conceptually, using a computer language is very much like using a natural language. In using language (of any sort), you typically begin with a real-world phenomenon you want to deal with. In the case of natural language, that is usually an *idea* you want to talk about (like the weather). In the case of computer languages, it is generally a *problem* you want to solve (like predicting the summer rainfall in south Texas).

The next step is *formulation*: fitting what you want to talk about (or solve) into the framework of the language you are using. Pope John Paul II can take the same ideas and formulate them in Polish, French, or Italian. A person who knows several computer languages can solve the same problem in COBOL, COMAL, or C. Natural language formulations are *expressed* through speech or writing, while computer formulations are run.

The *result* of speaking (or writing) or of running programs is to bring some reaction from others. A natural language audience may fall asleep, throw a cream pie, or go out and start a revolution. By solving problems, computer languages enable us to chart new courses of action. We may run out and bet our life savings on a horse race, or leave south Texas because the climate is too dry.

The actual running of a computer program involves additional steps. Figure 2.4 shows how these additional steps (left-hand side) mesh with the set of components for using computer languages that we just looked at (right-hand side).

Translator

To run a computer program written in a particular language, you need some means of making the computer "understand" the program you want to input. As we have said, to buy a computer language is to buy a *program* (typically written in another language altogether) that allows your computer to *translate* the lines of programming code you are writing (in a language like Pascal) into the "native language" of the computer hardware (ultimately, those binary instructions telling the computer whether to turn a switch on or off). These programs are generically called language *translators*. Since the "native language" of computers differs from machine to machine, you must buy the translator that is matched to the machine you are using. A Pascal translator disk for the IBM PC won't run on an Apple Macintosh, or vice versa.

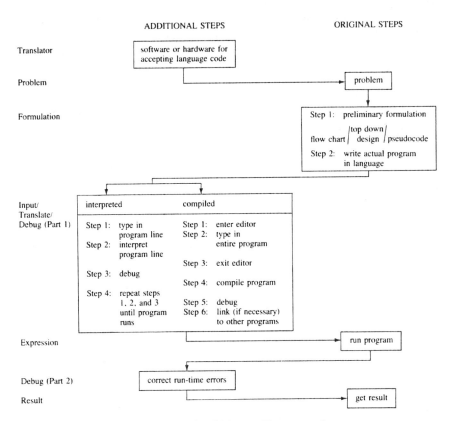

Figure 2.4. Steps for Using a Computer Language

Translators come in two varieties: *compilers* and *interpreters*. A language translator written as a compiler is called a *compiled language*. A compiled language is one in which the computer doesn't begin translating your program until you have typed the whole thing in. Languages that use interpreters are called *interpreted languages*. Every time you type a line of your program (and press the "return" or "enter" key), your entry is translated into code that is comprehensible to the machine hardware.

By convention, some languages are written with compilers (e.g. FORTRAN, Pascal), and others are written with interpreters (e.g. LISP). There is, however, a growing tendency to write both compiled and interpreted versions of languages. BASIC (which traditionally was interpreted on microcomputers) is now available in both compiled and interpreted versions for most machines, and the first interpreted versions of Pascal are beginning to appear.

Is one kind of translator preferable to the other? That depends upon what you want to do with the computer. Compiled programs run much faster than interpreted programs, so if speed is a factor, compilers may be more appropriate.

However, interpreted programs give more feedback as you go along, and are especially useful for people just learning programming or for occasional users.

There are two more useful things to know about compilers and interpreters. First, the term *translator* (to describe both compilers and interpreters) is becoming dated. It is more common today to speak of only *compilers*, and then to add the caveat that some so-called compilers are really interpreters. (Nonetheless, for reasons of clarity, we will retain the term *translator* when referring to compilers and interpreters collectively.) Second, some languages (e.g. FORTH) make use of *both* compilers *and* interpreters. In such languages, compilers tend to be used for those lines of code which are frequently reused, while interpreters are used when the programmer needs to interact with the computer line by line.

Problem and Formulation

The hardest part of programming languages isn't learning the programming languages themselves. It is figuring out how to recast your problem into programming language syntax. (Remember how the hardest part of algebra was putting "word problems" into equations, not solving the equations themselves?) There are dozens of books available on just this "formulation" part of programming.

There are several ways of doing this formulation. The most tempting (but usually the most disastrous) is to stare at the problem and then start writing lines of computer code. This strategy is like deciding to film a movie without first having a complete script. A few directors such as Federico Fellini can pull off this feat—and so can some experienced programmers. For most of us, though, the cost overruns of plan-as-you-go are enormous.

For many years, the conceptual cure-all has been the flow chart. A flow chart is a diagram that isolates the different steps to be taken in solving a problem. It tells you where to begin, how to proceed at each point where a decision or evaluation must be made, and when to end. Each block in the flow chart can then be converted into a line (or lines) of programming code.

An alternative (and more recent) approach has been to see the transition from a natural language statement of the problem to lines of programming code as a series of gradual transitions. You begin by writing out the problem in English. Next you restructure the problem so it reads as a series of logical steps. Then you reformulate those steps—still using English—in terms of the kinds of operations and decisions that computer languages use (e.g. add, compare, if . . . then . . . else). Eventually, you restate these increasingly computer-like statements using the syntactic conventions of the computer language in which you want to write the program. This gradual process is called *top down design* or *stepwise refinement* or *version-by-version programming*.

Another way of thinking about the reformulation from English to computer language is as a three-step process:

> English
> computer-like code
> computer code

The intermediate step here is generally called *pseudocode*. Pseudocode can be thought of as computer language in the abstract. It has the format of computer languages in general, without being written in any particular computer language. Pseudocode can also be thought of as an intermediate *stage* in top down design.

There are two caveats we need to add about pseudocode. The first concerns the name. The term *pseudocode* is ambiguous in the computer world. One meaning refers to this intermediate stage in the *construction* of a computer program. The other meaning refers to an intermediate stage in the *translation* of a Pascal computer program into machine language.

The second point about pseudocode is more subtle. Although pseudocode is typically described as an intermediate stage between natural language and *any* computer language, in actual fact, pseudocode typically looks very much like the popular computer languages taught in high schools and colleges (especially Pascal), but not very much like other computer languages such as LISP or FORTH.

In general, flow-charting is a technique associated with so-called unstructured programming. Top down design, along with the intermediate stage of pseudocode, tend to be associated with so-called structured programming (see the beginning of Chapter 3 and the entry on ALGOL in Chapter 5).

Input/Translate/Debug (Part 1)

Once the program is coded (i.e. written in a computer language), it must be entered into the computer. With *interpreted* languages, you enter a line of programming code by directly typing it in. The editor (which lets you enter text, make corrections, or change things around) is always available, mixed in with the interpreter itself. As soon as the line is entered, the interpreter translates it into machine-executable code. If you have made a syntactic error (like forgetting a closing parenthesis), the machine immediately informs you that you have a "bug" (that is, a mistake) in your program. Depending upon how the interpreter is written, you may be told only that there is a mistake somewhere in the line. Alternatively, the error message might explain just what the bug (or bugs) might be. Some of the more modern interpreters even correct simple mistakes for you. Each line in the program is entered in succession, just this way.

With *compiled* languages, you begin quite differently. The first thing you type is the command to enter the editor. (The editor is a separate program— typically part of the operating system.) You then type in your program, correct any typographical errors, and exit the editor. It is only at this point that you begin to use the language translator by giving the command to compile your program. On a microcomputer that runs only one language at a time, you simply give the "compile" command. On a large machine that has several resident languages, you must specify which language compiler you wish to invoke.

Occasionally, the program will compile the first time around. More typically, you will get one or more error messages indicating "bugs" in your program. Once you figure out what the problem is, you must reenter the editor, make the corrections, exit the editor, and then try to compile the program again. In most cases the compiled version is actually stored on the disk. When you want to rerun a program, you simply call up the compiled code and don't need to recompile the code again. In interpreted languages, each line of original source code must be reinterpreted each time the program is run. This process can become quite time-consuming.

Compiled languages often require one more step—called *linking*—before actually running your program. Some languages, such as FORTRAN, COBOL, and C, let you write complex programs containing other programs stored somewhere else (written by you or someone else). Rather than physically typing these programs into your new program, you use a linker program to join together the compiled versions of these existing programs with the compiled version of your new program.

Expression

Finally the program is ready to run. For interpreted and compiled languages alike, there is a simple "run" command. With luck, you get a result straightaway.

Debug (Part 2)

Unfortunately, luck is not always with you. What you get instead is one or more error messages. These are *run-time errors*, that is, bugs that don't show up until the computer follows through the actual lines of programming code step by step. Remember that when the computer interpreted or compiled the program earlier, it was merely translating, line by line, from one language to another. At run time, the computer actually attempts to make sense of all those lines, taken together.

The first kind of bugs we saw (while interpreting or compiling) were typically *syntactic* mistakes. The errors we encounter at run time are generally *semantic* mistakes, that is, mistakes in the way we put statements *together*. If failure to include a closing parenthesis is a syntactic mistake, a semantic mistake might be failure to include a "then" statement if you have an "if" statement several lines earlier. Syntactic mistakes are usually easier to find than semantic mistakes. Syntactic errors can generally be located if you are sufficiently painstaking in your proofreading. Since semantic errors can involve problems in the way the program has been logically conceived, they often prove stubbornly elusive.

Result

When the program runs and produces a result, we can evaluate our findings and act upon them. However, we must be careful not to act too hastily. A program may compile immediately and run without a hitch, but yield an answer that is totally wrong. The program still contains a semantic error, but one that did not show up during the second debugging phase. Here you have to rely upon *human* knowledge of the problem, including knowledge of what might be a likely solution. The computer can help you pinpoint your mechanical mistakes. As of now, though, it can do little about faulty reasoning.

The Growth of Computer Languages

We have talked about computer languages conceptually (how they differ from natural languages) and practically (how they work on machines). Our next step is to look at them historically: how these languages emerged in the first place and how they have developed. To do so, we need to understand the symbiotic relationship between computer hardware and software, and the evolution of the hardware upon which computer languages necessarily depend.

THE SYMBIOSIS OF HARDWARE AND SOFTWARE

The most obvious link between hardware and software is memory space. Languages that need large amounts of RAM can become widespread only when there is affordable hardware with sufficient memory space. When microcomputers had only four kilobytes of internal memory and their disk space was meager as well, the average person could not hope to use memory-hungry languages like LISP and Ada. As the price of internal machine memory declines, and the amount of memory available on disks increases, users will be able to choose among a wider range of languages.

The symbiosis between hardware and software becomes even more interesting when we begin to talk about functional equivalences. Anything you can put into software (including language translators, applications programs, or even data) can also be built into hardware. That is, the motherboard of the computer (i.e. the large plastic board that holds the basic hardware) has a microchip (or microchips) with the programs or data burned into ROM (i.e. permanent memory locations). Built-in software is commonly called *firmware*.

In the early days of microcomputers, no languages were "resident" in hardware. If you had an Apple II and wanted to write a program in BASIC, you first had to load a copy of the BASIC language translator into RAM (i.e. temporary memory locations).

As microchip technology improved (and prices began to fall), it became feasible to build more programs into the hardware itself. Some computer companies built several languages into their hardware. Other companies built special-purpose computers (e.g. calorie counters) that had resident data banks with the number of calories in a small tossed salad or in a hot fudge sundae, and a program that calculated your quota for the day. A third avenue (taken by Texas Instruments for its home computer) was to build programs that were sold like software but ran like hardware. Instead of using standard floppy disks, TI's personal computers ran with "cartridges" that had ROM chips built into them. By inserting a cartridge, you actually extended the machine's hardware capabilities.

Despite contemporary symbiosis, computer hardware and software have undergone separate evolutions. An obvious way to distinguish between generations of hardware and software is in terms of continuity. In hardware, when you enter a new generation, the previous one eventually declines in the face of new technological superiority.

The case of computer languages is very different. The notion of "generation" is more loosely metaphorical with computer languages than with computer hardware. New generations of computer languages generally *add to* the types of computer languages already present. So far, only one of these types has been replaced by its historical successor (though many dozens of individual languages have faded from view).

HARDWARE GENERATIONS

We commonly talk about five generations of hardware. These generations—along with their major characteristics—are summarized in Figure 2.5.

In the nearly four decades since the building of the first computer, four trends have characterized hardware development. First, computers continue to become *more powerful*. They are able to process growing amounts of information using increasingly sophisticated memory and processing devices. Second, hardware continues to become *more reliable*. Chips don't burn out as easily as they used to, and random errors caused by hardware flukes have become much less frequent. Third, hardware continues to become *more compact*. The computing power of an IBM mainframe or a VAX minicomputer can now be housed on a single microchip, and powerful hand-held computers are becoming a reality. Finally, hardware continues to become *less expensive*. The price of powerful computers has fallen from the millions of dollars to the thousands into the hundreds. Already the cost of software—even for the home computer user—is beginning to match or outstrip hardware expenses. A growing number of users now choose their hardware on the basis of software needs.

LANGUAGE GENERATIONS

Talk of "generations" in computer languages is much less neat. Terminology for discussing computer language generations isn't standardized. In fact, some people avoid using generational terms altogether, and speak instead of "levels" of computer languages.

Low-level languages are directly tied to particular machine hardware, while *high-level languages* can, in principle, be used on any machine. Historically, low-level languages developed first, and high-level languages followed almost a decade later. Low-level languages include machine languages and assembly languages, while high-level languages include the likes of FORTRAN, Pascal, and Modula-2. We'll need to keep in mind that the low-level/high-level distinction was created to describe just one class of computer languages, a group called imperative/algorithmic (see Chapter 3). The term *high-level* may not be appropriate for describing some of the other language types we will be talking about in this book.

TIME	GENERATION	DESCRIPTION
1940s	First Generation (vacuum tubes)	The earliest digital computers used thousands of vacuum tubes to conduct electricity. The first such computer, the ENIAC, was developed by John Mauchly and Presper Eckert in 1946 at the University of Pennsylvania, and used over 18,000 vacuum tubes. Mauchly and Eckert's work was partially based on earlier work by John Atanasoff at Iowa State University.
late 1950s	Second Generation (transistors)	The invention of transistors in the late 1950s improved the functioning of computers in many ways: transistors were smaller than vacuum tubes, produced much less heat, and were far more reliable.
1964	Third Generation (integrated circuit chips)	The development of integrated circuits in 1964 enabled computers to be even smaller, to run faster, and to be yet more reliable. Because integrated circuits (that is, many electrical circuits placed on a single slice of silicon) were relatively inexpensive, it became possible for thousands of companies to afford computers.
mid-1970s to present	Fourth Generation (large and very large scale integrated chips)	Continued development in electronics in the 1970s made it possible to put an ever-increasing number of circuits on a single chip (known first as large scale integration and now very large scale integration, or VLSI). With the development of VLSI, computers became yet smaller, yet more reliable, and yet less expensive. VLSI technology made the microcomputer revolution possible.
present and future	Fifth Generation (parallel processing)	These machines are still on the drawing board. In 1981, the Japanese announced a national project to create the next generation of computers that would, among other things, function with ordinary language input. Similar projects were soon announced in Europe and in the United States. Current prototypes for these machines use several microprocessors simultaneously (so-called parallel processing) rather than a single processor (i.e. following von Neumann architecture).

Figure 2.5   Generations of Computer Hardware

First-generation languages are generally defined as low-level languages—machine languages and assembly languages. Machine language (or machine *code*) is made up of sequences of binary numbers (0's and 1's) used for turning switches on and off in the computer hardware. Machine language came into being, by definition, with the development of the first computers. Yet these are not languages in any serious sense. They are only sets of notes to ourselves on which switches to turn on and off. Assembly languages are more natural-language-like shorthand codes for machine language. Each line of assembly code directly corresponds to a sequence of machine code. Assembly languages use mnemonic terms like ADD (see Figure 2.2 above) in place of binary sequences of 0's and 1's.

Second-generation languages are more confusing. The name is usually applied to *early* versions of the first high-level programming languages like FORTRAN and COBOL in the latter half of the 1950s and the early 1960s. As our understanding of how to program computers became more sophisticated, new languages were developed that incorporated more modern syntactic conventions.

Another novelty of these emerging languages was that they could (in principle) deal with any kind of problem, while the original (second-generation) languages had specialized functions (science and mathematics in the case of FORTRAN, and business in the case of COBOL). These newer languages, like PL/I and ALGOL, came to be called *third-generation languages*. More recent languages developing out of this tradition (e.g. Pascal, C, or Ada) are still called third-generation languages.

At the same time, though, the early languages (e.g. early FORTRAN, early COBOL) began incorporating some of these more modern structures and functions. What was originally a second-generation language (e.g. early FORTRAN) now became a third-generation language (later FORTRAN). All of these languages taken together (that is, the revised second-generation languages along with the newer third-generation languages) are generally called high-level languages to contrast them with low-level (= first-generation) languages, i.e. machine code and assembly language.

There has been much recent interest in a *fourth generation* of languages. The meaning of this term tends to be confusing, but for somewhat different reasons. In the business world, people speak of "fourth-generation languages" when referring to language-like interfaces that allow personnel with no formal training in computer languages to access large data bases. These languages include Query-by-Example (QBE), Intellect, Themis, and Clout. Typically, such languages are *non-procedural* or *descriptive* languages, in that the programmer specifies *what* the problem to be solved is ("What city has the largest population in the United States?") rather than *how* the computer should solve the problem. This non-procedural approach to programming is used not only by modern business-oriented languages but also by more general-purpose languages like PROLOG or Smalltalk.

Is there a *fifth generation* of languages in the offing? When talking of "fifth-generation machines," the "fifth" generally refers to hardware and to a general

GENERATION	First	Second	Third	Fourth	Fifth
CLASSES OF LANGUAGES	machine, assembly	e.g. early FORTRAN early COBOL	e.g. later FORTRAN later COBOL Pascal Ada	non-procedural	natural language-like
LEVEL	low	high			
YEARS	1940s	1950s early 1960s	1960s to present	1980s	1990s

Figure 2.6   Generations and Levels of Computer Languages

approach to computing, not to a fifth generation of languages. The languages now being used for fifth-generation machine prototypes tend to be non-procedural, so the term *fourth-generation languages* currently suffices. However, as work progresses on fifth-generation hardware (and conceptual design), a new "fifth generation" of languages may eventually emerge that has the external appearance of at least a subset of natural language.

Figure 2.6 on page 31 summarizes the language levels and generations we have been discussing.

As in the case of computer hardware, the development of computer languages can be characterized by four trends. First, computer languages continue to become *more structured*. By a structured language, we mean one in which the lines of code are grouped into logical units rather than being strung together laundry-list fashion. Second, computer languages continue to become *more sophisticated*. Although the von Neumann architecture is still only capable of executing a very limited number of operations (basically addition, subtraction, comparison, and movement of information from one location to another), programmers can now use high-level languages to help them conceptualize problems and hence do their encoding more abstractly. The language translator bridges the gap between the high level of abstraction at which the programmer is working (e.g. conditional statements) and the low level at which the hardware functions (e.g. addition, comparison).

Third, there continues to be *increasing variety* in the kinds of computer languages available. Users can now select a language that is well suited to their application needs, their previous experience in programming, and even their pocketbooks rather than having to choose only among chocolate, vanilla, and strawberry (which has typically meant BASIC, FORTRAN, and COBOL). And fourth, languages continue to become *less machine-dependent* through the establishment of national or international language standards.

CHAPTER 3

Form and Function

Computer languages are initially confusing because there are so many of them. In the popular press, several dozen are talked about. Among computer experts, the list reaches into the hundreds. And the number is still growing. However, the chaos begins to subside when we begin to cluster computer languages into *types*.

Language Types

Think of all the vehicles in the nearest parking lot. There are various ways they could be grouped. They might be arranged by color, number of doors, or model year. Alternatively, we might organize them by manufacturer, maximum number of passengers, or urgency with which they need to be washed.

In general, there are three common ways we classify things. We can consider what they look like, that is, their *structure*. We can divide up items with respect to what they do, that is, their *function*. And finally we can ask where items came from, that is, their *genealogy*. In the case of the parking lot, a structural classification would separate front-wheel-drive cars from those with four-wheel drive or rear-wheel drive. A functional classification would distinguish between mass-transit vehicles (buses), commodity-carrying vehicles (trucks), family vehicles (station wagons or sedans), and pleasure vehicles (sports cars). And a genealogical classification would contrast the products of Ford with those of GM or Chrysler or Rolls-Royce.

Computer languages can also be classified along structural, functional, and genealogical lines. These classifications lend coherence to the plethora of languages described in the literature. They also help us understand some of the buzz words (like *algorithmic* or *non-procedural*) commonly used in talking about languages. Most importantly, thinking about computer languages in terms of types is invaluable when deciding what computer language—or languages—to learn.

Structural Classification

The most obvious way to classify computer languages is *structurally*: What do the languages look like? Not surprisingly, many structural distinctions are the

ORIENTATION	COMMON TERMINOLOGY	BRIEF DESCRIPTION
Hardware	high-level vs. low-level	degree of dependence of language organization upon computer hardware
Translator	interpreted vs. compiled	method of converting high-level code into machine code
Structure	structured vs. unstructured; structural unit	extent to which computer program is divided into internally coherent units
Data	numerical vs. symbolic; graphics	data type that language handles most easily

Figure 3.1   Structural Classification of Computer Languages: Familiar Distinctions

result of functional differences—that is, what problems various languages handle especially well—and genealogical differences—that is, how languages developed historically.

A major stumbling block in doing structural classifications of computer languages is that practitioners don't all agree upon the categories. Some categories (e.g. *low-* vs. *high*-level languages) are quite common, while others (e.g. *extensible* or *object-oriented* languages) are not. Another problem is that some languages (especially the more recent ones) don't neatly fit into the traditional typologies. Even more confusing is the choice of terms themselves. It sometimes isn't clear whether two labels (e.g. *algorithmic* and *imperative*, *descriptive* and *non-procedural*) mean the same thing or not.

Since there are many ways of grouping computer languages in terms of structure, we'll first divide up the various classifications themselves into two broad categories. The first category contains the ways of categorizing computer languages by structure that are *familiar* from popular discussions of computer languages in computer magazines and introductory textbooks. These are summarized in Figure 3.1. There are also less obvious—yet more interesting—ways of dividing up computer languages by structure. We will call these *conceptual* distinctions, and summarize them in Figure 3.2.

FAMILIAR DISTINCTIONS

When we speak of classifying computer languages, several questions readily come to mind. Is the language a high-level language or a low-level language? Is it interpreted or compiled? Is the language "structured" or "unstructured,"

ORIENTATION	COMMON TERMINOLOGY	BRIEF DESCRIPTION
Organizing Principle	imperative/algorithmic vs.	programs consist of instructions (imperatives) on how to carry out procedures (algorithms)
	functional/applicative vs.	programs consist of functions that are applied to data
	object-oriented vs.	programs consist of objects that are manipulated to obtain results
	FORTH vs.	programs consist of words that are built up of words already defined
	logic programming vs.	programs consist of statements in first-order predicate calculus
	query	programs consist of questions to be answered
Procedures	procedural vs. non-procedural/descriptive	does the program tell *how* to reach a result or *what* result is wanted?
Extensibility	closed grammar vs. open grammar	are the terms of the language all predefined, or can the user create new terms?
Program/Data	distinct vs. unified	does the language formally distinguish between analysis of programs and analysis of data?

Figure 3.2   Structural Classification of Computer Languages: Conceptual Distinctions

and what are its basic units of analysis? Is it numerically oriented or symbolically oriented, and can it handle graphics?

Hardware Orientation: High-Level vs. Low-Level

A simple way to divide up computer languages is by looking at their relationship to computer hardware: Is the language dependent upon particular hardware? *Low-level languages* (here, meaning assembly languages—we'll ignore machine code) are hardware-specific. By "hardware" we mean the actual microprocessor that is the heart of the computer. And so, there is one assembly language for the Intel 8086, another for the Mostek 6502, and yet another for the Motorola 68000. *High-level languages* are independent of specific hardware. These are second- and third-generation languages like COBOL and Pascal. In principle, the same lines of code can be run on any machine—assuming that there is a standard version of the language and that you have the appropriate language translator designed for that machine (see Figure 3.3).

An "intermediate" category of languages is now emerging. Included here are languages like C, FORTH, and Modula-2. These languages function like

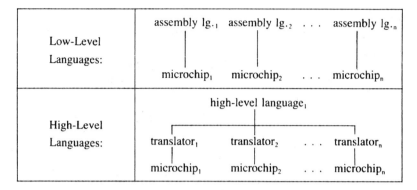

Figure 3.3   Hardware-Oriented Classifications

high-level languages, but also allow you to address some hardware functions directly (as assembly languages can), thereby increasing the speed at which programs compile and run. However, unlike assembly languages, these languages remain essentially hardware-independent.

Translator Orientation: Interpreted vs. Compiled

Computer languages can also be classified with respect to the way they are translated into machine code. As we saw in Chapter 2, code for *compiled languages* is translated after the entire program has been typed in, while *interpreted languages* are translated after entering each line.

Structure: Structured vs. Unstructured; Structural Unit

Like patriotism or promoting the public good, the notion of "structure" in computer programming is roundly lauded, though few people clearly define it. Perhaps this is because the term actually has at least three distinct meanings. To add to the confusion, the first two meanings are applicable only to the class of computer languages known as imperative/algorithmic languages (which we will be looking at shortly). The third meaning applies more generally to the whole spectrum of computer languages.

(1)   Language-Directed Structure
So-called *structured languages* are those whose syntax breaks programs down into components. These components may be called "blocks" or "procedures" or "modules" or "packages," depending upon the language and the syntactic function of the component. This formal notion of "structured languages" did not develop until the late 1960s and early 1970s. As a result, languages such as BASIC and COBOL and FORTRAN (which predated the emergence of so-called structured programming) retroactively came to be labeled *unstructured* languages. Programs written in these languages followed a single linear sequence of commands, rather than being broken down into components.

(2)   User-Directed Structure

Underlying the creation of structural subcomponents in programming languages was a more general approach to programming that encouraged users to think about the problem to be coded in a logical fashion that decomposes larger problems into smaller ones. This approach, which has come to be known as top down design, or stepwise refinement, or version-by-version programming (see Chapter 2), can be used regardless of the particular language in which the problem will eventually be coded. The notion of user-directed structure predated the subsequent introduction of explicit structured syntax into programming languages in the late 1960s and early 1970s.

Both language-directed and user-directed notions of structuring are direct outgrowths of the conceptual approach to programming embodied in imperative/algorithmic languages. The history of this development, along with a more detailed explanation of these first two meanings of *structure*, appears in Chapter 5 in the entry on the language ALGOL. For it was the developers of ALGOL and their students who first articulated the notion of structured programming.

Over the last decade, there has been an enormous shift in much of the computer world (specifically, the world of imperative/algorithmic languages) toward the use of structured programming. In fact, BASIC and FORTRAN and COBOL, which began as unstructured languages, now also appear in structured versions.

(3)   Structural Unit

A very different way of thinking about structure is to ask what the basic unit of analysis is in a given computer language. Is it a single line of programming code, or a group of lines that are clustered in some meaningful way? Can new units be constructed out of old ones? Comparing basic units of analysis offers one of the simplest yet starkest contrasts between computer languages.

Data Orientation: Numerical vs. Symbolic; Graphics

A final common structural classification considers the type of data involved in the problems you want the computer to solve. The majority of computer languages (including FORTRAN, COBOL, Pascal, Ada, and APL) are explicitly designed for dealing primarily with *numbers*. A second group of languages are constructed for easy manipulation of *symbols* (primarily alphabetic characters, punctuation marks, and numbers as characters). These include LISP, SNOBOL, and PROLOG. Finally, a few languages are particularly good at dealing with *graphics*. The best-known examples here are Logo and FORTH.

Conceptual Distinctions   ← SHOULD BE UNITALISIZED ; ALL CAPS ; etc.

Conceptual distinctions between computer languages are at once more subtle and complex than the familiar distinctions we have just looked at. In the long run, though, they are generally more important.

Most of the familiar distinctions are *contingent* rather than *necessary*. BASIC is BASIC whether it is compiled or interpreted. FORTRAN is still FORTRAN if you structure it. And LISP is still LISP if you add sophisticated number-handling abilities to it. The conceptual distinctions, however, are not contingent. Rather, they indicate critical presuppositions underlying different languages and language types.

In this section, we will consider four conceptual issues concerning the structure of computer languages: What central organizing principle governs the construction of the language? Is the language procedural or not? Is the language's grammar extensible? And does the language distinguish between programs and data?

Distinctions Among Organizing Principles

Present-day computer languages can be divided into six systematically distinct approaches to problem solving. Five of these approaches are represented by more than one language, while the remaining approach is not distinct from the language that exemplifies it (see Figure 3.4).

(1)   Imperative/Algorithmic

The names *imperative* and *algorithmic* refer to the same set of computer languages. The terms themselves derive from the von Neumann architecture of the machines on which these languages run. *Imperative* indicates that these programming languages are giving instructions as to what values should be placed in the computer's memory locations. *Algorithmic* tells us how these instructions are given: namely, through algorithms, that is, statements telling us how to carry out procedures.

Imperative/algorithmic languages are the best known and most widely used of all computer languages. The entries in Chapter 5 on FORTRAN, COBOL, BASIC, ALGOL, and Pascal illustrate how these languages work.

(2) Functional/Applicative

The oldest alternative conception to computer language design is *functional*, or *applicative*, languages. Again, both terms are applied to the same group of languages. Don't be confused by the terms: *functional* has nothing to do with the functional classification of computer languages we will look at later in this chapter, and *applicative* has no relationship to applications programs like Visicalc or Lotus 1-2-3. Rather, both terms come from mathematics.

In mathematics, a function is a way of relating elements of one set (the domain) to elements from another (the range). For example, a function for finding the square of a number associates ''square(x)'' with ''x^2.'' In a functional language, these functions are *applied* in order to solve the problem in which we are interested. Hence the name *applicative*.

Three separate attempts have been made at conceiving of computer languages in terms of mathematical functions. The earliest was LISP, a so-called *list-processing* language, developed in the late 1950s and early 1960s at MIT. *List processing* means that the basic elements in the language are either ''atoms''

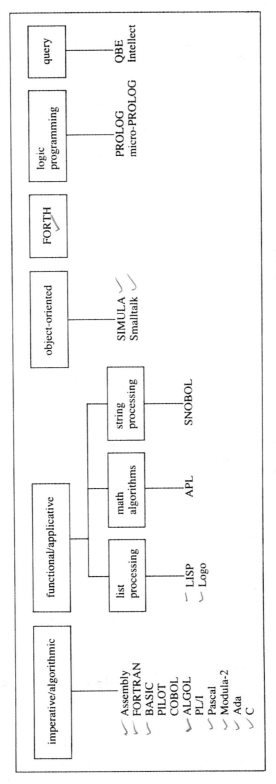

Figure 3.4 Distinctions Among Organizing Principles

(typically, strings of characters) or lists, which are series of atoms or other lists. A second functionally conceived language is APL (*A Programming Language*), developed by Kenneth Iverson at Harvard around 1960. APL is organized in terms of *mathematical algorithms*. A third well-known functional language is SNOBOL (*StriNg Oriented SymBOlic Language*), developed at Bell Laboratories in the mid-1960s. As a *string-handling* language, SNOBOL was designed to deal with large quantities of characters much as imperative/algorithmic languages were designed to handle numbers. The entries in Chapter 5 on LISP, APL, and SNOBOL explain how each of these types of functional/applicative languages works.

(3) Object-Oriented

Object-oriented languages such as SIMULA and Smalltalk use a radically different way of thinking about programming. These languages are structured in terms of *objects*, where an object is defined as an area in computer memory that serves as a basic structural unit of analysis. In the process of writing programs, users create new objects out of existing ones.

The notion of an object in SIMULA or Smalltalk is somewhat complex to explain, especially because its definition has shifted over time. For more detailed and precise definitions, see the entries on SIMULA and Smalltalk in Chapter 5.

(4) FORTH

FORTH is a language unto itself. Like object-oriented languages, it is made up of a small set of units (here *words*) that are used for constructing new words. The notion of a word is best understood in the context of the entry on FORTH in Chapter 5.

(5) Logic Programming

A fifth conceptual approach to programming is *logic programming*. The best-known example of logic programming is PROLOG (*PROgramming in LOGic*), a language developed in the early 1970s at the University of Marseilles. Logic programming is a form of theorem proving. A PROLOG program essentially evaluates theorems to see if they are true.

Logic programming as a genre of computer languages has begun attracting considerable interest since PROLOG was adopted by the Japanese as the language for programming the fifth-generation machines they are designing. The entry on PROLOG in Chapter 5 explains what a logic programming language is.

(6) Query

Finally there are *query* languages. These are languages that require little or no knowledge of formal programming conventions. Users specify what problem they want solved and what data may be relevant. The language translator itself then determines how to solve the problem.

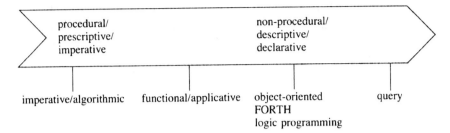

Figure 3.5   Procedural Distinctions

Query languages are becoming increasingly popular in the business world. Common examples are QBE (*Query-by-Ex*ample) and Intellect (see entries in Chapter 5). We will examine query languages more closely in the next section of this chapter ("Functional Classification").

Procedural Distinctions: Procedural/Prescriptive/Imperative vs. Non-procedural/Descriptive/Declarative

It has become increasingly common to divide up computer languages by whether they are *procedural* (or *prescriptive* or *imperative*) or *non-procedural* (also called *descriptive* or *declarative*). As Figure 3.5 indicates, a procedural/non-procedural classification tends to be one of degree.

Comparing Figure 3.5 (Procedural Distinctions) with Figure 3.4 (Distinctions among Organizing Principles), we find distinct parallels. At the left end of the spectrum are imperative/algorithmic languages, whose programs tell the computer *how* to solve a problem. By "how" we mean that they present an algorithm which instructs the hardware to behave in a particular way. At the far right end of the spectrum are query languages. Their only demand upon the user is to specify *what* problem is to solved. It is the responsibility of the original programmer who wrote the query language translator to figure out how to convert that request into the specific instructions the computer hardware will need to produce an answer to the query. Other language types lie somewhere in the middle. LISP, for example, is largely procedural. PROLOG can be used either procedurally or declaratively.

In talking about procedural versus non-procedural languages, we need to be careful not to confuse the word *procedural* with the notion of "a procedure" that we talked about earlier. (A procedure is a structural unit in terms of which a programming language like Pascal is organized. However, not all procedural languages use procedures.)

Extensibility Distinctions: Closed Grammar vs. Open Grammar

We speak of computer languages being *extensible* if users can construct new language elements (out of old ones) without changing the language itself. The new language elements generally become structurally indistinguishable from the

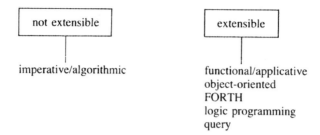

Figure 3.6   Extensibility Distinctions

primitive elements built into the original language. Think of mixing oil paints on a palette. You can achieve little color variety by applying the oils straight from the tubes. However, by mixing the oils, you can produce colors that did not exist before. These new colors now become part of your working palette.

Imperative/algorithmic languages are not extensible in this sense. If I add fifteen new elements to Pascal, the resulting language is no longer Pascal. I may call it a *dialect* of Pascal. It may even be superior to the existing standard. But it isn't the same language anymore.

All of the other five language types are extensible (see Figure 3.6). Languages of these five types each come with some basic elements (e.g. functions in LISP, words in FORTH, objects in Smalltalk) built in. The programmer then creates new elements to solve the problem at hand.

Comparing the extensibility scale (Figure 3.6) with our six language types (Figure 3.4) and the procedural/non-procedural spectrum (Figure 3.5), we once again notice similarities. Imperative/algorithmic languages are not only procedural but non-extensible. Query languages are highly descriptive and highly extensible. While the details of the rest of the correspondences are not precise, we are beginning to get an increasingly rich notion of what constitutes a conceptual type of computer language.

Program/Data Distinction: Distinct vs. Unified

All computers require both that we represent data (information) and that we manipulate these data (e.g. organizing pieces of information, calculating results, or presenting results). However, the *emphasis* is not the same in all computer languages. Consider two extremes. Imperative/algorithmic languages focus on the *program* itself. Their goal is to *calculate* a result that is distinct from the original data. Query languages focus on the *data* themselves. Their goal is to *select, organize,* and *present* information that is already stored in a data warehouse (see Figure 3.7).

The distinction between programming orientations is evident in the very way in which languages at either end of the spectrum conceive of appropriate programming style. With imperative/algorithmic languages, users are encouraged

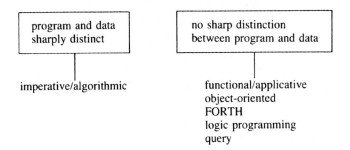

Figure 3.7   Program/Data Distinctions

to write programs that are as data-free as possible. Instead of putting values of variables directly within the program itself, actual data values are typically inserted only when running the program. This way, the same program can be reused without having to rewrite the original lines of code to reflect new data values. Languages on the right-hand side of the spectrum don't aim at such methodological abstraction. Programs containing constants are as much prized as those containing variables.

But differences in the relationship between program and data go deeper still. In imperative/algorithmic languages, procedures for manipulating data and the data to be manipulated are taken to be two distinct kinds of entity. Procedures state the form data can take, summon data when they are wanted, and spew out new data in the process of executing a program.

Many non-imperative/algorithmic languages work quite differently. No clear distinction—or no distinction at all—exists between data and programs. Such languages include LISP, Smalltalk, FORTH, PROLOG, and query languages. In LISP and PROLOG, for example, statements of fact have the same structure as instructions. And in query languages, the only ''instruction'' is to deliver an answer to a question.

Once again we find strong correspondences with other conceptual distinctions. Imperative/algorithmic languages separate data from programs, are non-extensible, and are procedural. Query languages don't distinguish between data and programs, are highly extensible, and are non-procedural. Other languages, as usual, lie somewhere in between.

Taken together, these four conceptual distinctions make up sharply distinct approaches to computer programming. On the left side of the spectrum, the user basically operates in terms of predefined constraints, reworking the problem to fit the mold. On the right side of the spectrum, there are still constraints, though much looser ones. The user has more say over the way in which a problem can be approached. At the same time, though, users are faced with the additional responsibility of figuring out what the relevant questions are that must be asked. Instead of beginning with a conceptual sketch that is to be elaborated, they start out with a sparser canvas.

Functional Classification

Instead of classifying languages with respect to their *structure*, we can look at computer languages *functionally*: What kinds of tasks was the language designed to carry out? What tasks does it do best? What other types of problems can the language be used to solve?

Computer scientists traditionally distinguish between *special-purpose* and *general-purpose languages*. *Special-purpose languages* are designed or used for limited kinds of applications. COBOL, for example, was designed to process business data. FORTRAN was created to do scientific calculations. And LISP was invented for doing work in artificial intelligence. The term *general-purpose language* has been applied to languages such as BASIC, PL/I, or Pascal, which were created for working at a large range of tasks.

Yet there are difficulties with this dichotomy. To begin with, functions can evolve over time. Modern airplanes were developed for wartime use, but now fly millions of commercial and private passengers a year. In much the same way, today's programming languages are often used for purposes other than the ones for which they were initially developed. Smalltalk is a good example. Alan Kay designed the language to develop children's creative abilities, though Smalltalk is now used for large-scale business simulations and for work in artificial intelligence. Similarly, some would argue that FORTRAN has evolved from a special-purpose language to a general-purpose language as the needs of its programmers have broadened (e.g. FORTRAN is now commonly used not only in science and engineering but in high-resolution graphics programming).

Alternatively, a language's functions may be underutilized. FORTH, for example, was intended as a general-purpose language, and indeed many loyal hobbyists use it that way. Currently, though, FORTH has become a favorite among many scientists working in astronomy, physics, and robotics, and strikes many novices as a special-purpose language.

Yet a third possibility is that the "general-purpose" or "special-purpose" designation for a language is a matter of dispute. Logo offers a classic case. Logo's detractors argue that the language is only good for doing basic geometry, while its advocates state emphatically that Logo can perform the same range of tasks as other general-purpose languages.

The notion of general-purpose languages was introduced in the early 1960s, at the same time as third-generation languages. General-purpose languages like BASIC, PL/I (and later Pascal) were general *in comparison with* languages like FORTRAN and COBOL that were designed to do just one kind of programming. Yet all of these languages were heavily numerically oriented. In the ensuing twenty years, our uses for programming languages have expanded enormously. A so-called general-purpose language like Pascal isn't "general" enough to be able to handle symbol manipulation or graphics as easily as it handles numbers.

The very terms *special-purpose languages* and *general-purpose languages*

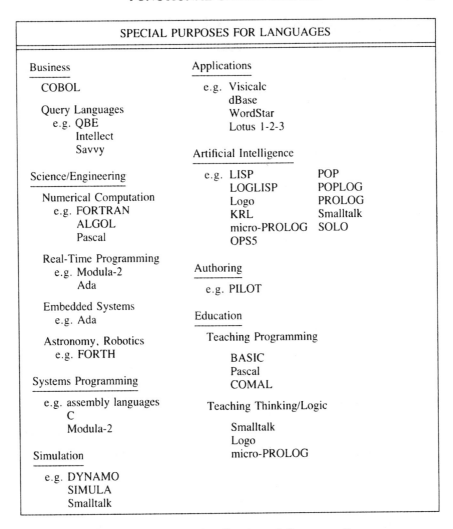

SPECIAL PURPOSES FOR LANGUAGES

Business

COBOL

Query Languages
  e.g. QBE
       Intellect
       Savvy

Science/Engineering

Numerical Computation
  e.g. FORTRAN
       ALGOL
       Pascal

Real-Time Programming
  e.g. Modula-2
       Ada

Embedded Systems
  e.g. Ada

Astronomy, Robotics
  e.g. FORTH

Systems Programming

e.g. assembly languages
     C
     Modula-2

Simulation

e.g. DYNAMO
     SIMULA
     Smalltalk

Applications

e.g. Visicalc
     dBase
     WordStar
     Lotus 1-2-3

Artificial Intelligence

e.g. LISP   POP
     LOGLISP   POPLOG
     Logo   PROLOG
     KRL   Smalltalk
     micro-PROLOG SOLO
     OPS5

Authoring

e.g. PILOT

Education

Teaching Programming

     BASIC
     Pascal
     COMAL

Teaching Thinking/Logic

     Smalltalk
     Logo
     micro-PROLOG

Figure 3.8 Functional Classification of Computer Languages

are becoming outdated. While acknowledging the *potential* expandability of languages to deal with new functions, it is more useful to focus on the *actual* uses to which particular languages are generally put. We will therefore speak not of "special-purpose languages" but of "the special purposes" for which languages are actually used.

Figure 3.8 lists the common functions of computer languages, and indicates some of the languages especially suited to those functions (either by original design or through current usage). Languages appear in more than one category if they serve multiple functions.

BUSINESS: COBOL AND QUERY LANGUAGES

The purpose of computer programming in business is to associate related elements of data (such as commodities, prices, date-of-purchase, stock on hand) into simultaneously accessible units called records. Different records or items within the records are then selected for examination. For example, a business manager may want to access all employee salaries and raise them 5 percent or may want to see how many items have sat in inventory for more than six months.

The first language designed especially for business applications was COBOL. Even today, COBOL remains at the center of American data-processing departments from the Department of Defense to small independent insurance agencies.

For thirty years now—almost as long as there have been high-level languages—occasional voices have called for computer languages that are usable by the average layman without professional computer training. Advocates have ranged from Grace Hopper in the 1950s to the designers of COBOL, BASIC, and SNOBOL in the 1960s. Yet in none of these cases was the goal fully realized. Query languages were the first actual "user-friendly" computer languages, and they did not appear until the 1970s and 1980s.

(1)   What Is a Query Language?

A query language *asks questions* (of a body of data) rather than *issuing commands* (which is what imperative/algorithmic languages do). But here the simplicity ends. There are *two* types of languages that function by making queries: *query languages* (also known as non-procedural or fourth-generation languages) and *logic programming languages*. An easy way to distinguish between these two types of languages is in terms of function: while query languages are heavily used in business and in library information retrieval systems, logic programming languages tend to be used in artificial intelligence.

(2)   Query Languages and Data Base Management Systems

The world of business depends upon computers to keep track of vast amounts of data: How many company employees from northern California earn more than $30,000 per year? What are the social security numbers of the president and chief executive officer?

COBOL was created in the 1960s to help cope with the vast amounts of data (though relatively simple levels of computation) that were characteristic of the business world. As the use of computers in business expanded in the 1960s and 1970s, the amount of data to be processed expanded exponentially. The problem was no longer simply writing programs to manipulate the data, but keeping track of the data themselves. Like the collection of books in the British Library, business data were in desperate need of a rational cataloging system.

The result was the rise of data base management systems (DBMSs). Since their entry into the business world almost twenty years ago, DBMSs have evolved into varied and often highly complex bookkeeping systems. Over the years, a large number of DBMSs have developed. The early group, developed for mainframes or minicomputers, include INGRES, System R, ORACLE, ADABASE, and DATATRIEVE. With the growth of microcomputers, a whole new collection of DBMSs has appeared, including Lotus 1-2-3, Multiplan, the dBase series (I, II, and III), and the R:Base series (2000, 4000, and 5000).

As DBMSs became more complex, they assumed a special status of their own. Instead of merely using data bases as input to formal programming languages like COBOL, programmers saw maneuvering within the data base to be a goal within itself. Yet with the increasing complexity of data bases, it became ever harder, especially for non-computer professionals, to figure out how to use the data bases.

There were two issues involved: control and efficiency. Many business people wanted to know how to access their own files, rather than having to relegate the task to data-processing departments. More importantly, data-processing departments were simply unable to keep up with the flood of programming requests.

(3)   Formal Query Languages

An attempt at a solution to these problems came in the early 1970s. Formal query languages (that is, English-like systems for asking questions of data bases) required less training. Consequently, they enabled a wider group of business people—from secretaries to executives—to use the company data bank.

Formal query languages were typically paired with independent DBMSs. The language QUEL was used to access INGRES; SQL accessed System R. In other cases, the query languages and data bases went by the same name and constituted a single system (e.g. QBE, NOMAD). In Chapter 5, we will look at QBE (also known as Query-by-Example) as an instance of formal query languages.

Query languages improved user access and reduced programming time, but other problems remained. While a query language is less difficult to learn than COBOL, it still has formal, arbitrary commands that have to be learned. By the late 1970s, a number of people began asking whether natural language might not be used to access DBMSs directly.

(4)   Natural Language Front Ends

The idea became increasingly plausible as research in artificial intelligence (and especially natural language processing) developed primitive models for computers to analyze rudimentary English sentences. The turning point came when these models were applied to the business world.

The result was the development of natural language tools that could literally be stuck on the "front end" of either more formal query languages or data bases directly. The user typed in natural language, and the program would make

the necessary "translations" to a syntax that was comprehensible by the query system or data base. For example, instead of having to type in a query like
> LIST ALL COMPANY STATE, SALES81, FOR
> STATE = 'RI'.AND.SALES81>1000000

you simply typed
> List all companies in Rhode Island with
> sales over 1,000,000.

In the last decade, three basic types of systems have been developed for dealing with natural language. The first actually performs linguistic analysis upon natural language input, looking for nouns and verbs, subjects and objects. In Chapter 5 we will look at the natural language system called Intellect as representative of this group.

A second approach lets the program itself produce a "menu" of natural language words and phrases, from which the user makes selections. Depending upon each selection made, additional screens of natural language options are made available. The advantage of this system over actual natural language processing is that all queries are guaranteed to be understood and understood correctly. A system currently using this approach to natural language front ends is Texas Instruments' NaturalLink (see Appendix).

With the third approach, users produce their own natural language. However, instead of analyzing the sentence syntactically or semantically, the program applies a pattern matching algorithm to the input. The meaning of the user's inquiry is determined by matching its pattern with the existing linguistic patterns already stored in the program. This is the approach taken by Excalibur Technologies' language known as Savvy (see Appendix).

SCIENCE AND ENGINEERING

The heaviest use of computers is traditionally in science and engineering projects. Computers were first developed to perform calculations on large amounts of numerical data or many iterations on the same data, and the mainstream of computer language developments has been of imperative/algorithmic languages (like FORTRAN, ALGOL, and Pascal) designed for numerical calculations.

As computer scientists began using computers in novel and increasingly complex ways, a need developed for running programs in "real time," where the results of a computation are immediately used to direct events in the real world. Special "real-time languages" (including Modula-2 and Ada) have been developed to control everything from traffic lights to robot production on an assembly line.

One special use of real-time languages is in "embedded systems," where the computer itself becomes part of a piece of machinery that has other primary functions. Embedded systems can be found today in automobiles, refrigerators, and even nuclear warheads. (For a fuller discussion of both real-time languages and embedded systems, see the entry on Ada in Chapter 5.)

With the emergence of non-imperative/algorithmic languages, some of the functions previously performed by languages like assembly or FORTRAN are now carried out in other languages. The use of FORTH in astronomy and robotics exemplifies this trend.

SYSTEMS PROGRAMMING

As we saw in Chapter 2, today's computers utilize several kinds of programs. Besides language translators and the programs you are writing for those translators to act upon, there are programs for operating systems, editors, debugging tools, and more. In brief, you need programs to make the whole system function and, if possible, to function as one integrated unit. This kind of programming is known as *systems programming*.

Over the years, special languages have been used for doing systems programming. This programming has traditionally been done in assembly language, which is compact and runs quickly. Other languages that have been used for systems programming include Mesa and Concurrent Pascal, though the most popular language for writing systems programs today is C. In addition, in a growing number of general-purpose languages (e.g. FORTH and Modula-2) the necessary systems programming is written in the languages themselves.

SIMULATION

Computers can be used to simulate outcomes of multiple events in the real world. Simulation models (and simulation languages) are used when you don't want to (or can't) perform real experiments. Simulations allow you to do experiments on systems that don't exist at all (like a hypothetical new shopping plaza in Dallas). They enable you to experiment without disturbing an existing system, where such disturbance might be harmful or costly (like seeing how much the addition of twenty new flights at rush hour from Chicago's O'Hare Airport will delay current takeoffs and landings). And simulations are useful for laboratory experiments where manipulating the objects in the real world could destroy the system you are working with (e.g. determining the stress tolerance of the World Trade Center in New York).

In the past few decades, a whole science of simulation has developed. One of the best-known simulation models is "systems dynamics," developed at MIT by Jay Forrester. Forrester's work with systems dynamics was heavily publicized in the early 1970s when the Club of Rome (a group of several dozen private citizens concerned with understanding such world trends as population growth, rising levels of pollution, and social disorder) asked Forrester to apply systems dynamics to their current study of "The Predicament of Mankind." They wanted to know, for example, if natural resources on earth declined at rate X, and population rose at rate Y, what would be the effect on the material standard of living (Z).

Forrester undertook to simulate the possible outcomes of dozens of hypothetical changes. To aid in the process, he made use of a computer simulation language he had developed called DYNAMO.

Underlying all computer simulation languages is the assumption that it is possible to represent the dynamic behavior of a system (i.e. its movement through time) by means of well-defined rules. However, there are two very different ways in which the change can be represented in the simulation model. It can be seen as *continuous* over time or as divisible into *discrete* instances in time. Note that we are talking here about the way in which the *model* looks at change, not at how change is actually occurring in the real world. (One might, for example, use a discrete simulation language to model behavior that is continuous in the real world—much as motion pictures appear to the view as continuous motion but are really composed of discrete frames of film.)

Continuous simulation languages are most useful when the activity to be modeled is not divisible into discrete units. A good example might be a model of the velocity of a spacecraft or a model of the gradual loss of soil nutrients in a particular farming area. The best known of the continuous simulation languages is probably DYNAMO.

The majority of simulation languages today are *discrete simulation languages*. They are most appropriate when the real-world activity to be modeled is easily divisible into discrete events. One example might be the circulation system of a library, where the charging out or returning of a book is an event distinct from all other events. Two of the best-known discrete simulation languages are SIMULA and Smalltalk, which largely derives from SIMULA. Several other well-known discrete simulation languages are SIMSCRIPT, GPSS, and OPS.

APPLICATIONS

In the late 1970s, nearly all serious computing was done with large machines. While a number of microcomputers were appearing on the market, there was almost no software for them. To operate a computer, you needed to write your own program (usually in assembly language or BASIC; FORTRAN didn't yet run on micros).

The microcomputer invention became the microcomputer revolution when software began to appear that removed the major burden of programming from the shoulders of potential users. The earliest round of such software appeared in three practical areas which were relevant to general users: financial spreadsheets, management of data bases, and word processing.

(1) Spreadsheets
Anyone who has filed an income tax form knows how time-consuming it can be to perform successive arithmetic calculations on a set of numbers. You must take 5 percent of the figure on line 25, divide the result by 10, and then subtract

$2000 from the quotient. Yet the real tedium comes when you find an error in one part of your calculations, for everything following it must be recalculated.

The problem of doing such calculations and recalculations becomes even more acute in the business world. Suppose I run a fast-food restaurant, where my profit is heavily dependent upon the volume of food I sell. The lower the prices I charge, the higher the volume of sales I can expect, but the lower the profit I make on each item. I therefore need to calculate where I should set my prices in order to maximize the amount I can charge per item *and* the volume of each item sold.

Traditionally, accountants have used spreadsheets to answer these kinds of questions. (A spreadsheet is a series of columns and rows in which a set of numbers is entered in one column and then manipulated in another—e.g. multiplied by 5%, divided by 10.) Such calculations used to be done by hand, using paper and pencil, sometimes augmented with a slide rule or calculator. Since the mid-1950s, you would write a program in FORTRAN to do the calculation for you, but that required considerable time and money, as well as access to a large computer.

A breakthrough came when two students at Harvard Business School decided to write a microcomputer program that would simulate the accountant's spreadsheet. They called the result Visicalc.

Many people argue that the appearance and successful marketing of Visicalc was directly responsible for catapulting microcomputers into the public eye. Visicalc enabled business people to save themselves vast amounts of time they would otherwise spend on performing repetitive calculations. And the cost of the software (and even the hardware on which to run it) was trivial compared with the cost of their own time or of doing the same work on a large computer.

Spreadsheets have continued to be one of the pylons upon which the microcomputer industry rests. Many other spreadsheet programs have appeared, though Visicalc (and its successor Supercalc) remain among the best known.

(2) Data Base Management Systems

The management of large data bases on computers had already become an important business function even before the appearance of microcomputers. However, the success of early spreadsheet programs made it obvious that microcomputers might also be used for data base management systems.

Since data bases can contain both numerical and symbolic information (i.e. words and, these days, pictures), the potential for data base applications programs was even wider than the market for spreadsheets. Not surprisingly, dozens of data base management applications programs have appeared on microcomputers. Among the earliest was dBase. Other well-known systems include PFS File, the R:Base series, and Multiplan.

(3) Word Processing

To millions of computer users today, the computer is nothing more than a glorified typewriter. Both have keyboards, and both have a mechanism for making the image of the character you strike on the keyboard appear on some visual medium. In the case of the typewriter, that process is strictly mechanical: the pressing of a key directly causes the making of an impression on a piece of paper. With the computer, the process is much more indirect (pressing a key activates a program built into the computer's ROM chips, which eventually activates a program causing a visual representation to appear on a CRT or at a printer). Yet from the perspective of the average user, the result is equivalent.

The overwhelming advantage of computers over typewriters comes in correcting mistakes. Traditionally, revising a text has meant typing it all over again. Because computers allow the movement of information from one part of memory to another, the computer makes it possible to make as many changes as you wish on a document, and only then print out the results. If there are still changes to be made, only the changes need to be entered. This use of computers as glorified typewriters came to be known as word processing.

Word processing was well established in major businesses in the United States long before the development of the microcomputer. Several companies (the best known being Wang and IBM) produced "dedicated" computers that did only word processing. Such machines tended to be easy to use, but relatively expensive and not extendable to other computing functions.

A major breakthrough came when special word-processing applications programs were developed for microcomputers. These programs not only cost a fraction of their office machine counterparts but could be run on general-purpose microcomputers (which could obviously be used for other functions such as spreadsheets, data base management systems, and programming in traditional computer languages).

Among the earliest word-processing programs for microcomputers were Apple Writer (for the Apple II series) and WordStar (which ran on many computers under the operating system CP/M). Since the writing of letters and documents is an activity common to most of the American population, word-processing programs have proliferated and continued to sell extremely well. Among contemporary word-processing programs are Microsoft Word, PFS Write, and Perfectwriter.

The sale of these three types of applications programs fueled the sale of microcomputers, which, in turn, generated new types of applications programs. As visual resolution on video display monitors improved, graphics applications packages began to appear (many specifically designed for displaying business charts and graphs). Other applications functions have included everything from desk calendars for keeping track of your daily appointments to programs for logging what day and time you use your computer.

The best-known trend for applications programs in the mid-1980s has been to integrate several computing functions (e.g. spreadsheets, data base management, and graphics) into a single applications program. The same data that you derive from your data base can be manipulated with your spreadsheet and then displayed in a bar chart. Lotus 1-2-3 was the first such integrated applications program, but many are following in its wake.

ARTIFICIAL INTELLIGENCE

In the summer of 1956, a group of academicians met at Dartmouth College to explore the conjecture that "every aspect of learning or any other feature of intelligence can in principle be so precisely described that a machine can be made to simulate it." The conjecture was formulated by John McCarthy (who later invented LISP) and the field of inquiry it engendered came to be known as artificial intelligence.

The study of artificial intelligence (or AI) is, in principle, as broad as the study of human intelligence. Included are the production and perception of natural language, the capacity to see, and the ability to draw logical inferences or to reach a decision on the basis of incomplete information. Moreover, it encompasses formulating generalizations and learning from one's mistakes.

There are two ways of thinking about how a machine might approximate human intelligence. In the first model, the goal is to achieve the *same result* as a human would, although the process followed by machine and man need not be similar. (This model of shared result but distinct process describes how computers do arithmetic computation.) In the second model, the goal is not only for the computer to achieve the same result as a person but to do it following the *same procedure*.

In the early years of work on artificial intelligence, only a handful of people took the basic goal of simulating intelligence (by whatever model) seriously. However, in the 1960s and early 1970s, the success of early chess-playing programs made it clear that computers could engage in some activities thought to involve the equivalence of human intelligence, and the debate turned to the two models.

In the later 1970s, it became clear that some of the discussion was circular. Since we don't really understand how people comprehend language or how they distinguish visual images or, more generally, how they learn anything, computer simulations of intelligent human behavior became theoretical models for human behavior itself.

While much of the circularity remains today, the primary thrust of work on AI has gone in new directions. As work on artificial intelligence growing out of universities and private research institutes has begun to bear commercial fruit, AI has attracted a burgeoning audience. Natural language front ends to query languages are based upon research in artificial intelligence. However, many commercial applications of artificial intelligence are now in the area of so-called expert systems, that is, computer programs that simulate the decision-making behavior of an expert in a particular field of knowledge. An expert systems program contains a large data base of information and a set of rules (or sometimes rules of thumb, called heuristics) for making decisions. Some of the best-known expert systems are written in the areas of medicine, chemistry, and oil prospecting.

Artificial intelligence programming has been almost exclusively dominated by two languages: LISP and PROLOG. In the United States, nearly all AI programming has been done in LISP. In much of Europe, and in Japan, the language of choice is often PROLOG.

Like the little-enders and the big-enders in *Gulliver's Travels* who regularly came to blows over which end to crack open an egg, proponents of LISP and PROLOG often speak as if theirs is the only viable language. Conceivably, a new language will emerge in coming years that incorporates the best features of each. Attempts (such as LOGLISP and POPLOG) are already underway.

AUTHORING LANGUAGES

An increasingly important role of computers is to make education more efficient, more effective, and more enjoyable. The original problem with constructing computer-aided instruction (CAI) was that you needed to know a computer language in order to write programs. The vast majority of educators who had use for CAI programs either didn't know how to program or lacked the time needed to write the necessary volumes of code in BASIC or FORTRAN or Pascal.

A new type of programming known as authoring languages has gradually emerged to fill this gap. The languages themselves (PILOT is the best known) are often imperative/algorithmic in orientation. However, people using these languages to construct CAI programs don't need to understand *how* the programs operate. Instead, users are presented with a simple set of commands that enable them to construct lessons, drill sections, and examinations.

EDUCATION

There is an enormous amount of talk about the importance of "computer literacy" in today's schools and colleges. Though defining "computer literacy" is problematic at best, many of its advocates argue that it includes learning to program.

Even if we assume that learning programming is a good thing, there is still the question of why. What do we accomplish in teaching beginning programming? And what languages are good for these purposes?

Two distinct answers are given to these questions (although in practice the two answers are sometimes combined). The first presupposes that students are going to learn programming, and asks which languages are best for getting started. BASIC was developed so that college students could begin programming without a mathematical or computer science background. Pascal was explicitly invented to teach computer science students good programming style (where "good" meant "structured" programming). And COMAL, a language combining the best of BASIC and Pascal, was developed in Denmark for similar pedagogical reasons.

A very different use of programming in education is exemplified by Smalltalk, Logo, and micro-PROLOG. The advocates of each of these languages are not particularly concerned that children learn to program computers. Rather, they are interested in developing children's cognitive abilities—to teach them how to think more clearly. Whether computer programming (with these or any other languages) accomplishes such a goal remains to be seen.

Figure 3.9 summarizes the variety of education languages that have evolved over the past two decades. The figure is constructed to highlight the conceptual and functional differences between these languages. We will return to these differences in Chapter 5.

Genealogical Classification

The third way of categorizing computer languages is *genealogically*, looking at their historical relationship with each other. Like human languages, computer languages are often direct historical descendants of earlier languages. Old English is the linguistic ancestor of Middle English, and LISP is the direct progenitor of Logo.

In the case of human languages, it's not always obvious why two languages look similar. Language 1 might be a direct descendant of Language 2 (like Middle English and Old English). Alternatively, Language 1 may have borrowed some elements from Language 2, though the languages remain distinct from one another. (English, for example, is historically a very different language from Hindi or Arabic, though it has borrowed the word *pajamas* from the one and *assassin* from the other). Finally, two languages may resemble one another simply because they are human languages. All natural languages share many properties (e.g. every natural language has a way of asking questions and a way of saying "no"). These similarities are not the result of genealogical relationships or historical borrowing. They are part of the definition of natural language.

The same three possible relationships exist for computer languages. One language may be the direct descendant of another. A language may borrow elements. And two languages may have something in common just because they are both computer languages.

There is, however, one essential difference in the relationships between human languages on the one hand and computer languages on the other. Change in natural language is rarely under anyone's control. What's more, most linguistic change is so gradual that few speakers notice it.

By contrast, programmers consciously create computer languages and can

CONCEPTUAL ORIENTATION	PURPOSE	LANGUAGE	YEAR	DIRECT ANCESTOR	COMMENTS
imperative/algorithmic	teach programming (plus teach clear thinking)	BASIC	1964	FORTRAN, ALGOL	first for college students, then for children
		Pascal	1971	ALGOL	college students
		COMAL	1973	BASIC, Pascal	lower-school children
functional/applicative	teach creative thinking	Logo	1968	LISP	also used to teach programming (especially for older students)
object-oriented	teach creative thinking	Smalltalk	early 1970s	SIMULA	educational applications tapered off in late 1970s, may be revived in 1980s
logic programming	teach logic	micro-PROLOG	early 1980s	PROLOG	assume that logic underlies most education

Figure 3.9 Education Languages

form them any way they choose. They combine together elements from radically different parents or create new elements that never existed before. As a result, it is not self-evident how to draw a genealogical tree for computer languages. Not everyone agrees that Language 2 descended from Language 1 (rather than from Language 3). And even if there is agreement on primary lineage, there is still frequent debate on which older languages were sufficiently important as influences to warrant mentioning.

In the genealogical charts that follow, computer languages are divided into the same six conceptual categories we used when talking about structural classifications of computer languages: imperative/algorithmic, functional/ applicative, object-oriented, FORTH, logic programming, and query languages. The reason is obvious: computer languages (or language families) historically arise when someone develops a new organizing principle through which computers can be used to solve problems. Once the idea has been given form, the resulting languages can undergo the same kinds of borrowing or merger— or even death—characterizing natural languages.

The most elaborate genealogical relationships exist among the imperative/ algorithmic languages. Dozens of languages have sprung from three ancestors: FORTRAN, COBOL, and especially ALGOL. The genealogical chart in Figure 3.10 presents major developments within these three language families, while Figure 3.11 indicates some important languages of mixed genealogy. Languages that will be discussed in detail in Chapter 5 are enclosed in blocks. Next to each language name are the approximate dates during which the language was developed. More precise information on dating is given in Chapter 5.

Figure 3.12 offers genealogies for the other major language groups, indicating relevant influences from imperative/algorithmic languages and from one another. As in Figures 3.10 and 3.11, languages in Figure 3.12 that are treated in detail in Chapter 5 are enclosed in rectangular blocks.

Some languages fall in the cracks, not neatly fitting into one conceptual category or another. MUMPS (imperative/algorithmic and functional/applicative) and LOGLISP (functional/applicative and logic programming) are examples. Such "exceptions" illustrate the protean possibilities of computer languages. A decade from now, this organization of computer languages into six genealogical families (deriving from six conceptual types) could even be largely outdated.

Common Elements of Computer Languages

[It is] mandatory to *distinguish between what is essential and what ephemeral . . .* [in a computer language]. For example the inclusion of a coherent and consistent scheme of data type declarations in a programming language I consider essential, whereas the details of varieties of *for*-statements, or whether the compiler distinguishes between upper- and lowercase letters, are ephemeral questions.

Niklaus Wirth, Turing Award Lecture, 1984

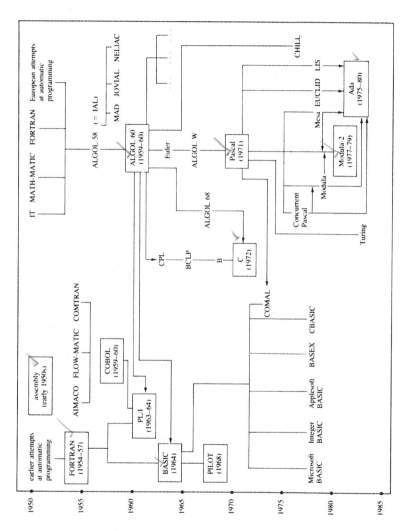

Figure 3.10 Genealogical Classification of Computer Languages:
Imperative/Algorithmic Languages

58

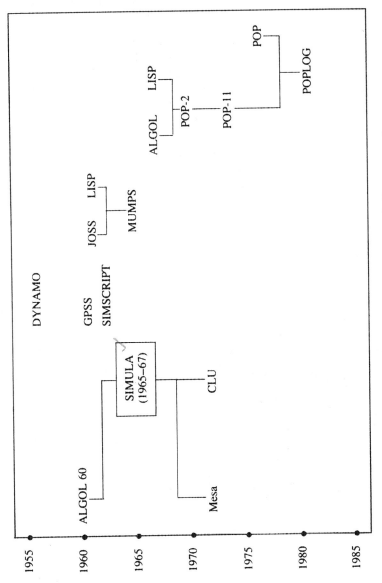

Figure 3.11 Genealogical Classification of Computer Languages: Mixed Genealogies

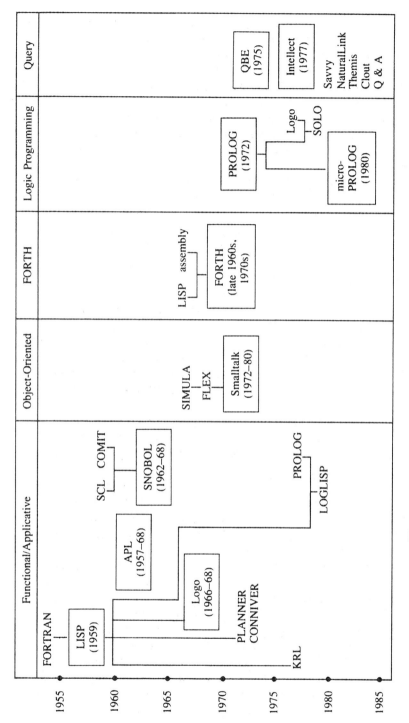

Figure 3.12 Genealogical Classification of Computer Languages: Other Families

Thus far we have been looking at ways in which computer languages can differ from one another. We can now see what these languages have in common.

Any language—whether a computer language or a natural language—must do three things. It must *represent* information (or data) relevant to solving a problem. It must *manipulate* that information to produce a solution to the problem. And the result must admit of *interpretation* by the interlocutor or user.

We already spoke about the representation and interpretation components of language in Chapter 2 when we looked at what you actually "do" when you use a programming language. We now need to look at the manipulation component.

A computer program enables users to perform three essential operations: organize, calculate, and present. A single program may encompass one or all of these functions.

Organizing information is probably the fastest-growing use of computer languages. You can alphabetize a thousand names, or place a thousand test scores in ascending numerical order (that is, you can *sort* information). More generally, computer languages enable you to look for—or to impose—coherence or patterning upon otherwise random data.

The best-known function of computers is to *calculate results*. If I want to know the average rainfall in Santa Clara County on the twenty-seventh day of September for each year over the past century, I can feed in the procedure for doing the calculation, feed in the relevant data, and get a result.

Finally, a computer can give answers or *present results*. In imperative/algorithmic languages, an answer is usually the result of organizing information and then performing a calculation. With functional/applicative languages, results come about (as the name says) from applying the function that has been used to represent the problem. In logic programming or in query languages, the result is the answer to a query as to whether or not something is the case (or, alternatively, a query as to what that something is).

These essential functions—organizing information, calculating results, and presenting results—are carried out by means of a basic structural apparatus. It is frequently said that all computer languages share a set of structural elements. (Conversely, to have those elements is to be a computer language, and so applications packages are often called computer languages.)

Yet we must also be aware that the "standard" list of common elements is *not* standard to all programming languages. To begin with, these features generally apply to imperative/algorithmic languages. Moreover, as computer languages (but imperative/algorithmic and functional/applicative languages in particular) have evolved, newly developed features have emerged that have been adopted into subsequent new languages or incorporated into new versions of older languages. To contemporary users, it may seem as if these features existed since the early days of FORTRAN, but history often proves otherwise. And so our contemporary notion of common structural elements in computer languages reflects a montage of components rather than accurately mirroring each computer language, past and present.

I. PROGRAM FORMATTING

	Imperative/Algorithmic	Functional/Applicative	Object-Oriented
Structural Units:	statement	atom	object
	block	list	
	procedure	function	
	module		
	package		
	subroutine		
	library routine		

FORTH	Logic Programming	Query Language
word	fact	query
	rule	
	query	

II. DATA FORMATTING

Identifiers

Variables
  variable declaration
  type declaration/type checking
  global vs. local variables

Data Types
  integer
  real
  boolean
  char
  pointers
  user-defined

Data Structures
  basic types:

record	string	linked list
array	stack	binary tree
file	queue	table
set	list	vector

static vs. dynamic structures

data abstraction:
  data encapsulation
  information hiding

Arithmetic Capabilities
  floating point vs. fixed point numbers
  double precision numbers

Parameters
  formal vs. actual parameters
  variable vs. value parameters

III. DATA MANIPULATION	
Assignment Statements/ Initialization of Variables	Control Structures linear sequence

Operators
  arithmetic
  relational
	selection
	  if . . . then . . . (else)
	  case
	  GOTO

Functions
  arithmetic
  transfer
  boolean
	looping
	  while
	  repeat
	  for

	procedures/functions
	Recursion vs. Iteration

	Sorting
	  e.g. selection sort
	       bubble sort
	       insertion sort
	       quicksort

	Searching
	  e.g. sequential search
	       binary search
	       hashing

IV. INPUT/OUTPUT	

Input
  e.g. READ/READLN/INPUT
	Formatting
	  format statements
	  prettyprint

Output e.g. WRITE/WRITELN/PRINT	

V. MISCELLANEOUS SYNTACTIC ISSUES	
Line Numbers Reserved Words	Comments Punctuation and Capitalization

Figure 3.13   Common Elements in Computer Languages

For the novice, the most difficult part of learning computer languages is having no idea what kinds of structural elements to expect. Learning a computer language has often been compared with learning a foreign language. Whatever the appropriateness of the metaphor might be, there is one all-important distinction between computer language learning and foreign language learning. When learning a foreign language, we already know the *structural outline* of natural languages, since each of us speaks at least one of them as a native. To learn a foreign language is mostly to learn how that new language differs from the language (or languages) we already speak. We don't have to learn all over again that languages can name things, make requests, or ask questions.

Computer languages are just the opposite. None of us learns BASIC or C or QBE as a "native" language. When we first learn a computer language, we can't formulate hypotheses in advance about what the language will be like. We don't know to expect assignment statements or DO loops. There is nothing "natural" or "intuitive" about the construction of computer languages. Rather, they are artificially devised to parallel (more or less directly) the structure of computer hardware, which is itself a man-made artifact.

Figure 3.14 summarizes many of the structural elements you are likely to encounter in contemporary computer languages. These structural elements are divided up into five major categories:

I.   PROGRAM FORMATTING
II. DATA FORMATTING
III. DATA MANIPULATION
IV. INPUT/OUTPUT
V.   MISCELLANEOUS SYNTACTIC ISSUES

The rest of this chapter consists of summary definitions of these elements.

There is, of course, a problem with trying to give such brief definitions in a contextual vacuum: They don't tend to make sense. Yet *not* giving these definitions of structural elements in computer languages can itself be problematic. As we have said, if you don't know what kinds of structures to expect when you encounter a new computer language, you needlessly complicate the learning process. What's more, if you want to *compare* computer languages, it is imperative to know what to compare with what. To know that procedures in imperative/algorithmic languages have a role similar to functions in LISP. To know that the range of available data structures or control structures varies from language to language.

Think of the rest of this chapter as a reference dictionary: a place you will refer back to as you read individual language entries in Chapter 5. However, the list of structures in Figure 3.13 is *not* intended to be exhaustive. Equally importantly, the explanations are here to help clarify your understanding of what computer languages have in common, not to explain how to use these structural elements in doing actual programming.

I. PROGRAM FORMATTING

Every language, regardless of whether it is structured or unstructured, has some basic unit (or units) of analysis into which it can be decomposed. These units can be sorted into the six conceptual language types we identified at the beginning of the chapter.

Imperative/Algorithmic

statement:
Statement is the generic name for an instruction in a programming language. In unstructured imperative/algorithmic languages, the statement is also the basic unit of analysis.

block:
The block is a unit of analysis in ALGOL-based languages. Typically a block is composed of declarations (e.g. of variables, procedures, functions) plus the programming statements indicating what data manipulation will be brought about. These programming statements are bounded by the words BEGIN and END (or their equivalents).

procedure:
The procedure is also a unit of analysis in languages of the ALGOL family. The purpose of procedures is to decompose problems into subproblems. Each procedure serves as a small program (i.e. within the larger program) for solving a subproblem.

module:
The notion of a module was first introduced by Niklaus Wirth in the language Modula, and then developed in the language Modula-2. Like the block and the procedure, the module is a means of breaking down larger problems into smaller ones. In using modules, however, it is possible to "hide" many programming details that distract the user from the program's basic outline. Modules are also able to "communicate" with each other, either sharing information or hiding it, as necessary.

package:
The package in Ada is essentially comparable to the module in Modula-2. Packages enable the programmer to "hide" programming details or communicate with one another. By minimizing the clutter of programming details, packages make it comparatively easy to maintain programs over time.

subroutine:
Subroutine is a generic label for a collection of statements that can be invoked more than once. Procedures, modules, and packages might all be viewed as special forms of subroutines. However, the term *subroutine* is most often used with unstructured imperative/algorithmic languages (e.g. BASIC, FORTRAN) in which there is no other unit of analysis for clustering together lines of programming code.

library routine:
A library routine (or library function) is a subroutine that is stored in a so-called library to be used on other occasions (either by the programmer who developed

it or by other programmers who have access to that library). Programming libraries are very common among imperative/algorithmic languages where the same kinds of data manipulation (e.g. finding numerical averages, alphabetizing lists) take place in many programs. There are vast libraries of FORTRAN subroutines, and there are coming to be extensive C libraries.

Functional/Applicative

atom:
As in traditional chemistry, the atom in LISP is the smallest unit of analysis. It is not decomposable into smaller parts. Atoms are combined together to form lists. An atom can be a single character or a string of characters.

list:
The list is the essential (and only) data structure in LISP. Lists are composed of atoms or of other lists. Lists are used in defining functions in LISP.

function:
In LISP, the function is the unit of analysis via which all programming takes place. Programming in LISP consists of defining and evaluating functions. The function is also the minimal programming unit in other functional/applicative languages (e.g. APL, SNOBOL). Be aware that the term *function* is used in other language types as well (especially within the ALGOL family among the imperative/algorithmic languages). The meaning of *function* is somewhat different in these non-functional/applicative languages.

Object-Oriented

object:
The object is the basic unit of analysis in object-oriented languages such as SIMULA and Smalltalk. Like the function in LISP or the word in FORTH, both data and programs are formulated in terms of objects. Again as in LISP and FORTH, the object in object-oriented languages is the means via which the language becomes extensible.

FORTH

word:
The word in FORTH is the counterpart of the function in LISP and the object in object-oriented languages. The word is used for expressing all data and programs and for creating new words in the language.

Logic Programming

fact:
A fact in a language like PROLOG is a statement of information that is contained within a data base.

rule:
In logic programming languages, rules are used for expressing relationships between facts.

query:
Logic programming languages use queries to ask questions about facts and rules which are contained in the data base, or to infer new information from existing facts and rules.

Query Languages

query:
The meaning of *query* in query languages is less precise than in the case of logic programming languages. In query languages, the term *query* is a generic indicator for the process by which a user extracts information from a data base.

II. DATA FORMATTING

All imperative/algorithmic languages distinguish between the *expression* (or formatting) of data and *algorithms* for manipulating these data. In non-imperative/algorithmic languages the expression and manipulation of data are often interwoven or even formally indistinguishable from one another.

Identifiers

An identifier is a name associated with a process or an object in a programming language. Identifiers are typically composed of alphanumeric characters (that is, numbers and letters). Each programming language sets its own requirements on what letters and numbers are permissible. Identifiers can be used to name constants, variables, or program units (e.g. procedures).

Variables

variable declaration:
Most programming languages require users to specify ("declare") at the beginning of a program the variables that will assume different values in the course of the data manipulation part of the program.

type declaration/type checking:
In the process of declaring variables, many programming languages require that users also state the *types* of data that are legitimate values for those variables (e.g. real numbers, integers, boolean values). Type declaration can become quite finely differentiated, especially in the ALGOL-derivative languages. Pascal, Modula-2, Ada, and C are examples of so-called strongly typed languages.

In addition to declaring the type of data that a variable can legitimately hold, it is also possible for a programming language to provide means of checking whether any inadmissible values have been assigned to those variables. This is known as type checking. It is possible for a language to be strongly typed (i.e. in the original declaration of variables) while not enforcing strong type checking. C is an example of such a language. (Ada, on the other hand, has both strong typing and strong type checking.)

global vs. local variables:
The actual assigning of values to variables can take place in one of two ways. Global variables remain "active" throughout the entire program, meaning that they can be used (or changed) at any point in the program. Local variables are "active" only within some limited subset of a program (such as a procedure), meaning that they are undefined outside of that subset.

Data Types

The power of a programming language derives in part from the kinds of data the language can handle and the distinctions among types of data that it can make. Generally speaking, the more modern the programming language, the more data types it recognizes.

integer:
The integer (i.e. whole number) is the most basic data type. All computer languages have means of handling integers.

real:
The data type *real* refers to variables that are able to take real numbers (i.e. with decimal points) as values. Some of the earlier programming languages could not handle real numbers (e.g. Integer BASIC).

boolean:
The data type *boolean* refers to the values "True" or "False."

char:
Variables that are type *char* are variables that take an alphabetic character as their value.

pointer
Some of the more modern ALGOL derivatives (especially Pascal and its offshoots, and C) use pointers to specify the address in memory of another piece of information.

user-defined:
Several of the more modern languages also allow programmers to define their own data types.

Data Structures

Data structures are the formal means programming languages have for showing relationships among individual pieces of data. Over the years, data structuring has become one of the most important areas of study in computer science. Typically, the more modern the programming language, the more kinds of data structures it has available.

One of the criteria generally used for determining whether a particular programming language is well suited to a given programming task is to see whether the language has built into it the data structures that will make the problem at hand reasonably easy to program. LISP, for example, has the list as its basic data structure. Many other languages (e.g. Pascal) do not have the list data structure, but allow you to create the equivalent of it with the data structures which are resident.

basic types:
Over the years, a large number of data structures have evolved. The ones you are likely to encounter are listed in Figure 3.13. (In addition, many languages allow users to define their own data structures.) Don't expect, however, to find all of these data structures within a single language.

static vs. dynamic data structures:
When a computer compiles and runs a program, it must set aside physical space in the Read/Write Memory locations (RAM) in which to store the data and program. With static data structures, a specific amount of memory is set aside at compile time, and cannot be altered (i.e. increased or decreased) during the actual running of the program. With dynamic data structures, the amount of memory space initially established is allowed to expand or contract when a program actually runs.

data abstraction:
A very important trend in modern imperative/algorithmic languages has been to separate low-level implementation details from overall conceptual structure. This move is seen in the "module" structure of Modula-2 and the "package" structure of Ada. More generally, the term *data abstraction* is used to describe

the separation of implementation details of data structures from their logical description. To the extent that the language structure itself dictates this abstraction, we speak of *data encapsulation*. To the extent that the abstraction is imposed by the actual program writer, we speak of *information hiding*.

Arithmetic Capabilities

One of the ways in which the early imperative/algorithmic languages were differentiated from one another was in their capacity for handling numbers. Many of the early languages (e.g. early versions of FORTRAN) which used to have limited arithmetic capabilities have subsequently added more sophisticated ways of formatting arithmetic expressions.

floating point vs. fixed point numbers:

There are two different ways in which computer languages can represent real numbers (i.e. numbers with decimal points). In floating point notation (also known as scientific notation), decimal expressions are represented with a single digit to the left of the decimal point, which is then multiplied by the appropriate power of 10. Depending upon the number of places to the right of the decimal point that the computer hardware is able to handle, it is possible to lose some precision in floating point notation.

In fixed point notation, the location of the decimal point is fixed in whatever location is appropriate for the number being represented (e.g. with two places to the right of the decimal point when representing U.S. currency; with one place to the right of the decimal point when representing readings from an average automobile odometer). Fixed point arithmetic is commonly used in business languages such as COBOL, where precision (down to the last penny) must be maintained.

double precision numbers:

Double precision numbers allow the programmer using floating point representation to specify a larger number of places to the right of the decimal point than is normally possible. This is brought about by using two rather than one memory location (in RAM) for holding the number.

Parameters

formal vs. actual parameters,
variable vs. value parameters:

Parameters are formal means by which different components of a program can "communicate" with one another. Structurally, a parameter list is composed of the names of variables. The selection of variables determines the kind of communication that takes place. For more discussion of parameters, see the entry on Pascal in Chapter 5.

III. DATA MANIPULATION

Regardless of the conceptual category to which a programming language belongs, all languages must be able to perform roughly the same types of manipulations. The differences between language types are manifested in the way in which this manipulation takes place. The names given below for data manipulation are generally the names used in talking about imperative/algorithmic languages. In the case of other language types (e.g. functional/applicative, logic programming), these same processes may go by different names (and look very different syntactically).

Assignment Statements/Initialization of Variables

A fundamental type of data manipulation in any program is the association of variables with values. In imperative/algorithmic languages, variables are given initial values, which can be altered by subsequent assignment statements.

Operators

All computer languages have a basic set of operators for manipulating data. The most common are:

arithmetic:
These operators perform such basic arithmetic procedures as addition, subtraction, multiplication, and division.

relational:
Relational operators compare two values and yield a boolean result (e.g. establishing the truth or falsity of the statement that the value of one variable is larger than the value of another).

Functions

Nearly all computer languages have built into them some rudimentary functions for manipulating numbers or characters. Languages that are numerically oriented tend to have more of these functions than languages that are symbolically oriented. In extensible languages (e.g. LISP), these functions often are not supplied as part of the basic language but can easily be defined by the user.

arithmetic:
Arithmetic functions include, for example, built-in means of taking square roots, squaring numbers, or taking the sine (or cosine) of a number.

transfer:
Transfer functions include truncating or rounding off fractional numbers.

boolean:

Some languages have special built-in functions for testing whether a program is at the end of a line (eoln) or at the end of a file (eof). When the end-of-line function evaluates to "True," there are no more data items on a given line of input to be read into the current program. When the end-of-file function evaluates to "True," there are no more data items in the entire file to be read.

Control Structures

Control structures lie at the heart of data manipulation in any programming language. Control structures quite literally direct the "flow of control" in a program, that is, they tell the computer what sequence of steps to follow.

Traditionally, some of the sharpest distinctions between languages came in the level of sophistication of their control structures. However, now that languages freely borrow syntax from one another, these distinctions are beginning to blur.

linear sequence:

The simplest possible control structure is to proceed in linear order, one statement at a time. This is the most typical control structure used in so-called unstructured languages like FORTRAN, COBOL, and BASIC.

selection:

A second approach to controlling the flow of a program is to use selection: In case X happens, do Y; if not, do Z. The most common selection control structures are *if . . . then . . . (else)* statements, *case* statements, and *GOTO* statements.

looping:

A third important control structure is the use of looping: Do activity X until Y happens. The most common looping structures are *while*, *repeat*, and *for* loops.

procedures/functions:

The fourth type of control structure uses procedures (and, in several imperative/algorithmic languages, their near cousins, functions). Procedures are declared in the data formatting part of the program and then invoked as control structures in the data manipulation part of the program.

Recursion vs. Iteration

One of the most important—though initially difficult to explain—concepts in manipulating data in a program is the distinction between recursion and iteration. In iteration, the same set of actions (e.g. increasing a number by one, squaring the result, and then subtracting two) might be carried out a number of times.

The procedure is carried out exactly the same way the tenth time through as it was the first. The number of times the procedure is executed is determined by some factor *outside of* the procedure itself.

In the case of recursion, the definition or operation of a procedure or function is also carried out a number of times. Here, however, the execution of each new operation is dependent upon the result of the previous one. As an analogy, think of the progress of a weight lifter. Every day he lifts 200 pounds of weights. Yet the very act of lifting the weights changes the weight lifter (i.e. muscles grow stronger). Therefore, the activity of lifting the same 200 pounds is not identical from one day to the next because the actor (the weight lifter) himself keeps altering as a result of his activity. Each recursive procedure takes the weight lifter nearer to some goal (perhaps becoming the strongest man in the world). However, unlike the case of iteration, the number of times a recursive procedure is executed is determined by some factor *inside of* the procedure itself. We look at recursion in more detail in the entry on LISP in Chapter 5.

Sorting

One of the most important ways in which computers manipulate data is to sort them (e.g. alphabetizing or placing in order). Over the years, several standard techniques have been developed for sorting data. In each case you compare two values, and then order them accordingly. Sorting techniques differ from one another in the ways in which they select values to be compared. Some of the best-known sorting techniques are listed in Figure 3.13.

Searching

Entries in a data base are of little use if they cannot be accessed. Searching is a fundamental data manipulation for locating a specific item. In many instances, search time is reduced if the list of items to consider has already been sorted. There are many standard search techniques, including sequential search, binary search, and hashing.

IV. INPUT/OUTPUT

For a computer language to function, it needs some means of taking in information and issuing results. Most computer languages have built-in functions for inputting and outputting information. However, it is also possible to place these input and output functions in separate programs or libraries where they can be invoked when needed. By removing input and output functions from the language itself, the language becomes more compact. More importantly, programmers can tailor input and output functions to the specific machine they will be using, thereby at once taking advantage of specific hardware properties while retaining the machine-independence of the language code itself. The early versions of ALGOL had no input/output functions, and C still does not.

Among languages in which input/output functions are incorporated as part of the language itself, the means used for accomplishing these tasks are quite similar. Input functions are indicated with such words as READ, READLN, or INPUT. Output is directed with such words as WRITE, WRITELN, or PRINT.

In addition to functions for directing information in or out, most computer languages have some means of indicating what form the output should take. The most common technique is known as a format statement, which specifies such things as where the output should appear on the printed page or how many decimal points should be expressed in a floating point number. Some languages also have so-called prettyprint format devices that automatically adjust the spacing and punctuation on a page (e.g. eliminating unnecessary spaces between symbols, adding the correct number of right-hand parentheses in a LISP function).

V. MISCELLANEOUS SYNTACTIC ISSUES

Line Numbers

Several computer languages (especially the earlier unstructured languages) numbered the lines of code in a program. Such ordering was used both to facilitate editing and to provide references for GOTO statements. Today, it is rare to find line numbering in computer languages, since, at least among the imperative/algorithmic languages, structured programming provides many alternative reference points in editing, and GOTO statements have been all but eliminated in favor of calls to procedures.

Reserved Words

Every computer language sets aside a small number of words whose meanings are defined by the language translator. Reserved words perform the basic operations of data formatting and data manipulation. These words cannot be used for identifiers (i.e. names for variables, procedures, or functions that the user independently defines in a program).

Comments

Nearly every computer language provides a means by which users can insert information into a program that explains what a particular line of code is doing. Using syntactic devices like brackets or parentheses (the convention differs from language to language), the translator ignores these comments when it comes time to compile or run the program.

Punctuation and Capitalization

Every programming language has a number of arbitrary syntactic rules stipulating where words must be capitalized and what punctuation must be used. These are by far the least interesting part of programming, but they also tend to be the most frustrating. For even if you have clearly thought out a problem, selected appropriate data structures and control structures, and written out the code 99 percent correctly, a single misplaced comma or blank space can keep your program from compiling or running. Many of the modern language translators tend to be more "forgiving" than their earlier counterparts, and will either ignore or automatically correct slight discrepancies in syntax.

PART II

SURVEY OF COMPUTER LANGUAGES

CHAPTER 4

Getting Started

Part II is a comprehensive overview of the major computer languages you are likely to have heard of or might want to learn. The languages themselves are presented, in alphabetical order, in Chapter 5. Chapter 4 provides background that will help you select a computer language, learn a language, buy a language translator—and read Chapter 5.

Choosing Among Languages

IS THERE A BEST LANGUAGE?

Many of the best computer languages are well suited for some tasks but not very efficient for others. If we could learn computer languages as easily as we change our clothes, we might use seven or eight different languages, each for a special purpose.

But it is not practical for most of us to become computer polyglots. The average computer user will do well to program in one or two languages. And so languages must be chosen carefully, and then stretched to fill a multiplicity of needs. It's obviously better to be able to write a slightly awkward program (that runs) in a language you know well than not to be able to write a program at all because you don't know the language that is tailor-made for the task.

This book will provide enough information on the range of languages now available to enable you to choose the language that best suits your needs. But do you know what those needs are? Will they remain the same over time? What's more, the language that interests you may not yet be readily available for the machine you own (a problem with Smalltalk, for example), or there may not yet be good documentation on the market to help you learn the language of your choice.

Finally, the languages of today might not survive the decade. If you bought a microcomputer in 1977, you helped fuel a revolution, but the machine itself will soon be ready for the museum. Prepare for the likelihood that the computer language you select now won't look nearly as appealing even a few years hence. The legendary longevity of FORTRAN, COBOL, BASIC, and LISP belongs to an earlier era when the computing world was controlled by a handful of programmers. (Very few people even knew how to *write* a computer language.) These older languages predate the microcomputer, and predate the phrase "user-friendly."

Should you therefore hold off learning a computer language until the dust settles? Obviously not. With that logic, we would never have started driving automobiles (which once constantly broke down), buying video cassette recorders (which used to record only a half hour's worth of tape), or using microcomputers (which started out with no screen, no keyboard, and almost no memory).

SHOULD YOU LEARN MORE THAN ONE?

How much do you need to learn? To be good at computer programming, you need to know a language well and use it often. Just as your high school French deteriorates if you don't practice, unused computer languages fade from memory. With such caveats, how can one reasonably advocate that general users come to know not one computer language but several?

Many people are already becoming computer multilinguals. Besides computer science students and professionals, there are two main groups: hobbyists who have outgrown BASIC, and children in school. A growing number of school systems are resolving the question of which language to teach by offering several languages seriatim.

In a typical scenario, Logo is taught to the youngest children, BASIC is introduced in the upper elementary school years, and Pascal is presented in junior high school or high school. Underlying this sequence are several suppositions: First, that Logo is easier than BASIC, and BASIC is easier than Pascal. Second, that there is a logical progression from one language to the next. And third, that these are the three best languages to teach. As we will see in Chapter 5, these assumptions are strained at best, and perhaps simply wrong.

Most people studying computer programming are *not* becoming multilingual. They are taking courses in *either* FORTRAN *or* BASIC *or* Pascal. Often they complete these courses believing that what they have learned is "computer programming," when they have actually learned "computer programming in a particular language." Such students may be wholly unaware that other languages even exist. Or if their existence is acknowledged, it is assumed these other languages obviously must not be as good as the one in the course.

The greatest virtue of learning more than one programming language (or at least getting an overview of several) is *perspective*. A sense of what a computer language is and of the various ways in which languages can be constructed. An understanding of the range of uses that a computer can have and the alternative ways in which programs can be written to develop those uses.

CRITERIA FOR CHOICE

How do you decide where to begin? Here are some criteria to consider.

Needs

Assess your current reasons for wanting to learn computer programming. Are you interested in "general education," or do you have specific problems you want to be able to solve? If your goal is general education, identify some plausible applications for what you will be learning. If your goal is specific tasks, consider whether the same language you select now will have other uses in the future.

Many American colleges argue that regardless of your programming interests, you should begin by learning a computer language that embodies the "principles of programming." Pascal is the current favorite. For users who will limit themselves to imperative/algorithmic languages, the choice is a good one. Pascal is a structured, clearly defined, comparatively simple language. Moreover, during the past decade it has become a benchmark against which to compare other imperative/algorithmic languages.

But what if you are primarily interested in graphics or natural language analysis or data base management? Other languages from other language families would be preferable. Moreover, these other languages embody *different* "principles of programming" (e.g. the importance of functions, extensibility, and data bases). In most computer science departments, a language like LISP is generally available only to advanced computer science students. Humanities students—for whom a list-processing language will probably be more useful than an imperative/algorithmic language—rarely know LISP exists. (Britain has been far more innovative than the United States in the use of list-processing and logic programming languages with non-science students, promoting the use of such languages as micro-PROLOG, POP-11, and now POPLOG.)

Prior Background/Availability of Teaching Materials

Some languages are especially easy to learn if you already know related languages. Learning Pascal, for example, is facilitated by knowing ALGOL, and prior knowledge of SIMULA simplifies the learning of Smalltalk.

When languages are *not* related to one another, learning a new computer language may actually be complicated by one's previous experience. The way that FORTRAN, for example, approaches a problem sharply differs from the way LISP or PROLOG would go about it. It might even be more difficult for FORTRAN programmers to feel comfortable with LISP than for rank novices. (A similar point applies to languages *within* a single language family. New programmers in Ada—a Pascal derivative—are warned not to write Ada programs with a Pascal "accent.")

Another pedagogical difficulty may be the availability of teaching materials. Many existing handbooks, especially on the newer languages like C and Ada, and the newly popular languages like LISP and Smalltalk, assume you are already familiar with computer languages and are a competent programmer in at least one of them. The rank beginner is typically at a disadvantage.

For many years, computer languages were taught by the apprenticeship system. After a small amount of elementary instruction, the learner was thrust into a world of practitioners and told to learn by example. Sometimes even the basic instruction was missing. David Touretzky, author of an excellent book on LISP, has described the traditional "teaching" of LISP this way: If you wanted to learn LISP, you hung around MIT until you met some people who knew LISP. Then you went out to a local Chinese restaurant and discussed LISP programs until the language began to make sense.

Not everyone can hang around MIT, and not everyone likes Chinese cooking. The work of Edsger Dijkstra and Niklaus Wirth on structured programming did a great deal to define and articulate the principles of computer programming (at least for imperative/algorithmic languages). Within the last few years, a growing number of legitimate "beginners''" books have begun to appear on most of the available languages. There are, however, hundreds of brightly covered, well-reviewed books now in the stores that are largely unusable for intelligent laymen who want to begin learning a computer language on their own.

Time

How much time you have for learning and using the language may also influence your choice. If you only want to write a few programs to calculate the family finances, learning a complex language like Ada is probably a waste of time. The language C has become a case in point. In the early 1980s, C became very popular among professional systems designers who wanted a concise, powerful language enabling them to take shortcuts. Novices who knew nothing about programming heard rumors that C was the "in" language to learn, and many invested in expensive C compilers. Yet C generally *isn't* a good beginning language. While it can be learned from scratch, C's virtues are largely lost on people without prior background in computing.

The U.S. Army Language School in Monterey, California, is rumored to "rank" foreign languages by the amount of time it takes to learn them passably well. While French might be a fifteen-week language, Russian is perhaps a twenty-week language and Mandarin Chinese a forty-week language. Computer languages could be given similar ratings. Using a scale of 1 to 10 (with 10 being the most time-consuming), PILOT might receive a rank of 1, micro-PROLOG a rank of 2, BASIC a rank of 3, and Pascal a rank of 4. LISP might be ranked 6; C, ranked 7; and Ada, ranked 10.

Rankings—both with computer languages and with natural languages—don't just reflect syntactic complexity. A language with simple syntax may still be difficult to learn to use properly. LISP, for example, has less distinct syntax than Pascal, but much of the difficulty in learning LISP comes in deciphering the layout of code on the page.

Cost, Availability, Compatibility

Finally, there remain the practical questions of cost, availability, and compatibility with other computing needs. We will postpone the discussion of these factors until later in the chapter when we talk about actually buying a computer language.

Learning a Language: The Question of Method

Educators generally agree that not all people learn the same way. The issue is not so much one of intelligence as one of cognitive style. Some very bright people don't do well at learning foreign languages (Einstein failed his foreign language entrance examination to college), while many not-so-smart people learn to pass for native speakers. There are those who do best by learning "principles" in advance, while others prefer to begin concretely and then derive principles through empirical generalization.

This book emphasizes the "principles." The main reason is that computer languages are so different from anything we are used to calling a language. By knowing in advance the sorts of structures and actions to expect, the empirical components of the language begin to make sense more quickly, and understandable fear of the unknown is essentially eliminated. If you encounter some syntax you don't understand in the original language, you have a "bird's-eye view" from which to puzzle things out. Moreover, if you go to learn a second computer language but don't understand the principles underlying the first one, there is little basis for generalization to the new task.

The movement toward "top down design" emphasizes principles rather than programs. The *last* thing you do in working out the top down design of a computer program is write actual lines of code. Before that, you think first about the logical components of the problem and then about the generic kinds of computer structures that might be used for representing the problem in *any* computer language. Syntax becomes a low-level detail.

Of course, teaching principles rather than programs can be taken to extremes. At some time you need to learn specific syntactic details to do actual programming. Equally importantly, the level of "principles" that are explained must be appropriate to the audience. Six-year-old children learning Logo don't need to know about functional/applicative languages, and twelve-year-olds learning micro-PROLOG need not understand the first order predicate calculus. However, these principles *are* relevant for teachers who must decide whether their school system should teach Logo or micro-PROLOG.

Buying a Language

Once you have chosen a language, you need to obtain a language translator (i.e. a compiler or an interpreter). If you will be running the language translator on someone else's mainframe or minicomputer, you are ready to begin. However, if you will be programming on your own microcomputer, you need to buy the translator (unless, of course, it is already built into ROM). Before sprinting to your local computer store or placing a mail order, mull over the following considerations.

Cost

Computer languages come in all price ranges. The price structuring reflects both the reputation of the software house and the amount of money that market analysts believe customers will pay. Translators written with the hobbyist in mind (e.g. most versions of FORTH, 8-bit versions of LISP, some versions of Pascal) tend to be reasonably priced. Languages for which a corporation will probably pick up the tab (e.g. COBOL, C, FORTRAN) can often be far more expensive.

An extremely important development in language translators is the recent move by several software houses to produce complete, efficient, and very inexpensive compilers for the larger languages. This trend was begun in late 1983 with Borland International's release of Turbo Pascal. Two years later, inexpensive compilers were released for Modula-2. Given the growing number of programmers working at home on microcomputers, it seems likely that this trend towards the "democratization" of powerful software will continue.

Before choosing a particular language implementation, *definitely* read reviews of the possible options in the computer magazines, and talk with friends. *Infoworld, Byte, MacWorld, PC World, PC Magazine,* and *Personal Computing* are good places to look. If you have difficulty locating reviews, write or call the distributor of the language you are considering. Look for a computer dealer who will let you try out the software before buying it. (Be forewarned: Since most dealers only stock the most popular languages—and then only the most popular implementations—this strategy often won't work.)

Availability

By now you know that not all languages—or language implementations—run on all machines. The availability of languages is a function of the marketplace. While you may want to run, say, MUMPS on your Macintosh, perhaps no software writer has shared your priorities. Many users end up selecting machines on the basis of the languages they will run.

Compatibility

If you only want to write and run programs on your own machine, you needn't worry about compatibility. Yet given the volatility of the computer market, this decision may prove unwise. A language translator specially tailored to your machine may produce superb programs that are not directly transferable to other machines. By choosing a standardized implementation (i.e. for which the code you write can be run directly on different machines, using different translators), you may save yourself a lot of recoding in the future.

Also remember that some languages have versions that run under different operating systems, even on the same physical machine. There are versions of BASIC that run on the Apple IIe under DOS 3.3 and versions that run under CP/M. When you select a particular computer language implementation, be sure your machine has the proper operating system for running it. Just because the salesperson said the language will run on an IBM PC doesn't mean it will run on *your* IBM if you lack the appropriate operating system. (NOTE: You sometimes even need a special *version* of an operating system. A program running under DOS 2.1 might not run properly under DOS 1.1.)

In the same vein, be certain that your machine has enough RAM and ample disk drives. Some languages are extremely memory-hungry. A $500 computer language is of no use if you can't load it and run it.

Speed

A perennial problem with using microcomputers is speed. Some machines (and some programs) run very quickly, while others allow time for your morning calisthenics between input and response. The speed problem can come from hardware design, limited memory space, a slow operating system, or the design of the language translator itself (compiled languages are generally faster than interpreted; low-level languages are faster than high-level languages). Some software manufacturers sell versions of languages that run much faster than their competitors. However, when considering the speedier versions, be sure they have all the other desirable features of the more lethargic competition.

Support

The least considered but most important criterion in buying a computer language is support. If there are problems, is there a place to turn? Some language translators come with excellent documentation, while the manuals for others are hopelessly confusing or absent altogether.

Many software manufacturers provide user support, either by telephone or by electronic bulletin board. While such support may seem utterly pedestrian when deciding which language to learn, one long bout of being unable to get your programs to compile or run will rapidly change your opinion. Again, read the reviews and check with friends. Don't necessarily judge a software house by its size. Some mom-and-pop operations provide excellent support. (Admittedly, others never even fill your orders.) A number of software houses have toll-free hot lines, while others leave your long-distance call on hold while you listen to Muzak and watch the phone bill rise. As in all cases of computer purchases, *caveat emptor*.

Preview of Chapter 5

There are by now many hundreds of computer languages in use in the United States alone. To include them all here would produce a very thick volume that would be both superficial and largely irrelevant to most readers. On the other hand, to select just a handful of languages (as is common in books on computer languages) presents a skewed view of the range of possible languages and their relationships with one another.

Our solution here is to discuss twenty-two languages in some detail. The entries are selected not only to be representative of the languages you are likely to encounter but also to provide the background necessary to understand how and why computer languages differ from one another and what languages we are likely to be using in the future. These languages are either historically important (e.g. ALGOL), currently widely used (e.g. LISP or Pascal), or promising for the future (e.g. micro-PROLOG).

The Appendix at the end of the book presents much briefer information on a number of additional languages.

Organization

Each of the major language entries is presented through the same basic format. The entries all begin with a "language profile" that summarizes the important features of the language: the meaning of its name; its structural characteristics; its primary functions; its genealogy; its major versions or dialects; and a collection of special characteristics (including such things as memory requirements, ease of learning and use, availability, and important terminology). The rest of each entry contains sections on why the language came into being, how to think about solving problems in that language, the evolution of the language, the future of the language, and information on how to use the language (including what you need to know about buying a translator and what else to read).

This standard format encourages comparison between languages. By juxtaposing the "profile" charts on two languages, you can quickly see the most significant similarities and differences. Many of the major language entries also contain direct comparisons with other languages. The comparisons may be based on structural grounds (e.g. differences between BASIC as an unstructured language and Pascal as a structured language), functional grounds (e.g. Logo vs. micro-PROLOG as languages for teaching thinking), or genealogical grounds (e.g. the derivation of Logo from LISP). In most instances these contrastive discussions appear in the entry for the language which is historically more recent. However, there is frequent cross-referencing.

The mechanics of actual programming in each language are explained to the extent necessary to offer a gestalt of how the language works and why it has the shape it does. This is not a "how to" book on any language in particular, and syntactic detail is therefore kept to a minimum. As a result, the chapter does not present full program samples for each language. Often the syntactic conventions necessary to make a program actually run (e.g. where you put the semicolons, how to assign values to variables) obscure the principles that make a particular language interesting and distinct from other languages. When you get to the point of learning the nuts and bolts of a particular language, all these details will, of course, be necessary, but they will also make sense. For now, this degree of syntactic clutter merely makes languages look far more complex than they actually are.

We have also avoided the common temptation to write programs in each language solving the same problem. Readers would have to know considerably more about the syntactic conventions of each language for these programs to make much sense. What's more, the enterprise itself is of dubious value. As we saw in Chapter 3, not all languages are equally well suited for solving the same types of problems, though all can be contorted into solving any problem. We don't need ten or fifteen examples of contorted—and, for the novice, unreadable—programs to prove the point. To show each language in its best light, we would need a minimum of four or five different problems in each of the twenty-two languages.

As an alternative, we present comparative programs *in context*. The same problem is solved in Logo and LISP to illustrate the strong degree of similarity between the two languages. Another problem is solved in BASIC and APL to show just how compact an APL program can be. And so on.

HOW TO READ CHAPTER 5

The entries in Chapter 5 are presented alphabetically—from Ada to SNOBOL. This arrangement has the advantage of enabling you to find each language discussion without having to resort to the index. It also neatly avoids the dilemma of where to put languages that could logically be categorized in several places.

The problem, of course, with an alphabetical listing is conceptual coherence. The entry on SNOBOL immediately follows the discussion of Smalltalk, but the two languages have little connection with one another. Reading Chapter 5 straight through is probably not the best way to proceed.

Instead, you should devise a plan. Use the structural, functional, and genealogical classifications in Chapter 3 to select areas that interest you. You may want to know more about logic programming, artificial intelligence languages, or the ALGOL family.

Within an area you can generally begin at random. But once you have read an entry, you will be guided to other, related entries. For example, if you begin by reading about SIMULA, you will find yourself logically turning next to the section on Smalltalk. The entry on BASIC naturally leads back to discussion of Pascal. Once you have chosen a place to begin, the path of possibilities is still wide but no longer random.

You will sometimes encounter a major language discussion that has a "prerequisite," a recommendation that you read another language entry first. The section on micro-PROLOG, for example, suggests you initially read the section on PROLOG, and the discussion of Logo directs you first to LISP. All of the sections (including micro-PROLOG and Logo) *are* self-sufficient. However, in cases such as these where a sizable portion of the entry constitutes a comparison with another language, it obviously makes sense to concomitantly learn something about that other language.

In structuring your reading, it is important not to get bogged down in historical anecdotes or in syntactic detail. Halfway through a discussion of objects in Smalltalk or MATCH statements in PILOT, it is easy to forget why this language might be worth learning (as opposed to some other language that looked so interesting just a few moments ago). Remember to keep your reading in perspective.

CHAPTER 5

The Languages

Ada

PROFILE
NAME named for Augusta Ada Byron, Countess of Lovelace, and inventor of the stored program

STRUCTURE
Familiar Distinctions:
  hardware: high-level
  translator: usually compiled
  structural unit: package
  data: numerical
 	
Conceptual Distinctions:
  organizing principle: imperative/algorithmic
  procedures: procedural
  extensibility: not extensible
  program/data: distinct

FUNCTIONS specifically designed for military emedded systems, but use may broaden
GENEALOGY 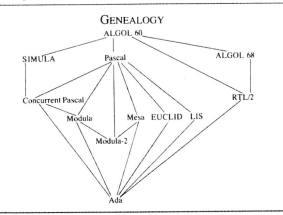

Ada (Continued)

Years:　1975–83 (ANSI Standard)

Authors:　Jean Ichbiah (and design team at Cii Honeywell-Bull, France)

Impetus:　U.S. Department of Defense needed single language which was tailored for programming embedded systems in real time and which could be easily maintained

Evolution:　multilayered definition and design process for both the language and the software environment
validated compilers only now becoming available

VERSIONS/DIALECTS

Standard:　ANSI Ada　(NOTE: The DoD holds a trademark on Ada, and legally no one else can produce a subset, superset, or variant of any kind)

SPECIAL CHARACTERISTICS

Memory Requirements:　especially large

Ease of Learning/Use:　basic structure not difficult, but a very large number of details

Availability:　validated compilers slowly becoming available; non-authorized subsets currently sold for microcomputers

NOTE: To understand Ada's structure and purpose, it helps to be familiar with the history and structure of earlier ALGOL-based languages. Review the entries on ALGOL and Pascal first, and then read Ada in conjunction with the entries on Modula-2 and C.

WHY ADA?

The camel, it is said, is a horse created by committee. Each of its features seems reasonable in isolation, but the composite (at least to the Western eye) is ungainly.

Ada is the ultimate language created by committee. But unlike ALGOL (also produced by a communal effort), Ada was sponsored by the ultimate organization: the United States military. And the military plans on a grand scale. While the first draft of ALGOL 58 was completed by a handful of people in a few days, more than a thousand computer scientists had a hand in designing Ada. In fact, it took several years just to finalize the *specifications* for the language (that is, the description of what structural elements the future language would need to contain).

Why all this effort to create one computer language?

Real-Time Languages and Embedded Systems: The Problem of Reliability

Much of the computer programming done by the U.S. military is used for controlling military hardware—tanks, airplanes, nuclear bombs. To control such hardware, a computer program must operate in *real time*, that is, while the tank is rolling or plane is flying. A navy fighter pilot can't wait for results to be returned from the computer center the next day.

A *real-time computer language* controls or responds to stimuli occurring in the real world. The control of traffic lights in response to the actual number of cars crossing an intersection would be one example. A hospital monitoring device that detects heart rate—and sends appropriate signals to a central nursing station in case of dramatic changes—would be another. These systems contrast with "atemporal" languages, where no event in the real world (such as changing a light from green to red) is dependent upon *when* the computer processes a particular datum.

Real-time programming languages have become increasingly important over the past ten or fifteen years. These languages control everything from nuclear power plants and industrial robots to dishwashers. Several dozen such languages have been developed on both sides of the Atlantic. Among the better known are JOVIAL, CORAL 66, RTL/2, LIS, EUCLID, PEARL, Mesa, Modula, and Modula-2.

Real-time systems can operate in one of two ways. The controlling mechanism (a computer) can be housed outside of the device it is controlling (e.g. a traffic light). Alternatively, the computer (and program) can be *embedded within* a larger mechanical system (such as a robot or a pilotless plane). Conceptually, then, embedded systems are a type of real-time system, and real-time systems are a type of programming system. In practice, so many real-time systems have been developed to deal with embedded systems that the terms *real-time* and *embedded* are often used interchangeably.

The development of software for real-time embedded systems is far more exacting than software written for atemporal systems. Real-time systems are typically large and complex, making coordination of the programming effort a problem in itself. Real-time systems must be able to respond to external events within a guaranteed response time. (Learning your patient had a cardiac arrest twenty minutes ago is of little use.) Further, real-time systems must be able to interface with standard computer peripherals (like printers and modems) as well as with non-standard input and output devices like traffic signals and robot arms.

But the absolutely critical feature of a real-time embedded system is its need for *reliability*. The program must not only work. It must work flawlessly. In the case of process control (e.g. the use of robots in industry), errors can lead to lost production, and therefore to loss of money. In the case of military embedded systems (e.g. aircraft navigation or the control of a nuclear warhead), a programming error could result in enormous loss of human life.

In designing a real-time language, then, the most important criterion is *security*: can programming errors be detected *automatically* before any damage is done? Typically such detection is the job of the compiler.

How do you avoid undetected errors? One of the very best ways is to guarantee that a datum entering the system is a legitimate value for the relevant variable in the program. The best means of guaranteeing the correctness of such values (or for detecting illegitimate values) is through strong data typing and type checking.

As we saw at the end of Chapter 3, a data type is a category of acceptable values that a variable can take. For example, a language may distinguish between *integer* and *real* data types. If a variable is declared to be of type integer, then 2.56 (a real number) is not an acceptable value for that variable. Similarly, 2 is not a proper value for a variable of type real (though 2.0 is).

Some computer languages are very stringent about both data typing and type checking. In a language with strong typing and strong type checking, a program may not compile if you assign an illegitimate value to a variable (i.e. a value that does not belong to the declared data type). Other languages (like C) are more lax, either converting data that are not properly typed (e.g. converting 2 to 2.0) or simply allowing values that do not belong to the declared data type (e.g. accepting the value 2.56 for a variable that was declared to be of type integer).

Strong data typing automatically enables programmers to catch a significant number of errors that regularly creep into programs. One reason Niklaus Wirth built strong data typing into Pascal was that he wanted to enable students just learning programming to identify their mistakes quickly and easily. On the minus side, though, strong data typing requires programmers to know how the program will be used while they are still writing it. What if you don't *know* what kind of data will be used (or even the kinds of variables you will need) when you are starting out? The advantage of weak data typing is the flexibility it affords programmers.

When comparing strong vs. weak data typing and type checking among atemporal languages, the debate typically reduces to personal style and experience. Highly structured languages tend to be strongly typed and checked, as are languages used in pedagogy. Languages used by professional programmers are often less strongly typed or, if strongly typed, less strongly checked.

In an atemporal system, if a weakly typed (or weakly type-checked) language inappropriately accepts an inadmissible data value (e.g. where the inadmissible value comes from a malfunctioning input device), the worst consequence is an incorrect answer generated on the screen or printout. The programmer can scrutinize the results, find the error, and correct it at leisure. The situation changes radically when we talk about real-time systems. If an inadmissible value should be accepted in a real-time system, the damage is immediate. A traffic light shifts from green to red every three seconds, or a satellite is catapulted off course.

Thus, real-time programming must have strong data typing (and type checking) as a safeguard against errors creeping in during the input or manipulation of data. The consequences of errors can be disastrous. Discussions of Ada necessarily keep returning to this critical issue of language and program reliability.

Given the importance of embedded systems in military activity, it is hardly surprising that the Department of Defense (DoD) should be interested in identifying a suitable real-time language. But which one?

Scaling the Tower of Babel: The Cost of Productivity and Maintenance

In the early 1970s, the DoD decided to review its expenditures on computer software. A study it commissioned revealed that in 1973 the DoD spent between $3 billion and $3.5 billion on new software and software maintenance. In breaking down these figures by function, more than half of that amount (56%) was being spent on embedded computer systems. (Data processing consumed 19%, and scientific computing a scant 5%.)

While COBOL and FORTRAN largely functioned as standards in data processing and scientific computing, respectively, the linguistic landscape for embedded systems was chaotic. At least 450 different computer languages and dialects were used by the DoD for embedded systems in the early 1970s.

The practical consequences of this veritable Tower of Babel were devastating. Obviously, programs written in a language specially designed for one application could not readily be transferred to another. Programmers beginning work on a project would often have to learn a new language or dialect. Worse still, very few of these hundreds of languages had appropriate software tools to aid in writing new programs. Beginning a new project was like reinventing the wheel.

Yet the real nightmare came not in writing programs but in maintaining them (e.g. in correcting bugs in existing programs, adapting programs to new machines or new language standards, or altering the functions of programs). With an average programmer turnover rate of every two years, people responsible for maintaining programs over a decade or so often had no connection with the authors of a program or the authors of the language in which the program was written.

The outlook was bleak. The report estimated that by 1990 the cost of software for military embedded systems alone would approach $35 billion (up from less than $2 billion in the early 1970s).

By 1974, the DoD decided to act. Groups from each of the military departments proposed adopting a common programming language to be used in defense systems. The search that would eventually lead to Ada had begun.

Jousting with Straw Men: The Development of Ada

In January 1975, the Defense Advanced Research Projects Agency (DARPA) of the Department of Defense established a High Order Language Working Group (HOLWG). Its charge was:

> To produce a minimal number of common, modern High Order [= high-level] Computer Languages for the DoD embedded systems applications and to assure a unified, well-supported, widely available programming support environment for these languages.

The "minimal number" was eventually reduced to "one." The call for a "support environment" (i.e. in addition to the language itself) reflects the DoD's perception that it needed to lower software development costs.

The project was divided into several steps:
(1) language
    a. definition and evaluation
    b. design
(2) environment
    definition and design
(3) implementation
    language and environment

Step (1) took five years, and step (3) is only now bearing fruit. Throughout the ordeal, the definers and designers coined a stream of titles that injected levity into the otherwise hard-nosed business of designing an extremely complex computer language.

The flow chart below summarizes the evolution of the language that came to be known as Ada. Language design and development milestones are on the left-hand side, and developments of the Ada Programming Support Environment (APSE) are on the right.

(1a) Language Definition and Evaluation

The first step was to create a "job description" for the new language. These specifications underwent several drafts. The first, aptly named STRAWMAN, was produced in 1975. It was replaced by WOODENMAN later in 1975, which was superseded by TINMAN in 1976.

TINMAN (which was a *specification* of what the new language should be like, not a language itself) was compared against a large number of existing languages currently in use or potentially suitable for embedded systems. (NOTE: Modula-2 had not yet been invented, and C was not on the list—see the comparative discussion of Ada, Modula-2, and C near the end of the entry on Modula-2.) None of the languages examined was found to meet the specification requirements, though PL/I, ALGOL 68, and Pascal were judged possible starting points. The result of this comparison with existing languages was a new requirements document known as IRONMAN. Completed in 1977, IRONMAN became the starting point for actual design.

LANGUAGE Definition and Design		ENVIRONMENT Definition and Design
High Order Language Working Group (HOLWG) established by DARPA at DoD STRAWMAN, WOODENMAN	1975	
TINMAN	1976	
IRONMAN	1977	
RED, GREEN, BLUE, YELLOW STEELMAN (RED and GREEN competing)	1978	SANDMAN, PEBBLEMAN
GREEN selected (Jean Ichbiah of Cii Honeywell-Bull, France)	1979	
Ada Reference Manual	1980	STONEMAN
	1981	development of actual software environments
Revised Ada Reference Manual	1982	(continued)
validation of early Ada compilers; ANSI Standard for Ada approved	1983	(continued)
continuing validation of compilers; as of January 1984, Ada must be used for new mission-critical programs	1984	(continued)
(continued)	1985	(continued)

(1b) Language Design
DARPA (the Defense Advanced Research Projects Agency) now issued an open
invitation to software designers to write a language that met the IRONMAN
specifications and that took either Pascal, PL/I, or ALGOL as a base. Of the
almost three dozen entries received, four were selected to continue in the
competition. All four, it turned out, were based on Pascal. Each of the four
sponsoring organizations was then funded for six months of further study, and
each was assigned a code name: RED (Intermetrics), GREEN (Cii Honeywell-
Bull), BLUE (Softech), and YELLOW (SRI International).

The result of these four contracts was a final requirements document known
as STEELMAN. Two of the contestants—RED and GREEN—were invited to
complete languages meeting the STEELMAN specifications. The final evaluation
was made in the spring of 1979. The winner was the GREEN language, the
product of a design team led by Jean Ichbiah of Cii Honeywell-Bull in France.
The language was named Ada, in honor of Augusta Ada Byron, Countess of
Lovelace. Ada was the inventor of stored programs, and hence the first real
computer programmer.

For the next year and a half, the language Ada underwent testing and
evaluation. The first Ada Reference Manual was issued in July 1980, with a
revised version appearing in 1982.

(2) Environment: Definition and Design
Alongside the development of the Ada language itself was a parallel effort to
develop a standard software environment. This environment would include not
only the language translator but debugging aids and project management support
facilities as well. As we saw in Chapter 2, the creation of environments alongside
languages is becoming increasingly popular in the programming world.

The definition and design of the Ada Programming Support Environment
(APSE) parallel the development of the Ada language, but on a smaller scale.
First there was a series of specifications documents: SANDMAN, PEBBLEMAN,
and STONEMAN. Work began in 1978 (by which time the definition of Ada
itself was nearly complete). Specifications were laid down not only for the
software environment but for the administrative framework necessary to support
Ada. The final planning stages were completed by early 1980, a few months
before the first Ada Reference Manual was issued. By late 1980, multiple
contractors had been selected to begin the actual design of the APSE, using
STONEMAN as their specifications guide.

In the process of designing the Ada language and environment, three important
administrative moves were made. An Ada Joint Programs Office was established
to coordinate all DoD Ada activities. The DoD took out a trademark on the
name ''Ada,'' thereby legally preventing anyone from producing a subset or
superset of Ada or any Ada-like language. And the DoD established a mechanism
for validating Ada compilers that were produced by private parties or under
government contract. Unless a proposed compiler meets the DoD's validation

test, its manufacturers cannot publicly claim that it translates the Ada language. (Without such validation, it is obviously impossible to be awarded government contracts to program in Ada.)

(3) Language and Environment Implementation
Implementation of the Ada language and environment is a slow process that will continue through the 1980s. The first validated compiler (actually an interpreter) was developed at New York University, and designed largely as a teaching tool. The second validated compiler was produced by ROLM and Data General for the Eclipse minicomputer, and the third was developed by Western Digital for its Micro-Engine (a microcomputer). Several dozen other compilers— on large and small computers—are now undergoing validation testing. By the end of the decade, validated compilers should be ubiquitous.

THINKING IN ADA

Ada's Split Personality

Two major design considerations underlie the structure of Ada. On the one hand, the DoD needed a highly reliable, sophisticated real-time programming language to control embedded systems. On the other, the DoD was wallowing in a sea of languages. Many programs using these languages were written inefficiently, and maintenance was extremely costly. Thus, the DoD's new language needed to be at once complex and simple.

The character of Ada heavily depends upon one's perspective on programming. In the eyes of Ada's creators, the language is actually very simple if you look at its underlying structure (without becoming bogged down in detail). In the eyes of Ada's critics, the language is totally unwieldy, too large for any single human being to fathom in its entirety.

Just what did Ada's designers have in mind for the language, and how do their goals explain these paradoxes?

Production and Comprehension

Linguists distinguish between the ability to *produce* a linguistic utterance and the ability to *understand* what someone else has said. Very young children who produce only one- or two-word sentences typically understand far more complex language. Adults learning foreign languages are often better at one skill than another, being able, for example, to ask directions in a foreign language but not being able to understand the native's response.

The production/comprehension dichotomy also applies to computer languages. APL and FORTH are sometimes dubbed "write-only languages" because while it is reasonably straightforward to write programs in them, it is often difficult— even for the original programmer—later to make sense of what has been written.

The symbols used to write APL or FORTH code tend to be very short, and to bear few clues as to their meaning. Yet unless you readily recognize the meaning of these symbols, a line of code can easily begin to look like hieroglyphics.

In other cases, language designers have been especially concerned that people can read programs written by others. COBOL is the first well-known example. COBOL designers put a lot of effort into making COBOL code readable by business managers, but expended less energy on making COBOL an easy language in which actually to write programs (see the entry on COBOL in this chapter).

Ada is the second major language in which designers have given precedence to program readability over writability. The IRONMAN language specification explicitly required that

> The language should promote ease of maintenance. It should emphasize program readability over writability. That is, it should emphasize the clarity, understandability, and modifiability of programs over programming ease.

Jean Ichbiah, who implemented the IRONMAN specification in the language that came to be known as Ada, justifies his decision:

> For many years the emphasis had been on creating languages that made it possible to write programs very fast. It took years for the software industry to realize that this was an improper goal: The development of a large program may take less than two years, whereas that same program may have to be maintained for over 20 years. Even if it takes a little longer to write it, it is far more important that a program be readable than writable. For 20 years after the program is written, programmers will have to read it to maintain it. And the easier a program is to read, the easier it will be to maintain.
> Interview with Ichbiah,
> *Communications of the ACM*, October 1984

Thus, the Ada language is intentionally more complex in the eyes of the software writer than it is in the eyes of later program users. Ada programmers tend to have to write a lot of "extra" lines of code which make the structure of a program self-evident to such future users.

Packages: The Key to Ada Design

The central notion underlying the construction of Ada is the *package*. The idea of the package is hardly unique to Ada. It ultimately derives from blocks and procedures in ALGOL, and is similar to modules in Modula-2.

Packages have three functions. First, they conceptually divide a large program into units (much the way that Pascal does with procedures). Second, they enable programmers to hide the details of a package not only from users but also from other packages. And third, where appropriate, they allow communication with one another (akin to Modula-2's *import* and *export* features across modules). Our discussion here will focus on the use of packages to hide programming details.

In arguing that Ada is conceptually a simple language, Ichbiah suggests an analogy between Ada's construction and the way the average person uses a digital watch:

> Consider a watch. We can view it as an Ada package. It has a set of entry points: a procedure (or button) called *Select* to select a given function of the watch; a procedure called *Set*, to reset the data; and a procedure for displaying the current time. This is the user's view of the watch.
>
> If there were nothing more to the watch than these buttons, it would not be able to perform its functions. There has to be something inside the watch: a mechanism to *implement* all the promises on the outside. In Ada, you can collect all the facilities you want to provide into a package. The user's view of these facilities is defined by a *package specification*; it is the *visible part* of the package. The programs that provide their mechanism are what we call the *package body*.

Like the *Set* button on a watch, the *package specification* is all that the average Ada program user needs to know of the package. And like the clockwork mechanism that actually sets the watch, the *package body* is what the software developer needs to know to write a program in Ada.

To see how this distinction works, consider the overall structure of an Ada package:

```
               PACKAGE SPECIFICATION
package PACKAGE_NAME is
     (type declarations)
     (variable and constant declarations)
     (program and task specifications)
private
     (full declaration of private types)
end PACKAGE_NAME;

               PACKAGE BODY
package body PACKAGE_NAME is
     (subprogram bodies for all specifications in
          visible part)
     (additional type, variable, and constant
          declarations)
     (additional subprograms and tasks)
begin
     (program statements)
end PACKAGE_NAME;
```

The *package specification* (i.e. the part the user generally needs to deal with) contains a sequence of declarations, divided into two kinds. The first (including type declarations and the declaration of variables and constants so familiar from Pascal) is known as the *visible* part of the package specification. The second is the *private* part, and includes the declaration of types that are used in special ways allowing the user greater control over the program.

The *package body* is the place in which the operations indicated in the package specifications are actually spelled out. That is, the lines of code for manipulating data are placed here. The body may also contain additional declarations needed to operate the package, but these details don't need to be known outside the package body.

Packages are written and then stored in a library until needed. To use an Ada package, it must be embedded within a program frame (much as a procedure in Pascal only functions in terms of a larger program). A complete Ada program for even a simple problem may seem quite long. However, this degree of detail is intentional, since painstaking declarations and specifications make a program less prone to error now and easier to read in the future.

THE EVOLUTION OF ADA

Since compilers are only now appearing for Ada, relatively few programmers have had much experience with the language. Yet given the vast development effort and the enormous level of interest that the language has generated, it is already clear what the major issues will be in the evolution of Ada. One is the question of function: Is Ada merely a special-purpose language for handling embedded systems, or is its potential range of functions far broader? The other question concerns Ada's size: Is it too big?

Special-Purpose or General-Purpose Language

When DARPA first formed the High Order Language Working Group in 1975, its immediate interest was in defining a language to use in embedded systems. Over time, the DoD's immediate interests have focused on "mission-critical" programming (e.g. guided missiles rather than controlling traffic or operating dishwashers). The DoD issued a directive that by January 1984 all newly initiated mission-critical projects must be programmed in Ada.

Yet we shouldn't forget that Ada was designed to be conceptually clear and therefore easy to maintain over time. Since the needs for readability and maintenance are the same in business and scientific programming as they are in embedded systems, current users of COBOL and FORTRAN might reasonably switch to Ada. Ichbiah indicates that many programmers in both business and industry are exploring Ada. Several American universities are even experimenting with teaching Ada as a beginning programming language because of its high degree of structuring and its potential for revealing progressively more details of the language as students become increasingly proficient. Since Ada derives from Pascal, this move toward making Ada a general-purpose language is hardly surprising.

Is Ada Too Big?

But there is a problem: Ada's size. Unlike COBOL or FORTRAN or Pascal, Ada is a huge language. Is it *too* big, as many people argue? Articles—and rebuttals—dot the pages of the *Communications of the ACM* over the past several years.

One type of argument questions whether Ada can ever become a general-purpose language. Critics of Ada's size argue that much of the detail available in Ada is unnecessary for the general programmer. Potential programmers avoid the language, not wanting to become mired in superfluous structure.

A second argument is even more serious. Is Ada too big a language for running special-purpose embedded systems (the function for which Ada was designed)? The issue is whether such a complex language can offer flawless reliability.

A true story illustrates the problem. At 4:21 A.M. on July 22, 1962, the National Aeronautics and Space Administration launched a Mariner spacecraft from Cape Canaveral, bound for Venus. Two hundred and ninety seconds later, the vehicle was ordered destroyed. Mariner I had deviated significantly from its intended trajectory and was less likely to reach Venus than some yacht cruising off the Florida coast.

Something was awry with the equation used to edit data on the booster position and velocity of the Atlas guidance system, which was to propel the satellite into space. The debacle was eventually traced to the way in which the underlying FORTRAN program controlling operations allowed the program not to declare all variable types, instead providing a default convention. The lack of compulsory type declarations in FORTRAN produced a program that malfunctioned.

But how does the failure of Mariner I involve Ada? Unlike FORTRAN, Ada is a strongly typed (and strongly type-checked) language. Presumably at least this error would not have arisen if the Mariner computers were programmed in Ada.

According to Tony Hoare (ACM Turing Award recipient in 1980), the problem runs much deeper. There is no way, Hoare argues, that a sprawling language like Ada can ever be fully comprehensible to users, and so programmers may unwittingly introduce errors. Since Ada is designed to run mission-critical projects, such mistakes can be disastrous.

In his Turing Award Lecture, Hoare made an impassioned plea against Ada:

> Do not allow this language in its present state to be used in applications where reliability is critical, i.e. nuclear power stations, cruise missiles, early warning systems, anti-ballistic missile defense systems. The next

rocket to go astray as a result of a programming language error may not be an exploratory space rocket on a harmless trip to Venus: It may be a nuclear warhead exploding over one of our own cities. An unreliable programming language generating unreliable programs constitutes a far greater risk to our environment and to our society than unsafe cars, toxic pesticides, or accidents at nuclear power stations.

In less apocalyptic terms, Niklaus Wirth reinforced Hoare's point in his own 1984 Turing Award Lecture:

> Even if the effort of building unnecessarily large systems and the cost of memory to contain their code could be ignored, the real cost is hidden in the unseen efforts of the innumerable programmers trying desperately to understand them and use them effectively.

Wirth's notion of a reasonably sized language compiler is about five thousand lines (the size of Modula-2). By contrast, an Ada compiler is several hundred thousand lines long.

Yet unlike the language's critics, Ada's designers don't find the language too large. Ichbiah, in direct response to Hoare's critique, retorts that Hoare and his colleagues lose the forest for the trees by looking at the language with the eyes of mathematicians rather than architects—focusing on detail rather than on overarching structure. "The human mind," says Ichbiah,

> has an incredible ability to understand structures. Provided it understands the major lines of a structure, it will make inferences and immediately see the consequences. When you judge something, the complexity is not in the details but in whether or not it is easy to infer details from major structural lines.
>
> From this point of view, I consider Ada to be very simple.

THE FUTURE OF ADA

The future of Ada hinges on three questions: Will Ada succeed in being highly reliable and easily maintained? Will the public find Ada too large to learn and too unwieldy for doing general-purpose programming? And how much clout will the Department of Defense choose to exercise?

Reliability and Maintainability

The first mission-critical software is only now being written and installed in embedded systems. It will be several years before Ada's success or failure can be assessed. Structurally, Ada incorporates all known precautions to ensure program reliability. It remains to be seen whether Ada's size undermines the reliability (and ease of maintenance) of the system, or whether the use of packages to hide detail reduces the "cognitive" size of the language.

Public Response

The programming public may well turn to Ada as the next conceptual step beyond Pascal. Should the DoD decide to issue a subset of Ada, public response could be extremely positive.

The Long Arm of the DoD

Ada could readily become a widely used language (even given its current size) if the Department of Defense extended its directive on which DoD programming must be done in Ada. As of now, only new mission-critical work requires programming in Ada. But extensions of this directive are not difficult to envision.

Business programming could as easily be done in a rich ALGOL-based language like Ada as in COBOL. Admittedly, two strong forces mitigate against such a change: the enormous backlog of programs written in COBOL, and the growth of query languages that already challenge further expansion of COBOL for data processing (see the entries on QBE and Intellect).

Scientific programming is the application most readily convertible to Ada. Despite the vast libraries of FORTRAN programs, much scientific programming is already done in ALGOL-derived languages, and there is no conceptually distinct competitor (such as query languages in the case of COBOL).

What about artificial intelligence (AI)? The AI community has always drawn substantial funding from DARPA. And it was DARPA that initiated the development of Ada. Will AI researchers soon be programming in Ada?

The answer, as of now, is ''no.'' American AI researchers have almost always programmed in LISP, a language better suited to their purposes than highly structured imperative/algorithmic languages (be they ALGOL or Pascal or Modula-2 or Ada). Besides, they say, their work is not mission-critical.

But might not AI programming *become* mission-critical? As AI researchers create increasingly ''intelligent'' programs for controlling the movements of machines, we can expect future military embedded systems to be guided by ''intelligent'' programs which, as of now, are written in LISP. It will be interesting to see how the interaction between Ada and LISP develops.

USING ADA

Buying ADA

Full (and validated) versions of Ada are still few in number and generally too expensive for home consumption. However, this situation is rapidly changing. The best place to look for new Ada compilers is current computer magazines. But be aware that some versions of Ada even now being offered are (unauthorized) subsets of the language. They may be useful for learning and experimentation, but should not be mistaken for the full (and authorized) language.

What to Read

An understanding of Ada requires some grasp of real-time and embedded systems. This bibliography includes entries both on real-time and embedded systems and on the Ada language itself.

Real-Time Languages and Embedded Systems:

BOOKS

Young, Stephen J. (1982). *Real Time Languages: Design and Development.* Chichester (Eng.): Ellis Horwood.
   An especially clear explanation of what real-time languages are, how they work, and what some of the major real-time programming languages look like. Much of the book is comprehensible even to novices.
Downes, Valerie A., and Stephen J. Goldsack (1982). *Programming Embedded Systems with Ada.* Englewood Cliffs (N.J.): Prentice-Hall International.
   A useful book that presents Ada in the context of its uses in embedded systems.

The Language Ada:

BOOKS

Books on Ada are rapidly beginning to proliferate. Here are just three suggestions.

Shumate, Kenneth (1984). *Understanding Ada.* New York: Harper & Row.
   A useful and gentle introduction to Ada that will be understandable to novice and experienced programmer alike.
Ledgard, Henry (1983). *Ada: An Introduction.* New York: Springer-Verlag.
   A text written to accompany the Ada Reference Manual. Ledgard is well known for his clarity in writing about computer languages, and this book is no exception.
Barnes, J. G. P. (1982). *Programming in Ada.* Reading (Mass.): Addison-Wesley.
   The most technical of these three books, this one was written by a member of the Ada design team working with Ichbiah.

ARTICLES

(1984). "Ada: Past, Present, Future—An Interview with Jean Ichbiah, the Principal Designer of Ada," *Communications of the ACM* 27 (no. 10):990–997.
   A candid discussion with Ichbiah that we have drawn upon several times in our entry on Ada.
Fischer, David A. (1978). "DoD's Common Programming Language Effort," IEEE *Computer*, March, pp. 24–33.
   A readable history of early motivations for the development of Ada.

(1981). "Ada," IEEE *Computer*.

A special collection of articles on Ada that surveys the development of both the language and the software environment.

PERIODICALS

Ada Letters

A newsletter published by AdaTech, the SIGPLAN (Special Interest Group on Programming Languages) Technical Committee on Ada of the ACM. The newsletter is informal, up-to-date, and has information both on Ada itself and on activities involving the use of Ada.

Ada Information Clearinghouse Newsletter

A newsletter put out by the Ada Joint Programs Office. It contains official announcements from the Department of Defense as well as general information on developments involving the use of Ada.

Journal of Ada, Pascal, and Modula-2

A source of more technical articles on Ada.

ALGOL

PROFILE
NAME
*ALGO*rithmic *L*anguage
STRUCTURE

Familiar Distinctions:
  hardware: high-level
  translator: compiled
  structural unit: block
  data: numerical
 	
Conceptual Distinctions:
  organizing principle: imperative/algorithmic
  procedures: procedural
  extensibility: not extensible
  program/data: distinct

FUNCTIONS
general numerical analysis in scientific computing
GENEALOGY

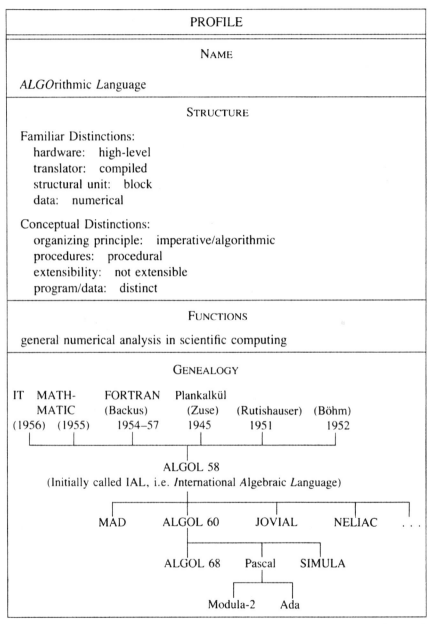

(Continued)

ALGOL (Continued)

Years:	1958–68
Authors:	International Committee—Zurich (1958), Paris (1960)
Impetus:	European need for general algebraic language; American desire to produce standard algebraic language
Evolution:	three successive published standards widely adopted in Europe; never penetrated FORTRAN barrier in U.S. most influential as source for subsequent languages like Pascal and Ada

VERSIONS/DIALECTS
Standards: ALGOL 58, ALGOL 60, ALGOL 68
Versions: ALGOL W, S-ALGOL

SPECIAL CHARACTERISTICS
Memory Requirements: large
Ease of Learning/Use: average (though less explicit syntax than Pascal)
Availability: widely available in Europe, but use largely restricted to mainframes in the U.S.

WHY ALGOL?

ALGOL is the unsung hero of the imperative/algorithmic computer language revolution. Many of the distinctive characteristics we associate with modern computer languages (including structured design and the rich use of data and control structures) derive from ALGOL. Better known in Europe than in the United States, ALGOL is the progenitor of many of the best-known modern computer languages, including Pascal, Modula-2, and Ada. Our primary interest here in ALGOL is less the structure of the language itself than the enormous *influence* it has had.

The ALGOL Saga

The story behind the creation of ALGOL has much of the drama of an Old Norse saga. Strong factions meet in battle. Cunning rivals brute strength in determining the victor. And there are morals to be learned from the tale. The history of ALGOL (the name simply means *ALGO*rithmic *L*anguage) falls neatly into four periods: a prologue, ALGOL 58, ALGOL 60, and ALGOL 68. (The meanings of these names will become clear.)

(1) Prologue

In the 1950s, the American computer world underwent a programming revolution. By 1957, so-called algebraic languages emerged, such as IT, MATH-MATIC, and of course FORTRAN, which allowed programmers to function like people solving numerical problems with paper and pencil. These new "high-level" languages freed programmers from having to write in machine code or its conceptual equivalent, assembly language. What's more, it became increasingly possible to write programs whose code could directly run on any computer (i.e. using the appropriate machine-specific translator).

This burst of potential of high-level languages engendered a veritable language explosion. While machine-independent languages were now possible, major computer manufacturers began developing proprietary versions of high-level languages. In fact, most programming groups around the country seemed determined to create their "own" languages as well.

The result was chaos. Languages running on one machine wouldn't run on another. Programmers had to learn new languages if they moved. In self-defense, the major computer users' groups in America requested that the ACM—Association for Computing Machinery (the central professional organization of computer scientists)—study the prospects for creating a single national programming language. An ACM committee met in early 1958. Its major decision was that, whatever else happened, FORTRAN should be rejected as a possible candidate because of its close ties to IBM (the creator of the language—see the entry on FORTRAN). For the ACM to endorse FORTRAN would have been like the U.S. Department of Transportation endorsing United Airlines or Ford Escorts.

Around the same time, a group of European computer scientists were also searching for a "universal" computer language. A German organization known as GAMM (Gesellschaft für angewandte Mathematik und Mechanik, that is, Society for Applied Mathematics and Mechanics) had contacted the American ACM in October 1957, requesting cooperation on the design of a universal algorithmic language.

GAMM's search had been going on since 1955. In the 1950s, continental Europe was far less developed in computer software implementations than the United States. Several paper-and-pencil attempts had already been made at developing algorithmic languages (including work by Zuse as far back as 1945, work by Rutishauser in 1951, and work by Böhm done in 1952 and published in 1954). But postwar Europe was still searching for an actual language to implement. A major consideration was to avoid domination by IBM, which meant avoiding the language FORTRAN. An equally important consideration was a "passion for orderliness." The Europeans wanted a language that not only worked but had the neatness of a German village and the precision of a Swiss clock.

(2) ALGOL 58

The independent interests of the Americans and Europeans were joined in a meeting at the end of May 1958 held in Zurich at the ETH (Eidgenössische Technische Hochschule, that is, the Swiss Federal Institute of Technology). Out of this eight-day meeting, the initial version of the ALGOL language emerged. It was first known as IAL (*I*nternational *A*lgebraic *L*anguage) and then renamed ALGOL 58.

The first published version of ALGOL 58 was acknowledged by its creators to be incomplete. In fact, one reason for publishing this first version was to gather comments from the computing community. As we shall see, though, the incompleteness of the design is partially responsible for the cool reception the language and its immediate successors were to receive in the United States.

The birth of the language itself was fraught with complications and interventions. A classic case of computer midwifery was the resolution of a deadlock over the representation in ALGOL of the decimal point. In the United States, the decimal point is denoted with a period, e.g. 10.6, while in Europe, it is denoted with a comma, e.g. 10,6. After days of discussion, one member of the European delegation pounded the table, declaring he would *never* use a period to represent a decimal point. The Americans were equally adamant: what could be more absurd than using a comma for a decimal point! Joe Wegstein (a member of the American delegation) finessed the debate by suggesting that the ALGOL language be officially represented at three separate levels:

>   a *reference* language, defining the ALGOL language itself
>
>   a *hardware* language, which would be represented differently on different machines
>
>   a *publication* language, for actually publishing books or articles on ALGOL

Both sides were rapidly mollified, assured they could, in the publication language, continue to represent decimal points the way they had since childhood. Unfortunately, this political solution added to the confusions that came to surround ALGOL and to detract from its potential American following.

(3) ALGOL 60

The published report on ALGOL 58 generated considerable interest in both the United States and Europe. In fact, with the first announcements of ALGOL 58, IBM began considering whether to implement the language on its machines.

European involvement was at least as intense, given the considerable stake Europe had in the development of an international language. If the ALGOL effort failed, Americans could always fall back on other languages. But for the Europeans, ALGOL's failure would leave them with nothing.

A second international meeting of a now expanded group of Europeans and Americans was held in Paris in January 1960. A number of changes were then introduced into the language. One of these was the adoption of a new notation for describing the ALGOL syntax. The notation, developed by John Backus (creator of FORTRAN), was known as BNF or Backus Normal Form. Another major change between ALGOL 58 and ALGOL 60 was the development of the notions of block structures and procedures.

ALGOL 60 had an explosive effect upon computer language design. While ALGOL 58 spawned several new languages (e.g. MAD, JOVIAL, and NELIAC), it was ALGOL 60 that served as a prototype for SIMULA and Pascal and, indirectly, for C, Modula-2, and Ada.

(4) ALGOL 68
ALGOL 68 is the result of continuing refinement of ALGOL 60. However, unlike ALGOL 60, ALGOL 68 has not been especially widely used and has exercised little influence on other languages.

ALGOL, FORTRAN, and IBM

We have said that ALGOL was well received in Europe but not in the United States. We have also mentioned that both the ACM and GAMM were leery of a commitment to FORTRAN and, in the case of the Europeans, to IBM. Just what was the relationship between ALGOL, FORTRAN, and IBM?

There is a literal story, but an allegorical one as well. The allegorical tale is embedded in the very name ALGOL. ALGOL simply means "*ALGO*rithmic *L*anguage." But many of the European framers of the language also recognized "Algol" as the name of the second-brightest star in the constellation Perseus. The amount of light emanating from Algol changes, for roughly every 69 hours the star is eclipsed by a large dark body, its partner star, which is about six million miles away. Yet Algol always manages to regain its brilliance.

The double meaning was not lost on the Europeans: the ALGOL language was not to be eclipsed by FORTRAN. Primed for a FORTRAN assault, some European countries deliberately underwrote the success of ALGOL. The German Research Council, for example, decided that all computers used at German universities should be equipped with ALGOL. The Council placed this requirement upon institutions ordering computers funded by the German Research Council. Since the Council provided 95 percent of the monies for all research computers, the adoption of ALGOL was guaranteed. This political move precisely parallels moves in the United States to adopt COBOL: The Department of Defense offered grants for the purchase of computers only if the computers ran COBOL (see the entry on COBOL).

The American side of the story is hazier. Critics of IBM and FORTRAN are quick to point out that IBM regularly supplied FORTRAN free of charge to its customers, making FORTRAN the obvious language of choice in research institutions across the country. Alan Perlis, a member of both the Zurich meetings in 1958 and the Paris meetings in 1960, observes that when ALGOL 58 was announced in the United States, IBM had already committed enormous resources to the development and propagation of FORTRAN. For IBM to add ALGOL to its machines (or to use it to replace FORTRAN) would have substantial financial ramifications. John McCarthy (the inventor of LISP), who was also a member of the American delegation, describes the battle between ALGOL and FORTRAN more bluntly: "I really thought one of the goals of ALGOL was to knock off FORTRAN."

IBM, of course, has its own account of what happened. When ALGOL 58 was first announced in the United States, IBM did express interest. According to John Backus, it was IBM *users* (through a users' group called SHARE), not IBM itself, that rejected ALGOL 58. This rejection came in part because ALGOL 58 was not a "finished" language. It lacked means of doing input and output, and before 1960 the syntax was difficult to describe clearly. American computer users had to choose between FORTRAN—which was already implemented and debugged—and ALGOL, which was not yet "usable." Their choice was FORTRAN. In the words of Backus, "IBM didn't see that it could expend the rather enormous expense it would have taken to support something that its major customers didn't want."

Whoever was ultimately responsible (IBM or its users), the die was cast. ALGOL never developed in the United States, and FORTRAN became the lingua franca of the scientific computing community not only in the United States but, with the expansion of IBM, around the world.

The final story has an ironic twist. While the United States rejected ALGOL in early 1960s, twenty years later the American computing scene has become heavily dominated by ALGOL's progeny.

THINKING IN ALGOL

NOTE: Our discussion of ALGOL programming will concentrate on three important syntactic constructions introduced by ALGOL 60, the version of ALGOL which has been most influential.

Backus Normal Form

For all their variety, natural languages together share some basic syntactic conventions that aid in constructing representations. All natural languages are composed of sentences. All natural languages have means of asking questions and making statements. They all seem to have the equivalent of nouns and verbs, and all make some use of word-order rules in determining how words are combined into sentences.

The conventions for computer language syntax are less developed. Since computer languages (unlike human languages) are consciously constructed by people, these same people need to devise efficient and clear syntactic conventions for representing the very syntax itself. The original syntactic description of FORTRAN was one such attempt, as was the original syntactic description of ALGOL 58. The contribution of John Backus (later reinforced by Peter Naur) was to propose a representation of computer language syntax that was efficient and clear. This same syntactic format, originally proposed for what was to become ALGOL 60, is now commonly used to represent the syntax of other computer languages.

We need to be careful to distinguish between the syntax of a computer language itself (e.g. the rules of ALGOL 60) and the way in which those rules are represented in a formal description of the language. When we talk about a "means of representing computer language syntax," we are not talking about the syntactic properties that make computer languages different from one another. Instead, we mean the essential structures that apply to all computer languages— the computer equivalent of sentences, nouns, and verbs in natural languages.

The principle behind Backus Normal Form (BNF) is very simple. The basic rules of the computer language (in this case, ALGOL) are expressed through a set of *equations*. On the left-hand side is the word to be defined. On the right-hand side is the definition. For example, if we have an element in the language called a *declaration* that is defined as a "procedure declaration" or a "variable declaration" (don't worry about the meaning of the terms for now), the definition would be written in BNF like this:

$$< \text{declaration} > :: = < \text{procedure declaration} > \mid < \text{variable declaration} >$$

Both the term to be defined (*declaration*) and the pieces of the definition (*procedure declaration, variable declaration*) are enclosed in angle brackets. The symbol ":: = " denotes "is defined as," while the symbol " | " means "or." And so the above definition reads: "A declaration is defined as either a procedure declaration or a variable declaration."

Backus explains that the notation has no intrinsic connection with computers or computer languages. In fact, Backus borrowed the idea directly from the work of the logician Emil Post, who was writing on problems in symbolic logic in the early 1940s.

One final note on Backus Normal Form. Many writings in computer science state that BNF means Backus *Naur* Form, named after John Backus *and* Peter Naur, another of the European participants in the planning of ALGOL. Peter Naur did read about Backus's notation just before the 1960 meeting in Paris at which ALGOL 60 was designed. Naur was impressed with the notation and was instrumental in getting it adopted as the formal representation of ALGOL 60 syntax. Yet despite his role, Naur himself confirms that at least originally BNF meant Backus *Normal* Form. And indeed Post, writing in 1943, proposed a notation which he called "normal form."

Blocks and Procedures: The Beginnings of Structured Programming

The European "passion for orderliness" is clearly evident in the development of two structuring devices, the block and the procedure, that add logical coherence to the writing of ALGOL programs. Without explaining all the details of how blocks and procedures work, we can get a sense of what they were designed to accomplish, and why they have been so important in the development of modern computer programming.

In Chapter 3, we distinguished between *structured* and *unstructured* programming. The differences between these two approaches derive both from the disparate syntactic tools that languages have available for organizing lines of programming code and from the conceptual attitudes that programmers have toward the task of encoding real-world problems into lines of programming code. Not surprisingly, the availability of syntactic tools reinforces the shaping of conceptual attitudes.

We might clarify the distinction with a metaphor. Consider a university professor preparing to leave for work in the morning. In principle, the procedure is straightforward: wake up, bathe, get dressed, organize your papers, leave the house.

The structured approach to this sequence of events might look like this:

Instructions for getting out of the house in the morning:

1. get up
    remember where you left your glasses the
        night before
    get out of bed
    turn off the alarm clock once you have your
        glasses and can see the clock
2. bathe
    go into the bathroom
    find a clean towel
    turn the hot water on and let it run before
        getting into the shower
    shower
    dry off
3. get dressed
    turn on iron
    get out clothes
    iron clothes
    turn off iron
    put on clothes
    put on watch
4. organize papers
    remember what classes you will see today, and
        put appropriate papers in briefcase
    remember what appointments you have today,
        and put appropriate papers in briefcase
    remember what work you want to do today in
        library, and put appropriate papers in briefcase
5. leave the house
    remember to bring your briefcase
    remember to turn out the lights, lower the
        heat, and lock the door

When it comes time to follow these instructions, the professor can look first at the short list:

1. get up
2. bathe
3. get dressed
4. organize papers
5. leave the house

For each item, she can reference a list of subtasks.

Now consider the same sequence of events from an unstructured perspective. The individual events become an undifferentiated laundry list of activities. Taken in order, they would look like this:

1. remember where you left your glasses the night before
2. get out of bed
3. turn off the alarm clock once you have your glasses and can see the clock
4. go into the bathroom
5. find a clean towel
6. turn the hot water on and let it run before getting into the shower
7. shower
8. dry off
9. turn on iron
10. get out clothes
11. iron clothes
12. turn off iron
13. put on clothes
14. put on watch
15. remember what classes you will see today, and put appropriate papers in briefcase
16. remember what appointments you have today, and put appropriate papers in briefcase
17. remember what work you want to do today in library, and put appropriate papers in briefcase
18. remember to bring your briefcase
19. remember to turn out the lights, lower the heat, and lock the door

In the unstructured approach, individual events are not clustered into subgroups. When our professor wants to review the steps for leaving the house in the morning, she must look at nineteen of them instead of five.

But the problem with the unstructured approach is not simply numbers. In unstructured programming, the very order of lines in a program need not reflect the order of events in the real world. In unstructured programming, as you are proceeding from one line of programming code to the next, you might be instructed to jump to another part of the program (indicated by the address of a memory location in assembly language, or a line number in a language like FORTRAN or BASIC). After running through these lines of code in the "detour," you return to the regular linear progression. We assume the original programmer had a good reason for constructing the program in this unexpected order. Yet the reason is often unclear, and the resulting program can be difficult to read.

In a worst-case scenario, the unstructured version of our program might look like this:

1. remember where you left your glasses the night before
2. JUMP to 10
3. go into the bathroom
4. find a clean towel
5. turn the hot water on and let it run before getting into the shower
6. shower
7. dry off
8. turn on iron
9. JUMP to 13
10. get out of bed
11. turn off the alarm clock once you have found your glasses and can see the clock
12. JUMP to 3
13. get out clothes
(etc.)

The shapers of ALGOL (especially ALGOL 60) wanted the language to reflect the logical order of programming activity and distinction between a conceptual overview of a program (e.g. organize papers, leave the house) and the details of how a program is to be carried out (e.g. remember what classes you will see today). It is for these reasons that *blocks* and *procedures* were introduced.

(1)   BLOCKS

In Algol 60, a block is the formal name for a program. It consists of the *name* of the program, a *declaration* of variables, arrays, and such that will be used in the program, and the program *statements* themselves. All-importantly, though, the contents of the block are bounded by the terms BEGIN and END, which visually delimit the program. The structure looks like this:

```
name
     BEGIN   declarations
     statements

     . . .
     END
```

A block can occur within another block. The reason for embedding one block within another is to show the conceptual distinctions between the action of the outer block and the inner block, while at the same time indicating the relationship between the two. A block embedded within a block would look like this:

```
name
    BEGIN declarations
    statements
    . . .
    name
        BEGIN declarations
        statements
        . . .
        END
    statements
    . . .
    END
```

(We are ignoring punctuation in this and the previous schematic example.)

(2)   Procedures

Procedures in ALGOL 60 look very much like blocks, but serve a different function. Like blocks, they have names, BEGIN-END boundaries, declarations, and statements (plus other dimensions we will ignore). Schematically, here is a procedure in ALGOL 60:

```
type PROCEDURE name-of-procedure (parameters)
    BEGIN declarations
    statement
    END
```

Unlike blocks, procedures function as self-contained entities that can be invoked at more than one point in the same program. Procedures are contained *within* blocks. Blocks are always followed through in logical sequence, while the name of a procedure in a program is really a shorthand for the instruction "go somewhere else to get the exact instructions on how this is to be done." The call to use a procedure in ALGOL is like the use of the word *refrain* in a songbook. Many songs are composed of several verses which are separated by the singing of a refrain. The refrain is usually printed out only once. The word *refrain* indicates "go to the written-out version of the refrain to get the actual words."

To see how procedures work in ALGOL, return to our case of the professor. Suppose we want to write a program outlining more of her day. Assume that she goes through the routine we have detailed in the morning, but upon returning home in the evening, she once again bathes, irons a new set of clothes, and dresses again before going out to dinner. The use of procedures allows us to define the bathing and dressing processes just once each, and then "call" these procedures each time the full program requires them to be used. The procedures are "declared" in the very beginning of the block structure (along with the declaration of variables and arrays). In the main set of statements in the block structure, procedures look much like other statements.

A fuller version of our professor program, using ALGOL-like syntax, would look like this:

```
PROFESSOR-KURTZ'S-DAY
        BEGIN   variable declarations
                array declarations
                procedure declarations
                    GET UP (parameters)
                        BEGIN declarations
                        remember where you left your glasses. . .

                        . . .
                        END
                    BATHE (parameters)
                        BEGIN declarations
                        go into the bathroom

                        . . .
                        END
                    GET DRESSED (parameters)
                        BEGIN declarations
                        turn on iron

                        . . .
                        END
                    ORGANIZE PAPERS (parameters)
                        BEGIN declarations
                        remember what classes you will see. . .

                        . . .
                        END
                    LEAVE HOUSE (parameters)
                        BEGIN declarations
                        remember to bring your briefcase

                        . . .
                        END
                    DRIVE TO SCHOOL (parameters)
                        BEGIN declarations
                        statements

                        . . .
                        END
                    DO WORK (parameters)
                        BEGIN declarations
                        statements

                        . . .
                        END
```

```
        DRIVE HOME (parameters)
            BEGIN declarations
            statements
              . . .
            END
GET UP
BATHE
GET DRESSED
ORGANIZE PAPERS
LEAVE HOUSE
DRIVE TO SCHOOL
DO WORK
DRIVE HOME
BATHE
GET DRESSED
END
```

THE EVOLUTION OF ALGOL 60

The Rise of Structured Programming

The most significant contribution of ALGOL to computer programming is not the set of syntactic conventions (such as BNF or blocks or procedures) which have become so prevalent in modern imperative/algorithmic languages, but the conceptual approach that came to be known as structured programming. While structured programming can be implemented through syntactic devices, the idea of structuring goes beyond syntax.

Why were notions of structuring absent from the design of early computer languages whereas they have become almost gospel within the last decade? Were early programmers simply sloppy, or is there a more rational explanation?

A sociological profile of the programming world from the 1940s to the 1970s provides some of the answer. In the first decades of computing, the number of people involved was extremely small. People learned to program not by taking courses but by becoming apprentices, working alongside someone who already knew how to program. Since there were practically no textbooks, one learned hints and shortcuts along with basic principles. Most of the early programming was done in the United States, where this "tinker with it until it works" attitude has long been a hallmark of American approaches to things mechanical. It was in these early days that the notion of "hacking" in computing was developed at the Massachusetts Institute of Technology. (Admittedly, such tinkering—coupled with ingenuity—was often necessary to fit programs into the very limited amounts of memory space then available in the computer hardware.) By contrast, in Europe there was far less programming being done. And for those who did learn to program, the method was more formally pedagogical: instruction by example.

The world of computing began to change drastically by the mid-1960s. The number of computers was growing exponentially, requiring a comparable cadre of new programmers. The informal apprenticeship system would no longer do. Formal classes in computer languages, textbooks, and the rest became a standard part of the curriculum of post-secondary education in both the United States and Europe. However, it was the Europeans who almost single-handedly developed the conceptual tools that now underlie the teaching of programming to the masses on both sides of the Atlantic. The change in teaching styles was born everywhere of necessity.

Within the history of structured programming, a small number of landmarks, well known within the computer science world, led up to contemporary assumptions that "good" programming is synonymous with "structured" programming. The major players are two Europeans, Edsger Dijkstra and Niklaus Wirth, augmented by several of their colleagues (again, mostly European). The simplest way of telling the story is with an annotated chronology of publications. Full references to these works appear in the "What to Read" section at the end of this entry.

(1)   1968: Edsger Dijkstra

Dijkstra is renowned for enunciating outspoken criticisms of early computer languages. Typical favorites are that FORTRAN is an "infantile disorder" and that "the use of COBOL cripples the mind; its teaching should, therefore, be regarded as a criminal offense." (FORTRAN and COBOL are both unstructured languages.)

Such comments are not surprising, since Dijkstra is also the father of structured programming. He participated in the development of ALGOL 60, and later wrote a textbook on it which was published in 1962.

In his 1968 articles, Dijkstra made two critical points. The first concerns the distinction between a *program itself* and the *process taking place* when a program actually runs. To quote Dijkstra:

> Although the program made by the programmer is his final product, the computations evoked by it are the true subject matter of his trade: he has to guarantee that the computations—the "making" of which he leaves to the machine—evoked by his program will have the desired effect.

That is, the logical running of the program within the central processing unit may have little correspondence to the physical sequence of code that the programmer writes in a high-level language. (The entry on assembly language in this chapter exemplifies just how different a high-level representation can be from the way a problem is actually solved at the hardware level.)

Dijkstra's second point concerns the difficulties that human beings have in making the conceptual leap from programming code to the process taking place as a program actually runs on a computer. Again, Dijkstra:

The mental aids available to the human programmer are, in fact, very few. They are enumeration, mathematical induction and abstraction, where the appeal to enumeration has to satisfy the severe boundary condition that the number of cases to be considered separately should be very, very small. The introduction of suitable abstraction is our only mental aid to reduce the appeal to enumeration, to organize and master complexity.

That is, if we want to avoid having to enumerate in our programming code every single step that actually takes place when a program runs, we need to form abstractions that serve as "shorthands" for whole chunks of code that can be reused. These abstractions help us to "summarize" the major steps happening in a program, removing the detail that fills up pages of code.

Dijkstra's objection to languages like FORTRAN and BASIC is that they do little to aid in this "abstraction" process. Instead, they leave wide conceptual gaps between the sequence of instructions in the programming code itself and the process taking place when the program actually runs. These gaps are most clearly seen in the famous GOTO statement, a carryover from the JUMP statement used in assembly language. JUMP statements let you physically jump from one point in the programming code to another, where the rationale for the jump is known to the programmer but is not part of the programming code itself. Over the past decade, the use of GOTO statements has decreased in direct proportion to the rise of structured programming.

(2)   1971: Niklaus Wirth

Wirth is best known as the creator of Pascal, the immediate and increasingly popular descendant of ALGOL 60. We will wait until the section on Pascal to consider the evolution and structure of Pascal itself. However, at this point we need to look at a programming technique that Wirth developed called "stepwise refinement" that underlies the way in which he envisioned programs in Pascal should be written.

In Chapter 2, when we discussed how computer languages work, we mentioned the all-important stage of *formulating* the problem. One method we discussed was the use of flow charts, and a second was what we called *top down design* (or *version-by-version programming* or *stepwise refinement*). Niklaus Wirth was responsible for developing this approach to problem formulation.

Stepwise refinement in programming is really nothing more than taking a large problem, decomposing it into smaller problems, and then continuing to break down those smaller problems into yet smaller ones. In everyday life, we do this same sort of thing all the time. If we are planning a trip abroad, we choose the countries we want to visit and our modes of transportation. Then we decide where in those countries we want to go and obtain the transportation schedules for getting ourselves from place to place. Next we might book plane or train reservations. All of this seems perfectly obvious, and one may reasonably wonder why it took until 1971 for someone to think of approaching computer programming this way.

We touched upon part of the answer earlier when we spoke about the explosion of computer use in the 1960s and the subsequent need for many more programmers than could easily be trained by the apprenticeship method. Wirth, himself a teacher of programming, decided to consider the pedagogical problem more closely.

Wirth was concerned with the *process* by which programming was then being taught. In Europe, programming was typically taught by examples. Students studied finished programs, and then tried to write programs like them—much like trying to learn medicine by watching someone else do a dissection. Unfortunately, students had little idea of how those sample computer programs had been constructed in the first place. If students needed to write altogether new programs (e.g. because the prototypes provided by the old examples wouldn't do for the programming problem at hand), they had no methodology for proceeding. Learning to program meant little more than memorizing the rules of syntax, and then relying upon your intuitions about how to transform an idea into a finished program using the rules.

Wirth believed that, instead, programming courses should teach *methods* for designing programs. His proposal for such a method was stepwise refinement of the problem, whereby the student works from an abstract natural language-like representation of the problem down to subproblems and eventually down to the writing of actual programming code. In Wirth's words:

> A guideline in the process of stepwise refinement should be the principle to decompose decisions as much as possible, to untangle aspects which are only seemingly interdependent, and to defer those decisions which concern details of representation as long as possible.

(3)   1972: Dahl, Dijkstra, and Hoare

It was not until the mid-1970s that the ideas behind structured programming became widely disseminated, especially in the United States. In America, FORTRAN, COBOL, and BASIC (all unstructured languages) were the primary languages in which most programming was done. With the publication of Dahl, Dijkstra, and Hoare's book, interest in and information about structured programming began to spread.

(4)   1974: special issue of *ACM Computing Surveys* on programming
         methodology

Articles in this issue by Wirth and Donald Knuth further articulated the message of structured programming.

THE FUTURE OF ALGOL

ALGOL is much like the mythical phoenix, which dies but from whose ashes a new bird arises. It is generally agreed that the days of ALGOL itself are numbered. The language is used only occasionally in the United States, and its use elsewhere is also diminishing. Yet the basic elements of ALGOL—and the conceptual thinking of its designers—remain very much alive in the language's principal descendant, Pascal, and in Pascal's own major progeny, Modula-2 and Ada.

USING ALGOL

Buying ALGOL

ALGOL 60 and ALGOL 68 are typically available on large computers at major research facilities in Europe and in much of the United States. However, for reasons we have talked about, ALGOL has not remained sufficiently popular to have an active part in the microcomputer revolution.

What to Read

There are two sets of recommended readings for ALGOL. The first is on the language itself, while the second is on structured programming.

The Language ALGOL:

BOOKS

Dijkstra, Edsger (1962). *A Primer of ALGOL 60 Programming*. London: Academic Press.
  Dijkstra's text on the 1960 version of the language.
Brailsford, D. F., and A. N. Walker (1979). *Introductory ALGOL 68 Programming*. Chichester (Eng.): Ellis Horwood; New York: John Wiley.
  Clear introduction to ALGOL 68, intended for mathematics undergraduates learning their first programming language.
Cole, A. J., and R. Morrison (1983). *An Introduction to Programming in S-ALGOL*. Cambridge (Eng.): Cambridge University Press.
  S-ALGOL is a version of ALGOL developed at St. Andrews University. It was expressly designed for teaching programming.

ARTICLES

Perlis, Alan J. (1981). "The American Side of the Development of ALGOL," in R. L. Wexelblat, ed., *History of Programming Languages*. New York: Academic Press, pp. 75–91, 139–147, 161–171.
  A delightful history of the development of ALGOL 58 and ALGOL 60. Much of the information in our discussion of ALGOL is drawn from Perlis's article. In the same volume edited by Wexelblat is an article by Peter Naur, "The European Side of the Last Phase of the Development of ALGOL 60."
Bemer, R. W. (1969). "A Politico-Social History of ALGOL," in M. Halpern

and C. Shaw, eds., *Annual Review of Automatic Programming,* vol. 5.
Oxford: Pergamon, pp. 151–237.
The title of Bemer's article captures the importance of non-computational
issues that underlay the creation of ALGOL. The first part of the article
complements information in Perlis's article.

Structured Programming:

NOTE: Most of the items listed here are referred to by date in the earlier section
"The Evolution of ALGOL 60."

1968   Dijkstra, Edsger W. "Stepwise Program Construction," essay published
in E. W. Dijkstra (1982), *Selected Writings on Computing: A Personal
Perspective.* New York: Springer-Verlag, pp. 0 [sic]–14.
Dijkstra, Edsger W. "Go To Statement Considered Harmful," *Communications of the ACM* 11 (no. 3):147–148.
1971   Wirth, Niklaus. "Program Development by Stepwise Refinement,"
Communications of the ACM 14 (no. 4):221–227.
1972   Dahl, O., J. E. W. Dijkstra, and C. A. R. Hoare. *Structured Programming.* New York: Academic Press.
Dijkstra, E. W. "The Humble Programmer," *Communications of the ACM*
15 (no. 10):859–866.
An autobiographical essay, delivered to the Association for Computing
Machinery upon receipt of its annual Turing Award. Dijkstra gives a
personal perspective on the development of programming as a discipline
and of structured programming in particular. An ideal place for the novice
and professional alike to begin reading.
1974   Wirth, Niklaus. "On the Composition of Well-Structured Programs,"
ACM Computing Surveys 6 (no. 4):247–259.
Knuth, Donald E. "Structured Programming with *go to* Statements," *ACM
Computing Surveys* 6 (no 4.):261–301.

APL

PROFILE
NAME
A Programming Language
STRUCTURE

Familiar Distinctions:
  hardware: high-level
  translator: interpreted
  structural unit: function
  data: numerical, character string
 	
Conceptual Distinctions:
  organizing principle: functional/applicative
  procedures: largely procedural
  extensibility: extensible
  program/data: not distinct

FUNCTIONS
data processing
GENEALOGY
no computer language precursors Years: 1957–68 Authors: Kenneth Iverson, Adin Falkoff (Harvard, IBM) Impetus: develop language suitable for data processing (NOTE: APL is pre-COBOL) that incorporates mathematical elegance Evolution: despite its pragmatic beginnings, APL has developed the reputation of being a difficult language
VERSIONS/DIALECTS
Standards: each version of the language is named for the hardware it runs on, e.g. APL/360

(Continued)

APL (Continued)

SPECIAL CHARACTERISTICS

Memory Requirements: large

Ease of Learning/Use: very logical language; difficult to read, especially if not well documented

Availability: generally available on mainframe computers; microcomputer versions now appearing

Miscellaneous: unique character set can activate complex function with single keystroke

---

WHY APL?

APL is a misunderstood language. It is best known for its one-line programs written with obscure symbols that don't appear on the standard computer keyboard. Like FORTH, it is often called a "write-only language," meaning that once a program is written, it is difficult for someone attempting to read the program—including the programmer—to figure out what the lines of code mean. APL is reputed to be very "mathematical," which leads most people to believe the language must be designed for complex scientific calculations and is comprehensible only to people with strong backgrounds in mathematics.

Like most myths, the public image of APL is based on a grain of truth. APL was explicitly designed with formal mathematical notation in mind. APL does require a special keyboard with unfamiliar symbols. And APL programs (especially when undocumented) can be as lucid as pronouncements of the Delphic Oracle. Yet behind this formidable façade is a simple and elegant language that was designed for much the same reasons as COBOL: to process ordinary business data.

Data Processing and Computers

Computers were first developed in the United States during World War II to calculate trajectories of artillery shells. It was over a decade before the uses of computers for processing commercial information began to be explored. One of the earliest efforts (by Grace Hopper and her colleagues at Remington Rand Univac), called FLOW-MATIC, was developed in 1956. The best known of the data-processing languages, COBOL, did not appear for another four years.

Meanwhile, Howard Aiken at Harvard was organizing a new graduate program in Automatic Data Processing. The program was announced in 1954, and one of the faculty members appointed to teach was Kenneth Iverson, who had recently completed his Ph.D. with Aiken. Iverson's Ph.D. was in applied mathematics, while his earlier training was in mathematics. The intellectual stage was set for the combining of formal mathematics, data processing, and computer languages.

Mathematics and Computer Languages

There is a widespread misconception (even among computer programmers) that the use of computers necessitates an understanding of mathematics. This belief has been nurtured by several historical coincidences. The earliest uses of computers involved mathematical calculations of the sorts done by physicists and engineers. Moreover, the earliest high-level language was FORTRAN, which was explicitly designed for doing scientific calculations. And finally, a large number of computer scientists have emerged from mathematics departments (and, in fact, many computer science courses and faculty members still reside in departments of mathematics). The majority of non-science students being introduced to computer programming are forced to think about cosine functions and double precision numbers, and come away reaffirming their beliefs that computers exist for solving mathematical problems.

This "mathematics" perspective on computers presupposes that the computer is a special-purpose machine—a mathematics-problem-solving machine. But the computer is much more. It is a general-purpose control machine, the limits of which we cannot yet begin to imagine. Computers can be used to adjust the fuel in automobile engines, send Christmas cards to our favorite uncles, draw pictures of cathedrals in southern France, translate Hungarian into Hindi, or analyze the syntax of *The Canterbury Tales*. And that is just the beginning.

Mathematics can be involved at three levels of computer programming. The best known of these is in using the computer as a "number-cruncher." Languages like FORTRAN and Ada typify the use of computer languages to perform complex mathematical calculations. A less obvious role of mathematics is as a "hidden layer" between the result of a program and the means by which the result is obtained. Many graphics programs, for example, use reasonably complex mathematical calculations in order to produce graphic images. In procedural languages, users themselves must deal with these equations, while in non-procedural languages (and in applications programs), users merely indicate the desired result, and the language translator figures out not only how to do the necessary calculations but what calculations must be done.

The third level of mathematics in computer languages is at once the most obvious and the most elusive. It is the level of mathematical representation or notation. All programming languages must be able to represent constants and variables, functions and arguments. They need a way of grouping together symbols that have something in common, and of using punctuation (like parentheses) to show what goes with what. And obviously, they need operators for performing mathematical manipulations like addition and subtraction.

This third level of mathematics is more evident in some languages than in others. In every computer language we recognize the representation of constants (e.g. 62) and variables (e.g. Let A = 44), the indication of simple arithmetic functions (e.g. 5 + 6), and the use of parentheses to group data together—e.g. (5 − 2)*(8/4). Data structures (e.g. arrays, lists, records) are used for clustering together like kinds of symbols (e.g. world records for the women's marathon; the first name on each page of the Palo Alto telephone book). Some languages (especially of the functional/applicative family) explicitly talk about "functions," "arguments," and "operators," while others use alternative language to express the same thing.

The "mathematical" flavor of APL comes directly from this third notion of mathematics. In designing APL, Kenneth Iverson combined his interest in the problem of data processing with his mathematical background. It was only natural that the means of representation he should use for describing his new computer language would include the terminology of functions and arguments and operators, which he has grown up with as a mathematician. John McCarthy— who also holds a Ph.D. in mathematics—did much the same thing in designing LISP, another functional/applicative language. As we will see, APL and LISP have a great deal in common in the mechanisms they provide for representing and manipulating data and in the names given (e.g. function, argument) to the means of representation and manipulation.

The Gradual Emergence of APL

APL began as a handwritten notation that only gradually evolved into an implemented programming language. Iverson began working on what was to become known as APL while he was teaching at Harvard in the late 1950s. His interest was in developing a notational tool that he could use for analyzing various topics in data processing, for teaching classes, and for co-authoring a book, *Automatic Data Processing*. Iverson left Harvard in 1960 for IBM, where he continued work on his still unnamed programming language with Adin Falkoff. Together they developed a machine description of the system for the new IBM 360, which appeared in the mid-1960s. The first actual implementation of the language was not running on the IBM 360 until the fall of 1966.

The name APL itself is an afterthought. In 1962, Iverson had published a book entitled *A Programming Language*, but the language being described lacked a name. During the implementation phase of the language (beginning in 1964), the language was named with the initials from the earlier book title.

THINKING IN APL

Almost all computer languages are genealogically related to some other language. The syntax of Pascal isn't strange if you already know ALGOL. Smalltalk looks vaguely familiar if you have earlier worked with SIMULA. The unique characteristic of APL is its lack of progenitors. Iverson and Falkoff consciously rejected the influence of earlier programming languages, and for a reason. They argued that earlier computer languages (e.g. assembly language, FORTRAN) departed from traditional use of mathematical notation, and they saw APL as a way of doing computer programming using traditional mathematical formalism.

Iverson and Falkoff stress that two main principles guided their designing of APL: simplicity and practicality. The novice first reading an APL program might find these claims hard to believe. Not only is much of the character set unintelligble, but those brief, cryptic programming lines seem anything but practical. This apparent paradox begins to resolve itself when we look at how the mathematical notation of a *function* underlies not only the conceptual organization of APL but the very character set through which it is represented.

Functions in Mathematics and Computing

We have said that APL is a functional/applicative language. In Chapter 3, we explained that in mathematics a function is a way of relating elements of one set (the domain) to elements from another (the range). A function for finding the square of a number associates x with x^2, yielding the function $f(x) = x^2$. The variable x is often referred to as an *argument*, while "square" is the name of the *function*.

In a functional/applicative language, a program consists of a set of functions. A basic group of functions is usually "built into" the language translator. For example, LISP and Logo have a number of primitive functions that come with the language program itself. The user can then extend the language, defining more functions by building upon these original primitives. (The same "boot-strapping" principle is used in FORTH, using built-in words to define new words, or in Smalltalk, using built-in objects to define new objects.)

Like most extensible languages, APL has a number of built-in functions for performing the normal set of operations programmers might be expected to need: adding numbers, rounding numbers off to the next higher integer, arranging items in a list in ascending or descending order, selecting items from lists, concatenating data items together. The major difference between APL and other extensible languages is the way in which these everyday functions are provided. In languages like LISP, the functions themselves are written out with English-like abbreviations—e.g. a LISP function for taking square roots might be called SQRT(X). In APL, the basic functions are represented by single symbols on the keyboard. Addition (PLUS in LISP) is simply represented with the operator " + " in APL. The APL symbol "⌈" (called "ceiling") represents the function "round to the next higher integer." The symbol "∇" is used in APL to define new functions (comparable to LISP's DEFUN). The simplicity and elegance of APL comes from the fact that even conceptually complex functions (e.g. to produce random numbers or transpose arguments within a matrix of arguments) can be done with a single symbol.

Visual Strangeness: APL's Character Set

The confusion and difficulty associated with APL derives in large part from the fact that, to achieve such conciseness, APL requires a special keyboard. Half the keyboard looks familiar (the usual numbers, capital letters, and punctuation), while the other half seems strange indeed. An APL keyboard looks like this:

The meanings of some of the operators are obvious. On the top row, for instance, the result of pressing the shift key plus the 3 key produces < (the symbol for "less than"). The result of the shift key plus the 4 key is ≤ ("less than or equal to"). Many of the other symbols are less obvious, some having been invented by Iverson. To add to the confusion for the programmer new to APL, some operator symbols can only be formed by striking one key, backspacing, and then typing another keystroke. For example, the operator ⍋ is used for sorting elements in ascending order. The symbol is formed by typing the delta symbol (i.e. Δ) with a shift-H combination, backspacing, and then typing a shift-M (|), yielding ⍋ .

Contemplating the APL keyboard, you may well be asking whether Iverson has achieved but a Pyrrhic victory: attaining the goal of simplicity of operators at the cost of an arcane symbol set that is not available on the average computer keyboard and that requires special effort to use even when it is available. Before condemning the symbol set, though, we need to remember that APL was initially devised as a handwritten notation (much like shorthand that secretaries use for taking dictation), not as a computer language to be input at a keyboard. Moreover, for a person familiar with the symbols, they are no more cryptic than the abbreviations for elements in the periodic table in chemistry.

APL as a Data-Processing Language

Despite the initial strangeness of the APL keyboard, the kinds of problems APL is typically used to solve are highly familiar. APL is especially well suited for sorting information, selecting items from lists, and performing simple mathematical operations (e.g. multiply by 10) upon all the numbers in a data file. In fact, one of the reasons that programs (i.e. functions) in APL can be so concise is that a single function can be written that acts upon all members of an argument that follow it. (In APL, unlike other functional/applicative languages, a single argument can contain an aggregate of elements.) This is precisely the sort of calculation that takes place in business all the time. In fact, many of the electronic spreadsheet programs running on microcomputers (from Visicalc to Symphony) use the same principle by letting you immediately see the results of, say, multiplying an entire column of numbers by 1.15, which might signify a price increase of 15 percent.

Programming in APL

APL has a sizable number of built-in functions directly accessible from operators on the keyboard. Without attempting to illustrate all of them, we can look at how APL handles some of the common functions we might expect to find in any computer language, and then see how APL performs more complicated operations with literally a few short strokes.

(1)   Arithmetic Functions

(a)   Multiplication

The simple multiplication function in APL works much the same way as in any other computer language, with one exception: multiplication is indicated in APL with the familiar arithmetic symbol $\times$ (for "times") rather than with the asterisk (*) that is typically used for indicating multiplication in the computer world, e.g.

          25 $\times$ 62

The real power of APL, however, comes from being able to perform operations on entire groups of numbers at a time. If, for example, we wish to multiply a list of numbers (called a *vector*) by the same single number (called a *scalar*), we would write in APL

          10   $\times$ 3   4   5   6
     (scalar)   (vector)

and get back the "evaluation of the function" (i.e. the answer):

          30   40   50   60

(Notice the convention that functions are typed in at a position that is indented five spaces from the left-hand margin, while the evaluation of the function is printed flush with the left-hand margin).

(b)   Ceiling and Floor, Maximum and Minimum

Frequently programmers need to round off real numbers to the next higher or lower integer. Many languages have built-in arithmetic functions (like Pascal's *round* and *trunc*) that round real numbers up to the next higher or down to the next lower integer, respectively. In APL, these same arithmetic functions are accomplished with a single stroke. The symbol $\lceil$ ("ceiling") is used to round upward, and the symbol $\lfloor$ ("floor") is used for rounding downward. For example, if we write

    $\lceil$ 3.1

we get back the response

    4

or if we write

    $\lfloor$ 3.1

we get

    3

The same functions can be applied to whole series of numbers (a vector) at one time:

    $\lceil$ 3.1   44.5   66.9
    4   45   67

In keeping with APL's principle of simplicity of representation, the same two symbols, $\lceil$ and $\lfloor$, are reused with new meanings in new circumstances. So far, we have looked at the meanings of these symbols when they are used with *single* arguments. However, when the same symbols are placed *between* two arguments, they now express the functions "maximum" and "minimum," respectively, e.g.

    6 $\lceil$ 7

    7

    6 $\lfloor$ 7

    6

Again, the functions "maximum" and "minimum" can be used with vectors, e.g.

    1   22   99 $\lceil$ 9   8   66
    9   22   99

(i.e. of the two numbers 1 and 9, 9 is the maximum; of the two numbers 22 and 8, 22 is the maximum; etc.)

(2) Sorting

Every computer language allows the programmer to sort items in a group in ascending or descending order. The elegance of APL comes from the fact that you perform sorting with a single function, accessed with a single keystroke. The function "grade up" ($\blacktriangle$) indicates the position of the elements that would be necessary to put the elements in ascending order, while the function "grade down" ($\blacktriangledown$) does the same thing for descending order. For example, if you type in

    $\blacktriangle$ 19   0   52

you get the response

    2   1   3

The response says that to place the entries in ascending order, begin with the number 0, which was originally in second position; then take the number 19, which was in first position; and finally, take the number 52, which was in third position. The same principle applies to descending position:

$$\downarrow \quad 19 \qquad 0 \qquad 52$$
$$3 \qquad 1 \qquad 2$$

(3) The APL "One Liner"

The most impressive attribute of APL is its ability to "compress" into a single line of programming code (typically a compound function) the same amount of computing power that would take many lines of code in other languages. A typical example might be a program that stores a series of numbers, takes the average of those numbers, and then prints out the result. In BASIC, the program might look something like this:

```
110 INPUT N
120 DIM A(N)
130 FOR K = 1 TO N
140 INPUT A(K)
150 NEXT K
160 S = 0
170 FOR K = 1 TO N
180 S = S + A(K)
190 NEXT K
200 PRINT S/N
210 END
```

Here is the equivalent program in APL:

$$(+ \; / \; A) \div \rho \; A \leftarrow \square$$

Reading from right to left (which is the order in which APL evaluates functions), the first symbol, $\square$ (called "square" or "quad" or "window"), indicates that the system will accept input from the user until the return key is hit. The next symbol, $\leftarrow$, the assignment arrow, assigns the data on the right of the arrow (i.e. what the user types in) as the value of the variable on the left side of the arrow (i.e. A). The fourth symbol, ρ ("rho"), counts the number of items that appear in a vector (in this case, the number of items that appear in the variable A). When we apply the division function ($\div$) using the number of items in A as the divisor, we get an average. Moving further left in the function, we find that the dividend is represented by $(+ \; / \; A)$. The function $+ \; /$ before the A indicates we should sum together the actual values that are successively assigned to the variable A.

Is the BASIC program really easier to read than the APL program? That depends upon one's point of view. The BASIC program clearly spells out each step in the calculation—all eleven of them. The APL program provides the equivalent information, but does so in a very small amount of space. The BASIC program may be easier to read for the user who doesn't have good recall of the meaning of APL's symbols. Yet the APL program is faster and probably easier to read for the person who is fluent in handling APL.

THE EVOLUTION OF APL

For many years, use of APL was largely restricted to a few cognoscenti in computer science departments. Without a special APL keyboard, it was not possible to run the language. Equally importantly, most would-be users assumed that the language was too "mathematical" to be appropriate for their purposes. Throughout the 1960s and 1970s, APL never offered a serious challenge to COBOL in the processing of business data.

Yet within the last few years, APL has begun experiencing a renaissance. The language is now available for microcomputers, and a spate of new books (or new editions of older texts) is beginning to appear. As the population of computer users rapidly continues to rise, a growing number of non-professional programmers are coming to appreciate the power and conceptual cleanliness of APL in comparison with the more cumbersome and stolid alternative, COBOL.

THE FUTURE OF APL

While the future of APL is far brighter now than it was a decade ago, the future of data-processing languages themselves remains in question. On the one hand, COBOL is so firmly entrenched in data-processing departments across the United States that it is hardly plausible to speak of unseating COBOL with another procedural language. On the other hand, with the growth of electronic spreadsheets, data base management programs, and natural language front ends (see the discussion in "Functional Classification" in Chapter 3, and the entries on Intellect and QBE in this chapter), COBOL itself is being severely challenged by user-friendly non-procedural systems. We will need to wait a few years to see how APL fares in the evolving data-processing marketplace.

USING APL

Buying APL

Translators for APL are traditionally found on mainframe computers. However, there are a growing number of versions available for microcomputers. IBM has a version of APL for its PC, as does the University of Waterloo (inventors of Waterloo FORTRAN—WATFOR—and Waterloo Pascal). Another important version of APL for microcomputers is APL*PLUS, distributed by a company called STSC.

What to Read

BOOKS

Bryson, Susan M. (1982). *Understanding APL*. Sherman Oaks (Calif.): Alfred Publishing Company.

    Part of the "Alfred Handy Guide" series on computer languages, this volume on APL is especially lucid. It succeeds in making APL an extremely rational and even simple-to-learn language.

Iverson, Kenneth E. (1962). *A Programming Language*. New York: John Wiley.

    The standard "definition" of APL, written by one of APL's authors before the language was actually implemented on a computer.

Gilman, Leonard, and Allen J. Rose (1984). *APL: An Interactive Approach*. 3rd edition. New York: John Wiley.

    The standard text for teaching APL as a programming language.

ARTICLES

Iverson, Kenneth E. (1980). "Notation as a Tool of Thought," *Communications of the ACM* 23 (no. 8):444–465.

    The title says it all.

Falkoff, Adin D., and Kenneth E. Iverson (1981). "The Evolution of APL," in R. L. Wexelblat, ed., *History of Programming Languages*. New York: Academic Press, pp. 661–691.

    In the style of APL itself, a clear and concise history of APL.

Assembly

PROFILE
NAME
language translator "reassembles" this abbreviated code into machine code
STRUCTURE

Familiar Distinctions:
    hardware: low-level
    translator: assembler
    structural unit: n.a.
    data: no distinction made between types of data (all are treated as contents in memory locations)
 	
Conceptual Distinctions:
    organizing principle: n.a.
    procedures: highly procedural
    extensibility: not extensible
    program/data: not distinct (both are treated as contents in memory locations)

FUNCTIONS
used when speed, control, memory space, and interfacing are important (e.g. systems programming)
GENEALOGY
results of many individual attempts at "automatic programming" Years: early 1950s Authors: many Impetus: simplify the task of machine-level coding (which has no redundancy, is tedious, and highly prone to errors) Evolution: importance of assembly language may diminish as high-level languages begin introducing some low-level features (e.g. C, FORTH, Modula-2)
VERSIONS/DIALECTS
Standards: different assembly language for each microprocessor

(Continued)

135

Assembly (Continued)

SPECIAL CHARACTERISTICS

Memory Requirements: moderate

Ease of Learning/Use: confusing because of strangeness; far more intel-
                        ligible if you understand something of the computer
                        hardware

Availability: available for every existing computer (though must be
                purchased separately for most microcomputers)

WHY ASSEMBLY?

In Chapter 2 we looked at how computer languages are used to represent information to the computer hardware. We saw that from the hardware perspective (see Figure 2.1), the only signal understood is high or low electrical voltage, where high voltage has the effect of turning on a switch, and low voltage turns it off. From the perspective of a computer program, these high voltage levels are represented by the binary number 1 and the low voltage is represented by binary 0.

In the earliest days of computers, to "program" a computer meant to write out long sequences of binary code (i.e. 0's and 1's). To run the program a technician would physically flip individual switches on or off according to the binary pattern. This is *machine-level* programming (or coding) because it directly addresses the machine hardware.

Yet machine-level coding is cumbersome and highly susceptible to error. There is no redundancy in a line of 0's and 1's. If you leave out a digit or if you inadvertently change a single 0 to a 1, the program either won't run at all or will give you the wrong results. Yet failure or error is not the worst of the problems. The real difficulty comes in *finding* the error amidst a heap of digits. After you stare at strings of 0's and 1's for a few minutes, they start blending into an indistinguishable mass.

All natural human languages have two important properties that make them reasonably efficient means of communicating information. On the one hand, they offer a *shorthand* for representing more complex entities or events in the real world. Instead of referring to a particular building as "a place from which airplanes take off and land," we can simply call it an "airport." On the other hand, natural languages have a high level of *redundancy*. That is, within a single linguistic message, there is enough additional information such that if I miss part of the message, I can usually reconstruct it from the remaining components. If I see the string of letters *a-i-r-b-o-r-t* (i.e. with a *p* being mistakenly replaced with a *b*), I can probably figure out from the rest of the linguistic signal that the intended word is "airport." In computer jargon, mistakes in natural language are relatively easy to debug.

In the early 1950s, computer users realized that communicating with the machine in its own "language" (i.e. using 0's and 1's to represent high and low voltage) was grossly inefficient. The first step away from the machine was to construct a series of *abbreviations* that represented the major manipulations taking place in the machine. The programmer would write his or her code using these abbreviations. Before the program actually ran, though, it was necessary to pass this abbreviated code through a translating program that converted the abbreviations back into the sequences of binary numbers that the machine hardware could understand. (Think of adding water to dehydrated soup.) The translation program was called an *assembler*, and the abbreviated codes came to be known as *assembly language*. The principle behind assembly languages was independently worked on by a number of people and constituted the first step in a move toward "automatic programming" that was to culminate in high-level programming languages (see the entry on FORTRAN in this chapter).

E Pluribus Unum

Assembly language is actually a generic term for a whole family of languages that closely resemble one another and are used for the same purposes. To program "in assembly" is to program in a *particular* assembly language, much as to travel "by car" is to travel in a *particular* car.

Assembly languages are designed for individual microprocessors. There is an assembly language for the Mostek 6502 (the microprocessor used in the Apple II series), an assembly language for the Motorola 68000 (the chip used in a number of modern machines, including the Apple Macintosh), an assembly language used for the Zilog 80, better known as the Z80 (a chip used in many microcomputers running under the CP/M operating system), and an assembly language for the Intel 8088 (used in the IBM PC). Mainframe and minicomputers also have assembly languages tailored to their individual hardware. These languages often go by the name of the machine on which they run, such as IBM 370 Assembly Language.

Pursue for a moment the analogy between automobiles and assembly languages. All automobiles must be able to engage in a basic set of operations. They must go forward and backward. They must be able to travel at varying speeds and to accelerate from one speed to another. And they must be able to stop.

Automobile manufacturers have devised many ways of accomplishing these same ends. Cars may have automatic transmission or standard transmission. They may have three, four, or five speeds. They may or may not have power steering. A vehicle may have front-wheel drive, rear-wheel drive, or four-wheel drive. But regardless of these variations, all automobiles still go forward and backward, travel at varying speeds, are able to accelerate, and are able to stop.

Despite their superficial differences, all assembly languages are also used to perform a rather small and homogeneous set of operations. These include four basic activities: *loading* information that is stored in memory locations into the central processing unit, *adding* two pieces of information together, *comparing* two pieces of information to see if they are the same or different, and *jumping* from one part of the program to another. Instructions written in one assembly language (e.g. Z80 Assembly) are quite similar to instructions written in another (e.g. Mostek 6502). However, there are just enough differences so that code written for one system won't directly run on a machine with another microprocessor.

This lack of portability of programs written in assembly language was one of the motivations for creating high-level languages, which are, at least in principle, portable. (In high-level languages, hardware differences are handled by the compiler or interpreter, which is specially written for each machine.) Moreover, as we will see in the next section, while assembly languages are simpler than machine code, they are still far less intelligible to the average computer user than are high-level languages.

Why, then, do we still use assembly languages now that high-level computer languages have been invented?

The Virtues of Assembly

Assembly languages have three major advantages over their high-level counterparts. The first (and generally most important) is *speed*. Because assembly languages address the computer hardware more directly than do high-level languages (i.e. they have fewer "translation" stages to go through before reaching the native machine code of 0's and 1's), assembly languages almost always run much faster than high-level languages. In many computer operations (such as systems programming, graphic displays, or arcade games), speed is critical.

Assembly language also gives the programmer greater *control* over what is happening in a program than do high-level languages. By "control," we mean the ability to instruct each individual component of hardware just what to do when. In high-level languages, the programmer can issue general instructions, but it is up to the predefined translator program to determine precisely how those instructions will be carried out. Finely tuned control over the computer becomes especially important when the computer is being used to interface with external real-world devices (e.g. turning off light switches or measuring the temperature of liquid in a flask). In the words of one author: "If you try to write a typical control program in a high-level language, you often feel like someone who is trying to eat soup with chopsticks."

A third advantage that assembly languages have had over high-level languages is *efficient use of memory space*. Up until almost yesterday, computer memory was extremely expensive, and it was very important to be able to fit programs into as small a space as possible. Because of the tight control that assembly languages allow its users over each location in memory, a good programmer can fit more lines of code into a given number of memory locations using assembly language than using a high-level language.

THINKING IN ASSEMBLY

To really understand how assembly language works, you need to know much more about the internal organization of a computer than we can go into here. Suffice it to say that all of the operations in assembly language are directly tied to the physical structure of the microprocessor itself and the other chips in the computer (e.g. RAM chips, ROM chips). When an instruction says "load," for example, it is telling the hardware to move some information from one spot to another. (Obviously, there is no porter carrying around bits of information. Rather, electrical impulses are being sent from one part of the computer to another.)

In this section, then, we will not attempt to explain the basic pieces of assembly language. Without understanding the hardware, there are too many places where the names and operations will seem totally arbitrary and unnecessarily complex. Don't be put off, though. Assembly languages are not nearly as difficult to learn as some critics make them out to be. As with learning to drive a car, it simply takes time to get oriented.

One of the conceptually tricky parts of learning to program in assembly comes in figuring out how to formulate the abstract problem you are interested in solving in terms of a very restricted set of syntactic rules like JUMP, LOAD, and ADD. In high-level programming languages, the conceptual distance between the problem itself and the lines of programming code is much smaller than in the case of assembly language.

What we can do in this section is develop a feel for what an assembly language program looks like, and how it differs from both higher-level and lower-level programming. For one of the important lessons to underscore with these examples is that contrary to much popular writing, assembly language is *not* the same thing as machine code.

Machine Code/Assembly Language/High-Level Language

Consider the simple task of adding the numbers 3 and 2 together. How can we get a computer to do it?

There are three distinct levels at which we might write a program. At the lowest level, machine code, the lines of programming code themselves are series of 0's and 1's. Actually, as we will see, these binary numbers are themselves represented with hexadecimal numbers, that is, using a base 16 number system instead of the base 2 number system of binary numbers or the base 10 number system used for our familiar decimal numbers. At the assembly

I. MACHINE CODE

location	op code	comment
0000	3E 03	load the number 3 into register A
0002	06 02	load the number 2 into register B
0004	80	add the number in register B to that in register A
0005	76	stop the computer

II. ASSEMBLY LANGUAGE (Z80)

label	operator	operand	comment
START:	LD	A,3	set A = 3
	LD	B,2	set B = 2
	ADD	A,B	A + B → A
END;	HALT		stop.

III. HIGH-LEVEL LANGUAGE (Pascal)

assignment statement	comment
A := 3;	assign A the value 3
B := 2;	assign B the value 2
A := A + B;	assign A the value of A + B

language level, the programmer uses English words that stand in place of these binary numbers. And in high-level programming, users write formulas that look very much like ordinary algebra.

The easiest way to compare these three levels of programming is first to present three solutions to the same simple arithmetic problem, and then to discuss each in turn. The labels across the tops of each program are there for purposes of explanation, and are not part of the programs themselves. The machine code and assembly programs are written for the Z80 microprocessor.

In the machine language program, the programmer needs to write out memory locations (i.e. locations in Read/Write Memory—RAM) and the operating codes ("op codes") for the actions that will take place at those locations. For example, at memory locations 0000 and 0001, the operation represented by the code "3E 03" takes place. The meaning of the "03" part is easy to guess: it corresponds to the number 3 that we want to add to the number 2 (although note that the code "03" is really an abbreviation for the *binary* number 0000 0011, and does *not* stand for the Arabic numeral 3). The "3E" part is also an abbreviation, this time for the binary sequence of numbers that reads "0011 1110." The instruction "3E" tells the computer to place the equivalent of the Arabic numeral 3 in a temporary storage area in the central processing unit known as register A.

Both of these abbreviations ("03" and "3E") are written in hexadecimal (i.e. base 16) numbers. Hexadecimal numbers use a single number or letter in place of four binary digits (e.g. "3" in place of "0011"). Since the instruction "0011 1110" takes up one full memory location, and "0000 0011" takes up another, we need to use two memory locations, 0000 and 0001, to house the first operation in the machine code program. Notice also that data (e.g. the number "03") and program instructions (e.g. load that number into register A—"3E") are not physically stored or manipulated in distinct ways.

The second line of code in the program works much the same as the first. Two memory locations, 0002 and 0003, are used to house the instruction (in hexadecimal code) "06 02." In normal binary code, this instruction would read "0000 0110 0000 0010." The third instruction (which takes up only one memory location, 0004) performs the addition: It takes the contents of register B (think of a register as a computer work space like a laboratory table) and adds it to the number that is in register A. The final line of code (located in memory location 0005) stops the computer because the problem is solved.

The assembly language program physically traces exactly the same steps as does the machine language program. The only difference is in the syntax that the programmer needs to use to represent the problem. To begin with, in assembly language, the programmer does not need to specify the precise locations in memory where the instructions are to be housed. And even more importantly, the programmer can use English (e.g. ADD) or English-like abbreviations (e.g. LD for LOAD) to represent the operations that will take place. Finally, by distinguishing between operator and operand, the program can reflect in the programming code the difference between an operation (such as loading a number) and the place in which the number is to be loaded (e.g. register A). In the machine code program, this information was combined into a single two-digit hexadecimal code (e.g. "3E," meaning "load into register A").

Finally, in high-level programming languages (like Pascal), the operation of addition is barely distinguishable from the way in which we might formulate the problem in algebra, e.g.

A = 3
B = 2
C = A + B

Ignoring trivial differences in punctuation, the only real difference between algebra and a high-level programming language is that in programming languages an expression can be written where the same variable that appears on the right-hand side can be assigned a new value on the left, i.e.

A := A + B

In a high-level language, the programmer approaches the operation of addition much the way as if there were no computer. Programmers need not concern themselves with the way in which the language translator reformulates the problem so that the computer hardware will understand it. (Of course, the high-level language compiler or interpreter needs to recast the problem into a form that approximates our machine language example.)

THE EVOLUTION OF ASSEMBLY

Assembly languages have altered very little since they were first developed in the early 1950s. The only "evolution" has been to increase the number of assembly languages as the variety of microprocessors grows.

The real change to have come about is not in assembly languages but in high-level languages on the one hand and computer hardware on the other. We said at the outset that assembly languages are useful because they allow greater speed, control, and conservation of memory locations than do high-level languages. However, within the last decade, at least three essentially high-level languages have emerged—C, FORTH, and Modula-2—that can function as reasonably low-level languages as well. C has largely replaced assembly language in doing systems programming in many programming shops. FORTH is renowned both for its speed and for the minuscule amount of memory space it takes. And Modula-2 is a highly structured modern imperative/algorithmic language (undoubtedly the most popular form of programming today) that is gaining an increasingly wide following. Meanwhile, the price of memory chips is falling dramatically, and the efforts necessary to squeeze large programs into small spaces may soon not be cost-effective.

THE FUTURE OF ASSEMBLY

As a result of changes in high-level languages and computer hardware, assembly language is losing some of its allure. It seems likely that assembly languages will always exist. They are the most direct way of addressing a particular microprocessor, and have an aesthetic appeal for programmers who always want to know just how their program is running on the machine. Moreover, even when doing systems programming in a language like C, it is still usually necessary to use assembly language for a few parts of the programming to "bootstrap" the other language. However, it seems likely that in the years to come, many programmers who felt driven in the past to use assembly (e.g. for reasons of speed) will now switch to higher-level programming language alternatives.

USING ASSEMBLY

Buying Assembly Languages

In order to run an assembly language, you need an assembler. Assembler programs are available on all mainframe and minicomputers. In the case of microcomputers, you generally need to purchase an assembler separately from the computer itself (much as you would purchase a high-level language like Pascal or C). That is, just because your microcomputer comes (by definition) with a microprocessor doesn't mean you can address it directly.

What to Read

Since every assembly language is different, if you want to learn to program in assembly you will need to obtain a book on the version of assembly language you will be using. Be aware that some publishers entitle their books on assembly language with the name of the computer that the language runs on rather than with the name of the microprocessor in the machine. Thus, a book on "Apple Assembly Language" describes the same language as "6502 Assembly," and a book on "IBM PC Assembly Language" is really about the language of the Intel 8088.

Listed below are just a few books to start you out. They are organized by subject.

GENERAL

Bishop, Ron (1979). *Basic Microprocessors and the 6800*. Rochelle Park (N.J.): Hayden Book Company.

The Motorola 6800 is a fairly simple microchip and its assembly language is a good place to begin. Bishop's book provides a solid introduction not only to 6800 Assembly Language but also to such necessary prerequisites as basic electronic principles, logic elements, number systems, digital arithmetic, and computer hardware.

Microprocessors (1979). Benton Harbor (Mich.): Heathkit Educational Systems.

Heathkit books and hardware kits provide an excellent grounding in electronics and computers. The volumes on microprocessors give a foolproof introduction to both machine code and assembly language for the Motorola 6800. The course requires a number of hours of commitment, but is well worth the effort.

Mansfield, Richard (1983). *Machine Language for Beginners*. Greensboro (N.C.): Compute! Publications, Inc.

This very clear manual explains how to do machine language programming on a variety of common microcomputers. The book assumes knowledge of BASIC but not of computer hardware.

Z80 Assembly

Leventhal, Lance A. (1979). *Z80 Assembly Language Programming*. Berkeley: Osborne/McGraw-Hill.

Mostek 6502

De Jong, Marvin L. (1982). *Apple II Assembly Language*. Indianapolis: Howard W. Sams.

Intel 8088

Schneider, Al (1984). *Fundamentals of IBM PC Assembly Language*. Blue Ridge Summit (Pa.): Tab Books.

BASIC

PROFILE

NAME

*B*eginner's *A*ll-Purpose *S*ymbolic *I*nstruction *C*ode

STRUCTURE

Familiar Distinctions:
    hardware: high-level
    translator: generally interpreted (originally compiled)
    structural unit: statement (originally unstructured; now often structured)
    data: numerical, simple graphics

Conceptual Distinctions:
    organizing principle: imperative/algorithmic
    procedures: procedural
    extensibility: not extensible
    program/data: distinct

FUNCTIONS

general-purpose, though especially popular in lower education (to teach programming)

GENEALOGY

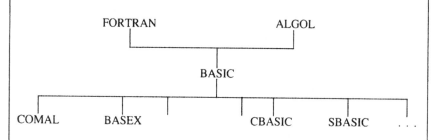

Year: 1964

Authors: John Kemeny and Thomas Kurtz (Dartmouth College)

(Continued)

BASIC (Continued)

Impetus:	provide college students with a simple way to start using computers
Evolution:	important role of time sharing, microcomputers, and interpreters very widespread in late 1970s, early 1980s challenged by structured languages, especially Pascal

VERSIONS/DIALECTS

Standards:	ANSI Minimal BASIC (1978) ANS BASIC (under development)—True BASIC
Others:	hardware proprietary systems: e.g. Applesoft BASIC, TI BASIC, IBM BASICA software house systems: e.g. Microsoft BASIC other systems: e.g. SBASIC

SPECIAL CHARACTERISTICS

Memory Requirements: small

Ease of Learning/Use: easy

Availability: readily available for all computers

WHY BASIC?

> BASIC has become the most widely known computer language. Why? Simply because there are more people in the world than there are programmers. If ordinary persons are to use a computer, there must be simple computer languages for them.
> Thomas Kurtz, "BASIC," 1981

For many computer users, "BASIC" is synonymous with "computer language." Hobbyists, occasional computer users, and the overwhelming population of schoolchildren often begin—and end—their programming experiences with BASIC. The language's popularity has generated vast amounts of software (and program listings) written in BASIC, along with seemingly endless courses and textbooks.

BASIC also has its naysayers. In the words of Edsger Dijkstra:

> It is practically impossible to teach good programming to students that have had a prior exposure to BASIC: as potential programmers they are mentally mutilated beyond hope of regeneration.
> "How Do We Tell Truths That Might Hurt?" 1975, from *Selected Writings on Computing*

How did BASIC come to generate such polarized opinions?

Centrality of the User

BASIC was created for one fundamental reason: to enable computer novices to use computers as easily and naturally as possible. The resulting syntax that has evolved over the years is strictly a product of this overriding goal. Whenever the syntax or implementation of BASIC appears to be hindering this goal, the language design is always seen as expendable. In the words of the language's authors: "In all cases where there is a choice between simplicity and efficiency, simplicity is chosen."

BASIC was developed in 1964 at Dartmouth College by John Kemeny and Thomas Kurtz. Yet the history of the language goes back another eight years. After Dartmouth's first serious encounter with computers in 1956, Kemeny and Kurtz (along with an assortment of students and associates) worked out a successive series of experimental languages intended to make the computer serve the programmer rather than vice versa. BASIC was the last in the series.

Unlike most computer languages (such as FORTRAN, COBOL, APL, PL/I, LISP, or ALGOL) that were created to help accomplish programming tasks, BASIC was explicitly designed for giving Dartmouth students entrée to the computer. But the issue was not simply to get students to begin using computers. It was to get them to use computers for a *purpose*.

In the early 1960s, computers were becoming increasingly important in business and industry. Kemeny and Kurtz reasoned that non-science students graduating from Dartmouth would be entering a world in which they would need to make managerial decisions about computing. "How," the authors wondered, "can sensible decisions about computing and its use be made by persons essentially ignorant of it?" Like Grace Hopper and the drafters of COBOL, Kemeny and Kurtz felt computer programming was too important to be relegated exclusively to professional programmers. The decision-making public would need to understand what was going on as well.

The overall model of computing that Kemeny and Kurtz proposed was as important as the BASIC language itself. They settled on a fourfold approach:
   (1)   "to devise a computer system that would be friendly, easy to learn and use, and not require students to go out of their way"
   (2)   "to develop a new language—again, one that was easy to learn and use"
   (3)   "to introduce students to computing as an *adjunct*" to another course
   (4)   "to operate the computer with open access," with an open-stack library serving as a model

The first goal was largely made possible by the system of time sharing (which we will turn to in a moment). The third goal is only now in the 1980s being incorporated into computer literacy curricula around the United States. (The importance of this third goal in the minds of Kemeny and Kurtz is starkly reflected in the page distribution of the 1967 version of their text, *BASIC Programming*: only 26 pages are devoted to the syntax of BASIC, and 88 pages are devoted to applications.) The fourth goal is still a wish rather than a reality at most American institutions of higher learning.

Time Sharing and Interactive Computing

BASIC as a philosophy of computing would not have been possible without the earlier development of time sharing. Time sharing as an approach to multiple-user computing was first developed at MIT around 1960. Previously, doing computer programming entailed writing out the lines of code, entering the code on punched cards, submitting the cards to the computer operator, and waiting for the results. When the program was finally returned, it typically hadn't run— or even hadn't compiled—because of errors, however minor. And so it was back to the drawing board: correct the errors, punch the necessary new cards, submit the stack again, and wait.

With time sharing, users could sit directly at a computer terminal (not a key punch machine) and interact with the computer *as if* the computer were solely at the beck and call of that user. No punched cards and, comparatively speaking, no waiting for results. In actual fact, the computer was attending to the needs of many users, though not simultaneously. Yet by working very quickly, the computer (like an efficient waiter) gave the illusion of being totally dedicated to each user.

In time sharing, we need to distinguish between the *means of inputting programs* and the *operation of the computer* itself. At base, the essential element of time sharing is that the computer hardware can seemingly handle more than one task at the same time. How those data are input (i.e. through punched cards or at a terminal) is a matter of convenience to the user. It does not influence what the computer does with the lines of programming code it receives. At Dartmouth, those two components of time sharing were combined: users input their programs at remote terminals around campus, and the computer seemingly dealt with several programs simultaneously. However, at many other computer installations around the country to this day, time-sharing machines are regularly used to process programs delivered on stacks of punched cards.

The significant variable, then, is not whether the computer is able to do time sharing, but how much *interaction* the user is able to have with the computer. "Interactive computing" is a matter of the degree to which the user can "converse" with the computer in a give-and-take dialog. The user types in a program; the computer returns a result. The user enters a correction; the computer accepts the correction and runs the program again.

Part of this "conversation" may entail the user being able to enter not only programs but also data to be processed while a program is actually running. The earliest versions of BASIC did *not* have any means of entering data at the terminal during the execution of a program. Not until 1966 was the INPUT statement added to BASIC, thereby making the language fully interactive. Before that, all data had to be entered in DATA statements at the beginning of the program itself.

Compilation vs. Interpretation

But there is a further possible meaning of "interactive computing," and that is having the computer respond to every line of code as you enter it. This level of "interacting" takes place when the language translator directly *interprets* each line of code entered (rather than waiting to *compile* the whole program at the end).

Nearly all versions of BASIC used today run under interpreters, not compilers. It is therefore surprising to learn that Kemeny and Kurtz designed BASIC as a *compiled* language. Interpreted languages did exist at the time (e.g. JOSS, LISP). Time sharing would have made an interpreted BASIC easy to implement, but the authors of BASIC chose not to do so.

Kemeny and Kurtz's reasoning was both pragmatic and pedagogical. The central computer on which BASIC originally ran at Dartmouth had very limited memory capacity. A compiled version of the language put less strain on the system than an interpreted version would have. But equally importantly, Kemeny and Kurtz did not want students to have their mistakes spelled out for them at the end of each line of code they entered (as happens with interpreted languages). By using a compiled version, students could type in their entire programs and have a chance to correct their mistakes before attempting to run the program. Even then, the original error messages given by Dartmouth BASIC were intentionally sparse.

The Evolution of BASIC: A Preview

The issue of *why* BASIC was created is reasonably straightforward. Yet the seemingly trivial issue of what we are talking about when we speak of "BASIC" is not. Within Dartmouth itself, BASIC has evolved dramatically over its twenty-year history. In the world of computing more generally, BASIC has been pushed and pulled, stretched and compressed into forms that Kemeny and Kurtz would hardly call BASIC at all. Writing in 1978, Kurtz concludes: "Rather than being a single language with dialects, BASIC is really a class of languages, all with a common core."

BASIC has evolved (especially in the last decade) in three essential ways. First, nearly all popular forms of BASIC are interpreted rather than compiled. Second, BASIC has undergone an important shift from being an unstructured language to becoming a structured language. And third, as more modern languages have appeared on the scene with sophisticated data structures and control structures, many versions of BASIC have absorbed some of these new features.

We will address these developments a little later in our section "The Evolution of BASIC." We mention them here to clarify which version of BASIC underlies our discussion of "Thinking in BASIC." Our choice is what we might call "vintage BASIC," that is, BASIC as developed in its first decade at Dartmouth. For this is the version that most users have come to know as "BASIC" through their use of the language on microcomputers.

THINKING IN BASIC

Linguistic Heritage: Small Is Beautiful

The syntax of BASIC is the least interesting part of the language. This is because, in the words of its authors, BASIC has no syntactic or semantic ideas that hadn't been thought of before. BASIC is entirely a syncretic language.

The languages shaping BASIC were, first, FORTRAN and, to a lesser extent, ALGOL. In fact, before deciding to create a new language, Kemeny and Kurtz had contemplated teaching the general Dartmouth student population either FORTRAN or ALGOL, but rejected the possibility because "the majority would balk at the seemingly pointless detail."

The alternative was to create a language that had *some* of the computing power of FORTRAN and ALGOL, but not all. At the same time, the goal of user accessibility dictated a syntax that was as English-like and unambiguous as possible. In the same way that the designers of COBOL (which predates BASIC by four years) incorporated as much ordinary English vocabulary into the structure of COBOL as they deemed possible, Kemeny and Kurtz chose short common English words (e.g. HELLO, LIST, RUN, GOODBYE) as system commands, rather than more technical words like LOGON, CATALOG, EXECUTE, or LOGOFF, which are still common in mainframe systems. The regrettable exception to the tendency toward natural language simplicity came in the naming of variables. For not very convincing reasons, BASIC represents variables with single alphabetical characters rather than allowing users to define their own more meaningful names (e.g. "Average" rather than "A").

There were other moves toward simplicity as well. One was the elimination of such mathematical nuances as the distinction between integers and real numbers (only integers were allowed, and hence the name INTEGER BASIC, an early version of BASIC running on the Apple II). Another was the inclusion of line numbers to facilitate editing (and to handle GOTO statements—the equivalent of JUMP statements in assembly language). Line numbers and GOTO statements (also found in other unstructured languages like FORTRAN and COBOL) were to become the rallying points around which later proponents of structured programming would attack these earlier unstructured languages (see the entry on ALGOL).

Language/Editor/Operating System

Users of BASIC often don't realize that what goes under the name BASIC is typically more than simply a language translator. It is also an editor and pieces of an operating system. The interconnectedness of these components is especially obvious in modern interpreted versions of the language. Users who have grown up on interpreted BASIC are often surprised to realize that in using other languages they must learn a whole set of operating system commands plus another set of editing commands before being able to use the syntax of the programming language itself.

Vintage BASIC: A Syntactic Overview

The early versions of BASIC contain the essential elements necessary to do elementary arithmetic tasks. The language has means of declaring data, assigning values to variables, jumping to other parts of the program, performing IF-THEN conditionals, creating loops with FOR-NEXT statements, and calculating results using standard arithmetic operators. Vintage BASIC also has some built-in functions (e.g. sine, square root) and allows the user to define several dozen more. In addition, BASIC uses subroutines to incorporate self-contained programs within larger ones.

All of these syntactic manipulations are familiar from other programming languages. What distinguishes vintage BASIC from more modern languages (including more modern versions of BASIC) is what is missing. It has very few data types, limited data structures, and only a handful of control structures. To write even moderately sophisticated programs in vintage BASIC, you need to jury-rig existing data structures and control structures to make them behave in more sophisticated ways.

Vintage BASIC predates the development of structured programming. One hundred lines of code in a structured language of the ALGOL family are decidedly easier to read than a hundred lines of BASIC. Unlike the continuous linear sequence in a BASIC program, a program in a structured language is divided into components (e.g. blocks and procedures and functions) that bear their meanings in their titles and show their relationships with one another in ways that are obvious once you learn the conventions.

To illustrate programming in BASIC, here is a standard program for converting degrees fahrenheit into degrees centigrade:

```
100 PRINT "FAHRENHEIT TEMPERATURE"
110 INPUT F
120 LET C = (F − 32) * 5/9
130 PRINT "CENTIGRADE TEMPERATURE:"; C
140 PRINT
150 GOTO 100
160 END
```

When the program is run, the computer types out

FAHRENHEIT TEMPERATURE?

(line 100) and waits for the user to input a value (e.g. 32) (line 110). Using this value, the program calculates the centigrade equivalent (line 120) and prints out the result as

CENTIGRADE TEMPERATURE: 0

(line 130). The program then skips a line (line 140) and returns the user to line 100 to input a new fahrenheit value.

BASIC and Pascal

Most of the debates about the choice of programming languages for use in general education end up contrasting vintage BASIC (an unstructured language) with Pascal (a structured language). Vintage BASIC is still the language most often taught in lower education, while Pascal is assuming this status in colleges and some high schools. Both languages were designed to be used by beginning programmers. Proponents of Pascal typically charge that students should learn structured programming, while advocates of vintage BASIC counter that their language has stood the test of time, being easy to learn and then use for a multiplicity of functions.

The comparison between Pascal and vintage BASIC is unfortunate. There are far more sophisticated versions of BASIC available today than vintage BASIC. What's more, it is not obvious that *any* imperative/algorithmic language is appropriate for students who do not intend to become professional programmers. (List processing, logic programming, or object-oriented languages may be more suitable.) Nonetheless, to understand what all the hullabaloo has been about, we will briefly compare how vintage BASIC and Pascal might go about solving the same problem.

Consider our program for converting fahrenheit temperatures to centigrade temperatures. The BASIC program read like a continuous laundry list, sequencing one statement after another. The same program in Pascal enables us to break down the program—even such a small one as this—into components.

The Pascal coding would look something like this (for convenience of discussion we have numbered the lines of code, but these line numbers are *not* part of Pascal):

```
1   PROGRAM TEMPERATURE;
2   VAR FAHRENHEIT, CENTRIGRADE: REAL;
3   PROCEDURE CONVERT;
4       BEGIN
5           CENTIGRADE := (FAHRENHEIT − 32) * 5/9;
6           WRITELN ('CENTIGRADE TEMPERATURE IS ,'
                CENTIGRADE)
7       END;
8   BEGIN
9       WRITE ('FAHRENHEIT TEMPERATURE: ');
10      READ (FAHRENHEIT);
11      CONVERT
12  END.
```

The first line of the program tells us (by name) what the program will be about, while the second line indicates what kinds of variables we will be using (here, real numbers). Lines 3–7 specify a procedure (here named CONVERT) which does the conversion of degrees fahrenheit to degrees centigrade, and prints out the result. This procedure is then used in the main part of the larger program (lines 8–12).

The main program writes out the prompt "FAHRENHEIT TEMPERATURE:" (comparable to BASIC's PRINT statement in line 100), to which the user responds by typing in a number (comparable to BASIC's INPUT statement in line 110). The elegance of the Pascal program comes in line 11: With a single call to the procedure CONVERT, the main program can invoke the procedure of lines 3–7 that is tucked out of the way. Lines 8–12 give a succinct statement of what the program is doing. If we want to know the details, there is another succinct location (lines 3–7) we can turn to. In the BASIC program, all parts of the program run together, giving us no visual or conceptual sense of what parts are subordinate to what other parts.

THE EVOLUTION OF BASIC

Around 1976, two fundamental developments took place that were to create a split personality for the BASIC language. One widely publicized event was to give BASIC enormous popularity among computer users around the world, while a second, quieter move would turn BASIC into a far more modern language than is generally known.

BASIC on Microcomputers

In 1976, Paul Allen and Bill Gates (who later founded Microsoft, Inc.) wrote an interpreted version of BASIC for the MITS Altair microcomputer. That version was based upon the original unstructured Dartmouth BASIC defined a decade earlier, complete with line numbers and GOTO statements. Their BASIC interpreter eventually became known as Microsoft BASIC, one of the most widely used versions of the language on the market today.

With the explosion of the computer market in the late 1970s and early 1980s, an interpreted version of vintage BASIC was adopted by millions of microcomputer users. And for many, BASIC was the only computing option. FORTRAN or COBOL was too "large" to fit into the memory space of the early microcomputers. Many hobbyists still learned assembly language, but assembly proved too distant from the real world of problem solving for most users.

And so it was a variant of vintage Dartmouth BASIC that came to be known as "BASIC" in homes, offices, and classrooms around the world. (The version is often dubbed "street BASIC.") The decade-long perseverance of this outdated form of the language resulted from two other developments. On the one hand, hardware manufacturers (especially Apple) decided to distribute an interpreted version of BASIC along with their machine (first as a disk and later built into ROM). On the other hand, educators, especially at the lower-school level, were giving microcomputers an enthusiastic reception. Not being computer scientists themselves, most teachers readily accepted street BASIC as the best that the computer profession had to offer. The more books and programs that appeared in BASIC, the more entrenched this version of the language became.

There is, of course, much variety within microcomputer versions of BASIC itself. BASIC has been customized by almost every computer manufacturer and several independent software houses. Applesoft BASIC isn't quite the same as TI BASIC or IBM's BASICA or Microsoft BASIC. Yet differences among at least the machine-specific versions of BASIC tend to be comparatively slight.

Structured BASIC

Just about the same time that Allen and Gates were repackaging vintage BASIC for distribution on microcomputers, the keepers of BASIC at Dartmouth were introducing new versions of the language that incorporated current ideas about what constituted good programming languages and good programming style. By 1976, Stephen Garland, a professor of computer science at Dartmouth, wrote a structured version of BASIC (called SBASIC) that was taught to Dartmouth undergraduates. Ironically, SBASIC may well be among the first structured programming languages taught to general students in the United States. (ALGOL was not seriously taught in the United States, and Ken Bowles's implementation of Pascal at the University of California at San Diego did not become well established until the late 1970s.) This, despite the reputation that BASIC still bears for being an unstructured language.

SBASIC incorporates many of the ideas of structured programming that emerged from the development of ALGOL and especially its descendant, Pascal. SBASIC eliminates line numbers, GOTO statements, subroutines, and primitive forms of conditional statements and looping statements, replacing them with more sophisticated ALGOL-like structures. Adhering to the principle of "simplicity above all else," nothing of the syntax of vintage BASIC remains sacrosanct. In fact, writing in 1978, Thomas Kurtz stated matter-of-factly that the GOTO statement, long the hallmark of BASIC programming style, "has an attractive simplicity for novices, but . . . should be discarded at an early stage in favor of structured constructs."

Structured versions of BASIC (or structured derivatives of BASIC) have proliferated in recent years. COMAL, for example (see Appendix), is essentially structured BASIC, and CBASIC, a compiled version of BASIC, incorporates some of the principles of structured BASIC. Given this transformation in the conceptual underpinnings of BASIC, one wonders if Dijkstra would feel that structured versions of BASIC also cause programmers to be "mentally mutilated beyond hope of regeneration."

THE FUTURE OF BASIC

BASIC's future is now uncertain. One very real possibility is that it will be replaced in classrooms by another language. The logical candidate is Pascal, especially since the Educational Testing Service (in Princeton, New Jersey) began offering Advanced Placement examinations in Pascal to high school students (see the entry on Pascal). Other options include Logo (especially versions including the more sophisticated LISP functions) and perhaps even PROLOG, micro-PROLOG, or Smalltalk.

Another scenario would be for vintage or street BASIC to remain as one of several languages that students learn in sequence. Some schools already begin by teaching children Logo, then progress to BASIC, and finally end up with Pascal. BASIC thus becomes a stepping-stone to "real" programming, much the same way that initial teaching systems such as Karel the Robot are used to teach students *about* programming before they actually *do* programming (see Appendix).

Alternatively, the general microcomputing community (including education) might replace vintage BASIC with a newer, more structured version of the language. Kemeny and Kurtz have recently taken the offensive here by developing yet another form of structured BASIC for micros. Their result, called True BASIC, bears strong resemblance to SBASIC and is essentially the same as the proposed ANS BASIC. If True BASIC successfully permeates the market, it may present a strong alternative to Pascal. According to Kemeny, Pascal can declare more kinds of structures than True BASIC, but True BASIC is superior in handling strings and graphics. Whether such differences are sufficiently important for two languages to persist remains to be seen.

USING BASIC

Buying BASIC

BASIC is available for any microcomputer you are likely to encounter. Often (e.g. in the Apple IIe or the IBM PC), the language is already built into the machine hardware. In other cases, it is available as a program that you purchase separately. Don't assume that a single hardware manufacturer follows a consistent policy as to whether BASIC is burned into a ROM chip. While the Apple IIe, for example, has BASIC built in, the Apple Macintosh does not.

What to Read

More books and articles are probably available on BASIC than on any other computer language. Because so many dialects of BASIC are customized to particular microcomputers, you will do best to purchase a book geared to the dialect of BASIC you will be learning. Both Applesoft BASIC and Microsoft BASIC have become standards in the world of microcomputing, so you may want to begin there if you will be using an Apple II series machine (for Applesoft) or a machine on which Microsoft BASIC will run (there are many).

Instead of making recommendations on basic learning texts, we will, instead, give references to a few books and articles that are of historical or comparative interest or that talk about the future of BASIC.

BOOKS

Kemeny, John, and Thomas Kurtz (1967). *BASIC Programming*. New York: John Wiley.

This is the original text on BASIC, written by its inventors. The simplicity of the language and the language's practical applications are both evident in the book.

Kemeny, John, and Thomas Kurtz (1981). *BASIC Programming*. 3rd edition. New York: John Wiley.

Published thirteen years later, this third edition of Kemeny and Kurtz's text illustrates the language's evolution.

Kemeny, John, and Thomas Kurtz (1985). *Back to BASIC: The History, Corruption, and Future of the Language*. Reading (Mass.): Addison-Wesley.

Twenty years after BASIC was created, its authors reflect on its history and make projections for its continuing potential. The book is a popularization and update of the article by Kurtz cited below.

Seiter, Charles, and Robert Weiss (1983). *Pascal for BASIC Programmers*. Reading (Mass.): Addison-Wesley.

An excellent comparison between Pascal and BASIC that simultaneously explains much about both of the languages.

ARTICLES

Kurtz, Thomas (1981). "BASIC," in R. L. Wexelblat, ed. *History of Programming Languages*. New York: Academic Press, pp. 515–549.

A clear statement (written in 1978) of the early goals behind the development of BASIC at Dartmouth.

"In Quest of True BASIC," interview with John Kemeny and Thomas Kurtz, ed. by Andrew Fluegelman. *PC World*, November 1984, pp. 120–128.

A candid and incisive interview with the authors of BASIC. Much of this material is discussed in more detail in the authors' *Back to BASIC*.

C

PROFILE
NAME
revision of a language called B, which was a revision of a language called BCPL
STRUCTURE

Familiar Distinctions:
    hardware: part high-level and part low-level
    translator: compiled
    structural unit: function
    data: numerical, text
 	
Conceptual Distinctions:
    organizing principle: imperative/algorithmic
    procedures: procedural
    extensibility: not extensible (though very important role of library functions)
    program/data: distinct

FUNCTIONS
systems programming (e.g. writing compilers, operating systems, text editors)
GENEALOGY

Year: 1972
Author: Dennis Ritchie (Bell Laboratories)

(Continued)

156

C (Continued)

Impetus:	create a general-purpose language suited to systems programming by combining high-level structured language with features to control low-level programming
Evolution:	spread to colleges and universities in the 1970s; became very popular in the early 1980s because of close ties with UNIX and availability on micros

Versions/Dialects

Standard:	work of Kernighan and Ritchie constitutes de facto standard work underway to develop ANSI standard
Others:	small versions for microcomputers (including Tiny-C and Small-C)

Special Characteristics

Memory Requirements:	moderate
Ease of Learning/Use:	confusing for beginners
Availability:	many implementations now available for microcomputers, but compare before you buy (they vary widely in price and features included)

NOTE: Before reading this discussion of C, review the entry on ALGOL. You may also want to read the sections on Ada and Modula-2 in conjunction with the entry on C.

WHY C?

Americans are a people given to fads. One year we all buy books on cats, and the next year the ultimate gift becomes a teddy bear. A particular restaurant may have had no business yesterday and be impossible to get a table at today— without the restaurant having changed its chef, menu, or decor. Computer languages can also go in and out of fashion. Ten years ago, BASIC was seen by many as an ideal language, while today many scorn it as primitive.

The programming language C has recently come into vogue. "Real" programmers, or so the hyperbole goes, program in C. How did C develop such a reputation? And is this good advice? The answer depends heavily upon whom you ask.

COMPUTER LANGUAGES

The Question of Purpose

C is composed of contrasts. It is at once a high-level and a low-level language. It is structured, while at the same time violating some of the cardinal rules of structured programming. And it is a special-purpose language whose designer, Dennis Ritchie, describes it as a general-purpose language.

Ritchie opens his classic textbook on C (*The C Programming Language*, by Brian Kernighan and Dennis Ritchie) by declaring:

> C is a general-purpose programming language . . . . [A]lthough it has been called a "systems programming language" because it is useful for writing operating systems, it has been used equally well to write major numerical, text-processing, and data-base programs.

Yet others describe C as a language written *by* a professional programmer *for* professional programmers. Much as assembly language can be used as a general-purpose programming language (but only professional programmers or dedicated hackers would tend to use it this way), C can be used for programming any problem, but it is not clear that the average programmer—especially the novice—would be well advised to do so.

Systems programming language or general-purpose language? How did this ambivalence of purpose arise?

Alphabet Soup: The History of C

The language C is the most recent in a line of languages constituting one of the lesser-known branches of ALGOL 60. As we saw in the entry on ALGOL, ALGOL 60 spawned most of the modern imperative/algorithmic languages that are in use today, including ALGOL 68, SIMULA, and the Pascal line (which, in turn, gave rise to Modula-2 and Ada). All of these are high-level languages that put increasing layers of distance between the programmer and the actual machine on which the program is running.

In 1963, a group of programmers in England decided to try a different tack. Like the designers of ALGOL 58 and ALGOL 60, they wanted to create a general-purpose language that would be appropriate for all types of problems (numerical and non-numerical) and would allow programmers to make use of all the computational subtleties of the computer without having to delve down to the level of machine code. (At that time, nearly all systems programming was done in machine code or assembly language.)

The creators of ALGOL 58 and ALGOL 60 had taken great pains to devise languages that offered precise definitions of algorithms. However, neither of the ALGOLs was fleshed out when it came to writing actual programs that ran on actual computers. Many of the implementation details were not part of the language specification. In fact, this lack of implementation specificity was largely responsible for American FORTRAN users deciding to stick with FORTRAN rather than risk a new language which could not immediately be implemented.

A joint committee, formed of members of the University Mathematical Laboratory in Cambridge and the University of London Computer Unit, decided to create a new language to help bridge this gap between algorithmic definition and actual implementation. At the same time, they believed it was important (if they were to have a single language for all programming functions) to allow the programmer, where necessary, to retain contact with the realities of an actual computer. That is, instead of making their language strictly "high-level" (i.e. more distant from the inner workings of the computer), they wanted a language that was at once machine-independent and explicitly oriented to the inner workings of the computer. It would still be a high-level language (compared with assembly language, which is always tied to a particular microprocessor) but it would function at a fairly low level (giving the programmer the ability to control the behavior of individual bits of information). The resulting language was called CPL (for *C*ombined *P*rogramming *L*anguage), since it represented the combined efforts of two universities.

CPL had many virtues, but one major drawback. The language was too large for most specific applications that users wanted to program. In 1967, Martin Richards (at Cambridge) decided to develop a smaller version of CPL specifically aimed at doing systems programming (including operating systems, compilers and interpreters, data base packages, simulators, text processors, and editors). CPL was already in principle well suited to these tasks because it was a fairly low-level language (without descending to assembly language or machine code). The new language was called BCPL (for *B*asic CPL) because it borrowed the syntactic richness and linguistic elegance of CPL while scaling down its size.

On the other side of the Atlantic in Murray Hill, New Jersey, Ken Thompson of Bell Laboratories was also involved in systems programming. In 1970, Thompson decided to use an even smaller distillation of this English line of programming and created a language named B (named, presumably, because he took only a part of BCPL and therefore needed only a small part of its name).

At the time, Thompson was working with Dennis Ritchie (also at Bell Labs) on developing a multifunction operating system that would be useful not only for running languages but also for software development. The operating system came to be known as UNIX. The UNIX system was written, as one might expect, in assembly language. In 1972, Ritchie decided to rework Thompson's language B (which, remember, had become a very small, specialized language). The new language was called C. (Ritchie leaves us to guess whether he was following Thompson in pulling out the next letter in the name BCPL or taking C as the next letter in the alphabet following B.)

One of the major differences between B and C was that C restored some of the generality that had originally existed in CPL. While C remains (like CPL and BCPL and B) a relatively low-level language, it includes some features generally associated with higher-level languages, such as a rich data-typing structure.

Soon after C was written, its power and flexibility became obvious. The

UNIX operating system was almost immediately rewritten in C. (Only a fraction of the program for UNIX still had to be written in assembly language in order to "bootstrap" the bulk of the code, which was written in C.)

C was a programmer's language—written by a programmer for programmers. In this sense, C was unlike most of its well-known predecessors. FORTRAN had been designed, in part, to accommodate scientists and engineers, who generally knew very little about computers but needed to program them. COBOL was explicitly created for the computer laity in the business world. Other languages, such as BASIC, took as their audience total novices. Even APL, despite its cryptic façade, was intended for business people to do their own data processing.

Living Dangerously

What does it mean to say that C is a programmer's language? The language itself isn't inordinately large (it has a moderate number of lines of code), and its range of data structures and control structures is typical of modern ALGOL-derivative languages such as Pascal and Ada.

Yet programming in C is different in a very fundamental way. Think of driving along a winding, mountainous road with a steep precipice on one side. If there is a solid guardrail separating the road from the precipice, you are in little serious danger, even if you veer off the road. If there is no guardrail and you are a very careful driver (who doesn't suffer from vertigo), you are physically just as safe as if there were a rail. However, if in the latter case you do swerve off the road, you could go careening over the edge.

Most modern ALGOL-derivative languages come complete with guardrails. If you make a mistake, the compiler will let you know (with an error message) so that you can correct the mistake before actually running the program. But not in C. Cruising along in C, you are perfectly safe as long as you make no mistakes of particular sorts such as data typing. If you *do* make a mistake, often you are taking your fate in your own hands. For the error messages (if they appear at all) may be less than comprehensible, and discovering the source of the errors on your own can present a genuine challange.

To get a sense of what all this means, let's take a closer look at how to think about programming in C.

THINKING IN C

Language of the Middle Range

Begin with the observation that C is at once a high-level and a low-level language. True low-level languages (i.e. assembly languages) have two decided advantages over high-level languages. On the one hand, they carry out processes very quickly. (Think of speaking directly to another person in a language he or she already understands, instead of having to go through a translator.) On the other hand, low-level languages offer the programmer very tight control over everything that is happening in the computer: each movement of data, each manipulation of information, each storage of a result. (Think this time of the difference between standard transmissions and automatic transmissions: both regulate the speed of a car, but standard transmissions give you much greater control over the vehicle.)

Yet low-level languages have disadvantages as well. To begin with, they are not portable. Each program must be recoded for each microprocessor it will run on. Moreover, the tight control that is inherent in low-level languages often exceeds the programmer's needs. If my goal is simply to add two numbers together, I don't really want to be bothered with having to specify that the first number should be loaded into register A, the second number loaded into register B, the contents of register A added to the contents of register B, and the result stored in register A (see the entry on assembly language).

The language C attempts to offer the best of both worlds. High-level abstraction when you choose to use it (along with portability of programs) without sacrificing control over individual bits of information when you need it. For example, in its "low-level" operation, C allows the programmer to conserve memory space (and therefore speed up program operation) by allotting different amounts of memory for variables whose values are signed integers and variables whose values are unsigned integers.

C is almost unique in offering these dual capabilities—but not quite. Modula-2 and FORTH also combine both high-level and low-level programming abilities for much the same reasons that C does: to enable the programmer to have tight control over the physical activity of the computer when necessary, while always offering the possibility of distancing one's thinking about a program from the details of a machine implementation.

The Issue of Data Typing

Since the development of structured programming in the 1960s, one fundamental change in high-level languages has been the introduction of rich data typing. By data typing, we mean specifying what kinds of values the variables in a program can take. Data typing is an extremely efficient way of keeping track of the sorts of information a program is designed to handle.

But the real value of data typing is less its organizational benefits than its power in preventing errors. (To understand why data-typing errors can be serious, see the entry on Ada.) Once we have declared what types of values variables can have, we obviously want a means of tracking whether any aberrant values have slipped in. That is, in addition to *typing* the admissible values in advance, we need a way of *checking* whether these types are being adhered to.

The line of languages deriving from the Pascal branch of ALGOL 60 (including Pascal itself, Modula-2, and Ada) offer not only strong *typing* (i.e. many distinct data types) but strong type *checking*. If a variable is assigned a value that violates the declared data type, the compiler lets you know immediately.

C works differently. Like Pascal and its descendants, C has strong data *typing*. You can, for example, distinguish not only between integers and real numbers but between long and short integers, signed and unsigned integers, floating point and double precision numbers. As we saw a moment ago, by being very precise about just how much room a value will take up in memory (e.g. 8 bits, 16 bits, 32 bits), it is possible to make extremely efficient use of memory space.

However, unlike Pascal and its offspring, C *does not check* to make sure you have indeed used variables the way you said you were going to in the writing and running of the program. In fact, C even allows you to use variables you haven't declared in advance. Instead, the compiler has a system of defaults that will, after the fact, assign data types for you. If you use a negative integer as a value of a variable that has not been declared in advance, the C compiler will assign the variable to type a signed integer for you. (Historically, this lack of type checking comes from the fact that C's predecessors, BCPL and B, did not have types at all, and therefore had no need for type checking.)

The C compiler attempts to figure out automatically what the appropriate data type for your variables is. But there is one hitch: The compiler doesn't always get it right. You can end up with default assumptions that are not what you intended, and have your program either not run at all or yield incorrect results. Even worse, it can be extremely frustrating trying to track down the problem, since the C compiler, not you, "wrote" the type declaration that yielded the mistake in the first place.

An experienced programmer can take great advantage of the flexibility that comes in not having to declare variables in advance (or being able to violate the original declarations). If errors arise, presumably users know enough about debugging techniques to find the mistakes. C is a language intended to be *used*, and used by people who already know how to program reasonably well. In this respect, it contrasts sharply with a language like Pascal, which was explicitly designed for *pedagogy*, for training people in good programming practices and, in the process, providing them with all the "guardrails" necessary to protect them against their own errors.

More recent versions of C have remedied this condition of "living dangerously" by introducing a program called "lint." The program (in Ritchie's own words) "picks bits of fluff from programs," that is, it does a lot of error checking for things such as type conflicts. Once a program has successfully passed through the lint filter, you are reasonably protected against future disasters.

Programming in C

Putting together a program in C is a little like assembling pieces of a component stereo system. The components are drawn from several sources and must be combined together to get a finished product.

C's modularity largely results from the important role of the C *library* in doing programming. Many programming languages make use of libraries to store programs that will be used in other programs. As with other languages, C's library contains programs (written by the user) that will be incorporated within other programs, as well as programs written by other people that may prove handy to a particular user. But C's use of libraries is particularly broad. Recall that C as a language is intimately linked with UNIX as an operating system and software development environment. UNIX is a multi-user system that allows programmers to share programs and files with one another. Therefore the C library (when C is running under UNIX) can easily import components from the libraries of other users on the system.

Another important use of the C library is to hold all the machine-specific details that are necessary to make an actual C program run. The C language itself intentionally does not contain the programming code necessary to do input and output functions. These functions (when running most efficiently) tend to be machine-specific, and one of Ritchie's goals in designing C was to make the language at once maximally efficient and machine-independent.

The flow chart below outlines the sequence of steps necessary to take a C program from start to finish:

What does the heart of a C program (that is, the source code that you write with the editor) look like? As a structured language, C breaks programs down into components (called *functions* in C) much the way that Pascal organizes programs into blocks and procedures. However, as a professional programmer's language, C also keeps excess detail to a minimum. For example, instead of writing out the words BEGIN and END (as Pascal does) when you are starting and finishing a self-contained unit of programming code, C reduces the syntax to a simple set of opened and closed curly brackets, respectively (i.e. { and }).

In the same vein, C uses a number of shorthand conventions for indicating

FUNCTION	COMPONENT	PROCESS
I. Write program	editor	produce C source code
II. Compile program	preprocessor	expand the C source code so it is readable by the compiler
	C compiler	compile the expanded source code into the computer's native assembly language
	assembler	convert the assembly code into relocatable object code (an intermediate stage of code not readable by either the programmer or the machine)
	linker	join together the relocatable object code with the necessary code from the C run-time library, and translate it all into executable code
III. Run program	loader	run the program

data manipulation. To increment a variable, for example, you can simply follow it by two "plus" marks, e.g.

    i ++

instead of having to write out a full assignment statement, i.e.

    i = i + 1

(Note that in C the assignment operator is the simple "equals" sign as opposed to the more familiar := from Pascal and its derivatives.)

Yet even Dennis Ritchie admits that some of C's shorthand can become quite difficult to read. Consider Ritchie's own example of the brief line of code containing the symbols

    * ++ *argv

If we assume that "argv" has been declared to be a pointer into an array of character pointers (don't worry about what these terms mean), then reading from right to left, these few keystrokes are to be interpreted as follows:

select the character pointed at by "argv" (i.e. *argv), increment it by one (i.e. ++ *argv), then fetch the character that *that* pointer points at (i.e. * ++ *argv)

This kind of cryptic coding in C is strongly reminiscent of APL. Each symbol has a precise meaning, and there is practically no redundancy. The meanings themselves must be memorized. Unlike languages such as BASIC, FORTRAN, or Pascal, the languages C and APL rarely allow the user to decipher the meaning of an unknown symbol from context.

To exemplify a simple program in C, consider the standard problem of converting between degrees fahrenheit and degrees centigrade. (You may want to compare this program with related programs found in the entry on BASIC.) Say we want to print out a table of numbers containing two columns: degrees fahrenheit on the left-hand side and their equivalents in degrees centigrade on the right. Assume further that we will begin at 50 degrees fahrenheit, and work our way up in increments of five degrees to 100 degrees fahrenheit, i.e.

Fahrenheit	Centigrade
50	
55	
60	
. . .	
100	

Remember that the formula for converting degrees fahrenheit to degrees centigrade is

$$\text{centigrade} = (5/9)(\text{fahrenheit} - 32)$$

The program in C for creating such a table of conversions would look like this (line numbers have been added here for ease of discussion, though actual C code has no line numbers):

```
1   /* program prints a conversion table from fahrenheit to centigrade in
        steps of 5 degrees, from 50 to 100 degrees fahrenheit */
2   main ( )
3   {
4       int lower, upper, step;
5       float fahr, cent;

6       lower = 50;      / * lower limit of table * /
7       upper = 100;     / * upper limit of table */
8       step = 5;        / * size of steps in table * /

9       fahr = lower;
10      while (fahr < = upper) {
11          cent = (5.0/9.0) * (fahr − 32.0);
12          printf(''%4.0f %6.1f \n'', fahr, cent);
13          fahr = fahr + step;
14      }
15  }
```

Most of the program is reasonably easy to understand. (But don't be deceived. The average C program quickly becomes more complex.) The first line is simply a comment, indicating what the program is about. Line 2 specifies that what follows is the main function (= component, procedure) in the program. The curly bracket that constitutes the third line is C's equivalent of Pascal's BEGIN of a BEGIN-END block (line 15 closes the block in this program). Lines 4 and 5 are type declarations for variables, and lines 6–8 declare the program's constants.

The data manipulation part of the program begins on line 9, which initializes the variable *fahr* (for *fahrenheit*) to the value of the constant *lower*, which in this case is 50. Lines 10–14 form a *while* loop: as long as the value of the variable *fahr* is lower than or equal to the value of the constant *upper* (in this case, 100), perform the fahrenheit-to-centigrade conversion, print the result, and increase the value of the variable *fahr* by the value of *step* (i.e. 5 degrees).

If you know Pascal (or any other modern ALGOL language), most of the code here is quite familiar. The only really strange-looking line is the print statement in line 12, which specifies such things as how many characters to print before and after the decimal point for each variable.

THE EVOLUTION OF C

The Changing Character of C

C began quietly as an in-house language at Bell Labs that was used in systems programming. During most of its first ten years, it spread among university-oriented computer science professionals, especially those involved in systems programming.

In the early 1980s, the public profile of C changed dramatically. In part this resulted from the growing popularity of the UNIX operating system. While there is no necessary connection between C and UNIX, the fortunes of the two have been closely tied: Not only is UNIX largely written in C, but both UNIX and C were designed for professional programmers.

C received another major infusion of support from microcomputer users. In 1978, Tom Gibson of Bell Labs wrote a scaled-down version of C (which he called Tiny-C) in order to teach the language to his son. This was followed by BD Systems C, and by Small-C (which derived from Tiny-C). All of these were designed for microcomputers, running under the CP/M operating system.

In the last few years, C has assumed a dominant role in the computer industry. Computer magazines are laden with advertisements for dozens of versions of C, along with library packages to make C run more effectively. The classified pages of daily newspapers are now calling for C (and UNIX) programmers much the same way they used to advertise for COBOL or FORTRAN programmers. Viewed from the eye of publicity alone, C would seem to be the most important up-and-coming language.

What C Isn't

There is a lot of talk these days about the "new" imperative/algorithmic languages: C, Modula-2, and Ada. The discussions seem to suggest that in choosing a programming language, a person might want to choose among these three. While in many instances the comparison between Modula-2 and Ada is apt, the inclusion of C in the discussion is more questionable. Modula-2 and Ada were designed to do real-time programming (that is, to control operations such as traffic lights and subway cars and guided missiles that function in the real world). Both Modula-2 and Ada *can* be used for more general-purpose programming, but they always have available the machinery to control real-time devices.

C does not. In fact, Dennis Ritchie makes it quite clear that C was not designed to handle more than one operation at a time (that is, it was never intended to do multiprogramming, which is a necessary component of real-time programming). What's more, says Ritchie, he cannot imagine C ever going in such a direction in the future:

> One direction for possible expansion of the language has been explicitly avoided. Although C is much used for writing operating systems and associated software, there are no facilities for multiprogramming, parallel

operations, synchronization, or process control. We believe that making these operations primitives of the language is inappropriate, mostly because language design is hard enough in itself without incorporating into it the design of operating systems. Language facilities of this sort tend to make strong assumptions about the underlying operating system that may match very poorly what it actually does.

THE FUTURE OF C

What, then, is C's future? In the short range, it is likely that the trend toward using C not only for systems programming but for a wide variety of general programming will continue. Due to C's relatively low level of functioning, its programs run extremely quickly, a critical consideration not only in writing systems programs but in writing applications packages and games. Moreover, despite our caveats, C isn't all that hard a language to learn, even with its subtleties and shortcuts. There is a growing cadre of people who have grown up writing programs, and C is a suitable next step beyond either unstructured programming (e.g. what we have called vintage BASIC) or main-line structured programming (e.g. Pascal), replete with the aesthetic rewards of creating very powerful programs with just a few lines of code.

One factor that could limit subsequent growth of C is that programs written in C are often difficult to read. As our discussion of Ada shows, the expenses involved in maintaining software over time are enormous, and languages that are difficult to read (like APL, FORTH, and, often, C) are far more expensive to maintain than languages explicitly written for their readability (e.g. COBOL and Ada). C has not been around long enough for vast libraries of programs to develop that need to be maintained by people who had nothing to do with writing them. As of now, C is not commonly used for writing programs that will be kept over the years and maintained by people other than the original authors (as happens in the case of COBOL or FORTRAN). If C *does* come to be used in programs that need to be maintained over time, it is plausible that some of C's less readable code will be exchanged for source code that is more transparent in meaning. Perhaps the preprocessor could then "strip down" all the verbiage before the source code is compiled without jeopardizing C's enviable speed of operation.

There are several other issues which may affect C's future. One is the policy that the Department of Defense takes toward the use of Ada. Should the DoD issue directives that general-purpose programming for the DoD needs to be done in Ada (not a likely but always a possible move), then the future of C (along with the future of many other computer languages) would become rather cloudy.

Another possibility is that the growing ranks of programmers trained in Pascal programming style will find C too unkempt. Modula-2 (a Pascal derivative) would provide them with a reasonable alternative to C, in that Modula-2 can be used for general-purpose programming and is, like C, especially well suited to systems programming because it can directly address low-level machine operations.

Finally, there is the possibility that systems programming itself will no longer remain the exclusive domain of professional programmers (who feel comfortable with languages like C and Modula-2), but will instead open up to intelligent novices who want to create their own computer languages. To create a computer language, you need to be able to write your own translator and perhaps your own operating system to drive it. Although such models do not yet exist, it is possible that non-procedural systems could be developed that would enable individual computer users (who know little about computing but a good deal about what they would like a computer to be able to do) to create their own systems programming in languages that are far more tractable—and far more English-like—than C.

USING C

Buying C

Compilers for C are available in all shapes, sizes, and price ranges. The computer magazines are brimming with suggestions on what to buy for your microcomputer. Some products are obviously better than others, and generally speaking, you do indeed get what you pay for. Some of the better-known (and more expensive) versions are Microsoft C, Lattice C, and Whitesmiths C. The magazines frequently run reviews (and often comparative reviews) of C compilers. For starters, try the February, July, and October 1983 issues of *PC Magazine* and the January and August 1983 issues of *Byte*.

What to Read

BOOKS

The titles listed below include one classic on C, three especially good books for learning the language, and a problem-oriented book. For other possibilities, you may want to refer to the annotated bibliography in the August 1983 issue of *Byte*.

Kernighan, Brian, and Dennis Ritchie (1979). *The C Programming Language*. Englewood Cliffs (N.J.): Prentice-Hall.
This is the acknowledged standard text on C. It is clearly written, yet remains largely unreadable to people who don't already know a good deal about programming in general, not to mention something of computer architecture and systems programming. Once you have introduced yourself to C in some other way (e.g. using one of the next three books listed below), you should return to Kernighan and Ritchie's text for the definitive word on the language.

Hancock, Les, and Morris Krieger (1982). *The C Primer*. New York: McGraw-Hill.

An excellent, non-intimidating place to begin learning C.

Plum, Thomas (1983). *Learning to Program in C*. Cardiff (N.J.): Plum Hall.

Plum not only writes lucidly on C but also runs a company (Plum Hall, Inc.), along with Joan Hall, which offers some of the best courses on C available.

Purdum, Jack (1983). *C Programming Guide*. Indianapolis: Que Corporation.

A third book which has developed an especially good reputation for teaching the C language.

Feuer, Alan R. (1982). *The C Puzzle Book*. Englewood Cliffs (N.J.): Prentice-Hall

A useful supplemental text for the above three books, Feuer's book is full of interesting programming exercises on C. It comes not only with solutions but with good explanations of the solutions as well.

Ritchie, D. M., S. C. Johnson, M. E. Lesk, and B. W. Kernighan (1978). "The C Programming Language," *Bell System Technical Journal* 57 (no. 6, part 2), July–August, pp. 1991–2019.

A dense but highly useful overview of C. The article is especially helpful in presenting the historical origins of C and in offering a critical assessment of the language's strengths and weaknesses.

Byte, August 1983.

The August 1983 language issue of *Byte* is devoted to the language C. While the articles are well written, most of them tend to be fairly technical. It may help to begin reading one of the three texts suggested above before turning to the articles in this issue of *Byte*.

COBOL

PROFILE
NAME
COmmon *B*usiness *O*riented *L*anguage
STRUCTURE

Familiar Distinctions:
  hardware: high-level
  translator: compiled
  structural unit: statement
  data: numbers and alphabetic strings
 	
Conceptual Distinctions:
  organizing principle: imperative/algorithmic
  procedures: procedural
  extensibility: not extensible
  program/data: distinct (with emphasis on data)

FUNCTIONS business
GENEALOGY

FLOW-MATIC   AIMACO   COMTRAN

COBOL

Years: 1959–60

Authors: CODASYL (*CO*mmittee/*CO*nference on *DA*ta *SY*stems Languages); Grace Hopper

Impetus: need for portable language that was suited to the needs of business (good file handling, fixed point notation, easy to read)

Evolution: rapidly grew to become the most widely used language on large computers
naive users replaced by data-processing departments

(Continued)

COBOL (Continued)

VERSIONS/DIALECTS

Standard: ANSI-74 COBOL

Others: COBOL 60   COBOL-80   CIS COBOL
       COBOL 61   (NOTE: 80 stands for chip,
               not year)   Level II COBOL

SPECIAL CHARACTERISTICS

Memory Requirements: fairly large

Ease of Learning/Use: easier to read than to write

Availability: ubiquitous on mainframes and minicomputers used in business (but not the academic world); becoming available for micros

WHY COBOL?

What makes an invention or discovery or product a household word? To begin with, the product itself must be good for something (like preserving food or digging ditches). But it must also be readily available and useful in a variety of ways. Asa Candler turned a druggist's formula for a soda-fountain drink into the first Coca-Cola fortune by creating a vast distribution network. The internal-combustion engine truly sparked a revolution when its uses were expanded from pumping water out of mines to running boats and trains and then lawn mowers and portable generators.

Before "computer" could become a household word, the machine had to be made readily available and had to expand in function. A huge piece of hardware costing a million dollars and good only for doing scientific calculation was of little interest to most people.

The world of business helped change all that.

Today, the vast majority of computer purchases are made by business. Not surprisingly, design decisions (of both hardware and software) are heavily dictated by business. In the late 1970s, the upstart microcomputer enterprise was catapulted to national recognition by the appearance of a piece of software called Visicalc, which allowed its users to prepare spreadsheets electronically on a microcomputer and to bypass data-processing departments and accountants alike. And almost twenty years earlier, business was largely responsible for the proliferation of first mainframes and then minicomputers into the non-scientific world through the invention of a new computer language known as COBOL.

The Needs of Business

In the mid-1950s, the business sphere had very little to do with computers. Most computer programming then was still done in assembly language, which was time-consuming and required many hours to learn in the first place. The earliest high-level languages were just being developed, the best known being FORTRAN. But their focus was very specialized: to encode algebraic formulas of interest to scientists and engineers. At the same time, since many groups in academia and industry were creating their own languages for use on their own machines, a babble of incompatible tongues was developing. As we saw in the entry on ALGOL, in the late 1950s both Americans and Europeans banded together to create a single "universal" language for encoding algorithms to reduce the growing chaos.

But neither ALGOL nor its predecessors (nor their successors) would do for business. There are two fundamental reasons why not.

(1) Data Formatting and Manipulation

At the end of Chapter 3, we looked at those elements that most or all computer languages have in common. We said that, conceptually, computer programs can be used to organize information, calculate a result, or present a result. We also saw that, structurally, the components of computer languages can be divided up into means of *formatting* data and means of *manipulating* data.

In all imperative/algorithmic languages, the part of the program in which the data themselves are expressed (what we are calling data formatting) is distinct from the section in which computations are performed upon the data (what we are calling data manipulation, but what is often called the program). But there is a further distinction we can draw among imperative/algorithmic languages: between the *emphasis* placed on data formatting and the *emphasis* placed on data manipulation.

High-level computer languages were invented to simplify the task of doing algebraic calculations. In FORTRAN, ALGOL, and almost all imperative/ algorithmic languages, the very reason for the language to exist was to do such calculations. The data upon which the calculations were to be performed were typically lists of similar items (e.g. 2000 temperature readings, 45 atomic weights) or items which were easily classified into simple groups (e.g. the temperature readings for January 1, the readings for January 2, etc.). The reason for putting the data into the computer was to come up with some new information that took these data as input and for which the calculation was either difficult or laborious. Rarely was the purpose to be able to *retrieve* the very information which you had earlier fed in.

The needs of business are very different. Of course there is a lot of basic calculation involved—adding up the total sales each month, calculating the commission that salespeople earn as a percentage of total sales. But the calculations themselves rarely go beyond simple arithmetic.

Of far more importance in business is the ability to store vast amounts of information and then retrieve just the piece you want upon demand. Moreover, unlike scientific data, business data tend to be organized into groups, and subgroups, and sub-subgroups. A gourmet hamburger chain may have five franchises. Each franchise has an owner, a manager, and a cook. Each owner has a staff of several members. Each member has a social security number, an annual salary, and a data of hire. And so on. For computers to be useful in business, there must be a convenient way of encoding and later retrieving these hierarchically arranged layers of data. COBOL was explicitly designed to emphasize data formatting rather than data manipulation.

(2) Ease of Use

In Chapter 1, we talked about the early computer "priesthood" which dominated the computer world before the coming of the microcomputer. Among the earliest fighters against this priesthood was one of the founders of the American computer establishment, Grace Murray Hopper. Sometimes called the "grandmother of COBOL," Commodore Hopper, then at Remington Rand Univac, created a language in 1955 known as FLOW-MATIC, which had a major influence on COBOL. (She also later supervised the development of test validation routines for COBOL while in the Navy.)

Hopper believed it was possible to create a computer language that could be used effectively by people who knew nothing about computers. In Hopper's words:

> We were . . . endeavoring to provide a means that people could use, not that programmers or programming language designers could use. But rather, plain, ordinary people, who had problems they wanted to solve.

This same philosophy was directly adopted into the design of COBOL. Jean Sammet, one of the creators of COBOL, simply states:

> It was certainly intended (and expected) that the language could be used by novice programmers and read by the management.

The word *management* here is very important. The designers of COBOL (as well as its precursors) believed that if a computer language were to be successful in the business world, it was critical that the people who made the decisions— the management—be able to understand the programs that helped dictate how those decisions were to be made (even if the management didn't write the programs themselves). Unfortunately, the ease-of-use goal was not fulfilled.

The Birth of COBOL: A Language Before Its Time

COBOL, like ALGOL, PL/I, and Ada, is a language written by committee. The language came into being because a small group of computer users from academia and industry felt the time had come to create a common business language. The group enlisted the assistance of the U.S. Department of Defense in sponsoring an expanded meeting in which an actual language could be mapped out.

The initial group met in early April 1959. By the end of May, the larger meeting was held at the Pentagon, and the following plan was laid out. Three committees were set up for actually devising the language: a Short-Range Committee, an Intermediate-Range Committee, and a Long-Range Committee. The job of the Short-Range Committee was to discover what was right or wrong with already existing business languages, primarily Grace Hopper's FLOW-MATIC; AIMACO (standing for *AIr MAterial COmmand*, a language developed by the U.S. Air Force in 1959); and COMTRAN (later renamed Commercial Translator, a language developed by IBM, also in 1959). The committee was charged with making a composite of these languages that could be used in the short run ("good for at least the next year or two"). That is, they were asked to create an *interim* language that would be used only until there was time actually to create a new language.

The tasks of the other two committees were less well defined, although it was assumed that it would take several years before they would be able to finish the new common business language. An executive committee was also set up to coordinate everything. The committee called itself CODASYL (which is sometimes said to stand for *Conference* on Data Systems Languages, and other times taken as meaning *Committee* on Data Systems Languages).

After three months of work, the Short-Range Committee reported its results to the CODASYL Executive Committee in early September 1959. Some alterations were made over the next few months, and the results were published in early 1960 under the name COBOL 60. Shortly thereafter, manuals and compilers began to appear, and the language was, quite literally, in business.

But what became of the "real" COBOL—the planned efforts of the Intermediate- and Long-Range Committees? A common business language was badly needed in 1960, and COBOL 60 was the only candidate available. The language itself was far from ideal, even in the eyes of its creators. In the words of Jean Sammet:

> I am certainly convinced . . . that had the Short-Range Commitee realized at the outset that the language it created (i.e., COBOL) was going to be in use for such a long period of time, it would have gone about the task quite differently and produced a rather different result.

COBOL has, of course, continued to undergo revision since 1960. But the language never received the design efforts that were originally intended. Popular judgments that COBOL is not a carefully constructed language do have some basis in historical fact. We should add, of course, that COBOL is not alone in this distinction. The history of PL/I is also one of rushing a language to implementation before it was actually ready for mass distribution.

COBOL and the DoD: Setting the Record Straight

Within the computer world, there persists a belief that COBOL is a direct product of the U.S. Department of Defense. Textbooks on COBOL typically imply that the U.S. government itself had decided in the late 1950s that data-processing applications had to be standardized (and hence called for the creation of COBOL). In fact, one author goes so far as to say that the committee responsible for creating COBOL was formed ''at the insistence of the Department of Defense.''

While it is true that the U.S. government is the largest single user of COBOL programs, it was a group of private citizens—representing academia, commercial users, and manufacturers—who first met informally to suggest an official conference to design a common business language. The group then approached Charles Phillips, Director of the Data Systems Research Staff of the Office of the Assistant Secretary of Defense, to ask the U.S. Department of Defense (DoD) to sponsor the meeting. In responding to this independent request for sponsorship, Phillips acknowledged:

> We were embarrassed that the idea for such a common language had not had its origin by that time in Defense since we would benefit so greatly from the success of such a project.
> From a lecture by Phillips to the ACM annual conference,
> September 1, 1959

Once the committee had done its work and a new common business language existed, the language specifications needed to be published. Again, the DoD was involved, but by default. Phillips made clear in February 1960 that ''there is no intent to characterize the report as a 'military document.' It will be published by the Government Printing Office as a government report.'' Unfortunately, bureaucracy crept in. Apparently there was a government regulation that the name of the government department requesting a publication had to appear on the cover. And so the words ''Department of Defense'' were emblazoned on the cover of the first published version of COBOL.

The DoD *did* later become directly responsible for the *propagation* of COBOL. The means was very simple: Charles Phillips issued a letter to computer manufacturers stating that henceforth the DoD would only purchase computers that had COBOL compilers. (In those days, it was both time-consuming and expensive to install a new language compiler, as well as to write one in the first place.) The only exception was for computers that would be used strictly for scientific computations.

There was no way the manufacturers could ignore the request of such a major customer, even if it meant abandoning languages they were already using for business applications. However, before we accuse the U.S. government of strong-arming the private sector, we should remember that the West German government did something very similar with the propagation of ALGOL.

It is often said that the DoD's current sponsorship of Ada is "just like" its earlier involvement with COBOL. The statement is simply not true. As we saw in the entry on Ada, Ada is a language commissioned by and created for the U.S. Department of Defense. COBOL was not.

THINKING IN COBOL

A Language Suited for Business

We have said that the needs of a language designed for business are different from those of a language used in science and engineering. What do these differences look like? The table below summarizes the major differences, using examples from COBOL and FORTRAN.

(1)   Data Formatting: Arithmetic Representation

Computers are of no use to business if they don't correctly balance the books. It may come as a surprise to learn that FORTRAN—and most of the other imperative/algorithmic languages—can have a problem here. The notation used to represent numbers in languages like FORTRAN, called *floating point arithmetic* (or floating point notation), limits the extent to which you can be precise. You can easily represent a number such as 2.54. Representing 2.54652 also presents no difficulty. But if you want a number with a lot of decimal digits, e.g. 2.54652791, you may be in trouble. Languages like FORTRAN must round off numbers to fit within a system-defined number of decimal points. For example, 2.54652791 might be rounded off to 2.5465279.

In the business world, "almost precise" isn't precise enough. If your datum is 2.54652791, that is what the program needs to record. By using *fixed point arithmetic* (that is, being able to specify exactly how many places you want to use to the right of the decimal point), you can ensure you don't misrepresent data or results because of limitations on the size of numbers (or number of decimal places) the machine can handle. COBOL uses fixed point arithmetic.

There have been several efforts to handle the problem of precision in other languages. A few versions of BASIC and Pascal now have fixed point arithmetic available as well as floating point arithmetic. Moreover, by using double precision floating point numbers in a language like FORTRAN, users can increase the number of digits to the right of the decimal point. Nonetheless, any subsequent digits are still rounded off.

(2)   Data Formatting: Data Structures

Recording and retrieving data are more critical activities in the business world than in science and engineering. It is therefore not surprising that the designers of COBOL placed heavy emphasis on constructing data structures that would allow programmers to record hierarchical relationships between many layers of data. COBOL has two built-in data structures: tables (which are like arrays in

NEEDS	BUSINESS	E.g. COBOL	SCIENCE/ENGINEERING	E.g. FORTRAN*
DATA FORMATTING				
1. arithmetic representation	dollars and cents must always balance	fixed point arithmetic	very precise, but only up to a given number of decimal points	floating point arithmetic
2. data structures	efficient means of storing business-style data (hierarchically arranged files)	hierarchically arranged records tables (= arrays)	comparatively little data structuring needed	arrays
DATA MANIPULATION				
1. computational power	limited to basic arithmetic	ADD, SUBTRACT, MULTIPLY, DIVIDE	sophisticated manipulation	many built-in functions (e.g. square root, sine, cosine)
2. file handling	sophisticated and varied means of dealing with files	sequential files, random (= direct access) files, indexed files	limited needs	sequential files

* Some modern implementations of FORTRAN provide additional data structures and additional types of file handling, but these are not part of standard FORTRAN.

other languages) and records. However, a critical feature of data structures in COBOL is that they can be embedded within one another. In fact, it is possible to embed almost 50 levels of data, one within another (e.g. a hamburger chain has five franchises, each franchise has an owner, each owner has a staff, and so on).

Scientific languages like FORTRAN are quite the opposite. Since the data commonly used in science have comparatively little internal structure, standard FORTRAN has but one built-in data structure (i.e. the array). As in most imperative/algorithmic languages, other data structures can be implemented (and additional structures are built into non-standard implementations). But the fact they are not part of standard FORTRAN means that FORTRAN is a more cumbersome language to use for processing complex arrangements of data than is COBOL.

(3)   Data Manipulation: Computational Power
The level of computation needed in business is generally limited to basic arithmetic operations. Accordingly, COBOL has just four arithmetic functions built in: ADD, SUBTRACT, MULTIPLY, and DIVIDE. Languages that are oriented toward science and engineering are designed with more built-in computational functions, such as square root, exponentiation, sine, and cosine.

(4)   Data Manipulation: File Handling
A business-oriented language must not only be able to organize data into records and fields; it must also be able to access that information efficiently. COBOL has three ways of dealing with files: *sequential* (i.e. accessing records in a file in the order in which they appear), *random* (or *direct access*) (i.e. being able to access any data item immediately, regardless of where it appears in a file), and *indexed* (i.e. accessing a record in a file on the basis of the *value* of a key data element of that record). Compare this multiplicity of access methods with a language like FORTRAN, which can only deal with files sequentially.

The Problem of Representation

We have said that COBOL was explicitly designed to be as English-like as possible in order to be readable by non-programmers. However noble the goal, it is sometimes more cumbersome to use natural language than to use abstract representations. It's much simpler to write $\sqrt{2}$, for example, than "take the square root of 2." And so the creators of artificial languages (such as mathematics) often decide to represent natural language with something else.

COBOL ends up with an awkward mix of choices about representation. In some instances, the English language is used where symbolic representations would almost certainly have done just as well. Favorite examples are the four arithmetic operators. Surely anyone who has been to grade school knows that the symbol + means "plus." Yet COBOL uses the English word PLUS to indicate addition. There are other terms in COBOL that seem just right. The COBOL word PICTURE (used in specifying the data type of a variable and the number of digits before and after a decimal point) does indeed help the user visually "picture" what the variable will look like. But there are other, more arbitrary symbols in COBOL that make APL seem almost semantically transparent in comparison. Take COBOL symbols like V (it means "virtual decimal point," i.e. where the decimal point would go if you wrote out the number normally) or 77 (which is used in declaring irreducible data elements).

The result is that COBOL looks at once too easy and too hard. And in fact, this is the way the language has been received by the business community and evaluated by its designers. Jean Sammet admits that while the design committee was very concerned that programs written in COBOL be *readable* by non-programmers (hence all the explicit English), there was too little care taken that it would be easily *learnable* by the people who were actually going to do the programming.

The failure of COBOL to achieve its "ease of use" goal is reflected in the fact that since its invention nearly all COBOL programs have been written by professional programmers. The people for whom the programs are being written typically don't understand them, and therefore there can be little connection between the program design and the use of program results.

The Face of Janus

Some of the strangeness of COBOL programs comes not so much from the problems of representation we have been discussing but from trying to make the syntax of COBOL keep pace with dramatic changes in the computer world since 1960. In some cases, COBOL seems anachronistic, looking back to the hardware of the days when COBOL was first created, while in others, the syntax seems quite modern, and one wonders why so many people complain that COBOL is an antiquated language.

Consider the question of anachronism. When COBOL was invented, all programming was done by feeding punched cards into a card reader. This information was then given to the computer, which spewed out the results onto a printer. Each row on a punched card was 80 columns across. Since the programming code had to be placed in the correct column in each row in order for the information to be read correctly, languages like COBOL (and FORTRAN) incorporated into their syntax the division of columns into subgroups. Certain kinds of information could only appear in the first eight columns; the next space had to be left blank; the following four spaces were reserved for another kind of information; and so on.

Modern programming languages designed to be typed directly onto a keyboard and displayed at a CRT typically have no such spacing requirements. Since COBOL is, these days, generally programmed using keyboards and CRTs, the restriction of certain kinds of information to certain columns makes no logical sense. Another holdover from the early days is the restriction of input to uppercase letters (a feature shared by most of the older languages), since earlier computers could not handle lowercase letters.

On the other hand, COBOL (like BASIC and FORTRAN) has developed a modern version that takes advantage of structured programming, a notion that was not conceived of until almost a decade after the invention of COBOL. Modern COBOL programs have BEGIN-END blocks indicating where a set of instructions begins and ends, much as you would find in ALGOL or Pascal. When teachers of programming complain that COBOL has outlived its usefulness since it is an unstructured language, they are talking about the versions of COBOL that have not undergone the more recent face-lift. (Similar comments are made about BASIC and FORTRAN by critics unaware of the newer structured versions.)

Programming in COBOL

The syntax of COBOL was consciously designed to make the purpose, implementation, content, and results of a COBOL program as clear as possible to people who don't know much about programming. That is, the very syntax itself explains what the program is doing at any given step. Pascal and its derivatives are some of the only other languages that were formulated to be "self-documenting."

To anyone familiar with COBOL programming, these goals are at odds with experience. For COBOL code is notorious for being unreadable. The most common epithet for traditional COBOL programs is "spaghetti code," since the lines of programming code often seem heaped together rather than logically sequenced. It sometimes becomes quite difficult to maintain COBOL programs over time because the current members of the data-processing staff can't figure out what a program is intended to be doing, much less how it does it.

Why the contradiction?

The most obvious reason is that early COBOL was an unstructured language. It was inherently filled with GOTO statements and subroutines which obliterated any logical connection between the order of lines of programming code on the page and the order in which the program was actually executed.

Less obvious, but more important, was that the activity of programming in COBOL became wholly divorced from the activity of managing the business for which the software was being written. The job of the programmer was to make the program run, not to make the program in any way reflect the business operations that the program was being written to help expedite. As long as management itself had no role in the construction of programs (for that was now the sole province of data-processing departments), there was no external check on programming style.

With this prelude, let's see what COBOL actually looks like.

(1) Program Divisions: IDENTIFICATION, ENVIRONMENT, DATA, PROCEDURE

Every COBOL program is divided into four distinct divisions, each identified by name. The divisions are then subdivided into smaller parts, some of which are optional and some of which are obligatory. The major sudivisions in two of the categories (ENVIRONMENT DIVISION and DATA DIVISION) are referred to as SECTIONS, while some of the other subdivisions are referred to as PARAGRAPHS.

Unfortunately, the customary way of writing COBOL programs does not indicate the logical relationship between divisions, sections, paragraphs, and so forth in COBOL programs. The outline below (which does *not* follow proper COBOL syntax) is offered to help you figure out which parts are on the same conceptual level as which others. This outline does not include all the possible pieces of COBOL programs, but only the ones we will be discussing here.

```
IDENTIFICATION DIVISION
    PROGRAM-ID
    AUTHOR
    DATE

    . . .

ENVIRONMENT DIVISION
    CONFIGURATION SECTION
        SOURCE COMPUTER
        OBJECT COMPUTER

        . . .

    INPUT-OUTPUT SECTION
        FILE CONTROL
            SELECT-entry

        . . .

DATA DIVISION
    FILE SECTION
        FD ( = FILE DESCRIPTION)
        data declaration for external files
    WORKING-STORAGE SECTION
        data declaration for irreducible data elements

    . . .

PROCEDURE DIVISION

    . . .
```

The IDENTIFICATION DIVISION gives the name of the program, the program's author, the date the program was written, and other documentation that may prove helpful to current users or to people working several years hence who may need to maintain the program. In many other programming languages, such information, if given at all, is embedded in an optional comment. The designers of COBOL wanted this information to be an inherent part of the very program itself. Yet since the compiler doesn't interpret any of this information, professional programmers are often tempted to be briefer here than one might like.

The ENVIRONMENT DIVISION describes two external factors which may affect the running of the program. Each of these factors is expressed in a separate section. The CONFIGURATION SECTION holds information that is specific to a particular machine implementation of COBOL. Even though COBOL was intended as a machine-independent standard, it was clear that different machine implementations would require idiosyncratic specifications. By building those idiosyncrasies into just one section of COBOL programs, it should then be trivially simple to export programs from one machine environment to another, since it would be clear where the changes needed to be made. (In practice, implementation-specific changes sometimes need to be made in other divisions as well.) The INPUT-OUTPUT SECTION of the ENVIRONMENT DIVISION provides information about external devices that the program will need to access while running.

The third part of a COBOL program is the DATA DIVISION. Structurally, the DATA DIVISION is roughly comparable to data declaration sections in other languages. Yet in a business language like COBOL, it is the heart of the program, since the organization and expression of data are all-important if files are to be correctly manipulated or even simply retrieved. The significance of data themselves in the business community is reflected in the meteoric rise of data base management systems over the past decade. Comparatively speaking, in the business world, doing calculations on data is relatively straightforward (though admittedly sometimes involuted). Knowing *what* to do the calculations on (if calculations need be done at all) is conceptually far more problematic.

Part four of a COBOL program is the PROCEDURE DIVISION. This corresponds to the heart of most *other* programming languages (especially in the imperative/algorithmic family). It is here that numbers are added and subtracted, that conditional statements, loops, and jumps from one part of a program to another take place. It is also here that COBOL programs (like programs in most unstructured languages) become unreadable.

Since the DATA DIVISION is so important in COBOL, we will look at it in more detail.

(2)   The DATA DIVISION

The DATA DIVISION is divided into several sections. The two most important are the FILE SECTION and the WORKING-STORAGE SECTION. Both are involved in declaring data that will be manipulated in the program. The FILE SECTION is used for working with data that come from external files, while the WORKING-STORAGE SECTION is used for declaring irreducible data elements that are *not* part of any of the records that appear in the external files.

Both sections use a similar format for describing what data look like. The format looks like this:

LEVEL	VARIABLE	PICTURE	DATA	SPACE
NUMBER	NAME		TYPE	ALLOCATION

(Only LEVEL NUMBER and PICTURE are technical words in COBOL; the others are simply ordinary language descriptions.)

Level number refers to the hierarchical level of embedding of the data being described. For example, for a hamburger chain having five franchises, with each franchise having an owner, each owner having a staff, and each staff member having a social security number, the restaurant chain might be level 1 (represented in COBOL as 01), each franchise level 2, each owner level 3, each staff member level 4, and the set of characteristics applying to each staff member (including social security numbers) being level 5. While this system of embedding (and corresponding level numbers) makes logical sense when talking about external files, we'll see it becomes more arbitrary when talking about independent variables.

The *variable name* is obviously the name of the variable being declared. It could be HONDO-HAMBURGER or Q (in the case of an independent variable). PICTURE (a term COBOL borrowed from one of its predecessors, COMTRAN) announces that what follows is a visual picture of what the data that can appear in the variable may be like, that is, what data type the variable's values can be and what space allocation the variable's values may be given.

COBOL has three data types:

numeric (represented by the number 9)

alphanumeric, i.e. a string of alphabetic or numeric characters (represented by the letter X)

alphabetic, i.e. only alphabetic characters or the space character (represented by the letter A for an alphabetic character or by B for a blank)

The types themselves are expressed as part of the description of space allocation. A numerical variable that takes up two spaces would be represented by the sequence 99. An alphabetic variable that is made up of three letters of the alphabet, followed by one blank, followed by one letter (e.g. representing the initials of each member of a class, matched with his or her grade average), would be represented by the sequence AAABA.

Since numbers in COBOL are represented without decimal points, it is necessary to show when declaring numerical variables just where the decimal point should go. This is done with the letter V (for "virtual decimal point"). And so a variable in COBOL that can have as its value a number with five digits to the left of the decimal point and three to the right (e.g. 53499.121) would be declared as 99999V999. Multiple examples of the same data type can be abbreviated using the number of iterations in parentheses, i.e.

99999V999 = 9(5)V9(3)

How are these data declarations actually used in COBOL? We'll first look at the declaration of independent variables (through the WORKING-STORAGE SECTION) and then move to the declaration of external files (through the FILE SECTION). (COBOL actually declares these in reverse order, but since independent variables are easier to deal with than files, we'll begin with the former.) In the process, we'll also see what some simple COBOL programs look like.

(3)   WORKING-STORAGE SECTION: Independent Variables

Assume we want to run a program that calculates the sum of a variable (which we will call SUM) plus another number (say 555). We need to declare the variable in the WORKING-STORAGE SECTION of the DATA DIVISION. We also have the option of initializing the variable (i.e. giving it an original value) in the DATA DIVISION. (Alternatively, we could do so in the PROCEDURE DIVISION.)

The data declaration might be stated as follows:

    77   SUM PICTURE 999 VALUE ZERO

77 is the level number assigned to independent variables. (Remember we said that level numbers don't all make logical sense.) SUM is the name of the variable being declared. The PICTURE of the variable is that it consists of three numerals (and no decimal point). The remaining terms on the declaration line indicate that the initial VALUE of the variable is set to ZERO (i.e. 0).

Here is what the entire COBOL program would look like:

```
0001      IDENTIFICATION DIVISION.
0002      PROGRAM-ID. COBOL EXAMPLE 1.
0003      ENVIRONMENT DIVISION.
0004      DATA DIVISION.
0005      WORKING-STORAGE SECTION.
0006      77 SUM PICTURE 999 VALUE ZERO.
0007      PROCEDURE DIVISION.
0008      MAIN-PARAGRAPH.
0009          ADD 555 TO SUM.
0010          DISPLAY SUM.
0011          STOP RUN.
```

The IDENTIFICATION DIVISION gives the PROGRAM-ID, i.e. the name of the program. (It might have given other information as well, such as the program's author or the date the program was written.) The ENVIRONMENT DIVISION is empty here, though we might have chosen to specify such things as the computer on which the program is being run. We have already talked about the DATA DIVISION. In the PROCEDURE DIVISION, there is one subsection (called a PARAGRAPH) that actually performs the computation of adding 555 to 0 (the initial value of SUM) and prints out the result, i.e. 555.

(4)   FILE SECTION: External Files

All imperative/algorithmic languages have comparable means of dealing with independent variables of the sort used in the previous example. COBOL's uniqueness comes in the ease with which it deals with complex files.

To work with files in COBOL, you need to use the ENVIRONMENT DIVISION and the DATA DIVISION in tandem. In the ENVIRONMENT DIVISION, you use the INPUT-OUTPUT SECTION (and more specifically, the FILE CONTROL portion of the INPUT-OUTPUT SECTION) to indicate where files are coming from, how data are to be accessed from them, and where the results should go. In the DATA DIVISION, you use the FILE SECTION to specify more information about the file, and then give the usual data declaration of level number, variable name, and variable PICTURE. To see how the pieces fit together, it's easiest to begin with the DATA DIVISION.

Assume that our data are made up of feeding records at the local zoo. Each record contains the name of an animal and the number of calories of food it must eat each day to maintain its weight. Assume the zoo has many animals, of which ten are lions. Assume further that each lion has a name (not longer than twenty characters) and that the number of calories to be recorded is less than 100,000 (i.e. it can be expressed in a five-place number). Schematically, the zoo's lion keeper might construct a record looking something like this:

    lions
            total of 10 lions
            name (no longer than 20 characters)
            calories (no higher than 99,999)

To create a formal record in COBOL corresponding to this schematic record, we need to construct a declaration in the FILE SECTION of the DATA DIVISION that shows what hierarchical relationship the "levels" of data have to one another, how many entries there are at each level, and what PICTURE each entry has. The resulting data declaration for our zoo program would look like this:

    01 LION-FEEDING-RECORDS.
        02 LION OCCURS 10 TIMES.
            03 NAME PICTURE X(20).
            03 CALORIES PICTURE 9(5).

The highest level of abstraction (indicated by the level number 01) is that of the lion-feeding-record itself. (There might be comparable records for baboon-feeding and elephant-feeding.) The lion-feeding-record contains ten sets of information (one for each lion). These are at one level subordinate to the main record, and hence indicated by the level number 02. For each lion, there is then another level of entries, which here contains two items each (NAME and CALORIES). Since both NAME and CALORIES are conceptually one level below the individual lion that they characterize, they both have the level number 03. A PICTURE is given for each variable at the lowest level. PICTURE X(20) indicates that the variable NAME can have up to twenty alphanumeric characters, while the variable CALORIES can have up to five digits (with no decimal point).

Now that the data to be accessed from the external file have been declared, we need to think about how to get them into the program. (Remember, we are thinking about the problem conceptually, not in terms of the order in which an actual COBOL program is written.) Within the FILE SECTION of the DATA DIVISION, we will need to describe the file (i.e. of lion-feeding-records) that we will be using in the program. Within the FILE CONTROL part of the INPUT-OUTPUT SECTION of the ENVIRONMENT DIVISION (COBOL terminology can indeed get confusing), we will need to specify where the files of information with the actual data (i.e. the lions' names and their caloric intake) will be coming from, and how the files are to be read (e.g. in sequential order).

To make all this happen in COBOL, we need some more terminology. For our purposes, we will forgo explanations of the additional terms and simply present the resulting program. Nonetheless, you can still get a reasonable idea of what a typical (albeit very small) COBOL program looks like that deals with external files of information:

```
0001   IDENTIFICATION DIVISION.
0002   PROGRAM-ID. FEEDING TIME AT THE ZOO.
0003   ENVIRONMENT DIVISION.
0004   INPUT-OUTPUT SECTION.
0005   FILE CONTROL.
0006       SELECT LION-FILE
0007           ASSIGN TO DISK
0008           ORGANIZATION IS SEQUENTIAL
0009           ACCESS IS SEQUENTIAL.
0010   DATA DIVISION.
0011   FD LION-FILE,
0012       LABEL RECORDS ARE STANDARD
0013       VALUE OF FILE-ID IS "file name"*
0014       DATA RECORD IS LION-FEEDING-RECORDS.
0015   01 LION-FEEDING-RECORDS.
0016       02 LION OCCURS 10 TIMES.
0017           03 NAME PICTURE X(20).
0018           03 CALORIES PICTURE 9(5).
0019   PROCEDURE DIVISION.
       . . .
```

*file name supplied by user

THE EVOLUTION OF COBOL

Over the past quarter century, "COBOL" has been synonymous with "computing" for a large number of people ("BASIC" and "FORTRAN" have, likewise, become synonyms for other constituencies). The longevity of the language is largely attributable to the enormous accumulation of programs written in COBOL as well as the equally impressive number of people who know how to write programs in it—but not in other languages.

Standards and Versions

COBOL's success in the business world is partially attributable to the development of standards which compilers must, at a minimum, adhere to. In the 1960s, a series of standards (COBOL 60, COBOL 61) came out of CODYSYL and were followed by the early computer manufacturers. A decade later, the American National Standards Institute authorized a standard version of the language, ANSI-74 COBOL, which has been the functioning norm for the past decade. (A new standard is rumored to be forthcoming.)

As many business operations have begun switching from mainframes or minicomputers to microcomputers, software developers have followed with microcomputer versions of COBOL. The names, however, can sometimes be confusing. COBOL-80 (marketed by Microsoft) is named for the microprocessor under which the language program can be run, not the year in which it was written. 80 refers to the family of microprocessors including Zilog's Z80 and Intel's 8080, which use the operating system CP/M (developed by Digital Research). CIS COBOL is an acronym for Compact-Interactive-Standard COBOL, a version of COBOL developed for microcomputers by MicroFocus back in 1976. (MicroFocus also has a more powerful version of CIS COBOL called Level II COBOL.) All three microcomputer versions of COBOL implement the ANSI-74 COBOL standard, and then add their own extensions.

Reactions to COBOL: Academic and Business

Despite its permeation of the business world, COBOL has not received universal acclaim in the world of computing. From the very inception of COBOL, the academic world has expressed out-and-out hostility. Consider the fact that a sizable number of the more prestigious four-year colleges and universities in the United States refuse to teach the language. To learn COBOL, you often must go to a state university, a two-year college, or a vocationally oriented college. The reasons are not totally clear, though both academics and the creators of COBOL have their own sides to the story.

Recall that COBOL was developed at about the same time as ALGOL. And while ALGOL was very much an intellectual's language, COBOL was expressly intended for doing the business of the workaday world. Moreover, while ALGOL and even FORTRAN before it were heavily computational languages, the conceptual level of computing that COBOL was designed to do could be performed by the average schoolchild. To the computer scientist, COBOL did not seem to be good for very much.

COBOL's advocates see the reception of their language somewhat differently. They argue that computer science departments have wrongly ignored the sophistication of COBOL that derives from its file-handling abilities. In fact,

Jean Sammet argues that COBOL has far *greater* power and complexity than ALGOL. However, says Sammet, the adherents of ALGOL (and its descendants) rarely looked closely enough at COBOL to find out. In the meanwhile, subsequent languages that include sophisticated data- and record-handling capabilities took their basic concepts from COBOL.

Over the past decade, a second group (this time coming from the business world itself) has begun voicing strong antipathy toward COBOL. These are the developers and users of query languages (and fourth-generation languages more generally). The movement is epitomized in the title of a book by James Martin, one of the group's prime movers: *Applications Development without Programmers* (1982, Englewood Cliffs, N.J.: Prentice-Hall). Working in the same spirit as Grace Hopper and the original designers of COBOL, a new group has stepped forward demanding that the people who intend to use the *results* of programs should be able to write the programs themselves. To make this possible, a whole new generation of languages must be developed that are at once powerful enough to produce the desired results yet truly easy to learn and use (as COBOL was designed to be—but did not succeed in becoming). The entry on Query-by-Example (QBE) exemplifies what such competing languages look like.

THE FUTURE OF COBOL

COBOL's future depends less on the strength of the language itself than upon the challenge that is presented by its two major competitors. The first challenge, as we just saw, comes from fourth-generation languages. Both COBOL and fourth-generation languages were intended to give business people without professional programming background the ability to write (and read) programs utilizing a syntax that was full of familiar English. Yet COBOL is not as transparent as its authors had intended, and it takes considerable time to learn to write complicated COBOL programs. Moreover, if we look at COBOL from the perspective of more modern programming languages that tend to be non-procedural and extensible, COBOL clearly comes across as a more traditional language in that its use is largely restricted to professional programmers.

But the future is by no means determined. As business people have enjoyed the freedom of writing their own data-organizing programs, data base management systems have become increasingly complex. It is now necessary to spend many hours (and even take courses—and then advanced courses) to figure out how to write the programs you are supposed to be able to write yourself. The time may not be far off when fourth-generation languages go the way of COBOL—thrusting the actual task of programming back into the hands of data-processing professionals and away from the control of those who need to use the results of the programs.

There is also the question of COBOL's other challenger: APL. APL may be a language whose time has come again. Created only a few years before COBOL, APL was also designed to process business data. The language had two problems: most novices (and even many computer professionals) found its tightly written programs difficult to decipher, and APL required a special keyboard to operate. But now APL is becoming available for microcomputers, the keyboard problem is being solved (with a special add-on microchip or a keyboard template), and there is always the potential for writing the language in a more readable form.

USING COBOL

Buying COBOL

COBOL compilers are available on every mainframe or minicomputer used in business—practically around the world. The growth of COBOL on microcomputers has been more gradual, partly because the language requires so much memory (which has only recently become available on micros) and partly because the early users of microcomputers (including many in the business world) eschewed languages they couldn't control themselves. Now the movement toward COBOL on microcomputers is coming largely from data-processing professionals whose older, large computers are being replaced with powerful small ones.

What to Read

BOOKS

So many books have been written on COBOL that it is difficult to recommend a small handful as being superior to others. Listed below is one good example of the older books, along with three newer books designed for using COBOL on microcomputers.

McCracken, Daniel (1976). *A Simplified Guide to Structured COBOL Programming.* New York: John Wiley.

Seidel, Ken (1983). *Microsoft COBOL.* Beaverton (Ore.): Dilithium Press.
A book on COBOL-80.

Fryer, Alan D. T. (1984). *COBOL on Microcomputers.* Indianapolis: Howard W. Sams.
This book is about CIS COBOL and Level II COBOL.

Stang, Norman (1983). *COBOL for Micros.* Sevenoaks (Kent, Eng.): Newnes Technical Books; Woburn, Mass.: Butterworth & Co.
Another book based on CIS COBOL.

ARTICLES

Sammet, Jean (1981). "The Early History of COBOL," in R. L. Wexelblat, ed., *History of Programming Languages.* New York: Academic Press, pp. 199–277.
A no-holds-barred look at the history of COBOL, written by one of its principal designers (who is also one of the main historians of computer languages).

FORTH

PROFILE

NAME
truncated form of FOURTH (for fourth-generation language)

STRUCTURE

Familiar Distinctions:
    hardware: high-level and low-level
    translator: interpreted and compiled
    structural unit: word
    data: not well suited to number-crunching; excellent for graphics
 	
Conceptual Distinctions:
    organizing principle: in family by itself
    procedures: largely non-procedural
    extensibility: highly extensible
    program/data: no sharp distinctions

FUNCTIONS
general-purpose, but especially used for astronomy, robotics, and graphics

GENEALOGY

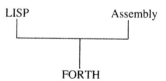

Years: late 1960s, 1970s

Author: Charles Moore (National Radio Astronomy Observatory)

Impetus: improve real-world applications programming

Evolution: gradual evolution in hands of Moore up to 1971
            slow spread in small number of areas in U.S. and in Europe;
            much recent interest

(Continued)

FORTH *(Continued)*

VERSIONS/DIALECTS		
Standards: FORTH-79 FORTH-83		
Others: fig-FORTH	microFORTH	MMSFORTH
polyFORTH	TRANSFORTH	

SPECIAL CHARACTERISTICS

Memory Requirements: extremely small (FORTH itself around 8K)

Ease of Learning/Use: can be tricky to learn and use (especially because it is so different from other languages)

Availability: becoming available for all computers; native language of Juniper Ace

WHY FORTH?

FORTH is the child of one man, Charles H. Moore, who wanted to become a more productive programmer. In the early 1960s, he reasoned that

> in 40 years a very good programmer could write forty programs. And I wanted to write *more* than that. There were many things out in the world to be done, and I wanted a tool to help me do them.
> Charles Moore, "The Evolution of FORTH, an Unusual Language," 1980

Moore worked at FORTH for over a decade before first using it in 1971 to write a radio-telescope data-acquisition program for the National Radio Astronomy Observatory.

The goal of FORTH is evident in its name. The letters F-O-R-T-H form a truncated version of the word FOURTH, indicating the fourth generation of computer languages. By the late 1960s, second- and third-generation languages like FORTRAN, COBOL, ALGOL, and PL/I had become the workhorses of the computer industry, largely replacing machine language and assembly language. Yet third-generation languages were conceived of as all-purpose languages, generally adequate but not efficient (or elegant) for real-world applications.

Talk began circulating in the programming world of the need for a new generation—a fourth generation—of programming languages designed with practical applications in mind. Moore's FORTH was to be such a language. He called it FORTH (rather than FOURTH) because the first computer on which he implemented the language, the IBM 1130, permitted only a five (not six) character name.

FORTH has indeed evolved into a powerful and genuinely unique language. But we need to be careful in our use of terminology. In the 1980s, when we talk about fourth-generation languages, we mean something quite different from FORTH. Like FORTH, contemporary fourth-generation languages are application-oriented. However, the typical applications of FORTH and the requirements FORTH imposes upon programmers tend to be quite distinct from contemporary fourth-generation languages.

FORTH has become known as a superb language for astronomy, robotics, and graphics. Contemporary fourth-generation languages are overwhelmingly oriented to business applications, especially to accessing large data bases. FORTH makes strenuous demands on its programmers, while contemporary fourth-generation languages are explicitly designed so users need to learn little or nothing about programming in order to use the language effectively. Both FORTH and contemporary fourth-generation languages are typically described as being non-procedural—focusing on *what* is to be accomplished rather than *how*. Yet an adequate statement in FORTH of ''what is to be accomplished'' requires considerably more knowledge of programming than does a comparable statement in contemporary fourth-generation languages.

THINKING IN FORTH

Unstructured imperative/algorithmic languages like FORTRAN and COBOL lead their users to think about programming in fairly similar ways: To solve a problem, you write a linear sequence of algorithms that bear at least a family resemblance to the way the hardware will process those algorithms. Structured imperative/algorithmic languages (e.g. Pascal, Modula-2) still work through algorithms, but they cluster those algorithms in modules that are self-contained units.

Spokesmen for non-imperative/algorithmic languages often warn new language learners that *their* language (e.g. LISP or PROLOG) approaches problem solving very differently than languages like FORTRAN or Pascal. For example, Patrick Winston and Berthold Horn, authors of a well-known textbook on LISP, caution that prior experience with another language ''can be something of a handicap'' to the would-be LISP programmer, ''for there can be a serious danger of developing a bad accent. Other languages do things differently, and function-by-function translation leads to awkward constructions.''

The same has been said of FORTH. Although FORTH is subtle and intricate, the rank novice may actually have an easier time learning it than seasoned professionals with entrenched presuppositions about how programming languages work.

Extensibility

The simplest way of pointing up FORTH's uniqueness is to cite the claim made by some of FORTH's strongest proponents that FORTH isn't a *language*. Instead it is a *grammar* that allows users to *write* a *new* language every time they write a new program. That is, FORTH is potentially an infinitely extensible system.

Any language has some degree of extensibility. By definition, all languages (natural languages and computer languages) are composed of a limited number of elements (such as words) and a finite set of rules for putting those elements together (called syntax). The power of language comes in the limitless ways in which you can conjoin elements using rules. Natural languages can also be extended by adding to their basic repertoire of elements through borrowing words (like *sputnik*), making up new words (such as *widgit*), or constructing new words out of existing words (e.g. *telecommunications* or *cranapple*). Similarly, languages can be extended by borrowing syntactic constructions or devising new ones.

On the contrary, the traditional computer languages have been closed systems. Machine (and assembly) languages have precisely defined sets of words and instruction codes. Similarly, imperative/algorithmic languages have predefined reserved words, data structures, control structures, and such. The programmer can use these elements and rules to perform novel tasks, but the language itself remains unchanged.

Most of the non-imperative/algorithmic languages tend to be more extensible—that is, more like natural languages. They allow users to create new elements, based upon the existing set, which can then be incorporated into the language. For some languages, this extensibility is an *option.* With FORTH, it is a *necessity.*

FORTH is a lot like German. The German language is notorious for the number of words it has that are made up of other words (like *telecommunications* or *cranapple* in English). In German, a telephone is a *Fernsprecher* ("far speaker"). A glove is a *Handschuh* ("hand shoe"). German does have a basic vocabulary (like the words for "far," "speaker," "hand," and "shoe"). But without the combination words, there are whole areas of everyday experience (like communicating at a distance and certain items of clothing) that would have no names.

FORTH takes the principle of word building in German one step further. While German *allows* its users to create new word combinations, FORTH *insists* that its users do so. The FORTH language is really a "language starter kit." It provides the user with all the essential tools necessary to build a program—and a language. Each program can be said to constitute a new language because in the process of writing a program, the user creates new words (out of older ones). Outside of a small shared core, the set of elements used in one program can look radically different from the elements in another.

Syntax is also extensible in FORTH. Programmers can construct new data types, data structures, and classes of operation.

The Word

The *word* is one of two especially distinctive components of FORTH. The idea of the word actually derives from LISP. In LISP, the basic unit for data manipulation is the *function*. Functions can themselves be made up of other functions. Similarly, in FORTH, both the indivisible units and the constructions made up of those units are called *words*.

Words in FORTH also resemble procedures in Pascal. Both words and procedures identify the subtask that is to be accomplished, and both can be embedded within other words and procedures, respectively. The difference is this: while procedures are names for lines of programming code that *use* the lexicon and syntax of the language, words that are newly defined actually *become part of* the FORTH language itself (as implemented by a particular programmer). In this regard, LISP functions (which can be defined by users and then incorporated into the language) are like words in FORTH.

The FORTH language that you buy comes with about 150 basic words built in. They denote familiar high-level programming notions (e.g. ABS takes the absolute value of a number, or BEGIN marks the beginning of a loop) as well as assembly-level notions (e.g. XOR initiates a bitwise logical exclusive OR) and notions unique to FORTH (e.g. a colon (:) is used to initiate the definition of a new word). However, in the *act* of writing a program, the user creates new words that are needed to solve the programming problem at hand. In fact, FORTH incorporates into its dictionary many of the *actions* that we are used to thinking of as *programming*. Another way of saying this is that defining new words in FORTH constitutes writing FORTH programs (much the way that defining new functions constitutes programming in LISP). Data and programs in FORTH (as in LISP) are not distinct.

To see how FORTH works, consider a program for squaring numbers. In BASIC, the program might look like this:

```
10 REM SQUARENUMBER
20 INPUT N
30 PRINT "The square of ";N;" is ";N*N
40 END
```

INPUT and PRINT are reserved words in BASIC (REM in line 10 indicates a comment), and multiplication is a defined arithmetic function. SQUARE-NUMBER has no status within the BASIC language.

Or consider the same calculation done in Pascal:

```
PROCEDURE SQUARENUMBER;
VAR n: INTEGER;
BEGIN
    WRITE ('The square of ',n,' is ', n*n)
END;
```

Again, PROCEDURE, BEGIN, WRITE, and END are reserved words, and multiplication is an arithmetic function, while the procedure SQUARENUMBER is not itself part of Pascal.

Now look at the same program in FORTH:

```
: Squarenumber DUP * . ;
```
is a word

"Squarenumber" is defined as a new word within the FORTH language. Outside of the new name "Squarenumber," the "word" (i.e. the entire line of programming code) is wholly composed of words that already exist in the language:

:   word indicating the beginning of a new
     definition (a so-called "colon definition")

DUP word that duplicates whatever is on the top
     of the stack (see below)

*   word indicating multiplication

.   word that prints a number

;   word indicating the end of the colon
     definition

The Stack

The stack is the second of the two central and distinct components of FORTH. For users who have studied computer hardware or data structures, the notion of a stack is familiar. But for many high-level programmers—as well as for novices—the term needs explanation.

In order to manipulate data (e.g. add two numbers together, alphabetize a list of names), you need to move the data out of the memory locations in which they are stored into the central processing unit (CPU). The CPU must then keep track of all the information while it is waiting to be acted upon by the arithmetic logic unit. Seen conceptually, the CPU *stacks up* the pieces of data to be manipulated.

Suppose we want to add together the numbers 6, 9, 2, 71, and 8. At the hardware level, the numbers and the request to add them will be put into RAM memory locations. When the addition request is acted upon, the numbers (and the addition request) will be dealt with by the CPU as if they were presented in a neatly stacked-up bundle:

+
8
71
2
9
6

All languages make use of such *stacks* somewhere in the translation from source code (what the programmer writes) to object code (what the computer hardware actually runs). Yet most languages hide the notion of the stack from the user. FORTH makes it explicit.

An easy way to see how the stack operates in FORTH is to see how FORTH handles arithmetic. (The same principles apply to non-arithmetic programs.) Consider the process of adding two numbers together. In doing normal arithmetic (or in writing algorithms for imperative/algorithmic languages), we might write out the problem something like

    71 + 8

or

    LET X = 71 + 8

The numbers to be added, 71 and 8, are separated by the sign of the arithmetic function to be performed upon them. Yet logically, we know that we have to have both numbers in hand *before* we can perform the arithmetic function of addition upon them. Logically, then, what we really mean is

  (a)   take the first number (71)
  (b)   take the second number (8)
  (c)   add the two numbers together

that is,

    71 8 +

This is the order in which the computer hardware actually looks at the program. First it takes the number 71 and *pushes* it onto the *stack*. It is usual to think of a stack as being like a pile of plates or trays held by an automatic dispenser in a cafeteria. The only plate or tray accessible to you is the one on the top. The cafeteria staff can add more plates (or trays) to the pile until the spring can be depressed no further. When a tray or plate is removed, it is *popped* off the stack. This is known as Last In, First Out (or LIFO) order.

To add 71 and 8, we first push 71 onto the stack and then push the second number, 8. When the addition instruction goes into the CPU, it pops the two numbers (71 and 8) off the stack, performs the function of addition upon them (in the arithmetic logic unit), and then pushes the result (i.e. 79) back onto the stack and eventually back to the data register (which holds information not actively being used).

The whole process looks something like the chart on page 197.

FORTH programs are written in the same order that the hardware stack physically functions. The addition of 71 and 8 is done with the FORTH expression

    71   8   +   .

(Recall that in FORTH, "." is the word used for printing a number—here, the result of the addition.) Placing the arithmetic operator *after* the numbers to be

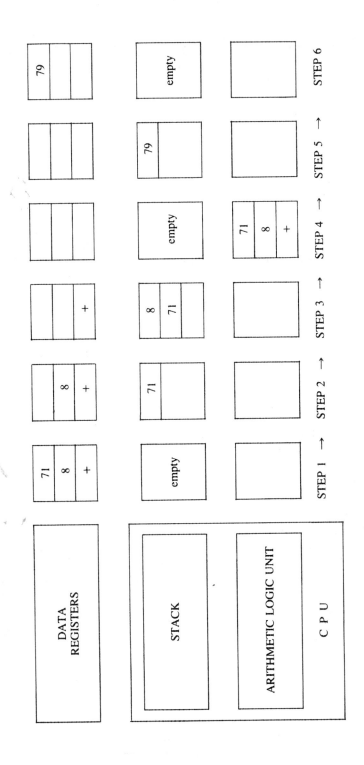

DATA REGISTERS

STACK

ARITHMETIC LOGIC UNIT

C P U

STEP 1 → STEP 2 → STEP 3 → STEP 4 → STEP 5 → STEP 6

operated upon is called *reverse Polish notation*. Reverse Polish notation is used in some forms of logic and has been implemented on several computers and calculators.

High-Level and Low-Level Language

We have said that FORTH was designed to help programmers write better programs and to write them more quickly. The stack facilitates programming by affording direct access to machine-level operations, without requiring programmers to cope with the clumsiness of machine code or assembly language. As a result, FORTH programs run extremely quickly, up to ten times faster than the same programs written in BASIC.

Yet FORTH, like C or Modula-2, is both a high-level and a low-level language. While FORTH allows programmers to control operations at the assembly language level, it does not require them to do so. The degree to which the language is high-level or low-level depends upon the needs and the programming experience of the user.

These low-level capabilities are responsible for a debate among FORTH users over whether a hardware-independent definition of FORTH is either possible or desirable. While many FORTH users advocate such a standard, Charles Moore argues that a machine-independent standard would not allow or encourage programmers to exploit the idiosyncratic low-level capabilities of the particular machine on which they are implementing FORTH. C manages to remain low-level yet machine-independent by placing all of its machine-specific instructions in a run-time library that is distinct from the language itself. Perhaps a FORTH standard could be achieved through a similar mechanism.

Interpreted and Compiled

A second paradoxical aspect of FORTH is that it is at once an interpreted and a compiled language. Some functions of the language run in the interpreted mode, while others run in the compiled mode. Normal input in FORTH is interpreted and executed directly, much as in common microcomputer implementations of BASIC. However, when a colon definition begins (signified by the FORTH word ":"), FORTH switches from interpreted to compiled mode. The colon definition is compiled into what is called threaded code (a term we will return to in a moment). To execute (i.e. run) one of these compiled colon definitions, the programmer types in just the name of the colon definition (such as the name "Squarenumber" from our discussion of words in FORTH a few pages back).

The effect of this dual system of interpreting and compiling is to make the system user-friendly (the interpreted mode) while at the same time making it run quickly and efficiently (the compiled mode). For similar reasons of combining ease of use with efficiency, several other computer languages combine interpreted and compiled modes (e.g. some versions of LISP).

Components of FORTH

Given all the strangeness (and paradoxes) of FORTH we have seen so far, we should not be surprised at finding one more. FORTH is not merely a language (or, if you prefer, a grammar) in the way that FORTRAN or COBOL or C is. Instead it is a complete software system. For reasons we have just seen, it has both an interpreter and a compiler. Like interpreted versions of BASIC, it also includes an editor and a debugger. But FORTH further contains its own operating system.

Perhaps the closest cousin to this multifaceted FORTH package is the p-system, developed by Kenneth Bowles at the University of California at San Diego to teach Pascal on mini- and microcomputers. The UCSD p-system contains an operating system, an editor, a debugger, a linker, and a loader. Yet unlike FORTH, the one element of the p-system that *is* now separable is the Pascal language itself: It is now possible to run languages other than UCSD Pascal under the UCSD p-system.

Threading

Like Pascal running under the p-system, the compiler for FORTH doesn't directly compile the source code (typed in by the user) into machine code that the hardware understands. Instead these languages are first compiled to an *intermediate* level of coding. In the case of UCSD Pascal, it is called *p-code* (for *pseudocode*). In the case of FORTH, it is commonly known as *threaded code*.   SRC —> Threaded code —>

Threading is a general programming technique that attempts to capitalize on the speed of machine language coding and the concise size of high-level programming by introducing an intermediate level of coding. This intermediate level (of threaded code) works by joining (or "threading") together subroutines which are, in turn, defined in terms of other subroutines. (The process is similar to the process by which FORTH defines new words in terms of previously defined words.)

As we saw earlier, colon definitions are compiled into this intermediate level of threaded coding and then actually executed later. Because FORTH *makes use of* the *technique* of threading, many people have mistakenly thought of FORTH itself as being a threaded language. This is not the case. The threading technique of compiling colon definitions could be replaced with some other technique (e.g. interpreting the colon definitions directly), and the resulting language would still be FORTH.

THE EVOLUTION OF FORTH

Most of FORTH's evolution took place before the language gathered a sizable following. Charles Moore worked alone on the language during the 1960s. In 1971, he produced the first modern FORTH grammar. The same year, Elizabeth

Rather became the second FORTH programmer. A few others (especially from the Kitt Peak National Observatory in Arizona) soon joined them.

A few "believers" (including Moore) left the observatory in 1973 to form FORTH, Inc., a company dedicated to producing applications programming in FORTH and FORTH systems. Over the next decade, interest in FORTH grew, but tended to be localized in a few geographic areas and among programmers particularly interested in some special applications.

Besides being the location of FORTH, Inc. (which produces versions of FORTH known as microFORTH and polyFORTH), California is home to the FORTH Interest Group (from which figFORTH derives, and which publishes a newsletter called *FORTH Dimensions*). A European FORTH User's Group (EFUG) was largely instrumental in creating a FORTH Standards Team that created FORTH-79. Back in the United States, the Institute for Applied FORTH Research in Rochester has been especially active in promoting the use of FORTH in astrophysics and robotics. And Richard and Jill Miller in Massachusetts have produced MMS (Miller Microcomputer Services) FORTH, an elegant and well-supported version of the language that resembles microFORTH.

The FORTH community continues to be racked by internal holy wars over standardization. The issue is not so much over whether one version is better than another, but whether it makes sense to fight over versions at all. If FORTH is not a language but a skeletal vocabulary and syntax, then the act of adding new elements to the language doesn't create a new version of the language (in the way that changing BASIC from an unstructured to a structured language can be seen as a fundamental change). Instead, it merely creates a new *implementation* of the grammar, which is what happens anyway each time a user writes a program.

THE FUTURE OF FORTH

As a language, FORTH is just now coming into the public eye. Articles are appearing in computer magazines with increasing frequency. A growing number of FORTH systems are becoming available, including MacFORTH for the Apple Macintosh. Yet courses on FORTH are still rare indeed, and the university community has all but ignored the language.

The future of FORTH is, in part, bound up with the question of whether FORTH is an appropriate language for many would-be users. The language has several advantages over languages currently more popular: It is extensible, fast, flexible, and generally quite portable. Yet FORTH remains more a professional programmer's tool than a language for the novice or casual user. Like APL, FORTH has been described as a "write-only language," in that it can be very difficult—even for the program's author—to figure out what a line of code means. Like C, FORTH lacks built-in safeguards that prevent programmers from making disastrous mistakes. Moreover, use of the stack and reverse Polish notation can hardly be called user-friendly. And finally, while it is true that

FORTH allows programmers to add new words or functions, the average computer user may lack the time, programming proficiency, or inclination to "flesh out" the language.

While admitting that FORTH is an "elitist" language, Charles Moore foresees that "FORTH is a language that a grade school child can learn to use quite effectively, if it is presented in bite-sized pieces with the proper motivation." But before replacing "grade school child" with "general user," we will have to see whether the potential power of FORTH is sufficient inducement for the general public to exercise the discipline necessary to learn the language (even in "bite-sized pieces"). And this will depend both upon the degree to which new versions of FORTH are constructed with the novice in mind (like the interpreted version of Pascal for the Macintosh) and upon the competition presented by other languages.

USING FORTH

Buying FORTH

FORTH is available for a wide range of microcomputers, running under most common operating systems. There is also a microcomputer known as the Jupiter Ace which has FORTH built in as the native code of the machine. (See the resources section below for sources of up-to-date information on new FORTH implementations.)

What to Read

BOOKS

Brodie, Leo (1981). *Starting FORTH*. Englewood Cliffs (N.J.): Prentice-Hall.
    A lucid (and humorous) introduction to the FORTH language and operating system, containing exercises and answers. Brodie works at FORTH, Inc.
Brodie, Leo (1984). *Thinking FORTH*. Englewood Cliffs (N.J.): Prentice-Hall.
    A thoughtful analysis of computer programming, seen from the perspective of FORTH.
Oakey, Steve (1984). *FORTH for Micros*. Sevenoaks (Kent, Eng.): Newnes Technical Books; Woburn, Mass.: Butterworth & Co.
    A clear teach-yourself book with exercises and answers.
Toppen, David (1985). *FORTH: An Application Approach*. New York: McGraw-Hill.
    As the title indicates, this book is useful in explaining how to write FORTH programs that interface with the outside world (e.g. converting analog signals to digital signals, controlling spectrometers).
Winfield, Alan (1983). *The Complete FORTH*. New York: John Wiley.
    Another well-done self-paced book with exercises and answers.

Byte, August 1980.

This issue of *Byte* features the language FORTH. It contains histories, overviews, tutorials, and sample implementations of the language. The article by Charles Moore is especially useful.

Other Resources

Because it is still difficult to get information on FORTH, here are some general resources that should prove helpful.

ORGANIZATIONS

FORTH Interest Group
P.O. Box 8231
San Jose, California 95155
FORTH, Inc.
2309 Pacific Coast Highway
Hermosa Beach, California 90254
The Institute for Applied FORTH Research
70 Elmwood Avenue
Rochester, New York 14611
Miller Microsystems Services
61 Lake Shore Road
Natick, Massachusetts 01760

MAGAZINES/NEWSLETTERS

FORTH Dimensions
published by the FORTH Interest Group
MMSFORTH Newsletter
published by Miller Microsystems Services
Journal of Applied FORTH Research
published by the Institute for FORTH Research
Dr. Dobb's Journal
frequently publishes articles on FORTH

FORTRAN

PROFILE
NAME
*FOR*mula TRANslation
STRUCTURE

Familiar Distinctions:
  hardware: high-level
  translator: compiled
  structural unit: statement
  data: numerical
 	
Conceptual Distinctions:
  organizing principle: imperative/algorithmic
  procedures: procedural
  extensibility: not extensible
  program/data: distinct

FUNCTIONS
science and engineering
GENEALOGY
earlier efforts at automatic programming | FORTRAN Years: 1954 (initial design), 1956 (first compiler), 1957 (commercially distributed) Author: John Backus (IBM) Impetus: simplify programming by enabling computer to take mathematical formulas as input Evolution: through success of IBM, remains most widely used language in science and engineering today

(Continued)

203

FORTRAN (Continued)

VERSIONS/DIALECTS			
Standards: ANSI FORTRAN-77			
ANSI FORTRAN-66			
Others: FORTRAN I	FORTRAN III	WATFOR	WATFIV-S
FORTRAN II	FORTRAN IV	WATFIV	RATFOR

SPECIAL CHARACTERISTICS
Memory Requirements: large
Ease of Learning/Use: average
Availability: widely available on mainframes and minicomputers; also now available on micros

WHY FORTRAN?

FORTRAN is the patriarch of high-level computer languages. During the past three decades it has had an enormous impact on the way we think about programming. Its most direct (and best-known) influence is upon the language BASIC, which is, in some ways, a simplified and more English-like version of FORTRAN. Although ALGOL (rather than FORTRAN) is the direct progenitor of nearly all *contemporary* imperative/algorithmic languages, FORTRAN remains the language that stimulated much of our thinking about the elaboration of programming techniques and even the conceptual underpinnings of programming.

Yet despite FORTRAN's success, the language was by no means unique for its time. FORTRAN grew out of a general movement, beginning back as early as 1945, to simplify the task of using computers to perform computations on numerical information.

The Quest for Automatic Programming

Computers were originally built in the 1940s to speed up mathematical calculations that would otherwise be computed by hand. In the early days of computers, numerical data and mathematical formulas for manipulating these data had to be manually translated into machine code (or, later, assembly language) before they could be fed into the computer. An obvious question was whether it was possible to construct languages that let you write the actual mathematical formulas you wished to use, input your data in Arabic numerals (rather than in 0's and 1's), and then have the machine automatically translate these formulas and data into machine code.

A number of people worked independently on both sides of the Atlantic on the problem that came to be known as *automatic programming*. Some of the major systems (though by no means all of them) are summarized below.

Automatic programming is a confusing term because it means different things to different people. In the 1940s and 1950s, it had at least three distinct meanings:

   (1) assembly language programming
   (2) use of a subroutine library
   (3) ability to accept algebraic language as input

All three of these techniques "automated" the programming process to some extent. Assembly language was actually little more than a series of mnemonic devices for representing the 0's and 1's of machine language, but it did simplify the programmer's work considerably. Subroutines (i.e. lines of programming code that could be used over and over again for representing common computing operations such as taking the square root of a number or computing an average) were hardly "automatic" in any usual sense of the term, but again they helped speed up programming. However, it was the third meaning of automatic—the ability to accept algebraic representations (e.g. constants, variables, and arithmetic operators like + and =)—that led to the creation of high-level languages.

Being able to enter algebraic representations directly drastically reduced the number of lines of code that a programmer had to write. As we saw in the entry on assembly language, the simple addition of two numbers in a low-level language might take up several lines of code (one to load into the CPU the first number to be added, a second to load the next number to be added, and a third to do the actual addition). In a high-level language like FORTRAN, the entire procedure could be handled with a single line of code:

$$K = I + J$$

where K = the resulting sum, I = the first number to be added, and J = the second.

The history of automatic programming and, within it, the creation of "algebraic languages" is surprisingly disjointed. For almost a decade, individual computer scientists were independently re-creating the wheel. It was often only after the fact that one group came to know that another individual or group had already created a very similar system. This situation did not result from any attempt at secrecy. There was simply a near-total lack of communication.

The development of FORTRAN is an excellent case in point. In describing the creation of the language, John Backus, FORTRAN's principal architect, points out that he knew nothing of the previous work of Zuse and Mauchly, never bothered to review Rutishauser's work carefully, and remained unaware of the work of Laning and Zierler (which very closely parallels the ideas in FORTRAN) until after the basic design of FORTRAN had been laid down.

Date Work Begun	Creator	Language Name	Description	Implementation	Comments
1945	Konrad Zuse	Plankalkül	first notation for an algorithmic language	not implemented	published in 1959 and 1972
1949	John Mauchly	Short Code	goal of accepting algebraic expressions	UNIVAC	published in 1952
1951	Heinz Rutishauser	—	notation for algorithmic language	not implemented	published in 1952
1952	Corrado Böhm	—	notation for algorithmic language	not implemented	published in 1954
	Alec Glennie	AUTOCODE	not algebraic	Manchester Mark I	very machine-dependent
1952–53	J. H. Laning and N. Zierler	—	algebraic world's first operating algebraic compiler (first running system to allow fairly natural mathematical expressions)	Whirlwind (MIT)	machine-independent published in 1954
1953	Grace Hopper	A-2	not algebraic	UNIVAC	machine-dependent
	John Backus	Speedcoding		IBM 701	direct precursor of FORTRAN
1954	John Backus (and Irving Ziller, Harlan Herrick, Robert A. Nelson)	FORTRAN	reduce time and effort in solving numerical scientific problems	IBM 704	
1955	Grace Hopper	MATH-MATIC		UNIVAC	same objectives as FORTRAN
1956	Alan Perlis et al.	IT		IBM 650	
1957–58		UNICODE		UNIVAC	hardware language

The Design of FORTRAN

The roots of FORTRAN itself are highly pragmatic. John Backus proposed to his boss at IBM the design of a language that would accept algebraic representation as input in order to reduce the costs of programming. As early as the 1950s, programming itself (along with debugging) was the major expenditure in the computing enterprise. And this was at a time when the cost of hardware was extremely high and wages paid for human labor were comparatively low.

Other designers of automatic programming languages had already recognized that if the programming process could be simplified, programming time and therefore costs could be reduced significantly. The problem was that programs written in the existing automatic programming languages all ran very slowly—much more slowly than comparable programs written in assembly language. In fact, for that reason, relatively few people in the early 1950s expressed much interest in automatic programming.

Backus's idea was to create a language that not only would accept algebraic formulas as input but would also run quickly. In fact, Backus has flatly stated that in devising FORTRAN he was far less concerned with the design of the language than with the speed of its compiler:

> We simply made up the language as we went along. We did not regard language design as a difficult problem, merely a simple prelude to the real problem: designing a compiler which could produce efficient programs.

For those who have complained for years that FORTRAN is an unnecessarily awkward language, the historical response is that no real effort was made to construct an elegant language in the first place. Backus justified this emphasis on efficiency over elegance as a matter of expedience:

> To this day I believe that our emphasis on object program efficiency rather than on language design was basically correct. I believe that had we failed to produce efficient programs, the widespread use of languages like FORTRAN would have been seriously delayed.

Whatever the merits of Backus's arguments, a radically different approach was taken in the design of ALGOL, a language which began a new era of programming by stressing elegance in the language design itself.

In reading about the history of FORTRAN, there are actually three separate dates to keep track of. The initial design of the language was done in 1954. By 1956 the first FORTRAN compiler had been built to run on the IBM 704 (a new machine announced by IBM in 1954). The public version of the compiler for FORTRAN was available in 1957 and was distributed to all IBM 704 installations.

The Competition

We have said that FORTRAN was not the only automatic programming language being developed. It was not even the only language that accepted algebraic expressions as input. One of the most serious contenders was MATH-MATIC, developed by Grace Hopper and her group in 1955 at Remington Rand to run on the UNIVAC. The language was implemented at the same time as FORTRAN.

Yet MATH-MATIC lost out to FORTRAN. Jean Sammet, a historian of computer languages, suggests that the problem with MATH-MATIC was really a problem with UNIVAC and Remington Rand. The UNIVAC was a less versatile machine than the IBM 704, and IBM also managed to market its machines more successfully than its competitors.

FORTRAN's other early potential competitor, actually developed a few years after FORTRAN, was ALGOL 58 (and then ALGOL 60). The history of the battle between FORTRAN and the ALGOLs is chronicled in the entry on ALGOL.

THINKING IN FORTRAN

Hardware and Software: The von Neumann Model

Assembly language programs approximate fairly closely the physical order in which the computer hardware actually processes a program. In principle, a high-level language is far removed from the workings of the computer hardware. After all, if one line of high-level programming code can correspond to three lines of assembly code, there must be a lot of work for the translator to do in order to put the high-level code in a form that the computer hardware can act upon.

In principle this is true, though in practice the "gap" between high-level programming code and machine implementation is not nearly as great as in "higher" high-level languages like PROLOG or Query-by-Example. Although it does so at a distance, a language like FORTRAN (and most of the other early imperative/algorithmic languages) parallels quite closely the order of events taking place in hardware. It is for this reason that FORTRAN is sometimes spoken of as a "von Neumann language" (i.e. paralleling the order of events occurring in a von Neumann machine).

As a result, for the FORTRAN user, the particular steps in a FORTRAN program and the order in which they appear may seem to be unnatural and even unnecessary. Yet there is a logic behind the code. That logic comes from the sequence of steps that the hardware will go through when it receives the object code version of the program (i.e. the version that has been through the FORTRAN compiler). Remember that Backus and his group explicitly designed FORTRAN to make the compiler run as quickly as possible, and the less rearranging of source code lines (i.e. what the programmer writes) that the compiler has to do, the faster it can complete its work.

Programming in FORTRAN

What does a FORTRAN program look like? Very similar to programs you have seen in any other imperative/algorithmic language, especially the older ones.

Consider a simple program for adding two numbers together. In this example, we have inserted, on the left-hand margin, a set of line numbers (which are *not* part of FORTRAN) to enable us to talk easily about the program:

```
1   C    THIS PROGRAM ADDS TWO NUMBERS TOGETHER
2        I = 6
3        J = 8
4        K = I + J
5        WRITE (5, 100) K
6   100  FORMAT (1X, I7)
7        STOP
8        END
```

We can think of each of the eight lines of programming code in terms of an ordered set of stations you must pass through (much as when you check into a hospital or go to register an automobile). The first station, line (1), is the comment station: tell the reader what the program will be doing. At the next station, we do programming steps stipulated in lines (2) and (3): assign integer values to the variables I and J. (We know the values must be integers rather than real numbers because FORTRAN requires that integer values—and only integer values—be assigned to the variables I, J, K, L, M, or N. Names for real constants and variables must begin with the letters A through H or O through Z.) At the third station, line (4) is set up: K (another integer variable) is assigned the value of the variables I and J.

The fourth station gives instructions on how the result is to be printed, i.e. line (5). The number 5 (i.e. after WRITE) is a preestablished code indicating the device on which the output will appear (e.g. a printer or a CRT). The number 100 is a "format label," which is actually an instruction to go to another station, i.e. the station that bears the sign 100. In our case, this is programming line (6).

The purpose of the FORMAT statement in line (6), which we were sent to by the format label in line (5), is to tell us what physical placement the output will have on the page. FORMAT statements clearly reveal FORTRAN's origins as a language coded on punched cards. There are 80 positions in a row on a punched card, and each piece of a FORTRAN program can only go in the column to which it is assigned. This holds true even when programming on interactive systems that use keyboards and CRTs. In line (6), the 1X indicates that one space will be written before the value assigned to K is itself written out. Moreover, the value of K will be written in a space that is seven columns wide and reserved for an integer (hence I7). The result that is printed will be justified to the right-hand side of the margin of the seven-column width.

All of this is more easily explained visually. For the above program, the result of K, i.e. 14, will appear as follows:

Column: 1 2 3 4 5 6 7 8 9 10 11 . . . 80

OUTPUT: 1 4

The final two stations of the program are two means (both necessary) of saying you are done. The STOP in line (7) is an instruction to stop computation. The END in line (8) is always the last statement in a FORTRAN program and indicates you have reached the end of a program listing.

THE EVOLUTION OF FORTRAN

The first commercial version of FORTRAN (FORTRAN I) was issued in 1957. An enhanced version, FORTRAN II, was issued in 1958 and established FORTRAN among a large body of users. Its successor, FORTRAN III, had far less acceptance. *Its* successor, FORTRAN IV (issued in 1962), became well entrenched in computing establishments around the country. The general spread of FORTRAN is due, in part, to IBM's free distribution of the language with its mainframe computers.

The first attempt at a real standard came in 1966, when the American National Standards Institute created ANSI FORTRAN (also known as FORTRAN-66). Meanwhile, the University of Waterloo in Ontario had been working on its own improvements to FORTRAN IV. Their interest was not so much in *using* FORTRAN to do computations as in *teaching* the language to students. Their first result, known as WATFOR (*WA*Terloo *FOR*TRAN), introduced a much faster compiler (useful for students, who frequently make mistakes and must recompile their programs many times) and a much improved system of error messages (again, especially invaluable for students). A subsequent version, WATFIV, increased the number of statement types available and improved capabilities associated with statements. WATFIV-S added principles of structured programming to FORTRAN. (Another version of FORTRAN with a memorable name is RATFOR, standing for *RAT*ional *FOR*TRAN. RATFOR is a programming system that provides the necessary constructs for writing well-structured programs in FORTRAN.)

A second national standard for FORTRAN was created by ANSI in 1977. Known as FORTRAN-77, the language included several features that had been developed in WATFOR and WATFIV.

In recent years, FORTRAN has continued to evolve to keep pace with developments in hardware and software. As in the case of COBOL and BASIC, FORTRAN has now been issued in "structured" versions that blur the earlier distinctions between the FORTRAN family and the ALGOL family. In addition, FORTRAN is now available for microcomputers.

THE FUTURE OF FORTRAN

Does FORTRAN have a future? The language's designers admit that the structure of the language itself was never of particular interest to them. John Backus long ago abandoned not only FORTRAN but other imperative/algorithmic languages that are, in his thinking, too tightly bound by constraints of von Neumann architecture. Backus presents his arguments in a well-known article, "Can Programming Be Liberated from the von Neumann Style?" (*Communications of the ACM*, 1978, vol. 21, no. 8, pp. 613–641).

Yet programmers continue to write new code in FORTRAN for much the same reasons that they continue to program in COBOL. COBOL and FORTRAN are both shackled with mountains of programs that would take thousands upon thousands of man-years to rewrite. Some companies are actually beginning to translate their formidable FORTRAN (or COBOL) libraries into more modern languages. However, the number of lines of code that would have to be converted is too immense for the task to be economically feasible on a large scale. In 1984, the price of converting a line of COBOL code to a modern fourth-generation language was almost $9.00 per line. At least as of now, there is no simple conversion program into which you can feed unstructured COBOL or FORTRAN code and get a modernized version out at the other end. Add in inflation, multiply $9.00 by millions of lines of code, and you can easily see the problem.

There is also an arsenal of FORTRAN (and COBOL) *programmers*—people who have programmed in FORTRAN or COBOL all of their working lives and people who make a living teaching other people to program in these languages. They pass on FORTRAN (or COBOL) to the next generation of programmers, and the language is perpetuated.

Will the cycle ever end? There are three possibilities. One (which does not seem at all likely) is that a decision will be made from above (e.g. by the U.S. Department of Defense) that as of January 1 no more projects of any sort will be funded for programs written in FORTRAN. This would be akin to the United States switching to a metric system of measurement, a move that once seemed inevitable but has now been dropped. As in the case of FORTRAN, there is too large an investment in an earlier system.

A second and slightly more plausible option is that FORTRAN will lose a war of attrition to newer languages. New generations of programmers will emerge who write in languages other than FORTRAN, and these programmers will, in turn, train their successors. The biggest alternative language challenge is coming from Pascal, which has generally replaced FORTRAN as the introductory computer language in American higher education, and from the derivatives of Pascal such as Modula-2 and Ada.

Perhaps the most likely possibility is that FORTRAN itself will continue to evolve in order to keep pace with changes in other languages, much as it has done with the introduction of structured programming, new data types, new data structures, and new control structures. As Tony Hoare quipped in the

January 1984 issue of the *Annals of the History of Computing,* "Whatever language we'll be using in the year 2000 we'll call FORTRAN."

USING FORTRAN

Buying FORTRAN

FORTRAN is almost universally available on mainframe computers. It can also be found on minicomputers used by scientists and engineers and on microcomputers with large memory capabilities used by the same audience.

What to Read

BOOKS

Among the myriad of books on FORTRAN, here are several suggestions that are especially clear, humorous, or both.

Didday, Rich, and Rex Page (1981). *FORTRAN for Humans.* 3rd edition. St. Paul: West Publishing Company.
This aptly titled text is commonly used for teaching FORTRAN to non-computer science students.
Kaufman, Roger E. (1978). *A FORTRAN Coloring Book.* Cambridge (Mass.): MIT Press.
You can indeed color in the pictures in this handwritten book, but you end up learning a lot about FORTRAN in the process.
Alcock, Donald (1982). *Illustrating FORTRAN (The Portable Variety).* Cambridge (Eng.): Cambridge University Press.
Another book in the same vein, also published by an otherwise staid press.

ARTICLES

The following two articles by John Backus give a clear sense of his thinking (and that of his fellow programmers) in the years when FORTRAN was created.

Backus, John (1980). "Programming in America in the Nineteen Fifties—Some Personal Impressions," in N. Metropolis et al., eds., *A History of Computing in the Twentieth Century.* New York: Academic Press, pp. 125–135.
Backus, John (1981). "The History of FORTRAN I, II, and III," in R. L. Wexelblat, ed., *History of Programming Languages.* New York: Academic Press, pp. 25–74.

Intellect

PROFILE

NAME
alternative names: ROBOT, IQS, ON-LINE ENGLISH

STRUCTURE

Familiar Distinctions:
   hardware: n.a.
   translator: n.a.
   structural unit: English phrase or sentence
   data: numerical and information categories

Conceptual Distinctions:
   organizing principle: natural language front end to query language
   procedures: non-procedural
   extensibility: extensible
   program/data: not distinct

FUNCTIONS
use natural language input to access large data bases

GENEALOGY

natural language processing research   formal
query languages

augmented transition networks (ATNs)

ROBOT/IQS/ON-LINE ENGLISH/Intellect

Year: 1977

Author: Larry Harris (now of Artificial Intelligence Corporation)

Impetus: use natural language processing techniques from artificial intelligence research to circumvent need for users to learn formal
query languages to access data bases

(Continued)

Intellect (Continued)

Evolution:	growing number of systems with same aims as Intellect entering the market (number of systems and their capabilities likely to explode in late 1980s)

VERSIONS/DIALECTS
Standard: n.a.

SPECIAL CHARACTERISTICS
Memory Requirements: very large
Ease of Learning/Use: in principle, nothing to learn
Availability: runs on large computers and on more powerful IBM PCs

NOTE: Read this entry in conjunction with the entries on QBE (in Chapter 5) and NaturalLink and Savvy (in the Appendix).

WHY INTELLECT?

Anyone who specifies solutions to problems as a sequence of primitive operations on a computer is indeed programming. The only difference is the level of abstraction of the primitives.
Larry Harris, "Language for End Users," 1985

Levels of Abstraction

Low-level languages reflect the way computer hardware actually processes lines of programming code. High-level languages conceive of problems in more abstract terms.

In the thirty years since the development of FORTRAN (the first widely adopted high-level language), many languages have appeared that remove the user further and further from the physical processing by the machine itself. Most discussions of this distancing between the low-level operation of the machine and the way a user thinks about the problem have dealt with the traditional imperative/algorithmic languages used for general-purpose computing. But the same issues can be raised in talking about computing in special-purpose areas using languages with other conceptual principles of organization.

Larry Harris, inventor of the language that came to be known as Intellect, analyzes the issue of distance between user and machine by talking about the use of computers in business. Harris begins by distinguishing among three levels of abstraction:

> physical: data as they appear in the actual storage medium (i.e. the computer)
>
> logical: how data look to applications programs
>
> conceptual: how users think about data

It is possible to think about a problem—and to program it—at all three levels. Professional programmers frequently work at the physical level (e.g. assembly language). But most people in the business world don't. With the growth of data bases in the 1970s, users increasingly began working with computers at the logical level. Data base management systems (DBMSs) were developed to map requests for information from the logical level to the physical level.

But for most business people, the problem was still not solved. For business problems originate at the conceptual level. Business users' primary concern is not with how data look to an applications program, but with how data look to users.

Formal query languages offered a first step in mapping from the conceptual level to the logical level. Most formal query languages, however, are still at least one step removed from the way business people normally think about a problem. The languages have very restrictive vocabularies and precise conventions for syntax and punctuation. But in their everyday thinking, people are used to the far-reaching flexibility of natural language. A more natural mapping, then, would be to begin with natural language (representing the conceptual level) and then convert it to the logical level at which DBMSs already operate.

From ROBOT to Intellect

This was Harris's plan. He set out to devise a computer language that would take natural language as its input and "translate" it into the more formal language that was already used to access large data bases. Drawing upon research in artificial intelligence, by 1977 Harris had created a language known as ROBOT that allowed users to input ordinary English sentences when questioning an existing data base on a mainframe computer. The responses the computer gave to such queries were of the same sort one could expect in using a formal query language (e.g. a list of natural gas customers in Boone, North Carolina; the home telephone numbers for all managers of Holiday Inns in the Denver area).

Over the years, the same ROBOT system has gone by several other names, including IQS, ON-LINE ENGLISH, and now Intellect. The Intellect system is currently sold by the Artificial Intelligence Corporation in Waltham, Massachusetts, of which Harris is president.

THINKING IN INTELLECT

Suppose we work in the personnel department of a Georgia bank and want some information on employees. We might ask of a data base

> Give me the names of all the tellers who work
>   in Atlanta.

Intellect would "translate" that query into something like

> Print the name of any employee with City = Atlanta
>   and Job = Teller.

Intellect would then follow the translation with an answer to the question, e.g.

> The number of records to retrieve is 432
>   Adams
>   Bray
>   Brown
>   Crowley
>   Greene
>   ...

What makes Intellect a natural language processing system (as opposed to a formal query language) is that the user, not the system, decides how to phrase the query. The same question could, for instance, have been asked in a number of ways:

> What are the names of all the Atlanta employees
>   working as tellers?
> Who are the Atlanta tellers?

or even the abbreviated

> Tellers in Atlanta?

In response to each of these four queries, Intellect would produce the same translation and the same response.

The Structure of Intellect

There are five components involved in running the Intellect system (see page 217). Since Intellect can run with several commercial data base management systems, the critical component to explore is the natural language parsing program that maps the user's natural language query into a formal query language representation that the DBMS program will understand.

The natural language parsing program in Intellect may seem like magic to

INTELLECT

```
        ┌─────────────────────┐
        │    USER'S QUERY     │
        └─────────────────────┘
                   │
                   │
            natural language

             parsing program
                   │
                   ▼
   ┌───────────────────────────────┐
   │   FORMAL QUERY LANGUAGE       │
   │                               │
   │      REPRESENTATION           │
   └───────────────────────────────┘
                   │
                   │
        data base management system

                 program
                   │
                   ▼
        ┌─────────────────────┐
        │     DATA BASE       │
        └─────────────────────┘
```

the lay user, but it is hardly unique in the world of artificial intelligence. In fact, in an article appearing in 1977, Harris himself explains that he makes use of a standard technique for doing natural language processing known as augmented transition networks (ATNs). The technique was developed in the early 1970s and has commonly been used for parsing simple English sentences.

The details of how ATNs work are too involved to go into here. Suffice it to say that the user produces a sentence, to which a set of analytic procedures are applied by the ATN program. Using these procedures, the ATN determines the grammatical structure of the sentence. If the sentence is ambiguous—e.g. "They are playing cards"—the system is able to produce two separate grammatical analyses. Once a natural language sentence has been analyzed in terms of a given set of syntactic categories, it is then easy to "translate" that analyzed sentence into a formal query language.

Consider the examples we gave at the beginning of this section:

> Give me the names of all the tellers who work in
>   Atlanta.
> What are the names of all the Atlanta employees
>   working as tellers.
> Who are the Atlanta tellers?
> Tellers in Atlanta?

Each of these user-generated sentences could be fed into the ATN, and the analyzed version that came out in each case would indicate that the following linguistic elements were involved:

(1) names of employees who
   (a) were tellers
   and
   (b) worked in Atlanta
(2) a request to print out the above list

These precise linguistic elements can then be restructured into a sentence that the formal query language can understand, in this case

Print the name of any employee with City = Atlanta
and Job = Teller.

(Some of the more English-like formal query languages have entries that look very much like this.)

If the syntax of Intellect is handled by the linguistic device known as ATNs, how does Intellect deal with vocabulary? There are three different categories of vocabulary that Intellect provides for. The first is a basic set of words (like *what, when,* and *count*) that are part of the Intellect system sold to every purchaser. A second set of words (such as *employee* or *title*) are provided as part of the customization of Intellect to a particular installation. If the installation is a bank, the words might include *interest, prime rate,* and *foreclosure.* If the installation is a department store, the customized vocabulary could include the names of major clothing designers whose fashions are sold by the store.

Finally, there is a third set of words that are the exclusive province of the user. A user can introduce a new word that the system doesn't already know (i.e. that isn't contained in one of the two existing sets). When the system encounters a new word, it gives the user an opportunity to provide a definition utilizing the already existing vocabulary. This "extensibility" of vocabulary is common among natural language front end programs of this type—systems like Themis and Clout (two of Intellect's competitors) are also extensible.

Powers and Limitations

Intellect was designed to allow users to formulate inquiries much as they would if questioning another person. As we have already seen, users can ask the same question in more than one way, introduce new vocabulary, or assume that the interlocutor (here, the computer) will recognize that a sentence is ambiguous and ask which of the possible meanings the user had in mind.

But Intellect has other natural language-like features as well. One of the most important is the use of pronominal reference. If I say, "Gilbert is an electronics engineer," and then go on to say, "He is well paid," you know that *he* refers to Gilbert. In Intellect, you can enter several queries in succession without having to specify all the information which is given in the first query (but presupposed in the later ones). For example, if I type in

Give me all the tellers who work in Atlanta.

and then ask

Who work in Athens.

Intellect can figure out that the *who* in the second query refers to tellers. In fact, Intellect even "knows" how to interpret the abbreviated

In Athens.

as meaning "who work in Athens." (Yes, there is an Athens, Georgia.)

But Intellect, like all the systems that accept natural language input, has severe limitations that salesmen of the new technology tend to neglect. As every researcher in artificial intelligence knows, no one yet understands how to analyze by computer the real natural language that you and I speak and write. The existing models of natural language processing (such as ATNs) only work successfully on very restricted subsets of ordinary language. Produce a slightly complex sentence, and most systems will either give an incorrect analysis or simply crash.

Only part of the problem lies in our as yet limited facility with computers. The main problem is that even *without* computers, linguists still know very little about how natural language works. We understand basic sentence types, but not the thousands of syntactic patterns that give human language its subtlety and richness.

In the world of artificial intelligence research, the common solution to this problem is to work with a *subset* of natural language rather than trying to use computers to analyze all of it. Contemporary projects on machine translation (e.g. between English and German) typically restrict themselves to limited cognitive and linguistic domains (e.g. chemistry or electronics or meteorology). In the case of monolingual projects working on natural language processing, the most successful have been front ends to data bases in the business world.

For the language of business is itself a subset of natural language. Despite its apparent variety, business discourse requires only a restricted number of questions to ask of a data base and necessitates only a restricted set of vocabulary items and syntactic constructions for asking them. Users of natural language front end systems such as Intellect very quickly learn which kinds of queries the system will be able to make sense of and which kinds it won't. Like Skinnerian pigeons, users adjust their behavior to maximize reward.

This is not meant as a criticism of such systems. Human beings naturally adjust their language to meet the needs of their interlocutors. Adults typically speak differently to young children than they do to one another, and we know to alter our language when speaking with, say, foreigners or people who are hard of hearing. We learn such "register shifts" as part of learning to speak. What we need to remember in the case of natural language front ends is that we *are* adjusting our language when we address them.

In the case of Intellect, we know what adjustments to make because the Intellect system itself gives us a translated version of our original query. If we type in

> Give me the names of all the tellers who work
> in Atlanta.

Intellect will print back

> Print the name of any employee with City = Atlanta
> and Job = Teller.

before giving the response. The "reworking" of the user's original utterance ends up serving as a tacit model for future user utterances as well as a check on Intellect's interpretation of the query.

Precisely this same modeling takes place when young children are first learning to speak. If a child says

> I don't want none of them.

her father might respond

> Oh, you don't want any of those?

The father (like Intellect) isn't overtly correcting the child's/user's language. However, with time, the novice learns how to produce statements that closely approximate or even precisely replicate the standard model.

THE EVOLUTION OF INTELLECT

While the design of Intellect is almost a decade old, the system has only begun to attract attention within the past few years. Part of the problem until recently has been Intellect's very hefty price tag, and the fact that Intellect only ran on a large computer with a limited range of data base management systems. More recently, the system has been made available on microcomputers and for other DBMSs.

THE FUTURE OF INTELLECT

The importance of Intellect is less its past than its future. And its future has two variables: short-range competition from other natural language front ends to DBMSs and its long-range prospects as a means of using ordinary language with a computer.

Short-Range Competition

The use of natural language front ends to DBMSs has become a veritable growth industry in the computer world. Some systems (like Intellect) work by analyzing the user's syntax, while other systems purport to analyze meaning by using a model of natural language semantics. With so many research and subsequent commercial projects appearing, it is hardly possible to publish an up-to-date list of them all and hope to be accurate.

Within the last few years, a flock of competitors to Intellect have begun to appear. These include Themis (marketed by Frey Associates in Amherst, New Hampshire), Clout 2 (marketed by Microrim in Bellevue, Washington), and Q & A (produced by Symantec in Sunnyvale, California).

In addition to these "analysis" models of natural language front ends, there are also systems designed from other conceptual perspectives. For a discussion of the pattern-matching approach, see the entry on Savvy (in the Appendix). For an example of the menu-driven approach, see the entry on NaturalLink (again, in the Appendix).

Long-Range Prospects

There is no question that computer systems that accept natural language will become commonplace in the future. The real issues involve the *amount* of natural language that the system can correctly make sense of and the *types* of data bases to which such natural language front ends are applied. As of now, both language base and data base tend to be restricted to the business domain. As linguistic research on natural language processing becomes more sophisticated, we can expect the range of comprehensible natural languages to increase. As this happens, the scope of data bases used is certain to expand from the current lists of employees and salaries to more sophisticated technical subjects, and then to general information sources like encyclopedias or even entire libraries.

USING INTELLECT

Buying Intellect

Intellect originally sold for approximately $70,000 and ran on a large IBM machine. The language is now available for an IBM PC and could well be issued for other microcomputers. The Artificial Intelligence Corporation has available a demonstration disk that will give you an idea of how the language works.

What to Read

ARTICLES

Harris, Larry (1985). "Languages for End Users," *Computerworld*, February 25, In Depth 1–8.
Harris explains his model of "levels of abstraction" that we discussed in the beginning of this entry.

Harris, Larry (1977). "User Oriented Data Base Query with the ROBOT Natural Language Query System," *International Journal of Man-Machine Studies* 9:697–713.
This article outlines very clearly not only what the ROBOT (= Intellect) language is but also how it works. It provides a useful antidote to the commercial hyperbole that surrounds the marketing of most natural language front end systems.

LISP

PROFILE
NAME
LISt Processing
STRUCTURE

Familiar Distinctions:
  hardware: high-level
  translator: generally interpreted
  structural unit: function
  data: symbolic (limited number handling)
 	
Conceptual Distinctions:
  organizing principle: functional/applicative (specifically list processing)
  procedures: largely procedural
  extensibility: extensible
  program/data: both programs and data are handled with functions

FUNCTIONS
artificial intelligence
GENEALOGY

FORTRAN   IPL   Lambda Calculus   (Smalltalk)

LISP

Logo

Year: 1959

Author: John McCarthy (MIT)

Impetus: neither FORTRAN nor precursors to ALGOL were able to handle list processing easily

Evolution: for the first two decades, LISP was only used by a small number of AI programmers;
considerable development of dialects in universities and industry;
sharp rise in interest in LISP in recent years with developments in AI (especially expert systems)

(Continued)

LISP (Continued)

VERSIONS/DIALECTS

Original Standard: LISP 1.5
Potential New Standard: COMMON LISP

Others:		
MACLISP	ZETALISP	P LISP
Franz LISP	INTERLISP	Q LISP
UCI LISP	GLISP	Mu LISP
SCHEME		

SPECIAL CHARACTERISTICS

Memory Requirements: large (programming is memory-intensive)

Ease of Learning/Use: not difficult in principle, but recursive programming can be confusing; until recently, part of the problem was lack of clear textbooks

Availability: available on mainframes, minicomputers, and is resident on some special-purpose machines (e.g. LISP Machine, Symbolics, Tektronix); full implementations becoming available on microcomputers with large amounts of memory

WHY LISP?

LISP and Artificial Intelligence

LISP is a language born of personal and immediate necessity. Much as FORTRAN (LISP's only slightly older brother) was created by John Backus to process numerical information using formulas of the sorts familiar to scientists and engineers, John McCarthy designed LISP to process symbols in a way recognizable to speakers of human language. Both McCarthy and Backus were intent upon raising computer programming to a greater level of sophistication (and general comprehensibility) than that offered by assembly language.

The emergence of LISP is inseparable from the development of what then seemed to be a contradiction in terms: artificial intelligence. For millennia, most of us have assumed that intelligence is a property of human beings alone or, by extension, of a few kindred creatures in the animal kingdom. Proposals that we might create machines that think have been the stuff that mythology or science fiction is made of.

The enormous memory capacity and computational abilities of the computer provided an obvious motivation for reopening the discussion of whether intelligent machines were possible. Whatever its other properties may be, human intelligence entails both memory and the ability to manipulate information.

The first "artificial intelligence" meeting took place in the summer of 1956 at Dartmouth (the school later to become well known for the development of BASIC). McCarthy, a professor at Dartmouth, began worrying about the inadequacies of existing algorithmic languages (such as FORTRAN and several others then in prototype) for handling symbols of the sort used in natural language. If the computer was to produce the sorts of manipulations that the human brain does, it would have to encode words (which, in turn, encode concepts). In the mid-1950s, FORTRAN and the like were strictly oriented to numbers.

McCarthy worked at the problem for the next two years. The real breakthrough came after he moved to MIT in 1958, where he and Marvin Minsky started an Artificial Intelligence Project. It was between 1958 and 1962 that McCarthy and his colleagues developed the first versions of LISP and began applying them to AI problems.

The Making of LISP

LISP is like an old-fashioned stew. Most (but not all) of its ingredients are recognizable. Over time, its flavor changes. New ingredients get added, and the identity of the original ingredients begins to fade.

The first established version of LISP, LISP 1.5, drew upon three sources of inspiration (which complemented McCarthy's own sizable contributions). These were FORTRAN, IPL (*I*nformation *P*rocessing *L*anguage), and a mathematical notation known as the lambda calculus.

From FORTRAN, McCarthy derived the model of using an algebraic syntax for processing symbols. In fact, there was a project at IBM in the late 1950s to develop an extension of FORTRAN called FLPL (*F*ORTRAN *L*ist *P*rocessing *L*anguage) that would manipulate lists of symbols.

IPL was actually a family of languages developed by Newell, Simon, and Shaw at Carnegie-Mellon for doing symbol manipulation. The problem with the IPL system was twofold. To begin with, it only ran on the RAND Corporation's JOHNNIAC computer, and McCarthy was to be working on an IBM 704. Equally importantly, IPL was a version of assembly language and lacked FORTRAN's ability to write programs algebraically.

The third borrowed ingredient came from the work of Alonzo Church, McCarthy's thesis adviser in mathematics at Princeton. McCarthy adopted Church's lambda (λ) notation for defining functions. The details of Church's work are not relevant here (McCarthy himself admits he didn't understand the rest of the book from which he took the notation). Suffice it to say that the mysterious lambda in LISP does have a known etiology.

McCarthy himself was to introduce the other critical ingredients that go into the making of LISP. These include the use of lists to represent information, a heavy dependence upon recursion (functions calling other copies of themselves), the representation of programs as data, and the creation of garbage collection to round up and recycle unused memory locations.

THINKING IN LISP

List Processing and AI

We have said that LISP was created to do AI programming. AI programming takes as its basic units symbols that represent either words in human language or the ideas that we use language to represent. In other words, AI programming seeks to represent what we know, and what we say about what we know.

Given the goals of AI, an AI language needs to be able to represent elements of knowledge, the properties of those elements, and the relationships between properties and elements. If we are talking about means of transportation, we may need to distinguish between self-locomotion (walking), animal locomotion (horses, camels, elephants), or mechanical locomotion (planes and buses and trains). We may cross-classify means of transportation by speed, price, and degree of comfort. From a contemporary perspective, this scheme looks much like a data base management system. And in fact, LISP is an excellent language for designing expert systems which are, in a sense, intelligent data base management systems.

LISP represents information in the form of lists. The list is the only data structure in LISP. As a result, LISP seems conceptually well suited for representing information that naturally comes laundry-list fashion. Transportation can be effected through self-locomotion, animal locomotion, or mechanical locomotion. Mechanical locomotion can be effected by planes, buses, or trains. Countries may have the properties of size, population, language, and climate, and soft drinks may have the properties small, medium, or large. Yet LISP also uses lists for representing information that normally has internal structure, such as natural language. The sentence "Where are the snows of yesteryear?" will be represented in LISP as a list of words: *where, are, the, snows, of, yesteryear.*

Notational Peculiarities

While the conceptual structure of LISP largely follows from concerns with AI programming, some of the terminology used in actual LISP programming still reflects the early hardware on which the language was first implemented. The clearest sign of anachronism is in the terms CAR and CDR, which are the primary means of manipulating symbols in LISP. The architecture of the IBM 704 (on which LISP originally ran) divided information into an address part, a decrement part, a prefix part, and a tag part. CAR refers to the "*Contents of the Address part of Register number,*" while CDR stands for "*Contents of the Decrement part of Register number.*"

Another note on hardware helps explain some apparent inconsistencies in the use of capitalization in LISP. The early computers had only uppercase letters, and everything—from language primitives to new data—was entered in capital letters. Now that contemporary machines have both uppercase and lowercase characters, some LISP systems (and programmers) have shifted *all* characters to lowercase (e.g. car, cdr), while others retain uppercase. The two notations are equivalent.

LISP as a Functional Language

To understand how LISP actually works, we first need to understand what is meant by a *functional* language. The notion of "function" in LISP comes from the notion of "function" in mathematics. In mathematics, a function is a way of relating elements of one set (the domain) to elements from another (the range). A function for finding the cube of a number associates x with x^3, i.e. cube $(x) = x^3$. Similarly, LISP has a function for cubing numbers, written

(CUBE X)

LISP programming is done by creating and evaluating functions. Whenever you run a program in LISP, you *read* information, *evaluate* it, and *print* the result. In most cases, you proceed through this read-eval-print cycle not once but many times, since functions in LISP are recursively defined: the value of one function depends upon the value of a previously evaluated function, and so on. In a moment we'll see how all this works.

The LISP language itself comes with about 200–300 functions already built in (depending upon which dialect—or implementation—you are using). It is up to the programmer to use these functions to create new ones. These new functions become indistinguishable from the ones initially defined. LISP, then, is a highly *extensible* language.

LISP programmers have been known to profess that LISP is the most extensible of computer languages. Such a statement overlooks, of course, the equally unlimited extensibility of languages like PROLOG and FORTH and Smalltalk. FORTH, for example, comes with only about 150 basic units called *words*. In the act of programming, the user creates new words out of these initial words, and then yet newer words out of the new words. In much the same way, the Smalltalk programmer is given an initial set of objects out of which can be created new, user-defined objects. As in the case of user-defined functions in LISP, user-defined words in FORTH or objects in Smalltalk are indistinguishable from the basic words or objects with which the system comes.

A final point to understand about functions in LISP is that functions are used to express both data and programs. Data are expressed as functions that bind values to variables, and programs are functions that define, manipulate, and evaluate. This all-encompassing role of functions in LISP is much like the all-encompassing role of objects in Smalltalk or clauses in PROLOG. From the perspective of the LISP translator, a LISP program is simply another data structure, since both data and program are expressed using the same syntactic structure: the list.

Basic LISP Building Blocks: Atom, List, S-Expression, Function, Argument

We have already begun using some LISP terms (*function* and *list*) without saying what they mean. Because almost everything in LISP is a function, and all the system-defined functions have names, there is a wealth of terminology we could introduce in talking about LISP. However, to keep things manageable, we'll restrict ourselves in this section to discussing the basic elements out of which all functions are built. In the next section, we'll look at a few of the important functions for doing real work in LISP.

The minimum, indivisible unit in LISP is the *atom*. Atoms are symbols— like X or *elephant*—that stand for something else. It is important to distinguish between these indivisible symbols and character strings (e.g. *e-l-e-p-h-a-n-t*) of the sort that Pascal might deal with. The LISP atom *elephant* is no more decomposable than the atom X.

Atoms, in turn, are used to build *lists*. Lists are nothing more than sequences of objects that are demarcated by a pair of parentheses. A list can contain a single atom, a collection of atoms, or a collection of lists, e.g.

> (elephant)
> (large white elephant)
> (large white elephant (standing in the corner))

One more term is used to refer to these basic LISP building blocks. *S-expression* (for *symbolic expression*) is a cover term for talking about both atoms and lists.

It is easy to confuse the meanings of the terms *atom*, *list*, and *s-expression*. A simple diagram illustrates how the use of these three terms overlaps:

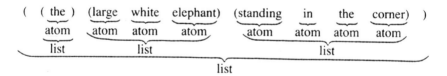

Everything that is an atom or a list is also an s-expression.

Atoms, lists, and s-expressions are used to make up functions. A *function*, as we saw, is an instruction to carry out some operation upon some entity (or entities) known as an *argument* (or arguments). As in mathematics, LISP functions are composed of a function name, followed by one or more arguments, i.e.

$$\underbrace{\text{function-name} \quad (\text{argument}_1 \quad \text{argument}_2 \quad \ldots \quad \text{argument}_n \quad)}_{\text{function}}$$

When confronted with a list of elements, the LISP translator always assumes that the first element is the name of the function, and subsequent elements are arguments. For example, given the function (and list (composed of atoms) and s-expression)

$$(\ \underbrace{\text{PLUS}}_{\substack{\text{function} \\ \text{name}}}\ \underbrace{5}_{A_1}\ \underbrace{3}_{A_2}\ )\qquad A\ =\ \text{argument}$$

LISP takes PLUS to be the function that operates upon the two arguments 5 and 3. The function PLUS evaluates the arguments and returns the value 8.

Sample LISP Functions

It should now be obvious that programming in LISP consists entirely of defining functions and evaluating them. Much of the power of LISP comes in the sophistication of its built-in functions and the unlimited range of new functions that can be defined.

Dialects of LISP differ from one another in their built-in functions, as well as in the names given to those functions. However, certain kinds of functions are common to all versions of LISP. While we cannot look at all of them, we will survey some of the most important.

(1) Functions for Binding Values to Variables: SETQ

Every computer language needs some way of specifying the actual value that a variable takes. In many languages, this is done with an assigment statement of the sort

LET   X = 25

LISP speaks, instead, of binding values to variables, and accomplishes binding by means of the SETQ (= *set q*uote) function. LISP's version of the above assignment statement would be

(SETQ   X   25)

where X is the variable and 25 the value assigned to it. The value 25 is bound to the variable X, much as the value of (PLUS 5 3) in

(SETQ X (PLUS 5   3))

is first evaluated (by the PLUS function) to 8 and then bound to the variable X by the SETQ function.

SETQ can also be used to bind values to variables where the values are "quoted," meaning that they always evaluate to themselves (hence, the name *set quote*). The idea of quoting in LISP is similar to quoting in imperative/ algorithmic languages, where the contents enclosed in quotation marks don't get evaluated. In BASIC, for example, if we have a string variable A$ that is given the value 5 + 2, i.e.

LET A$ = "5 + 2"

the value of A$ is literally 5 + 2, not 7. Similarly, in LISP, if we have the function

(SETQ X '(PLUS 5   3))

the value bound to X is PLUS 5 3, not 8. Quotation in LISP is indicated with a single apostrophe preceding the quoted element (which could be an atom or a list).

(2)   Functions for Defining Functions: DEFUN

In order for LISP to be extensible, it needs ways of defining new functions. There are several methods available. Choosing among them is sometimes a matter of personal programming style, sometimes a function of LISP dialect, and sometimes determined by simplicity considerations. Functions used to define new functions include DEFUN, LAMBDA (borrowed from Alonzo Church's lambda calculus), PUTD, and DEF. Since their basic purpose is the same (despite difference in detail), we'll illustrate how defining functions work with the function DEFUN.

The function DEFUN (= *de*fine a *fun*ction) is composed of three or four elements:

> DEFUN
> the name of the new function
> the argument(s) of the new function
> > (the arguments act as variables)

and sometimes

> the instruction for how the argument(s) will be used

A function to define a new function CUBED would look like this:

(DEFUN CUBED (X) (TIMES XXX))

The new function CUBED has one argument, X. The function CUBED is defined as a result of multiplying X times X times X.

Some defining functions have no instructions on how the arguments will be used. For example, we might define a function GROCERIES in which the arguments are categories on a grocery list:

(DEFUN GROCERIES (DAIRY PRODUCE CANNED-GOODS MEAT))

GROCERIES is the new function, taking four arguments (DAIRY, PRODUCE, CANNED-GOODS, MEAT).

(3)   Functions for Manipulating Lists: CAR, CDR

Since LISP programs are composed of lists, it is necessary to have some way of manipulating the list elements: selecting some elements (and ignoring others), changing the ordering of elements in the list, adding or deleting elements from the list, and so on. The two most common means of manipulating lists are (1) to select out the first element (the *head* of a list) and discard the rest and (2) to select everything *but* the first element of a list (the *tail* of the list) and disregard the first element. The names of the functions that accomplish these selections are CAR and CDR, respectively. As we said earlier, these names derive from the computer hardware on which LISP was originally implemented.

Consider a list such as

(the cat spied a rat)

If we take the CAR of this list, i.e.

(CAR (the cat spied a rat))

the value of the function that is returned is

the

Taking the CDR of the same original list, i.e.

(CDR (the cat spied a rat))

we get

(cat spied a rat)

CAR and CDR functions can be combined together, yielding unpronounceable functions like CADDR, i.e. a function that takes the CAR of the CDR of the CDR of a list of arguments. The CADDR of

(the cat spied a rat)

would be

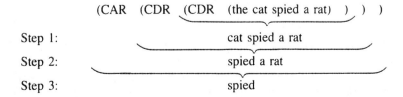

(CAR   (CDR   (CDR   (the cat spied a rat)   )   )   )

Step 1:   cat spied a rat

Step 2:   spied a rat

Step 3:   spied

(4)   Recursion

One of the most important means of constructing functions in LISP is with recursion. A recursive function is one which calls itself, that is, which has the function itself embedded within a larger function by the same name. By defining a function within a function of the same name, programmers can construct dynamic functions which change according to the changing value of the inner function.

The idea of recursion itself is quite simple and not restricted to computer programming. Think of the song "The Twelve Days of Christmas":

> On the first day of Christmas my true love gave to me
> A partridge in a pear tree.
> On the second day of Christmas my true love gave to me
> Two turtle doves
> And a partridge in a pear tree.
> On the third day of Christmas my true love gave to me
> Three French hens
> Two turtle doves
> And a partridge in a pear tree.
> (and so on)

Each day's gift is made up of two parts: something new plus what was given the day before. That is,

> first day: gift $= a$
> second day: gift $= b + a$
> third day: gift $= c + (b + a)$
> fourth day: gift $= d + (c + (b + a))$
> . . .

Recursion in LISP works much the same way. The value of the outer function (gift) is determined by the value of the inner function, which sometimes is a, sometimes is $b + a$, sometimes is $c + (b + a)$, and sometimes is $d + (c + (b + a))$. In the case of "The Twelve Days of Christmas," the value of the inner gift is changed by the rule "new gift for the day plus all previous gifts." In the case of LISP, other functions are used for altering the value of the inner list. One of the most common functions used for this purpose is CDR, which, as we just saw, returns the previous list minus its first element. In the example of "The Twelve Days of Christmas," it's as if we started on the first day with all twelve gifts, and each day eliminated the first one from the list.

Suppose we have a list of numbers and want to know if any of the numbers is even. We might adopt one of two strategies in making the determination. One possibility would be to go through the list one number at a time, asking whether the first, then the second, then the third (and so on) number is even. Alternatively, we might automate the process by asking the question recursively. We begin by asking if the first number of the list is even. If it is not, we then take the CDR of the original list, which leaves us with a new first number on the list. At this point we can ask precisely the same question that we did originally: Is the first number even? If the first number still isn't even, we take the CDR again and once more ask our original question: Is the first number even? The advantage of the recursive approach over the linear brute-force approach is that we don't have to keep track of which number in the list we are testing for "evenness." With the recursive solution, we are always testing the first number.

The LISP function for testing whether there is an even number in a list would look like this (we have added line numbers, which are *not* part of LISP, to facilitate discussion):

```
1    (DEFUN ANYEVENNUM (X)
2        (COND ((NULL X) NIL)
3            ((EVENNUM (CAR X)) T)
4            (T (ANYEVENNUM (CDR X)))))
```

Line 1 says that we are defining a function called ANYEVENNUM, which takes one argument, X. Line 2 specifies that if the list of numbers is nil (i.e. if the list has no numbers), we can conclude that the list has no even numbers. Line 3 looks at what happens if the list does have numbers in it. Specifically, it says that if the first item on the list (the CAR of the list) is even, then the function will return the value "True." If the first item on the list isn't even, the function defaults to line 4 of the program. Line 4 then invokes the original function ANYEVENNUM all over again by taking the CDR of the list X. The effect of taking the CDR of X is to make what used to be the second element of the list into the first element of the list. At this point the function goes back to test the condition statement in line 2. The continuous cycling from line 2 to 3 to 4 back to line 2 repeats until either you run out of elements in the list (i.e. the list X is null) or the first item on a list is an even number (the CAR of the list is even).

(5)   Other LISP Functions

LISP has numerous functions that allow it to perform the same kinds of operations we are used to finding in imperative/algorithmic languages. These include functions for doing arithmetic evaluation, functions for joining lists together, or functions for taking the intersections of sets. LISP has input/output functions, conditional functions, and functions that allow you to create loops, assignment statements, and even GOTO structures. However, what differentiates LISP from its imperative/algorithmic counterparts is that all of these programming activities are accomplished through *one* basic piece of syntax: the evaluation of functions. LISP uses functions for practically all the separate categories of data formatting, data manipulation, and input/output that typically require distinct syntactic constructions in imperative/algorithmic languages.

THE EVOLUTION OF LISP

Interest in LISP began very slowly in the 1960s. Artificial intelligence was a new field with few practitioners and few computers on which to run programs. The first "standard" version of the language, LISP 1.5, only had 100–150 primitives and used punched cards in batch mode. With the subsequent development of time sharing, LISP became one of the first languages to run on time sharing and run interactively. While most LISP implementations continue to run interactively, some recent implementations have returned to compilers to increase running speed.

Three factors—highly individual programming styles, considerable diversity in programming needs, and similar diversity in machines used for implementation—led to the emergence of a variety of LISP dialects. The two major dialects, MACLISP and INTERLISP, both developed out of Massachusetts research organizations. MACLISP was created as part of MIT's Project MAC, a major endeavor in the 1960s to explore the relationship between *man* and *computer*. (The "MAC" in MACLISP has nothing to do with Apple's Macintosh, a machine that postdates MACLISP by nearly twenty years.) The second major dialect of LISP, INTERLISP, was developed at Bolt, Beranek, and Newman (BBN), a research firm working on human language and computers. It was BBN that also developed the prototype for Logo.

Later diversification continued to develop at research centers involved in AI programming. Out of MACLISP, several new dialects emerged: Franz LISP (at the University of California at Berkeley), LISP 1.6 (at Stanford), which evolved into UCI LISP (at the University of California at Irvine), SCHEME (at Indiana University and MIT), and ZETALISP (used by LISP Machine, Inc., and Symbolics). Meanwhile, Xerox PARC (Palo Alto Research Center) adopted and modified INTERLISP. And so the LISP family tree looked something like this:

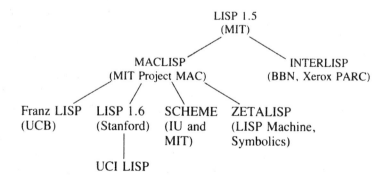

In recent years the number of dialects has continued to multiply as LISP has been implemented on additional machines (including microcomputers) and as the number of AI researchers continues to grow. Some of these additional dialects are:

SPICE LISP
P LISP
Q LISP
Mu LISP
GLISP
UTI LISP
Standard LISP
Portable Standard LISP

The community of LISP users has, in many ways, been unique in the programming world. In the areas of business and science and engineering, programming is typically a *public* activity. Programs are written to be used not only by oneself but by others. The same program is maintained over years and even decades. It therefore becomes very important for programming conventions in languages like FORTRAN or Ada or COBOL to be clearly established and formally shared. Private programming dialects or idiolects (that is, dialects used by a single person) are unthinkable in large data-processing departments or in the Pentagon.

The situation among LISP programmers is radically different. LISP programming has been a *private* activity. Most AI researchers using LISP work on their own projects and write their own programs. The programs are often used only once, and sometimes read only by the programmer who wrote them. Linguistically, there has been no pressure to conform to a standard LISP. Given the inherent extensibility of the basic language itself, it is not surprising that so many dialects (not to mention idiolects) emerged from such a small number of users over such a short period of time.

Another way in which the LISP community has been unique is in the development of its own hardware. The typical computer language is actually a *program* that runs as software on a general-purpose computer that can run many other languages as well. A VAX 11/780 can run FORTRAN *and* Pascal *and* BASIC *and* C . . ., as can an IBM PC or an Apple IIe. The purpose of the program is to translate the lines of code written by the programmer (source code) into another sort of coding (object code) that the machine hardware can "understand." This translation is typically made into the assembly language keyed to the machine's microprocessor. It is also possible to burn the language translator program into a ROM chip, thereby making it part of the hardware. This is commonly done in the case of BASIC.

For LISP, the integration of programming language and computer hardware has gone one step further. So-called LISP machines have been built in which the language translator is incorporated into the very wiring of the machine itself. The circuitry is specially optimized for doing the operations that LISP object code calls for. The method via which this is done is called *microcoding*.

LISP machines are now commercially manufactured by several companies, including LISP Machine, Inc., Xerox, Symbolics, Texas Instruments, and most recently Tektronix. To repeat, these machines are specially built for running

LISP (although other AI languages such as PROLOG and Smalltalk are now beginning to appear on these machines as well). No computer was ever built for the express purpose of running a single imperative/algorithmic language. However, the precedence set by LISP for a special-purpose machine has since been followed by at least one FORTH machine and a new PROLOG machine built by the Japanese fifth-generation project.

Interest in AI and LISP programming has mushroomed over the past few years. As the number of programmers—and the life of programs—has increased, so too has the need for greater language standardization. A new development in the LISP world has been the creation of COMMON LISP by a diverse group of AI researchers representing both universities and private industry. COMMON LISP, as the name implies, is intended as a unified, machine-independent standard to be adopted throughout the LISP community. The language is mainly influenced by ZETALISP, but also draws heavily from SCHEME and INTER-LISP.

Already, COMMON LISP is gaining strong acceptance. In the world of hardware, it has been implemented on supercomputers as S-1 LISP and on commercial time-sharing computers as NIL. Of more relevance to most readers, a subset of COMMON LISP known as Golden COMMON LISP will run on the IBM PC. And in the world of print, Patrick Winston and Berthold Horn, authors of the best-known book on LISP, have used the COMMON LISP dialect for the new second edition of their book.

THE FUTURE OF LISP

The Democratization of AI

Twenty years ago, computers were machines that took up entire rooms and cost hundreds of thousands of dollars. Today, microchips control everything from hand-held electronic backgammon sets to control panels in automotive dashboards, and are within the personal financial reach of nearly everyone.

The world of AI is undergoing a similar democratization. Once the language of an esoteric (and incomprehensible) few, LISP is gaining popularity among the general populace at an astounding rate. The public is clamoring to learn means to intelligently organize information. Just recently, this demand for training and hardware is beginning to be met. Articles, seminars, and new (and readable) textbooks are now appearing. New software for 16-bit microcomputers allows users to write sophisticated programs in COMMON LISP or to construct their own expert systems. It is possible that market forces will lead to further changes in the LISP language itself, making it more comprehensible to novices.

The Language Challenge: PROLOG and Ada

Yet LISP, of course, is not the only available language in which to do AI programming. Steady development and growing use of PROLOG in Europe and now in Japan have begun to influence the once "LISP only" American AI community. Occasional articles in the popular press, a few university courses, a new Tektronix microcomputer running PROLOG, and even new versions of PROLOG for Macintoshes and the IBM PC have begun to suggest that PROLOG is a possible alternative to LISP.

A second, though more circumscribed, challenge is coming from Ada. Sponsored by the U.S. Department of Defense, Ada was designed to be a new standard language for use in embedded systems. As of January 1, 1984, all new projects sponsored by the U.S. Department of Defense (DoD) that are "mission-critical" must be programmed in Ada.

The preponderance of American AI research is sponsored by the DoD. How will the new edict affect the programming habits of a community that remains committed to LISP? Many AI researchers dismiss the problem outright: either their work won't be viewed as mission-critical or the DoD will be counted upon to make an exception in their case.

The problem, of course, is that we can't always predict the uses to which basic research will be put. AI research on natural language processing or visual discrimination—now being programmed in LISP—could well find its way into the control panel of a Navy fighter-bomber or into an Army walking machine. The next few years will tell whether a real conflict between Ada and LISP will develop.

USING LISP

Buying LISP

Until recently, most LISP programming was done on time-sharing supermini-computers such as the VAX 11/780 or LISP machines. The cost of such hardware prohibited many people from having access to LISP. While there were implementations of LISP available on 8-bit micros (e.g. P LISP, Q LISP), the machines were not powerful enough to support the full range of LISP functions or to cope with the heavy memory requirements of running even moderate-sized programs.

This situation has now begun to change. Gold Hill Computers' Golden COMMON LISP runs on the IBM PC and provides a fairly substantial subset of COMMON LISP. The new Tektronix AI workstation provides Franz LISP for under $15,000 (a fraction of the cost of a traditional LISP machine). Moreover, with the current development of 32-bit microprocessors such as the Motorola 68020, we can reasonably look forward to full implementations of LISP available on micros in the near future.

What to Read

BOOKS

Touretzky, David (1984). *LISP: A Gentle Introduction to Symbolic Computation.* New York: Harper & Row.

As the subtitle says, a gentle (and clear) introduction to LISP. Makes no presuppositions about prior programming experience. Complete with exercises and answers. Based on MACLISP and COMMON LISP.

Wilensky, Robert (1984). *LISPcraft*. New York: W. W. Norton.
Another excellent introduction to LISP, but no answers to exercises. Based on Franz LISP.

Winston, Patrick H., and Berthold K. P. Horn (1984). *LISP*. 2nd edition. Reading (Mass.): Addison-Wesley.
For several years, the first edition of this book (1981) was the only widely available introduction to LISP. While the second edition (1984) is more readable than the first, it continues to presuppose a background in computers that the books by Touretzky and Wilensky do not. Contains exercises and answers. The first edition is based on MACLISP, while the second is based on COMMON LISP.

Steele, Guy L., Jr. (1984). *Common LISP: The Language*. Burlington (Mass.): Digital Press.
The complete reference guide to COMMON LISP.

ARTICLES

Hasemer, Tony (1984). "An Introduction to LISP," in Tim O'Shea and Marc Eisenstadt, eds., *Artificial Intelligence: Tools, Techniques, and Applications*. New York: Harper & Row, pp. 22–62.
An especially clear, brief overview of LISP.

Byte, August 1979.
A special issue of *Byte*, devoted in large part to LISP. The articles are fairly technical.

Logo

PROFILE
NAME
derived from Greek word *logos*, meaning "word" or "thought"
STRUCTURE

Familiar Distinctions:
  hardware: high-level
  translator: interpreted
  structural unit: procedure
  data: symbolic and graphic (contains graphics package using turtle)
 	
Conceptual Distinctions:
  organizing principle: functional/applicative
  procedures: procedural
  extensibility: extensible
  program/data: not distinct

FUNCTIONS
education (teaching thinking and geometry in particular) general-purpose potential (though rarely used as general-purpose language)
GENEALOGY
  Years: 1966–68 Authors: Seymour Papert (with Dan Bobrow, Wallace Feurzeig, Richard Grant, Cynthia Solomon, Frank Frazier, and Paul Wexelblat) (Bolt, Beranek, and Newman) Impetus: provide children with powerful language to encourage cognitive exploration and development (especially in geometry) Evolution: influence of Jean Piaget on Seymour Papert   1970s to date: refinement and testing out of MIT; worldwide use with children

(Continued)

239

Logo (Continued)

VERSIONS/DIALECTS
Standard: none
Dialects: e.g.   DR Logo   LOGO Computer Systems, Inc. CyberLOGO   Terrapin Logo TI Logo   TLC Logo

SPECIAL CHARACTERISTICS
Memory Requirements: small (48–64K)
Ease of Learning/Use: simple
Availability: readily available for most microcomputers

NOTE: Before reading this entry, read the entry on LISP.

WHY LOGO?

What distinguishes children from adults? Sometimes the criterion is age (e.g. ''over 21''). Other times it is the biological ability to procreate, or the fact of living in a separate household or being self-sufficient. But whatever the cutoff point, childhood is seen as a time for *learning*. Adults are expected to *use* what they have learned.

Half a dozen computer languages have expressly been designed to *teach* (as opposed to *use*) computer programming. BASIC, for example, was devised for teaching the principles of programming, while FORTRAN was intended for doing mathematical calculations. (Flight simulators are made for training pilots to fly airplanes, while airplanes are designed to be flown.) A ''doing'' language can be used for teaching, but often not as effectively.

In Chapter 3, we talked about six computer languages that were created for the purpose of teaching:

> BASIC
> Pascal
> COMAL
>
> Logo
> Smalltalk
> micro-PROLOG

The first three are imperative/algorithmic languages. Logo is a functional/ applicative language, Smalltalk is an object-oriented language, and micro-PROLOG is a logic programming language. The first three languages were essentially designed to teach programming techniques, while the last three were created to teach children to think by *using* computers and programming.

Why talk about all six languages in a discussion of Logo? Because of presuppositions made by the computing public. When most people think about using computer languages with children, two languages come to mind: BASIC and Logo. Some argue that Logo is a "better" language for children, while others favor BASIC. Curiously, neither side generally knows very much about the broader spectrum of programming languages of which BASIC and Logo are part. What's more, such debates tend to overlook other viable candidates (e.g. COMAL or micro-PROLOG) for the educational enterprise.

And so our discussion of Logo will be a discussion in context. We will look at the conceptual underpinnings of Logo, see how Logo works, and compare it with BASIC. At the same time, though, we will consider the other options that exist—and are coming to exist—for computer languages designed for pedagogy.

Computers and Pedagogy: What Is to Be Learned?

We teach children to read and write so they may decipher income tax forms, send letters to their grandmothers, and fathom Shakespeare. We instruct them in arithmetic so they may figure their taxes and balance their checkbooks. But why do we want them to learn computer languages?

Three rationales are commonly offered. The first (and most general) is the appeal to computer literacy: our world is increasingly populated with computers, and everyone should know something about them. The second argument is that of self-perpetuation: if we want a next generation of programmers, we need to teach people programming. And finally, there is the more abstract pedagogical argument that sometimes goes by the label "teaching thinking": the purpose of education is not to impart specific information, but to teach children *how* to learn. A computer language may (or so it is argued) aid children in the meta-learning process.

Historically, the imperative/algorithmic languages (e.g. BASIC, Pascal) have been used for the first two purposes (computer literacy and beginning programming). The last three languages (Logo, Smalltalk, and micro-PROLOG) were all invented with the explicit purpose of teaching children how to think, although the notion of what constitutes "thinking" differs in each case. (This is not to say that "thinking" is the only function these three languages have. In our discussion of Logo, we'll see that the language has some very pragmatic applications in the workaday programming world. The sections on Smalltalk and micro-PROLOG reveal similar diversity of function.)

To understand the Logo notion of "teaching thinking," we need to look at the pedagogical preoccupations of Logo's primary inventor and spokesman. We also need to be aware of the linguistic sausage skin into which he stuffed his educational visions.

Piaget, Papert, and Plane Geometry

The fact that Logo is so well known today is due to the energies and unflagging commitment of Seymour Papert, a mathematician and educator at the Massachusetts Institute of Technology. But the motivation behind the language and the particular area of thinking it emphasizes are equally due to the ideas of the Swiss developmental psychologist Jean Piaget.

Piaget's work has had a profound effect upon the way twentieth-century psychologists think about children's cognitive development. Piaget was interested in how children learn to comprehend and act successfully upon their physical and intellectual environments. A central notion in his model of intellectual development is that of *stages*. In the normal course of growing up, children pass through a series of cognitive stages in which what is being learned becomes progressively more abstract. In the early stages, children come to know their environment by acting upon it physically, manipulating objects, seeing things disappear and reappear, pouring liquids from squat jars into tall thin jars, and understanding that different shapes may bear the same contents.

Piaget argued that children find it more difficult to manipulate abstractions (such as found in arithmetic and geometry). Hence, children learn mathematics later in life. For unlike a ball that rolls behind a table or a liquid that is poured from a milk carton into a cake pan, abstract mathematical objects can't be physically manipulated. We can draw a picture of a square, but first we have to know something about pictorial representation and equality of sides. If we want to draw shapes only a little more complex (like a five-pointed star or a square within a hexagon), we need to know about Cartesian coordinates and angles and axes—hardly the stuff of which elementary education is normally composed.

Papert spent several years with Piaget, studying the normal stages of cognitive development. Papert reasoned that if it were possible to devise a physical equivalent of mathematical abstractions (that is, to make abstractions more like balls that can be rolled or liquids that can be poured), children should be able to master subjects like geometry much more easily. What was once abstract would become concrete. The normal stages of cognitive development could be accelerated because even young children can handle concrete information. Equally importantly, talking about numbers and shapes (necessary skills in algebra and geometry) might not be so intimidating to children if they could manipulate such numbers and shapes themselves, rather than merely performing for the benefit of a classroom teacher. "Math anxiety" might be curbed, and children might go from being uncomprehending mathematics imitators to intellectually independent manipulators of mathematical relationships. These relationships might not be new to the world of mathematics, but the fact they were new to the children creating them would make the children more independent and powerful thinkers.

Papert tells us that, as a child, he envisioned geometry quite concretely. In his research on cognitive development, the natural step was to ask whether computers (and computer languages) could be used to make geometry equally concrete for contemporary children. Papert's solution was to create a new computer language that combined, on the one hand, the underlying syntax of an existing language and, on the other hand, English-like commands and a powerful tool for producing geometric figures. The new language was Logo, and the graphics tool was known as turtle geometry or turtle graphics.

THINKING IN LOGO

Syntactically, Logo is essentially a scaled-down, user-friendly version of LISP. We can quickly get a basic sense of how Logo works by making a point-by-point comparison of the two languages.

Basic Logo Building Blocks: Number, Word, List, Procedure

Both LISP and Logo are constructed from a few basic building blocks out of which all programming is eventually done. Here are the basic correspondences between LISP and Logo:

ITEM	LISP	Logo
minimal unit	atom	number, word
units of manipulation	list	word list
means of manipulation	function	procedure

In LISP the minimal, indivisible unit is the *atom*, which is any individual letter (or number) or any string of alphanumeric characters. Atoms, in turn, are used for building *lists*. Both atoms and lists are referred to as *s-expressions* (or *symbolic expressions*).

Building blocks in Logo are quite similar. The minimal unit in Logo is either the *number* or the *word*. The meaning of *number* is self-evident: a number is a representation like 65 or −55.29. Words are a bit more involved. They are a cross between a LISP atom and a LISP list. Like a LISP atom, a Logo word is a string of alphanumeric characters that is separated on either side by white space. However, Logo and LISP differ with regard to decomposition. The LISP atom is not divisible. If the string *blackberry* is an atom in LISP, it is not divisible into *black* and *berry*. In Logo, however, words *are* divisible. The elements in a Logo word can be manipulated the same way as the elements in a LISP list (using the Logo equivalents of CAR and CDR and such).

But Logo and LISP do share the same meaning of the *list* itself. A list in Logo is a sequence of words separated by blank spaces. While LISP demarcates lists with the parenthesis notation, Logo uses square brackets (though these brackets do not appear as liberally as parentheses in LISP).

Lists are used in both Logo and LISP for building the basic elements used in programming. In LISP these elements are called *functions*, while in Logo they are called *procedures*. In each case, the name itself is followed by a set of data and/or instructions on how that function/procedure is to be carried out. In LISP, for example, we might have a function PLUS followed by two arguments representing numbers to be added, e.g.

$$(\underbrace{\text{PLUS}}_{\text{function name}} \quad \underbrace{5}_{A_1} \quad \underbrace{3}_{A_2})$$

In Logo, the same computation would be represented by a procedure PLUS followed by the numbers (a technical term in Logo) to be acted upon by that function:

$$\underbrace{\text{PLUS}}_{\text{procedure name}} \quad \underbrace{5}_{N_1} \quad \underbrace{3}_{N_2}$$

In both instances, either the PLUS function/procedure could have been defined by the user (in ways we'll look at in a moment) or it could have been built in as part of the language translator.

Sample Logo Procedures: MAKE, TO, FIRST, BUTFIRST

Just as the power of LISP comes from defining and evaluating functions, Logo's creative power comes from defining and executing procedures. Since Logo is a much smaller language than LISP, it doesn't come with as many built-in procedures as does LISP. However, the essential processes necessary for defining new units, assigning values to variables, and manipulating lists are often precise equivalents of one another. In this section, we'll look at several Logo procedures (along with their LISP counterparts):

PURPOSE	LISP	Logo
bind value to variable	SETQ	MAKE
define new function	DEFUN	TO
manipulate items on list	CAR, CDR	FIRST, BUTFIRST

(1)   Procedures for Binding Values to Variables: MAKE
The Logo procedure MAKE is used to assign values to variables. This is comparable to the SETQ function in LISP, or the assignment statement in imperative/algorithmic languages like BASIC or Pascal. If we want to assign X the value 25, we would say it the following way in BASIC, LISP, and Logo:

```
BASIC:     LET X = 25
LISP:      (SETQ X 25)
Logo:      MAKE "X 25
```

(Words in Logo are printed with a leading quotation mark. Since variables are words, Logo precedes the variable name X with a quotation mark.)

(2) Procedure for Defining Procedures: TO
As extensible languages, both LISP and Logo make heavy use of their respective means of adding new primitives to the system. In LISP, this is done with a

variety of functions (e.g. DEFUN, LAMBDA, PUTD), while in Logo it is done with the single procedure TO.

Remember that the LISP function DEFUN is composed of three and sometimes four parts:

(a) DEFUN (the function-defining function)
(b) the name of the new function
(c) the argument(s) of the new function
        (the arguments act as variables)

and sometimes

(d) the instructions for how the argument(s) will be used

A new LISP function CUBED would look like this:

(DEFUN	CUBED	(X)	(TIMES XXX))
function-defining function	name of new function	argument of new function	instructions for how argument will be used

To define a new procedure in Logo, you use precisely comparable components. The only thing different is the name of the procedure used to define the new procedure (along with some cosmetic differences in syntax). Instead of being called DEFUN, it is called TO. And so the same new procedure CUBED would be defined this way in Logo:

TO	CUBE	:X	X*X*X
procedure-defining procedure	name of new procedure	argument of new procedure	instructions for how argument will be used

        END

(The "dot" notation before the variable X is used in lieu of a leading quotation mark. Defining procedures in Logo end with the word END.)

(3) Procedures for Manipulating Lists: FIRST, BUTFIRST

The list data structure (common to LISP and Logo) is tailor-made for manipulating the items on the list. In our discussion of LISP, we considered two examples of list manipulation: isolating the first item of a list and isolating all but the first item on the list. Not surprisingly, Logo has its precise equivalents of these functions (as well as equivalents of other LISP functions for manipulating lists).

The LISP function CAR selects out the first item on a list. For example, the function

    (CAR (the cat spied a rat))

evaluates to

    the

In just the same way, the Logo function FIRST selects out the first item on a list in Logo. If we want to print out the first element on the Logo list

    [the cat spied a rat]

we write

    PRINT FIRST [the cat spied a rat]

and get back the result

    the

LISP's CDR and Logo's BUTFIRST work much the same way. The LISP function

    (CDR (the cat spied a rat))

and the Logo procedure

    PRINT BUTFIRST [the cat spied a rat]

both yield

    cat spied a rat

(We ignore punctuation here.)

Turtle Geometry

So far our examples of Logo have centered on familiar sorts of data: numbers and lists of symbols. But most people who know anything about Logo think of it not as a number-processing or even a symbol-processing language, but as a graphics language. Where do the graphics come in, and how do they relate to the functions of Logo we have been looking at so far?

    We said earlier that one reason Logo is considered to be such a powerful language is its relative ease of creating complex graphic images. These images are made possible by a special graphics package called "turtle graphics" that is incorporated into the syntax of Logo (much the way that all of ALGOL 60 is incorporated into the syntax of SIMULA). The rest of the Logo language is no more tailored for doing graphics than is LISP. However, with the addition of these special graphics commands, Logo suddenly begins to look like a very different language from LISP.

Why were graphics—and specifically graphics for constructing geometric shapes—incorporated into an otherwise symbol-manipulating language (i.e. LISP)? The answer lies in Piaget's and Papert's interest in how children learn geometry. Piaget, while known as a child psychologist to most of us, was also a highly creative mathematician. His theoretical interest in mathematics spilled over into his work on children, and his writings on cognitive development include such titles as *The Child's Concept of Number* and *The Child's Concept of Geometry*. For Papert, whose background was also in mathematics, it was natural to look to geometry as a fertile intellectual laboratory for investigating whether computers could help children make concrete certain abstract ideas that they usually only learn in their teens, and often with great difficulty.

Logo's "turtle graphics" package makes geometry concrete by way of a metaphor. Imagine that the cursor on the computer screen is actually an animate creature, say a turtle. Imagine further that the turtle can be made to move around the screen. You give it instructions on what direction to move in (its *heading*), how far to go, and how fast to move. Finally, imagine that the turtle is like a snowplow that can ride along the street with its blade either raised up or lowered. If you raise the "plow" of the turtle, the turtle moves about the screen without leaving a trace. If you lower the plow, it leaves a line in its wake. (Papert and his colleagues usually speak of the turtle raising and lowering a "pen," since some versions of Logo turtles graphics were done with a separate mechanical turtle that physically raised or lowered a pen on paper. Another obvious metaphor is to speak of the turtle's "nose.")

Commands to the turtle are given within the existing structure of Logo itself. Much of the time they constitute the "instruction" part of a TO procedure, that is, the procedure used for defining procedures.

Let's say we want to create a procedure for drawing a square. To do so, we create a new procedure called SQUARE, identify its arguments (i.e. variables), and specify how those variables are to be used. The Logo procedure would look something like this:

```
TO SQUARE :LENGTH
    REPEAT 4 [FORWARD :LENGTH RIGHT 90]
END
```

We recognize TO as the name of the procedure used for defining new procedures. The new procedure to be defined is called SQUARE. SQUARE has one argument, named LENGTH. That is, in carrying out the procedure SQUARE, the value of LENGTH may vary, depending upon the particular value we bind to it.

The instructions for the new procedure are spelled out in the second line. First we are told that something (i.e. what is specified in the list within the square brackets) will be done four times. (We assume that REPEAT is a procedure whose meaning has already been defined.) The action to be carried out is specified by two headings following in sequence: first FORWARD and then RIGHT. Each heading is further specified by a dimension. When given the procedure FORWARD, the turtle is to advance the amount that is given to the variable LENGTH. When given the procedure RIGHT, the turtle is to turn right 90 degrees.

Taken together, the pieces of the new procedure SQUARE work like this: The turtle begins at a home location, which is usually the center of the screen, with its "nose" pointing upward. Before we can do anything, we need to bind a value to the variable LENGTH. Say we give it the value 80 (meaning "move 80 units' worth of distance across the screen"). The turtle responds by moving 80 units forward (i.e. straight up on the screen). Then it turns its "nose" 90 degrees to the right. The instructions call for this procedure (move 80 units, turn 90 degrees to the right) to be carried out a total of four times, i.e.

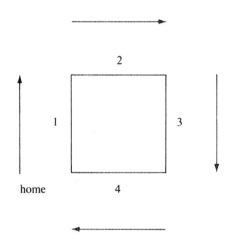

The power of turtle graphics comes from the fact that the user is free to create any kind of procedure that can be described by specifying directions and extents of movement. Procedures may repeat many times (as in the case of the square) or may be joined together with other procedures (e.g. letting you draw triangles within squares, or interesting geometric designs). You are in no way limited to the kinds of geometric shapes familiar from basic Euclidean geometry.

When most people see a Logo procedure like TO SQUARE, they think of the TO as a piece of descriptive English for drawing pictures, rather than as a formal piece of Logo syntax. But this same TO is used for defining new procedures of *any* sort—not just graphic images. Serious students of Logo often bemoan the skewed reputation that Logo has developed in the world of education. They tirelessly point out that Logo is a more general-purpose language than most people realize, and one whose utility extends not only down to kindergarten but up to college-level work.

The Logo defenders are, of course, right about Logo's power. Yet the creators of Logo are responsible for Logo's uneven reputation. When Seymour Papert writes about Logo in his book *Mindstorms* (a book that has become the ideological manifesto of the Logo movement in lower school education), he is essentially talking about the creative potential of turtle geometry, not of the parts of the Logo language that derive from LISP. If these non-graphic elements (which are, of course, still creative in that both languages are extensible) are largely overlooked by the general public, it is hardly the public's fault.

THE EVOLUTION OF LOGO

Logo was designed in the mid-1960s by a team of researchers and consultants at Bolt, Beranek, and Newman (BBN), a research firm in Cambridge, Massachusetts. In the early 1960s, BBN began pioneering computer-aided instruction systems, using the new time-sharing technology then being developed at both MIT and BBN (see the entry on BASIC).

The early projects at BBN were already geared to the teaching of mathematics. When Seymour Papert joined the group as a consultant, a new design effort was undertaken to create a language directly tailored to the needs of young children. It was decided that LISP should form the basis of the new language.

Although Logo was pilot-tested in elementary school classrooms as early as 1967, the general public didn't know much about Logo until it became available on microcomputers more than a decade later. BASIC was already becoming a standard fixture in many elementary schoc' classrooms when Logo was first introduced for the Texas Instruments 99/4 microcomputer in 1981 and then introduced for the Apple II shortly thereafter. The evolution of Logo is largely the story of Logo's challenge to BASIC.

BASIC vs. Logo: A Misguided Debate

Curiously, nearly all discussions of Logo emphasize the "creative" powers of the language and belittle its major classroom competitor, BASIC, as being too rigid. Yet there is little explanation of why Logo is supposed to allow such creativity and BASIC is supposed to stifle it. However, once we look at Logo as a functional/applicative language deriving from LISP, and compare it with BASIC as an imperative/algorithmic language deriving from FORTRAN and ALGOL, we can understand why the languages differ so much from one another.

Logo, like LISP, is an *extensible* language. Users can, therefore, create new units (called procedures in Logo, functions in LISP, words in FORTH, objects in Smalltalk) that are indistinguishable from the language's original set of primitives. There is no limit on the kinds of new units that can be created. You can devise units to write limericks, take cube roots, or draw an infinite series of concentric circles. It is not surprising to think of such a language as fostering creativity—but then so too does *any* extensible language. Since BASIC, like all imperative/algorithmic languages, is *not* extensible, it is no wonder that proponents of Logo characterize BASIC as rigid.

Logo uses its essential structural units (i.e. procedures) to divide up the programming task at hand. We saw in Chapter 3 that most computer languages today have some way of decomposing problems into pieces. Among modern imperative/algorithmic languages, Pascal uses procedures, Modula-2 uses modules, and Ada uses packages. Among other language families, LISP uses functions, Logo uses procedures, and so on. (NOTE: The term *procedure* does *not* mean the same thing in Logo as it does in Pascal.)

A language that decomposes larger problems into smaller ones is, pedagogically, preferable to languages that have no internal structuring. While Logo divides problems into subunits (procedures), the most commonly used versions of BASIC do not (although, as we saw in the entry on BASIC, contemporary versions of BASIC do tend to be structured).

Finally, there is the question of how much work it takes to get a result—especially an impressive one. One of the most impressive results you can get on a computer is a graphic design. Most computer languages have some means by which to produce graphics. However, in the earlier imperative/algorithmic languages, it took a lot of declarations and formulas and even special instructions for accessing the computer hardware to draw the most rudimentary designs. Although BASIC does have a special set of graphics commands (unlike its other imperative/algorithmic cousins), the results are hardly overwhelming. Logo, on the other hand, makes graphics not only easy but impressive.

Given the power of graphics, Logo quite naturally appears to be a far more powerful, creative language than BASIC. However, when we set Logo (and BASIC) within the spectrum of other computer languages, we need to be aware of two facts about graphics and computer languages. The first is that other computer languages exist (such as FORTH and Smalltalk) that are tailored for doing impressive graphics quite easily. And second, the special device that makes Logo graphics so impressive can be added to other languages (e.g. Pascal or PILOT) as well.

Debates over the relative virtues and vices of BASIC and Logo are really arguments about goals. If we want to teach children what common programming languages look like, then BASIC is a reasonable choice. The most frequently taught (and used) programming languages today are imperative/algorithmic, and so is BASIC. If we want children to learn how to formulate sequential instructions, then any procedural language will do, including BASIC *or* Logo. If the goal is teaching stepwise refinement of a problem, then a member of the ALGOL family (e.g. Pascal or COMAL) is preferable. If our goal is to teach children how to create new things that haven't existed before, an extensible language makes such creation comparatively easy. (It's easier to define a new idea in Logo than in BASIC.) And if we have reason to believe that graphic representation helps children think creatively, then we choose a language with a powerful graphics component. There are now several, including languages other than Logo, that incorporate turtle graphics.

THE FUTURE OF LOGO

User-Friendly Languages

As the use of computer languages expands from hobbyists and potential data processors to average citizens, computer languages are becoming increasingly transparent in their syntax. BASIC is easier to understand than FORTRAN, Logo is more English-like than LISP, and micro-PROLOG has a user front end that does away with some of the more arcane syntactic conventions of PROLOG. With the growth of query languages, it seems likely that at least some computer languages will continue this trend toward ease of use. Since Logo syntax is relatively simple to understand, Logo stands a chance of survival by the ease-of-use criterion.

Importance of Graphics

With the development of first 16-bit and now 32-bit microcomputers, it has become possible for the average person with a microcomputer to create original graphic patterns with increasingly high levels of resolution. The Apple Macintosh has further whetted the public's appetite for graphics capabilities. Computer languages that are graphically oriented—such as Logo—will have considerable advantage over languages in which graphics may be possible but are more cumbersome to create.

Non-procedural and Extensible Languages

There is a growing trend for newer computer languages (outside of the imperative/algorithmic family) to be both non-procedural and extensible. While Logo is highly extensible, it is still procedural. It remains to be seen whether its procedural character will constitute a liability in comparison with languages like Smalltalk that are (potentially) user-friendly, graphically oriented, and both non-procedural and extensible.

Artificial Intelligence (AI)

Perhaps the strongest—and least recognized—virtue of Logo is its potential for doing simple AI programming. As a direct subset of LISP, it is convenient for analyzing classes of information and the relationships between them because of its underlying list-based structure. Interest in AI and AI programming is developing at an astounding rate. Unlike LISP, Logo easily fits onto the average 8-bit machine and functions extremely comfortably on a 16-bit machine. It is quite possible that in the coming years the emphasis in Logo could shift from the teaching of geometry to children to the design of simple AI programs.

USING LOGO

Buying Logo

Because of the huge thrust to make Logo available in lower school classrooms, most computer manufacturers have at least one version of Logo. The majority of implementations require 64K memory, though smaller versions are also available (e.g. CyberLOGO, which focuses on turtle graphics rather than on the wider range of Logo procedures otherwise available).

What to Read

BOOKS

Papert, Seymour (1980). *Mindstorms: Children, Computers, and Powerful Ideas.* New York: Basic Books.
   The conceptual "bible" of Logo, in which Papert explains what Piaget's notions of cognitive development, Papert's and Piaget's thinking about geometry, and the development of computers have to do with the creation of Logo.
Abelson, Harold (1982). *Logo for the Apple II.* Peterborough (N.H.): Byte/ McGraw-Hill.
   A solid introduction to Logo, keyed to the Apple II version of the language.
Thornberg, David T. (1983). *Discovering Apple Logo: An Invitation to the Art and Pattern of Nature.* Reading (Mass.): Addison-Wesley.
   A very usable book demonstrating how to use turtle graphics to create the forms found in nature—or in the mind's eye.
Harvey, Brian (1985). *Computer Science Logo Style: Intermediate Programming.* Cambridge (Mass.): MIT Press.
   A more advanced book that explains some of Logo's sophisticated properties. Harvey presents Logo not simply as a language but as an approach to programming.
Allen, John R., Michael E. Burke, and John F. Johnson (1983). *Thinking about TLC Logo.* New York: Holt, Rinehart and Winston.
   The "TLC" stands for The LISP Company. A book filled with both slapstick and sophisticated humor. While the book appears on the surface to be meant for the utter novice, it actually contains an enormous amount of theoretical discussion of computer language issues. To the cognoscenti, the discussion can be both enlightening and provocative.
Abelson, Harold, and Andy diSessa (1981). *Turtle Geometry: The Computer as a Medium for Exploring Mathematics.* Cambridge (Mass.): MIT Press.
   The definitive book on the development and use of turtle geometry.
Tobias, Joyce, Sharon Burrowes, Jerry Short, and Tom Lough (1985). *Beyond MINDSTORMS: Teaching with IBM Logo.* New York: Holt, Rinehart and Winston.

A useful book for designing a lower-school curriculum in which Logo plays a significant role.

ARTICLES

Feurzeig, Wallace (1984). "The Logo Lineage," in Steve Ditlea, ed., *Digital Deli*. New York: Workman Publishing, pp. 158–161.
A brief but informative history of the early development of Logo and its conceptual roots in LISP.

Byte, August 1982.
Special issue on Logo.

micro-PROLOG

PROFILE
NAME
small version of PROLOG (*PRO*gramming in *LOG*ic)
STRUCTURE

Familiar Distinctions:
  hardware: high-level
  translator: interpreted
  structural unit: atomic sentence, molecular sentence
  data: no distinction between data and program
 	
Conceptual Distinctions:
  organizing principle: logic programming
  procedures: non-procedural
  extensibility: extensible
  program/data: symbolic

FUNCTIONS
education (teaching children to use first-order predicate calculus as aid to thinking) data base management artificial intelligence (especially knowledge systems involving large data bases)
GENEALOGY PROLOG | micro-PROLOG
Year: 1980
Authors: Frank McCabe, Keith Clark, Robert Kowalski, Richard Ennals
Impetus: use version of PROLOG on microcomputers as a way of teaching logic to children

(Continued)

Micro-PROLOG (Continued)

Evolution:	nearly all use of micro-PROLOG has been in England (deriving from experimental projects at Imperial College, London) now that a translator is available in the U.S., it remains to be seen how widely micro-PROLOG will be used

VERSIONS/DIALECTS

Standard:	only one dialect of micro-PROLOG is available, although it comes in versions for several microcomputers

SPECIAL CHARACTERISTICS

Memory Requirements: small (under 64K)

Ease of Learning/Use: easy

Availability: available for microcomputers in the U.K. and recently in the U.S.; can also be used as a front end on some PROLOG systems

NOTE: Before reading about micro-PROLOG, read the section on PROLOG. You will probably also want to look at the sections on Logo and Smalltalk in conjunction with this entry on micro-PROLOG.

WHY micro-PROLOG?

Several computer languages, including Logo and Smalltalk, were created to improve the education of children. Micro-PROLOG has the added distinction of having been designed to benefit the children of the language's authors. As its name suggests, micro-PROLOG is a user-friendly and somewhat scaled-down version of PROLOG.

In discussing PROLOG we observed that PROLOG is a version of logic programming, a field largely created by Robert Kowalski. We also saw that logic programming is based on the first-order predicate calculus. Both of these points are important in understanding the development of micro-PROLOG.

Kowalski, as head of the Logic Programming Unit at Imperial College in London, asked whether children of age ten or eleven could learn logic as a subject in its own right and could use logic as a means of thinking about other academic areas such as history and foreign languages. To answer the question, Kowalski began teaching logic at the local school his children were attending. Since PROLOG is a computer language based on logic, Kowalski and his colleagues at Imperial College decided to write a pared-down microcomputer version of PROLOG that children could use in the process of learning logic. The result was micro-PROLOG.

The micro-PROLOG project involved a number of people, including Frank McCabe (the primary author), Keith Clark (co-author of a text on micro-PROLOG), and Richard Ennals (author of a more general self-paced text on micro-PROLOG, as well as the person responsible for preparing and testing the original micro-PROLOG teaching materials). Since its invention in late 1980, micro-PROLOG has been used not only with schoolchildren but with college students as well.

Logic, Learning, and Language

The authors of micro-PROLOG have clearly enunciated their presuppositions about the role of logic in general pedagogy. The first supposition concerns the appropriateness of logic as a means of learning anything. Richard Ennals writes in his book *Beginning micro-PROLOG*:

> Logic can be said to provide a backbone for the various disciplines: in the past [logic] was taught through the medium of Latin and Euclidean geometry. Neither of these is now popular, and it can be argued that logic should be taught in its own right, as providing an insight into the workings of various disciplines through the representation and manipulation of knowledge. [p. 117]

When Ennals speaks of logic as a "backbone" for the various disciplines, he is talking about the "mental muscle" theory of learning, a once-popular approach to pedagogy. The thesis argues that in teaching children you must first develop their general mental ability through proper "exercise." Once they have developed their mental muscle, children can transfer general cognitive ability to more specific areas of learning. In the United States in the eighteenth and nineteenth centuries, Latin and Greek were two favorite means of "disciplining the mind." Mathematics joined the list in the nineteenth century, and logic also became a sometime candidate.

Around the turn of the twentieth century, a number of psychologists (the best known being E. L. Thorndike) began arguing that mental abilities were not transferable from one area of knowledge to another. If you wanted children to learn literature, then you had to teach them literature and not expect that what they knew about Greek or mathematics would improve their understanding of Shakespeare. One of the effects of this research was to reduce and eventually eliminate altogether Latin and Greek requirements in American colleges. Mathematics has suffered a similar fate (though it has not been entirely banished from required curricula). And logic as a formal discipline has not been a serious candidate for mental conditioning for quite some time.

Yet surely learning in one area *must* have *some* positive benefits for learning in another. If I know how to drive a car, won't the knowledge of how to control pedals, switches, and directions help me learn to fly a plane? If I have been trained as a competent detective, can't I expect my reasoning abilities to carry over if I switch professions and become a trial lawyer? And shouldn't knowing French, German, and Russian make it easier for me to learn Spanish?

The answer in each case is probably "yes," but not for any objectively provable reason. We talk a lot about the importance of "teaching people to think." However, since even cognitive psychologists don't yet claim to understand the nature of thought, we have no clear way of knowing how to *teach* thought. Latin or mathematics or French—or logic—surely can't hurt, but modern cognitive psychology has no way of concluding that it necessarily helps.

The second supposition behind micro-PROLOG concerns the value of studying logic as a way of improving one's command of the English language. Robert Kowalski, in an article, "Logic as a Computer Language for Children," states:

> It is a major objective of the [micro-PROLOG] project to teach the relationship between natural language syntax and its semantics, where as a first approximation the semantics are expressed in symbolic logic. This is thought to be an important object in its own right as a contribution to the more effective use of natural language: to teach the distinction between English sentences which are clear and precise and English sentences which are imprecise or meaningless.

Kowalski's argument about logic and language is somewhat tenuous. Kowalski is correct in saying that English, as a natural language, is laden with imprecision. In fact, since at least the middle of the seventeenth century, scholars and statesmen have been concerned about such imprecision. When the Royal Society of London was formed in the 1660s, its founding members decided that English was too imprecise a language to describe scientific phenomena, and actually created a new artificial language that was intended to eliminate all the ambiguities of natural language. This effort (like all of its successors) failed. We are still, therefore, burdened with using—and teaching—an imprecise language.

In examining Kowalski's assertion that by teaching logic we can improve children's facility with the English language, we need to be clear about what we mean by "logic." Throughout the twentieth century, formal logicians have repeatedly declared that ordinary language is *not* reducible to representation in logical notation. Some natural language constructions (especially those involving quantification and implication) do have *analogs* in logic. For example, the logical proposition

$$\exists(X) \, \forall(Y) \, X \supset Y$$

is translatable into the English "There exists an entity X such that for all entities Y, X implies Y." Yet the overwhelming majority of natural language has no equivalent in formal logic. There is no obvious way of using formal logic to say that perhaps it will snow on Mount Washington today or that the soft-shell crabs are better in Virginia than in Maryland.

Admittedly, it is common for teachers of writing or rhetoric to urge their students to be *logical* in constructing their arguments and precise in their choice of vocabulary and syntax. However, the admonition to be *logical* resides within the domain of ordinary language usage, and has no necessary connection with the technical discipline known as *logic*. Another way of looking at the distinction would be to say that the discipline of formal logic happens also to be logical.

Thus learning micro-PROLOG won't guarantee that children will be able to think "logically" (in the ordinary language sense of the term) in all work they undertake. Obviously, clear thinking in *any* domain of learning is useful. Moreover, since micro-PROLOG can be used not only to teach logic itself but to aid in the teaching of other subjects, we can eliminate the "transfer" problem entirely. And so we can think about the use of micro-PROLOG in the teaching of, say, history as a convenient tool for helping students to see logical relationships between historical events and causes. A similar argument can be made about micro-PROLOG and the study of natural language.

THINKING IN micro-PROLOG

To understand micro-PROLOG's structural makeup, we find ourselves repeatedly turning to comparison with PROLOG. First the differences.

One major distinction between PROLOG and micro-PROLOG is that micro-PROLOG is a much *smaller* language. PROLOG uses up a great deal of memory space and processor time. Like LISP, PROLOG can monopolize the resources of a small minicomputer to run only a moderate-sized program. Since micro-PROLOG was designed for 8-bit microcomputers, the PROLOG language needed to be pared down.

A second distinction is that micro-PROLOG is much more *accessible* to the naive user than is PROLOG. There are now several front end programs available (including SIMPLE and MITSI—for *Man in the Street Interface*) that allows users to avoid some of the syntactic strangeness of PROLOG, much of which is a holdover from its origins in Horn Clauses. In this section, which uses the front end SIMPLE, we will see what these syntactic differences look like.

LISP : Logo = PROLOG : micro-PROLOG

The relationship between micro-PROLOG and PROLOG resembles the relationship between Logo and LISP. Both parent languages require large amounts of memory and processor time to calculate functions or respond to queries. Both source languages are syntactically sparse (having few absolutely essential elements), but the syntax of each can seem arcane to novices.

Micro-PROLOG and Logo are scaled-down versions of their linguistic ancestors. While Logo was devised before microcomputers came into being, both Logo and micro-PROLOG have flowered as languages in their microcomputer implementations. LISP and PROLOG are primarily known for their use in artificial intelligence, while Logo and micro-PROLOG were primarily created to be used in education.

Essentials of micro-PROLOG Syntax

(1)   Conversing with micro-PROLOG: Sentences and Queries
The major components of micro-PROLOG closely parallel those of PROLOG. Only the terminology and syntactic conventions are really different.

What PROLOG calls a *fact*, micro-PROLOG calls an *atomic sentence*. What PROLOG calls a *rule*, micro-PROLOG calls a *molecular sentence*. PROLOG uses *prefix* notation to formulate items in the data base, while micro-PROLOG uses *infix* notation. PROLOG uses the syntax ?- to indicate a query, where micro-PROLOG uses the more familiar English *is* or *which*. And finally, PROLOG uses the colon notation (:-) to indicate the conditional formulation of a rule, while micro-PROLOG uses the English *if*. There are also some minor differences in punctuation.

(2)   Constructing an Initial Data Base: Atomic Sentences, Infix Notation
Atomic sentences (in PROLOG, *facts*) are entries in the data base that express relationships between individual entities. In micro-PROLOG, these relationships are stated in English-like syntax:

> individual-1   individual-2   individual-3

And so we might include in the data base the following atomic sentences:

leaves	cover	the-ground
Francis	kicked	the-cat
highways	are-part-of	modern-life
individual-1	individual-2	individual-3

Individuals can be specified by name (e.g. John) or as variables (e.g. x). Placement of the relationship (e.g. cover) *between* the two individuals (e.g. leaves . . . the-ground) is called *infix* notation. PROLOG, like LISP, uses *prefix* notation, meaning that the relationship (called the *predicate* in PROLOG or the *function name* in LISP) is placed at the beginning of the statement. And so in PROLOG we would indicate the English statement that leaves cover the ground with the fact

> cover(leaves, ground).

(3)   Adding to the Data Base: Molecular Sentences
Just as PROLOG has rules that state conditional relationships ("conclusion if condition"), micro-PROLOG has molecular sentences (sometimes also called

rules). Molecular sentences connect together two atomic sentences in the same way that PROLOG rules connect together two facts. Syntactically, micro-PROLOG uses the English word *if* to express conditionality, while PROLOG uses the more opaque :-. For example,

Language	Conclusion	if Condition
micro-PROLOG	Abraham father-of Isaac	if Sarah mother-of Isaac
PROLOG	father(abraham, isaac)	:- mother(sarah, isaac).

As in PROLOG, each molecular sentence in micro-PROLOG can have only one conclusion, though it may have more than one condition, e.g.

> Abraham father-of Isaac if Sarah mother-of Isaac and
> Sarah wife-of Abraham

(4)   Querying the Data Base: *is, which*
Once we have constructed a data base composed of atomic and, if we wish, molecular sentences, we can put micro-PROLOG to work by asking questions of the data base. In PROLOG, there is just one way to ask a question. The question syntax marker, i.e. ?-, is placed in front of the fact or rule to be queried, e.g.

> ?- cover(leaves, ground).
> ?- cover(X, ground).

The response to the first query might be "yes" or "no," and the response to the second would be the listing of arguments that are possible values of X, e.g. *leaves, snow, cherry blossoms.*
   Micro-PROLOG has different ways of asking questions whose answers are "yes" or "no" and questions whose answers are values of variables. Yes/no questions ("Is it the case that leaves cover the ground?") are posed with the English-like syntax

> is (leaves cover ground)

When the query has a variable whose value you are asking about ("Which is (are) the thing(s) that cover the ground?"), the syntax is a little more complex:

> which (x: x cover ground)

(i.e. "Which is the x such that x covers the ground?"). Like PROLOG, micro-PROLOG responds with all possible values of x.

(5)   Relationships in the Data Base: Genealogical Trees and Semantic
      Networks
Both PROLOG and micro-PROLOG allow users to create rules that have multiple
facts (or atomic sentences) in the right-hand side of the rules. In our discussion
of PROLOG, we used the familiar anthropological device of a genealogical tree
to show the relationship between several generations in the lineage of Abraham
and Sarah:

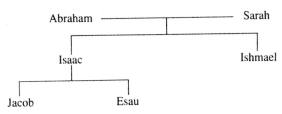

Using these relationships, we talked about who was a brother of whom ("X
is a brother of Y if X is male, X's parents are Father and Mother, and Y's
parents are the same Father and Mother"). We might also choose to talk about
the grandparent/grandchild relationship: "X is a grandparent of Y if X is the
parent of Z and Z is the parent of Y." Relabeling our genealogical tree, we see
that Abraham and Sarah are possible values of X, Jacob and Esau are possible
values of Y, and Isaac is a possible value of Z, i.e.

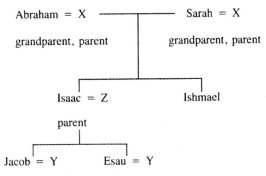

The PROLOG data base itself obviously contains information such as

         parent(abraham, isaac).
         parent(abraham, ishmael).
         parent(isaac, jacob).
         parent(isaac, esau).
         parent(sarah, isaac).
         parent(sarah, ishmael).

In micro-PROLOG this information would read

         Abraham parent-of Isaac
         Abraham parent-of Ishmael
         (etc.)

An alternative way of thinking about meaning relationships between objects is to use an artificial intelligence technique known as semantic networks. Semantic networks were developed in the late 1960s in order to represent the meaning of words and word relationships in English. For example, a semantic network representing a blue canvas chair that I own would look something like this:

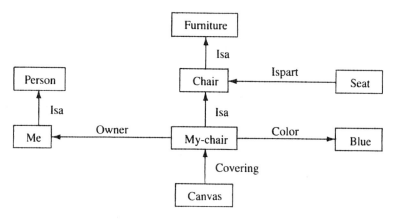

Neither genealogical trees nor semantic networks actually belong to the logic programming languages PROLOG or micro-PROLOG. The designers of PROLOG assume that users will figure out for themselves (in their heads or on scratch paper) the relationships between the entities and sentences that we have been illustrating with genealogical trees and semantic networks. In the case of micro-PROLOG, though, a major goal of the language is to *teach* children how to *work out* these relationships. That is, micro-PROLOG is as much a pedagogical tool for structuring data as it is a means of asking questions of a data base. Therefore, in the process of teaching micro-PROLOG, a representational model such as semantic networks can prove an important auxiliary educational component.

In his introductory materials on micro-PROLOG, Richard Ennals uses semantic networks to translate items of a micro-PROLOG data base into a visual representation. In the case of atomic sentences, the translation is unnecessary, e.g.

English:	Abraham is the parent of Isaac
micro-PROLOG:	Abraham parent-of Isaac
semantic network:	Abraham parent-of Isaac

With compound relationships, we can see how semantic networks become more useful:

English:	Abraham and Sarah are parents of Isaac
micro-PROLOG:	Abraham parent-of Isaac
	Sarah parent-of Isaac

semantic network:

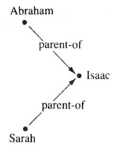

The real conceptual (and pedagogical) power of semantic networks becomes even clearer when we are dealing with rules. Consider the grandparent relationship we have just been looking at. In a semantic network, it would look like this:

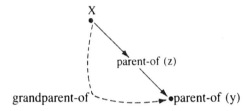

Consider the micro-PROLOG molecular sentence/rule

x grandparent-of y if x parent-of z and z parent-of y

The left-hand side of the rule ("x grandparent-of y"), that is the consequent, is represented in the semantic network by the dotted line connecting x and y via the grandparent-of relationship. The two conditions on the right-hand side of the rule ("x parent-of z" and "z parent-of y") are represented by solid lines in the semantic network connecting the arguments x and z, and z and y.

The difference between genealogical trees and semantic networks is the part of the data base they represent. The genealogical tree can only represent facts (i.e. atomic sentences). The semantic network can, of course, represent facts, but it can also represent rules (i.e. molecular sentences), which include both consequences (which need to be *derived* from facts) and conditions (i.e. the atomic sentences from which the consequences will be derived). Both genealogical trees and semantic networks are useful means of representing information. However, networks seem tailor-made for illustrating rules in logic programming, while genealogical trees are more limited in scope.

(6)   Familiar Syntax: Recursion and Lists

It is hardly surprising that micro-PROLOG, like PROLOG, uses both recursion as a means of data manipulation and lists as an important (though not exclusive) form of data structuring. Genealogical relationships are a good way of illustrating the use of recursion in micro-PROLOG. Remember that recursion means that we are calling the same function or predicate more than once in the process of running a program. However, the function/predicate changes its meaning each time it is used (unlike in the case of iteration).

To illustrate how recursion works in micro-PROLOG, return once more to the tribe of Abraham. This time, however, we will organize our data base slightly differently. Instead of thinking in terms of grandparents and grandchildren, we will think in terms of ancestors.

Consider the following data base:

atomic sentences:	Abraham parent-of Isaac
(facts)	Abraham parent-of Ishmael
	Isaac ancestor-of Jacob
	Isaac ancestor-of Esau
molecular sentence:	Abraham ancestor-of Jacob if
(rule)	Abraham parent-of Isaac and
	Isaac ancestor-of Jacob

The semantic network for the rule looks like this:

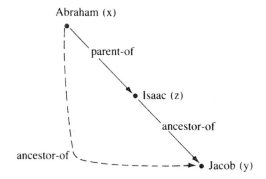

The new consequent we want to define is that Abraham is an ancestor of Jacob. We use two conditions (i.e. facts) to formulate this definition. The first condition is that Abraham is a parent of Isaac. The second (i.e. that Isaac is an ancestor of Jacob) utilizes this same "ancestor-of" relationship. In order to determine the meaning of "Abraham ancestor-of Jacob," we first need to evaluate the relationship "Isaac ancestor-of Jacob." Hence, the relationship "ancestor-of" is recursive.

The list in micro-PROLOG (as in PROLOG) is but one of several data structures available. In both languages, lists can take the place of a single argument in a fact or a rule, e.g.

Single Arguments	List
chimps love bananas	chimps love (bananas attention swings)
chimps love attention	
chimps love swings	

Not surprisingly, micro-PROLOG, like PROLOG and LISP, has means of manipulating items in a list (e.g. selecting out the first item, the rest of the items, and so forth).

(7)   Other Features: Arithmetic and Geometry
Finally, micro-PROLOG is able to handle basic arithmetic relationships, as well as to work with geometric shapes. While the built-in arithmetic relationships are elementary (LESS, SUM, and TIMES), micro-PROLOG, as an extensible language, allows users to define additional relationships such as QUOTIENT or REMAINDER. Micro-PROLOG's spartan (though adequate) arithmetic functions are reminiscent of the simple built-in arithmetic functions in Logo. Similarly, while micro-PROLOG does not emphasize graphics the way that Logo does, micro-PROLOG can produce results comparable to Logo's turtle graphics.

THE EVOLUTION OF micro-PROLOG

It is premature to talk about the evolution of a language that was so recently invented. Unlike BASIC and Logo, which are approaching their second decades, and Smalltalk, which has been around nearly as long, micro-PROLOG is barely five years old. Moreover, the language was not seriously introduced into the United States until 1985.

Logo vs. micro-PROLOG

Yet given the power of micro-PROLOG (plus its close ties with the increasingly important language PROLOG), it is likely that the next battle lines in education will be drawn between micro-PROLOG and Logo, much as the earlier pedagogical debate (at least in the United States) was between Logo and BASIC. We have already talked about the structural similarities between Logo and micro-PROLOG: both are user-friendly versions of existing artificial intelligence languages; both are extensible languages that are symbolically oriented but allow graphics. (One important difference is that Logo is a procedural language, while micro-PROLOG is generally non-procedural.)

What we haven't compared are the pedagogical presuppositions and functional goals that differentiate the languages. Yet these presuppositions and goals, as much as the languages themselves, may well determine relative use of Logo and micro-PROLOG.

(1)   Cognitive Presuppositions
Logo was designed as a language for *individual* discovery and creation, where differences among individual cognitive styles are encouraged. If no teacher ever interferes in a child's use of Logo, and no two children ever produce the same geometric results, the goals of Logo are satisfied.

Micro-PROLOG aims for a fundamentally different result. As least as of now, micro-PROLOG is used in formal classroom settings to supplement traditional means of teaching logical thinking and clear use of language. The definition of what constitutes "clear thinking" and "clear language" is already contained in the first order predicate calculus. This is not to say that children using micro-PROLOG are not creative in the data bases they construct and the queries they make. Far from it. However, the cognitive goals of micro-PROLOG are far more objectively identifiable than are the goals of Logo.

(2) Audience

Both Logo and micro-PROLOG were invented to be used by many types of people. But the intended range is different for the two languages, as are the actual audiences that have developed. Logo was designed to be used by people from elementary school to college and beyond, but the major developments in the Logo constituency have come at the younger end of the age spectrum.

By contrast, micro-PROLOG was designed to teach highly analytic skills to children who already have a preliminary round of education. The goal is not so much to encourage children to come up with new ideas as to discipline children in how to think about the ideas they already have. The first order predicate calculus presents a framework intended to facilitate clear thinking and language. Since analytic thinking is generally conceived of as an activity appropriate to children no younger than ten or twelve (and then on up through college age and beyond), the audience of micro-PROLOG has, in fact, been defined as including middle school, high school, and college students, but as excluding students just beginning their education.

(3) Areas of Use

Logo has overwhelmingly been used for the teaching of geometry. Despite its relative newness, micro-PROLOG has already extended across the curriculum. Logo's capabilities as an artificial intelligence language have not been exploited, while micro-PROLOG's potential as a data base management system—and generator of knowledge systems—*is* being developed.

THE FUTURE OF micro-PROLOG

The future of micro-PROLOG depends upon two factors: enthusiasm about PROLOG (coupled with dissemination of micro-PROLOG translators), and developments in other education-oriented languages. Since micro-PROLOG is intended as a microcomputer version of PROLOG (in a way that Logo was never intended to be viewed as micro-LISP), the acceptance of micro-PROLOG is directly tied to international response to PROLOG. The American artificial intelligence community could play a pivotal role here by continuing its recent overtures toward PROLOG as an alternative to LISP or as a language to be combined with LISP. It is fairly certain that the reputation of PROLOG will continue to grow. It is also clear that data base management (for which PROLOG and micro-PROLOG are especially well suited) will continue to expand in importance in the world of both specialist and novice computer users.

The unknown variable in predicting micro-PROLOG's future is Smalltalk. Smalltalk was originally invented to encourage children's thinking, somewhat in the same vein as Logo but using objects rather than functions as a means of extensibility and devising a whole user interface that both LISP and Logo lack. In recent years, the emphasis of the Smalltalk project at Xerox PARC has shifted from improving children's learning to assisting large computer companies in using Smalltalk for professional simulation systems. However, if Alan Kay's original Dynabook vision (which underlies the Smalltalk language) should come to fruition, Smalltalk, with its extensibility, non-procedural programming style, powerful visual orientation, and rich user interface, might surpass all other "education" languages, including micro-PROLOG (although micro-PROLOG might prosper in its non-education functions). It is also possible, of course, that as PROLOG and LISP begin to borrow elements from one another, and as LISP incorporates properties from Smalltalk, the pedagogical versions of these languages (i.e. micro-PROLOG, Logo, and Smalltalk for children) might blend into a single language.

USING micro-PROLOG

Buying micro-PROLOG

Micro-PROLOG was first written in Z80 assembly language to be run under the CP/M operating system. Currently micro-PROLOG is available for several 8-bit and 16-bit machines (including the Apple II series running under CP/M and the IBM PC running under MS DOS or CP/M-86). A new version for the Apple Macintosh also recently appeared.

What to Read

BOOKS

Ennals, Richard (1984). *Beginning micro-PROLOG*. New York: Harper & Row. (First published in 1983 by Ellis Horwood, Chichester, Eng.)
   An extremely readable self-paced text on micro-PROLOG. Recall that Ennals designed and evaluated the first teaching units on micro-PROLOG. The book also contains initial and final chapters on the motivations behind micro-PROLOG and its use in classrooms so far.
de Saram, Hugh (1985). *Programming in micro-PROLOG*. New York: John Wiley.
   Introductory text that parallels fairly closely the presentation of PROLOG found in Clocksin and Mellish's *Programming in Prolog*. Saram's especially well-written text is quite suitable for adult learners.

Conlon, Tom (1985). *Start Problem-Solving with PROLOG*. London: Addison-Wesley.

Conlon's book adopts a problem-solving approach to the teaching of micro-PROLOG.

Clark, Keith L., and Frank G. McCabe (1984). *micro-PROLOG: Programming in Logic*. Englewood Cliffs (N.J.): Prentice-Hall International.

A more formal text on micro-PROLOG, intended for readers with some familiarity with computers. Complete with exercises and answers.

Yazdoni, Masoud, ed. (1984). *New Horizons in Educational Computing*. Chichester (Eng.): Ellis Horwood; New York: Halsted Press (division of John Wiley).

An excellent survey of three computer languages used in education: Logo, micro-PROLOG, and POP. The micro-PROLOG section includes articles by Robert Kowalski and Richard Ennals, as well as by other members of the Imperial College logic programming project.

ARTICLES

Pountain, Dick (1984). Prolog on Microcomputers, *Byte* 9 (no. 13): 355–362.

One of the finest articles on micro-PROLOG in the American computer press. A very good place for a first look at the language.

Modula-2

PROFILE

*MODU*lar *LA*nguage	Nᴀᴍᴇ

Sᴛʀᴜᴄᴛᴜʀᴇ

Familiar Distinctions:
   hardware: high-level but access to low-level functions
   translator: compiled (or compiled and interpreted)
   structural unit: module
   data: largely numerical

Conceptual Distinctions:
   organizing principle: imperative / algorithmic
   procedures: procedural (but use of information hiding)
   extensibility: extensible
   program/data: distinct

Fᴜɴᴄᴛɪᴏɴs

systems programming, including real-time programming

Gᴇɴᴇᴀʟᴏɢʏ

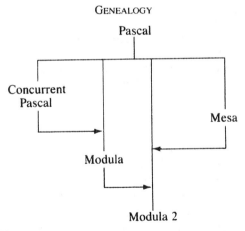

Pascal

Concurrent Pascal

Mesa

Modula

Modula 2

Years: 1977–79

Author: Niklaus Wirth

Impetus: design a general-purpose language that incorporates the principles of structured programming into a system powerful enough to do ''real'' programming

Evolution: language is still very new, but could replace Pascal

(Continued)

Modula-2 (Continued)

VERSIONS / DIALECTS
Standard: n.a.

SPECIAL CHARACTERISTICS
Memory Requirements: moderate (full implementation can run in 64K)
Ease of Learning / Use: fairly easy if you know Pascal, though modules can be tricky
Availability: growing availability for microcomputers; native language of Lilith

NOTE; Read this section in conjunction with the entries on Pascal, Ada, and C.

WHY MODULA-2?

> Complexity has and will maintain a strong fascination for many people. It is true that we live in a complex world and strive to solve inherently complex problems, which often do require complex mechanisms. However, this should not diminish our desire for *elegant* solutions, which convince by their clarity and effectiveness. Simple, elegant solutions are more effective, but they are *harder* to find than complex ones, and they require more time, which we too often believe to be unaffordable.
> Niklaus Wirth, Turing Award Lecture, 1984

Alles in Ordnung

From its very inception, the ALGOL family of languages (from which Wirth's Pascal and Modula-2 derive) has embodied the principle of order. Enemy of the "hack" or the "kludge," ALGOL and its descendants have created an approach to programming (which has come to be known as structured programming) in which all the pieces are clearly laid out and the execution of the program entails no sudden twists and turns. This principle of order underlies the original construction of ALGOL 58 and ALGOL 60, the creation of Pascal for teaching students how to think about programming, and the development of many ALGOL 60 and Pascal derivatives.

It is this same principle that Wirth once again invoked in his intellectual odyssey from Pascal to Modula-2. As we look at the origins of Modula-2, at Modula-2 itself, and at Wirth's comparisons of Modula-2 with a language like Ada, we will see the practical implications of this underlying approach to the art of programming.

Sequential, Concurrent, and Real-Time Languages

Most of the languages used by non-professional programmers were designed to do one thing at a time. In so-called *sequential languages* (which include FORTRAN, ALGOL, COBOL, BASIC, Pascal, and nearly all of the older imperative/algorithmic languages, as well as most languages of the other conceptual types), each action in a program is only initiated once the action of its predecessor is completed. This sequential processing of information parallels both conceptually and physically the sequential operation of the von Neumann computer architecture.

However, in more complex programming, it sometimes is desirable to make the computer (either literally or figuratively) do more than one thing at a time. This is referred to as *concurrent programming* or *multiprogramming*. In concurrent programming, a program is divided into distinct routines. Several of the routines are executed concurrently (though within each individual routine the processing of information is still sequential). Such concurrency may physically be occurring in the machine (through the use of more than one processor). Alternatively, concurrency may take place only at the logical level. That is, several processes only *seem* to be running at the same time, much as a time-sharing computer only *seems* to be attending to everyone's computing needs simultaneously (see the entry on BASIC).

There is an obvious advantage to concurrent programming. The "divide and conquer" strategy completes a task several times faster than if a job is carried through one step at a time. Sometimes the ability to do several things simultaneously is less a convenience than a necessity. Such necessity arises when a computer is controlling devices (like the traffic lights in Manhattan at rush hour or the movement of subway cars in the London Underground) in which the results of concurrent computations must be timed to coincide with one another. You want the traffic light in the southbound direction at Forty-second Street to turn green slightly after the traffic light at Forty-third Street does. And you want to be certain that two subways using the same track don't collide. When a concurrent program demands that the execution speeds of the processors be synchronized, we have entered the world of *real-time programming*.

Real-time programming is at once the darling and the nightmare of computer scientists. It enables computers to control the activity of a boundless number of devices in the real world, some of whose actions are too complex for any single human being to keep track of. At the same time, though, real-time programming is extremely difficult. The chance of error is enormous, not only because the programs themselves tend to be very complex (as do the languages used to write them) but also because the job of synchronizing two events can be exceedingly tricky.

As a result, languages used for real-time programming have tended to become extremely complicated. Ada is just the last in a long series of languages that have grown to resemble wild thickets as opposed to the neat English gardens so easily possible with sequential languages.

A fundamental requirement of any computer language is *validity* (or *reliability*). Do programs written in the language always do exactly what they are supposed to? Does the same program always run the same way? We have all heard stories about the isolated "bugs" buried deep within some well-known complex programs. In many cases, a computer program has sufficient leeway to tolerate an occasional mistake. Locating such bugs can be extremely costly, and we usually have the option of running the program over again (or writing our way around the bug) when such validity problems arise.

But in some cases we have no leeway. We need to know the program is entirely valid, entirely reliable. An early-warning radar system can't afford to misread a flock of Canada geese as an attack from the U.S.S.R. Not surprisingly, reliability is most critical in real-time systems. (See the entry on Ada for more discussion of real-time systems and the problem of reliability.)

Enter Niklaus Wirth.

In an article entitled "Toward a Discipline of Real-Time Programming" (1977), Wirth applied the *"Alles in Ordnung"* principle to the problem of synchronized control languages. *If* you are extremely disciplined in the way you do your programming (i.e. using the principles of structured programming growing out of the ALGOL tradition), *then* you have a chance of solving the problem of reliability:

> By adhering to a strict programming discipline and by using a suitable high-level language molded after this discipline, the complexity of reasoning about concurrency and execution time constraints may be drastically reduced. This may be the only practical way to make real-time systems analytically verifiable and ultimately reliable.

Wirth did not judge such a language to exist. His response was to create a new special-purpose language designed to handle real-time programming reliably. He called the language Modula.

From Modula to Modula-2

Wirth designed Modula in 1975. After introducing Pascal as a teaching language at the Swiss Federal Institute of Technology (its German abbreviation being ETH) in the early 1970s, Wirth had become interested in concurrent programming. In 1972, Per Brinch Hansen had begun working on an extension of Pascal that augmented its sequential capabilities with concurrent programming tools. Hansen's result was known as Concurrent Pascal. Wirth's own solution to the problem of concurrent programming (which, remember, encompasses real-time programming) was to create a *discipline* of real-time programming, *from* which he *derived* a new language. Since the principal aim of the language was to divide programs into *modules* that would then communicate with one another, Wirth called the language Modula.

Modula (sometimes referred to as Modula-1 in retrospect) was essentially a minimal subset of Pascal syntax with two major additions. One was the modular structure, which in essence divided a program into individual fiefdoms. Taken at face value, all that the program saw of the fiefdoms was their names and functions. That is, their internal structure was generally *hidden* from view. However, the fiefdoms could communicate with one another, imparting or receiving information about themselves.

Wirth's second major addition to Pascal was facilities for multiprocessing and low-level machine access. The reason for the addition of multiprogramming tools is obvious. The issue of low-level machine access needs some explanation.

Until the mid-1970s, there was still some doubt in the computer world whether high-level structured programming languages could be used effectively for solving "real" problems. One major issue was speed. Could these languages run quickly enough to do their work efficiently? Structured languages ran more slowly than unstructured languages, and all high-level languages ran more slowly than assembly language. In real-time programming or even general systems programming (e.g. the writing of compilers or operating systems), you couldn't afford to sacrifice speed merely for the sake of elegance.

But Wirth, at once a champion of structured programming and a practical man, was not ready to admit defeat. He asked himself whether the ineffectiveness of high-level structured languages was due to their being high-level or structured languages, or whether the difficulty really lay in the way the languages were being implemented. He concluded that the difficulty lay in implementation. If he could get a high-level (and, of course, structured) language to access low-level machine functions, he would be able to justify the use of a high-level structured language in place of assembly language. And so, in Wirth's words, "a major aim of the research on Modula [was] to conquer that stronghold of assembly coding, or at least to attack it vigorously."

While maintaining these same goals, Wirth soon altered his mode of attack. He "had become somewhat weary of programming languages and the frustrating task of constructing good compilers for existing computers that were designed for old-fashioned 'by-hand' coding." The turning point came in 1976 and 1977, when Wirth spent a sabbatical at Xerox PARC in Palo Alto, California. There he encountered the notion of a personal workstation (exemplified by the Xerox Alto) and the language Mesa (a Pascal derivative that was far more powerful than Pascal and ran on the Alto). Wirth's response was to shift his attention from software to hardware and to undertake to build his own computer *system* (hardware, microcode, compiler, operating system, program utilities) that would enable him to do real-time programming the way he felt it should be done.

The result was a project called Lilith. Using a single-processor computer, operated by a single programmer, the Lilith computer would combine state-of-the-art technology (as learned at Xerox PARC) with state-of-the-art programming (as crafted by Wirth, a master of disciplined programming). The entire system (from compiler to device drivers to graphics editors) would be written in that language.

Wirth wanted a language that combined two very different facilities: it would need to express algorithms at a very high level of abstraction (the trend begun in Pascal and continued in Modula) and at the same time be able directly to access machine facilities (traditionally the domain of assembly language). After considering existing languages, Wirth rejected them all. His alternative was to create a new language that was largely a hybrid between Pascal and Modula. The result was a general-purpose language that combined all aspects of Pascal with the modular concept, multiprogramming facilities, and the low-level facilities of Modula. The new language was named Modula-2.

Modula-2 is itself an example of the dual advantage of insisting upon using high-level structured programming while also keeping the solution to a problem small. The time elapsed between Wirth's original conception of the Lilith project and the actual running of Modula-2 on a completed Lilith was a scant two years. (Wirth pointedly compares this development time with the half decade it has taken to bring Ada from the drawing board to actual implementation.) Modula-2 was conceived of in 1977, defined in 1978, first run in 1979, and published and released in 1980.

THINKING IN MODULA-2

For Wirth, the construction of Modula-2 was largely motivated by his interest in reliable real-time programming. Real-time programming is a specialized computer language function. Yet the language Wirth created is a general-purpose language appropriate for any of the functions for which Pascal and its extensions have been used. To many potential programmers in Modula-2, then, the question is not so much how well Modula-2 does with real-time programming, but how Modula-2 compares with Pascal. This question is most easily answered in two parts: what indigenous problems exist in Pascal, and how does Modula-2 solve them?

The Problem with Pascal

Wirth had designed Pascal in the late 1960s to be a structured high-level language for teaching students the principles behind the art of good programming. While Wirth also intended the language to be applicable to real-world problems, he did not envision the scope of the problems to be especially large.

By the early 1970s, it was clear that Pascal was inadequate for meeting the needs of many users. There were two choices: switch languages or extend the existing Pascal standard. Many programmers felt Pascal's advantages were too good to relinquish. Chief among them were that Pascal provides a clear description of data structures and algorithms; that it protects the user against improper mixing of data types; and that it prohibits illegal values from being assigned to variables.

Many users decided to construct their own extensions to the language. But there were problems. Some of the attempts to extend standard Pascal to do real-time programming or to write operating systems simply did not work well. More importantly, as extensions proliferated, the need grew to standardize these extensions if programs were to remain portable across machines. Yet despite several attempts to define a standard extended Pascal, Pascal users were unable to agree upon which extensions should be incorporated into the standard.

Advocates of Pascal were not alone in acknowledging Pascal's shortcomings. One of the sharpest (and best-known) critiques came from Brian Kernighan, a major proponent of C. In an article entitled "Why Pascal Is Not My Favorite Programming Language" (1981), Kernighan identified eight major problems with Pascal. The items were reasonably technical (having to do with such things as whether arrays are of fixed size, whether the language allows separate compilation of subprograms, and what kinds of input/output facilities the language has). The upshot of the argument was that Pascal (presumably, unlike C) is a "toy" language, appropriate only for *teaching* programming but not *doing* programming.

Modula-2 offered a solution for Pascal loyalists. For Modula-2 not only provided the extensions to Pascal that so many of Pascal's users found lacking, but also directly answered all of Kernighan's objections.

Modula-2 and Pascal

Compare, for a moment, typical Western European houses with traditional Japanese houses. In Western Europe, the internal structure of a house is determined when the house is first built. The house is divided into floors, which are then divided into rooms. The walls between rooms are built of solid material and, for all practical purposes, are not movable. If there is a wall between two rooms, there is no simple way for people in the two rooms to communicate with one another. In traditional Japan, the arrangement is more flexible. Houses are still divided into rooms, but the walls are movable. It is therefore possible for occupants of different rooms to communicate with one another if they choose.

If Pascal is like a Western European house, Modula-2 is like a traditional Japanese dwelling. Both are divided into subunits—Pascal into blocks and procedures, Modula-2 into modules and procedures. What differentiates the two languages is the properties of these subunits and the interchange that can take place between subunits. In Pascal, there are language-wide rules as to how, for example, procedures can relate to one another. In Modula-2, the particular interaction between subunits (in this case, modules) can be defined for each module and each interrelationship between modules.

The Module

Structurally, a module is a collection of declarations that work together to perform a task. You can think of a module as a program within the larger Modula-2 program. So far, the definition of a module in Modula-2 resembles the definition of a procedure in Pascal. What makes the module distinct is the way in which it relates to other parts of the program. For modules, like Japanese houses, allow users control over how much the outside world (i.e. other modules) can see of what is going on in a particular module.

Modules are basically used for secrecy rather than for exposure. That is, modules are essentially designed to *hide* the information within them from other places in the program where the details of that program subcomponent don't need to be known. The notion of "information hiding" became very popular in computer science in the 1970s. It was part of a general attempt to construct ever higher-level languages in which a program might contain a considerable level of detail but the details were camouflaged when not needed. This principle of information hiding is found in many ALGOL and Pascal derivative languages, including Ada. In fact, the "package" in Ada (which also hides details of one program subcomponent from other components) closely resembles the module in Modula-2.

One of Modula-2's contributions was to refine the activity of information hiding by controlling the communication which the programmer *did* want to take place between modules. This is known as *importing* and *exporting* (think of opening a screen between two rooms in a Japanese house).

Importing is an activity that is very common in Modula-2 programs. In fact, the basic input/output functions of Modula-2 programs are drawn from (i.e. imported from) a library containing information on how input and output are done. Typical functions which need to be imported for even a simple program might include READInteger, WRITEInteger, WRITELine, or WRITEString. In Pascal, the functions for reading and writing information are contained directly within the main Pascal program itself.

Exports work much the same way, only in reverse. Information exported from a particular module is made available to other modules contained in the library.

Other Features of Modula-2

Modula-2's distinctiveness comes not only from its use of modules but also from the ways in which modules are handled by other features of the language. Here, briefly, are some of these other features.

(1) Separate Compilation

Modula-2 enables programmers to compile modules individually and then put them aside (e.g. when developing other modules) or incorporate them within a library for use in subsequent programs (see below). Other languages (e.g. FORTRAN) also offer separate compilation of subcomponents. However, Modula-2 has the advantage of checking the data types of each module (which Modula-2 assiduously declares) against one another when modules are linked together. In this way, it avoids errors resulting from illegal mixing of data types. In most other programming languages, the process of linking together subcomponents and being sure that data types don't clash can be a time-consuming and error-prone procedure.

(2) Libraries

Like many imperative/algorithmic languages (including FORTRAN and C), Modula-2 has a "library" in which it stores programs for building other programs. The range of library modules found in Modula-2 is especially rich. It includes not only program modules but also operations normally found in operating systems. Like pieces of an erector set, modules can be combined together to form larger modules, and pieces of different programs can be interchanged with one another.

(3)   Low-Level Systems Facilities

Part of Wirth's original motivation for undertaking the Lilith project was to create a language that could address machine hardware at both a high level and a low level, thereby obviating the need to resort to assembly language, whose conceptual structure predates the principles of structured programming. (Recall that FORTH and C also offer both low-level and high-level programming functions.) Modula-2 includes these low-level systems facilities as modules in the library. However, these facilities tend to be machine-dependent and therefore are not directly portable from one machine to another.

(4)   Multiprocessing

Wirth's interest in multiprocessing (concurrent programming) is what led to the development of Modula back in 1975. Most modern systems programming languages have multiprocessing facilities as part of the language. In Concurrent Pascal they are called *monitors,* in Modula they are known as *processes* and *semaphores,* and in Ada they go by the names *tasks* and *rendezvous.* In Modula-2 the same multitasking functions are accomplished using the simpler (and lower-level) concept of the *co-routine.*

THE EVOLUTION OF MODULA-2

Public Image

Much as in the case of Pascal, the computing public has taken several years to know and use Modula-2. Wirth does not announce his languages with great fanfare, but quietly uses them and makes them available to others who are interested.

The first (and for a long time, the only) book on Modula-2 was written by Wirth. It was published in 1982, but not widely circulated until 1983. Compilers only became readily available in the United States in 1984.

By the end of 1984, though, interest in the language began to mushroom in the States. *Byte* magazine devoted its August 1984 language issue to Modula-2. Several new books on the language began to appear. And in more innovative college classrooms, the language began to be taught alongside Pascal. There even seems to be a reasonable possibility that Modula-2 could eventually replace Pascal as the basic American "teaching language," with the added advantage that Modula-2, unlike Pascal, can be directly used for more sophisticated real-world and real-time applications.

Modula-2 Compared: Ada and C

For many people interested in programming languages, the real question in the evolution of Modula-2 is not so much its relationship with Pascal as its comparison with two of the other widely publicized languages of the 1980s: Ada and C. The comparison is somewhat unfortunate. While all three languages are ALGOL derivatives, they were not intended for the same purposes. C, the oldest of the three, was designed as a relatively low-level language for professional programmers doing systems development. Modula-2 and Ada were both developed to do real-time programming, but the scope of the two languages is radically distinct: Ada is an exceptionally large language and able to do many things in programming that Modula-2, a much smaller language, cannot.

Yet people interested in programming tend to talk about these three languages together and typically feel the need to choose among the three. Therefore, we offer here a succinct comparison of Modula-2, Ada, and C. (The summary presupposes you have read the sections on Ada and C.)

THE FUTURE OF MODULA-2

Modula-2 is so new a language that it seems premature to be making projections about its future. What we can do, though, is identify some of the factors that are likely to influence the future development and use of Modula-2.

System-External Factors

The first set of conditioning factors comes from the programming world outside of Modula-2.

(1) General Programming Trends

By now it should be evident that many of the newer (or newly popular) languages are moving in similar directions. As computers and their uses becomes more sophisticated, languages which have the capability of doing systems development and real-time applications are becoming more numerous.

The languages used for these (as well as other) functions are tending to share a cluster of properties. They often enable programmers to work at a relatively low level without having to resort to assembly language (e.g. Modula-2, C, FORTH). They typically depend upon some notion of modularity and communication between modules (e.g. Modula-2, Ada, SIMULA, Smalltalk). Extensibility is becoming more important, either through the development of libraries of compiled subprograms that remain distinct from that language or through user-defined components that become part of the language. (Functional/applicative languages such as LISP and APL originally led the way in user-defined extensibility, but now even Modula-2—an imperative/algorithmic language— can be said to be extensible.) And finally, a growing number of languages are making use of information hiding or data abstraction.

COMPARISON FEATURE	C	Modula-2	Ada
genealogy	ALGOL 60 — CPL — BCPL — C	Pascal Modula Modula-2	Pascal Ada
date work started	1972	1977	1975
data of first compiler	1972	1979	1983
size of compiler		c. 5000 lines	several hundred thousand lines
assumptions about user	already a competent programmer	very easy for Pascal programmers to learn	users with different backgrounds can access different amounts of language
original goal	systems programming (esp. compilers, operating systems) replace assembly language *not* intended for real-time programming	systems programming *and* real-time programming replace non-standard extensions to Pascal	embedded systems (which are, definitionally, real-time programs) replace diversity of languages at DoD
level of operation	high and low level	high and low level	high level
data typing	strong data typing	strong data typing	strong data typing
type checking	loose type checking (though lint program now does checking)	strong type checking	strong type checking
structural unit	function	module	package

279

(2)   Other Programming Languages

Modula-2's most important competitor is Ada. While the two languages were designed for solving problems on very different scales, Ada could nevertheless end up edging out Modula-2. Ada has the backing of the powerful U.S. Department of Defense (DoD). If the DoD says that its programming must be done in Ada, thousands of research establishments stand ready to fall into line. Moreover, many people in the programming world are repeatedly urging the DoD to define a subset of Ada that could be used for solving more general problems that don't require all the detail available in the full version of Ada. Were such a subset defined, it would presumably fill many of the same functions as Modula-2, while at the same time being upwardly compatible with fuller versions of Ada.

How much competition Ada will present is uncertain. There are as yet few validated compilers for Ada. The DoD still refuses to sanction a subset of Ada, despite its repeated suggestions that Ada is suitable not only for mission-critical embedded systems but also for general programming tasks. Within the next few years, there may be a shakeout within Ada, and between Ada and Modula-2.

The competition between C and Modula-2 is of a slightly different character. The original rush of interest in C came in the early 1980s, largely from programmers who had not grown up in the structured programming tradition. Although C ultimately derives from ALGOL, it comes from an offshoot of ALGOL 60 that developed quite separately from the ideas of structured programming propounded in the writings (and languages) of Dijkstra and Wirth (see the entry on C).

There is now a growing base of programmers trained in Pascal who have come to expect such design features as clear descriptions of data structures and algorithms, and protection against programming errors of the sort that can easily occur in C without warning. It is not clear whether C will retain its fascination for this new generation of programmers. Another important issue will be maintaining code over time—one of the major concerns and costs in software engineering. Given Modula-2's clarity, Modula-2 has a distinct advantage here over C. (See the entry on Ada for a discussion of the maintenance problem.)

System-Internal Factors

As a language, Modula-2 has two distinct advantages over its competitors. The first is the growing base of Pascal programmers. It is relatively easy to learn Modula-2 once you know Pascal. And second, Modula-2 is a highly tractable language because of its size. For programmers who insist on understanding how a language works in its entirety (and people like Tony Hoare and Niklaus Wirth maintain that should be every serious programmer), Modula-2 is not too large.

Another important variable will be the fate of the Lilith computer. BASIC gained its enormous popularity because microcomputer manufacturers began building BASIC directly into their hardware. LISP became firmly entrenched in the world of artificial intelligence with the proliferation of LISP machines. If the Lilith should achieve even reasonable popularity, Modula-2 could experience similar success.

USING MODULA-2

Buying Modula-2

Modula-2 is now available from a growing number of sources. It can be obtained from Wirth's home institution, the ETH, in Zurich. Modula Research Institute (in Provo, Utah) builds the Lilith computer, which includes Modula-2 software. Several software houses (including Volition Systems, Logitech, and Workman and Associates) already market versions for microcomputers.

What to Read

The first set of references focuses on the conceptual underpinnings of Modula-2, while the second set deals with particulars of the language itself.

Conceptual Underpinnings:

BOOKS

Hansen, Per Brinch (1977). *The Architecture of Concurrent Programs.* Englewood Cliffs (N.J.): Prentice-Hall.
Hansen, the inventor of Concurrent Pascal, discusses the structure of concurrent programming more generally.

ARTICLES

Wirth, Niklaus (1977). "Toward a Discipline of Real-Time Programming," *Communications of the ACM* 20 (no. 8):577–583.
Wirth's theoretical analysis of what *kind* of language is necessary to do real-time programming, and a description of his early attempts with Modula.
Wirth, Niklaus (1985). "From Programming Language Design to Computer Construction," *Communications of the ACM* 28 (no. 2):160–164.
In his 1984 Turing Award Lecture, Wirth discusses his intellectual evolution from Pascal to Modula to Modula-2.

The Language:

BOOKS

Wirth, Niklaus (1985). *Programming in Modula-2. 3rd Corrected Edition.* New York: Springer-Verlag.
This is Wirth's "official" definition of Modula-2. It is clearly written but, as is typical of Wirth's style, succinct.
Gleaves, Richard (1984). *Modula-2 for Pascal Programmers.* New York: Springer-Verlag.
Since most Modula-2 programmers today already know Pascal, this is a good book to start on. Gleaves is associated with Volition Systems, one of the current developers of a compiler for Modula-2.
Kaplan, Ian, and Mike Miller (1984). *Programming Modula-2.* Englewood Cliffs (N.J.): Prentice-Hall.
Another of the new crop of books on Modula-2.

Ogilvie, John W. L. (1985). *Modula-2 Programming*. New York: McGraw-Hill.

The author of this especially lucid text on Modula-2 works at Modula Corporation in Provo, Utah.

ARTICLES

McCormack, Joel, and Richard Gleaves (1983). "Modula-2: A Worthy Successor to Pascal," *Byte*, April, pp. 385–395.

An excellent place to begin reading about Modula-2.

Byte, August 1984.

Byte's annual computer language issue in 1984 is devoted to Modula-2. Most of the articles are quite clearly written. The issue gives at once a good conceptual overview of the language and a fair amount of detail.

Journal of Pascal, Ada, and Modula-2

An entire journal devoted to these three languages. The articles tend to be fairly technical, but quite up-to-date.

Pascal

PROFILE

NAME
named after the French mathematician Blaise Pascal (1623–62), who devised the first digital calculating machine

STRUCTURE

Familiar Distinctions:
   hardware: high-level
   translator: generally compiled
   structural unit: block, procedure, function
   data: largely numerical

Conceptual Distinctions:
   organizing principle: imperative/algorithmic
   procedures: procedural
   extensibility: not extensible
   program/data: distinct

FUNCTIONS
general-purpose (but numerically oriented); primarily developed for teaching programming

GENEALOGY

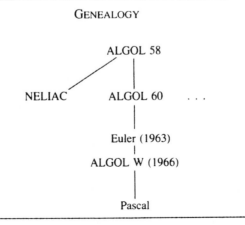

(Continued)

Pascal (Continued)

Years: 1968–71

Author: Niklaus Wirth

Impetus: improved upon ALGOL 60 by creating a concise and elegant language that incorporated the principles of structured programming within the language design itself

Evolution: within the last decade, has become the standard language for teaching computer programming in the U.S. (edging out FORTRAN and BASIC); growth spurred by development of p-code and implementations of Pascal and p-code on micros

---

VERSIONS/DIALECTS

Standard   ISO (International Standards Organization) Standard Pascal

Others: e.g.   UCSD Pascal
Waterloo Pascal
Macintosh Pascal
Turbo Pascal
Berkeley Pascal

SPECIAL CHARACTERISTICS

Memory Requirements: moderately large

Ease of Learning/Use: moderate

Availability: widely available

NOTE: For background on structured programming and Pascal's ancestry, read the entry on ALGOL.

WHY PASCAL?

> The subject [i.e. computer languages] seemed to consist of 1 percent science and 99 percent sorcery, and this tilt had to be changed.
> Niklaus Wirth, Turing Award Lecture, 1984

According to Alan Kay (the inventor of Smalltalk), there is typically a ten-year gap between the development of a good idea in the computer world and its implementation and dissemination to the public. Pascal is an excellent example.

In the first half of the 1980s, Pascal became the darling of computer science departments across the United States, replacing BASIC and FORTRAN as the language for introducing students to computer programming. Yet by that time, Pascal's creator, Niklaus Wirth, had already moved on to other programming concerns.

Pascal is important not only because of its current popularity but because of what it stands for—what it was created to accomplish. For these *goals* continue to be pursued not only by Wirth in his current work but by other language designers as well.

Pascal did not spring full-blown from the head of Wirth. Rather, as Wirth explains in his 1984 Turing Award Lecture to the Association for Computing Machinery, the language is deeply rooted in the syntax of ALGOL and the principles of structured programming.

From ALGOL to Pascal: History

The designers of ALGOL were intent upon constructing a well-thought-out language whose conceptual design was at least as important as its implementation. (Contrast this approach with John Backus's comment that the designers of FORTRAN were primarily concerned with the efficiency of the language's implementation, and were content to make up the syntax as they went along.) These early design efforts behind ALGOL were enhanced through the development of what came to be known as structured programming. The principal architects of structured programming were Edsger Dijkstra, Tony Hoare, and later Niklaus Wirth.

Wirth began his academic career at the Swiss Federal Institute of Technology (the Eidgenössische Technische Hochschule, or ETH) in Zurich, the same institute that was host to the ALGOL 1958 conference. Yet Wirth's introduction to computers did not come until 1960, when he had left Switzerland to study first at Laval University in Canada and then at the University of California at Berkeley, where he received his Ph.D. in 1963.

During his early years in the United States, Wirth worked on NELIAC (a dialect of ALGOL 58 developed by the Navy Electronics Laboratory in San Diego). Attempting to "condense and crystallize" the principles of the next version of ALGOL, ALGOL 60, Wirth devoted his dissertation research to creating another ALGOL derivative known as Euler. Working with Tony Hoare at Stanford, Wirth went on to design an improved (and extended) version of ALGOL 60 which came to be known as ALGOL W. The results were published in 1966.

After teaching at Stanford for several years, Wirth returned to Switzerland in 1967. Within three years, he and a team of three assistants had implemented yet another ALGOL derivative, which later became known as Pascal. The language specifications were published in 1971. By 1972, Pascal was being taught in programming classes at ETH in Zurich.

Design Principles

Wirth has designed several computer languages (including Euler, Pascal, Modula, and Modula-2). Common to all of these languages are several underlying principles that have, for many in the computer world, become synonymous with "good language design."

(1)   Occam's Razor: Never Multiply Entities Unnecessarily
As early as 1963, Wirth was concerned that computer languages were becoming more complex than necessary. In fact, in the abstract to his dissertation, Wirth wrote of the importance of eliminating "many of the non-fundamental concepts of programming languages."

(2)   Lucidity First
When Anatole France (a winner of the Nobel Prize for literature) was asked to name the three most important rules of writing, his response was: "Lucidity first, lucidity second, lucidity third." Wirth's language designs are models of lucidity. Even his syntactic notation serves as a natural extension of the algorithmic thinking that underlies his languages. The notation is never merely an arbitrary formalism stuck in to make the language work.

(3)   Principle, Not Technique
Wirth is acutely aware of the distinction between essential and ephemeral elements in computer languages. Implementation details (which change from language to language and even from installation to installation) are far less important than the fundamental principles underlying the languages themselves. Pascal (in particular) is designed to emphasize the concepts of structured programming, not fancy implementation techniques that easily change and are largely arbitrary.

(4)   Theory and Practice
It is often said that Pascal is a language designed for *teaching* programming rather than *doing* programming. Wirth admits this is historically true. In defining the language in 1971, he wrote that one of his principles of development was to "make available a language suitable to teach programming as a schematic discipline based on certain fundamentals of concepts clearly and naturally reflected by the language." Yet Wirth is also quick to add that he does not distinguish between pedagogy and practice: "I do not believe in using tools and formalisms in teaching that are inadequate for any practical task."

From ALGOL to Pascal: Structure

The major structural distinctions between ALGOL and Pascal can be thought of in terms of Wirth's language design principles. Pascal is a more elegant, more lucid version of ALGOL 60. Like ALGOL 60, it emphasizes principles rather than techniques, but unlike ALGOL 60, the standard Pascal language contains all the code necessary for implementation on computers.

Structurally, Pascal incorporates into its very syntax some of the ideas of structured programming that began to emerge in the late 1960s (i.e. well after the design of ALGOL 60). Pascal refines the ALGOL notion of breaking programs down into pieces (blocks, procedures, functions) and then defining ways of having those pieces "communicate" with one another. Pascal expands some ALGOL 60 features (e.g. adding new data types and data structures) while simplifying or clarifying others (such as the use of control structures and the way in which procedures and parameters operate).

ALGOL 60 is not a subset of Pascal (in the way that ALGOL 60 *is* a proper subset of SIMULA). Yet the design of Pascal is so fundamentally dependent upon the design of ALGOL that the intellectual inheritance—as well as the novelty—of Pascal is only clear when viewed in light of its progenitor.

THINKING IN PASCAL

> Programs should be designed according to the same principles as electronic circuits, that is, clearly subdivided into parts with only a few wires going across the boundaries. Only by understanding one part at a time would there be hope of finally understanding the whole.
> Niklaus Wirth, Turing Award Lecture, 1984

Modern structured programming languages—beginning with ALGOL and culminating with languages like Modula-2—are built upon an elegant and powerful model of modularity and communication. This model lies at the very heart of Pascal. Many of the details of Pascal programming (e.g. data types, control structures) are also computationally important, but their functioning is less central to understanding what makes Pascal unique. Therefore, we will devote this section to an examination of modularity and communication, for once this model is clear, the rest of Pascal is easily learned.

Portsmith, U.S.A.

To understand the Pascal model, we will begin with an analogy. By making the analogy fairly detailed, we can develop obvious metaphors for all the major components of Pascal that we will be talking about.

Consider the local organization of a town we will call Portsmith. It is made up of a central administration (composed of a mayor and a city council) plus the general population. Sometimes the population functions as an undifferentiated set of individuals, such as in voting for local or national officials. For other purposes, the population is organized into subgroups (e.g. the Policemen's Benevolent Association, the Lions Club, a Girl Scout troop, the local garden club).

Within Portsmith, certain rules of jurisdiction obtain between the central administration and the subgroups, and within the subgroups themselves. There are some conditions under which the mayor can govern the activities of the populace directly. In the case of a summer drought, for example, she may announce that no one is to water lawns. The local organizations also can exercise jurisdiction over their own activities. The Girl Scouts might choose to say the Girl Scout pledge at the start of their meetings, while the Lions Club might say the pledge of allegiance to the American flag. And so "pledge" means something different in each group.

There are many forms of communication that may take place within the town of Portsmith. The most important occurs between the central administration and the local organizations. For communication to be possible, the central administration must establish some ground rules. Each group states to the city council the issues that concern it (e.g. tax laws, use of the municipal center for a fund-raising activity). When the city council actually hears the organization's request, it fills in specific details (e.g. one organization may be tax-exempt while another may not be).

Once the ground rules have been established, two basic sorts of communication can occur between central administration and individual organizations. The first kind of communication is give-and-take. The mayor asks the Lions Club to discuss a proposal to build a new shopping center in town. The Lions Club meets, talks over the proposal, and hands back its recommendations to the mayor. In the second kind of communication, local organizations get input from the central administration, but are not expected to produce output in return. Consider the distribution of charitable contributions collected by Portsmith's United Way campaign. The mayor's office gives each local organization its allotted funds. The organizations spend the funds as they see fit, and are not required to give anything in return to the mayor.

Besides communication between central administration and local groups, the local groups may choose to communicate among themselves. The garden club, for example, might hold a special workshop for Girl Scouts earning merit badges in horticulture.

Portsmith and Programming Languages

All high-level programming languages have internal organization, lines of jurisdiction, and channels of communication between program components. Generally speaking, the central administration corresponds to the *main program*, the population corresponds to *linear sequences* of programming code, and subgroups correspond to *subroutines, procedures,* or *functions.* Jurisdiction is defined in terms of scope of *variables:* a variable is global (applying to the entire program) or it is local (applying to a particular subroutine or procedure). Communication is accomplished through the use of *parameters,* which are variables or expressions reaching from the main program to the subprogram or between subprograms.

Computer languages differ from one another in how they divide up programs into subcomponents, how the rules of jurisdiction work, and how communication between components is accomplished. While all languages can, in principle, carry out the same tasks, they differ considerably in the conceptual and syntactic clarity with which they do so.

ALGOL and its derivatives take the notion of program organization very seriously. In talking about ALGOL, we introduced the idea of *block structure* and of *procedures*. Pascal further refines the use of blocks and procedures, and develops an especially clear syntax for talking about jurisdiction and about communication within and across parts of the program.

Portsmith and Pascal

We can now look at the structure of Pascal by capitalizing on our extended analogy with Portsmith. To facilitate discussion, here is a table summarizing the correspondences:

SOCIAL ORGANIZATION	PORTSMITH	PASCAL
COMPONENTS:		
central administration	mayor, city council	main program
people	town's population (undifferentiated)	linear sequence of programming code
ORGANIZATIONS:	Policemen's Benevolent Association Lions Club Girl Scout troop garden club	procedures functions
JURISDICTION:		
central administration over groups	don't water the lawn during drought	global variables
within groups	Girl Scout pledge at each troop meeting	local variables
COMMUNICATION:		
I. between central administration and groups		
a. official relationships	hearings at city council meeting	formal parameters/ actual parameters
b. give-and-take	mayor presents shopping center to community groups, gets their opinions back	variable parameters
c. input only	United Way distributes funds to organizations to be spent as they please (no reporting back)	value parameters
II. between groups	garden club helps the Girl Scouts	parameter passing between procedures

Organization: Blocks and Procedures

(1)   Blocks

The basic principle behind structured programming is divide and conquer. By dividing a task into subproblems and then solving each of the subproblems, you end up solving the larger problem. A structured language like Pascal helps you keep track of the problem's subcomponents by labeling them with common-sensical names that become part of the program itself.

In some cases, the problem hardly needs dividing. Suppose you have just had a new parquet floor installed and been sent a bill of $1000. You want to figure out how much you owe per square foot. You know the room is 20 feet long and 30 feet wide. To program the problem, you need to state everything you are given (the length, the width, the price), declare the variables you will need to calculate square footage and cost per square foot, do the calculation, and print out the results. A Pascal program accomplishing the calculation might look like this:

```
PROGRAM PARQUETFLOORING (OUTPUT);
CONST   WIDTH  =  30;
          LENGTH  =  20;
          PRICE  =  1000;
VAR   AREA :   INTEGER;
        COSTSQFT :   REAL;
BEGIN
          AREA := WIDTH * LENGTH;
          COSTSQFT := PRICE/AREA;
          WRITELN ('The cost per square foot of parquet
          is ', COSTSQFT)
END.
```

Programs in Pascal are divided into a *heading* and a *block*. The heading is the line that contains the name of the program and any relevant parameters (i.e. channels of communication). The heading of this program is

PROGRAM PARQUETFLOORING (OUTPUT)

which tells us what the program is about (i.e. parquet flooring) and indicates that some information will be outputted from the program (in this case, written out at the terminal).

The rest of the program is entirely in the block. Blocks contain two main pieces: a set of declarations that tell you what the program will need to deal with and the main program itself that performs the manipulation of data. In PROGRAM PARQUETFLOORING, the declarations tell us what constants we will be using (i.e. width, length, and price) and their values. They also tell us what variables we will use (area and cost per square foot) and what data type the variables belong to. AREA must take an integer (e.g. 60 but not 60.65) while COSTSQFT can take a real number as its value. Pascal is a strongly typed language, which means that users must declare at the very beginning of the program what type of variables they will be using, and not change their mind in midstream.

The second part of the block, the main program, is bounded by the terms BEGIN and END. Contained within this BEGIN-END pair are the statements explaining how actually to solve the problem. However, the statements occurring between BEGIN and END make use of the information we have declared in the earlier part of the block (i.e. here the constants and variables). In our main program, we are instructed to calculate the area, calculate the cost per square foot, and print out the results. To make these first two calculations, though, we need the information we earlier declared as constants.

So far, the notion of a block doesn't seem to have accomplished very much other than grouping together declarations and program statements for manipulating information. In even slightly more complex programs, however, the beauty of the structure begins to come through. For Pascal allows users to embed pieces of programs within other pieces of programs. The block structure helps to keep things straight.

(2) Procedures

Pascal is best known for dividing problems into components that are individually named. There are two sorts of subdivisions in Pascal: procedures and functions. We will deal here only with procedures (procedures and functions are quite similar to one another).

A procedure is like a miniature program embedded within a larger program. It has its own heading and its own block structure. Procedures are *declared* in the declaration part of the larger program (i.e. the first part of the block of the larger program) and then *called* within the main program (i.e. the second part of the larger program).

The relationship between a procedure and the larger program can be shown schematically. The descriptions and line numbers on the left (which are not part of Pascal) explain what constitutes the program, the block, and the two components of the block. The program itself is in the middle. The comments that appear on the right-hand side and are enclosed in (*   *) markers are also part of the Pascal program.

Procedures are useful in four basic ways. First, they help us understand precisely what is going on in a program by separating essence from detail. Second, they enable us to use the same section of code more than once in a program without having to rewrite it in full each time. Third, procedures let us establish communication between parts of the program. And fourth, procedures allow us to incorporate units of code (i.e. subprograms) from another program into the one we are currently working on.

Even in a simple program, procedures allow us to separate the essence of a program from the surrounding syntax necessary to make it work. In the parquet

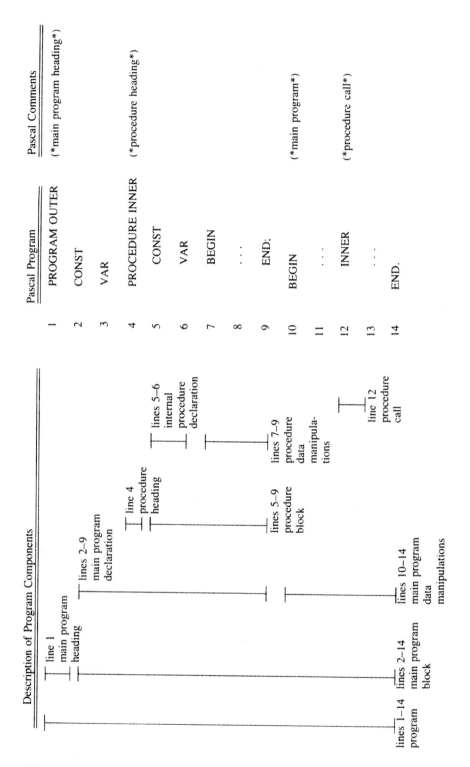

Description of Program Components

	Pascal Program	Pascal Comments
	PROGRAM OUTER	(*main program heading*)
1		
2	CONST	
3	VAR	
4	PROCEDURE INNER	(*procedure heading*)
5	CONST	
6	VAR	
7	BEGIN	
8	⋮	
9	END;	
10	BEGIN	(*main program*)
11	⋮	
12	INNER	(*procedure call*)
13	⋮	
14	END.	

line 1 main program heading

lines 2–9 main program declaration

line 4 procedure heading

lines 5–6 internal procedure declaration

lines 5–9 procedure block

lines 7–9 procedure data manipulations

line 12 procedure call

lines 10–14 main program data manipulations

lines 2–14 main program block

lines 1–14 program

flooring program, we might have defined a procedure to calculate the area and the cost per square foot and print out the answer. We would then call the procedure within the main part of the program doing data manipulation. The result would look something like this:

```
                    PROGRAM PARQUETFLOORING (OUTPUT);
                    CONST  WIDTH  =  30;
                           LENGTH  =  20;
                           PRICE  =  1000;
                    PROCEDURE CALCULATECOST;
                    VAR    AREA :   INTEGER;
                           COSTSQFT :   REAL;
Procedure                  BEGIN
Declaration                    AREA :=  WIDTH * LENGTH;
                           COSTSQFT :=   PRICE/AREA;
                           WRITELIN ('The cost per square foot is',
                               COSTSQFT)
                    END;
                    BEGIN   (* main program *)
                        READ   (WIDTH, LENGTH, PRICE);
Procedure Call              CALCULATECOST

Main Program        END.
Data Manipulation
```

This version of the program may look more complex than the original one—it is even longer than the original. Conceptually, though, the version with a procedure clearly presents what is happening in the program: a set of values is read in and the cost per square foot is automatically calculated and written out.

The power of procedures becomes more evident when we consider increasingly complex programming tasks. Suppose we want to calculate the cost per square foot of parquet flooring in not one but fifteen rooms. Instead of having to write out the formula for calculating cost per square foot fifteen times, we could simply call the procedure fifteen times.

Or suppose we wanted to use the results of one calculation as part of another calculation. To see if a building contractor's prices are fair, we might review what he charges per square foot to install parquet flooring, what he charges per day to paint rooms, and what he charges per hour to do rewiring. Our "hire contractor" program would then *call* each of the three procedures (for flooring, painting, and rewiring costs). We could decide on the basis of the results whether or not to hire the contractor.

Finally, the same procedures can be used in different programs entirely. Programs calculating cost per square foot of real estate could all use exactly the same lines of code. The programmer could simply declare the procedure CALCULATECOST in the declaration section of the appropriate program, and then call the procedure in the main data manipulation part of the program.

Jurisdiction: Global and Local Variables

In our comparison between Portsmith and Pascal, we saw that jurisdiction can work in two ways. Either the central administration can control action at the local level (e.g. whether the garden club can water the lawn at its headquarters during a drought) or local groups can have jurisdiction over their own activities (e.g. the Girl Scouts saying the Girl Scout pledge, the Lions pledging allegiance to the flag).

In Pascal, the analogous distinction is between global and local variables. Global variables are defined in the declaration of the main program and then applied everywhere they appear in the program (assuming they are not redefined by the local procedures). Local variables are declared within the declaration of the procedure block and function only within the level at which they are defined.

Consider a revised version of the parquet flooring example. Instead of declaring specific values for width, length, and price, we might declare these expressions as variables. The declaration part of the main program would now look like this:

```
                        PROGRAM PARQUETFLOORING;
global variables   ⊐⊏   VAR WIDTH, LENGTH, PRICE: INTEGER
                        PROCEDURE CALCULATECOST;
local variables    ⊤    VAR AREA : INTEGER;
                   ⊥        COSTSQFT : REAL;
                        BEGIN
                            . . .
                        END;
```

The variables WIDTH, LENGTH, and PRICE are *global* variables, which means they are defined throughout the program. The variables AREA and COSTSQFT are *local* variables, which means they are defined only within the CALCU-LATECOST procedure.

Communication through Parameters: Formal and Actual, Value and VAR

(1)   Formal and Actual Parameters

The elegance of Pascal is perhaps most vivid in the way that components of a program communicate with one another. Understanding how this communication takes place is often confusing the first (and even the fifth) time around. However, once users understand the principles governing parameters, they will not have difficulty working through actual examples in Pascal textbooks.

In the Portsmith analogy, the central administration established ground rules for communicating with local organizations. In Pascal, these ground rules are called *formal parameters*. They identify the basic categories through which communication will take place. Pascal's formal parameters are listed in the procedure heading. The Pascal equivalent of what local organizations choose to talk about are, not surprisingly, called *actual parameters*. They appear as calls to procedures and are found in the main program's data manipulation section. That is,

```
                    PROCEDURE OUTER;
                    CONST
                    VAR
city hall:          PROCEDURE INNER (FORMAL PARAMETERS);
                    BEGIN
                        . . .
                    END;
                    BEGIN
                        . . .
garden club:            INNER (ACTUAL PARAMETERS);
                        . . .
                    END.
```

The formal and actual parameters need to match in three ways. They must refer to the same thing, they must be of the same type (e.g. INTEGER, REAL), and there must be the same number of them. However (and this is initially the confusing part), they don't have to bear the same names. A variable referring to the number of citizens in Portsmith might be called CITIZENS as a formal parameter and COUNT as an actual parameter. The programmer only needs to be certain that the two sets of parameters are in the same *order* (and obviously that they refer to the same things and are of the same type).

(2)   Value and Variable Parameters

In Portsmith, some communiqués required responses (e.g. feedback on building a shopping center) while others did not (e.g. spending funds from the United Way). This distinction corresponds to the difference between VAR (for "variable") *parameters* and *value parameters* in Pascal. Again, the details can become confusing, but the principle is straightforward.

Pascal can communicate two sorts of information in the process of running a program. One (a *variable parameter*) is the equivalent of a slate which may be blank or which may already have information written on it. The procedure that receives the slate fills in an initial value or changes an old one (calculated in the course of running the procedure) and hands the result back to another part of the program. The procedure can communicate (i.e. pass along the filled slate) either with the main program or with another procedure.

Alternatively, Pascal can send along to the procedure a slate that is already filled (a *value parameter*) and not ask for anything in return. The procedure itself makes use of the parameter as it sees fit—analogous to the Lions Club spending its United Way funds. Thus, variable parameters can be used both to send information to and to receive information from a procedure, while value parameters can only take information in.

EVOLUTION OF PASCAL

From its quiet beginnings in Zurich in the early 1970s, Pascal has swept the higher education programming establishment, at least in the United States. Its success stems as much from a set of extraneous circumstances as from the virtues of the language itself.

Transferability and p-Code

With the growth of structured programming, along with a rising need for trained programmers, a number of people became interested in using Pascal for teaching programming. They began asking Wirth for Pascal translators that would run on their machines. The first Pascal compiler had been written for a CDC (Control Data Corporation) 6000, which was not a computer available to many people who wanted to run Pascal.

Wirth had several options: ignore the requests, write a whole stack of new compilers, or try something new. His solution was to rethink the problem of compatibility between machines.

High-level languages are normally translated into machine-level language, which can then be comprehended directly by a given microprocessor. That is, there is a one-to-many relationship between high-level languages and their implementation, i.e.

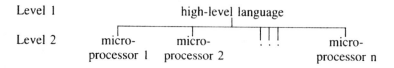

Wirth's idea was to add an intermediary stage. Instead of performing a rather sizable translation effort many times over between level 1 and level 2, he introduced a level 1a, i.e.

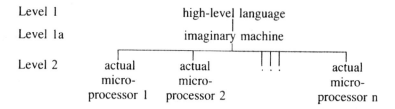

Wirth then wrote a new Pascal compiler that translated high-level Pascal down into a code (known as *p-code*) that would be understood by the imaginary machine. The task of translating this new version of Pascal into the "native" machine language of the actual microprocessor was now quite simple, for the distance between p-code and native machine codes was much less than the distance between high-level Pascal and machine code.

The Pascal Explosion

Wirth's idea found its most important audience at the University of California at San Diego, where in late 1974 Kenneth Bowles worked out a Pascal operating system and compiler to be used on mini- and microcomputers. Bowles went on to develop an entire *system*, containing not only the compiler but also a text editor (for writing and editing programs), an assembler (to do the second step of translation between p-code, i.e. level 1a, and the machine code of the host microprocessor, i.e. level 2), a linker (to join together separately compiled or assembled program modules), a file-handing utility (for general-purpose file manipulation), and a set of utility programs (e.g. to maintain the program library and to format disks). The entire package came to be known as UCSD Pascal.

Bowles's system was configured, tested, and ready for distribution to other university campuses and to people in industry by the summer of 1977. However, it was not until almost a year later, when *Byte* magazine published an article in May 1978 on the UCSD Pascal System, that UCSD Pascal began to receive national attention.

As the use of the UCSD Pascal System spread, it became obvious that the same "system" principle (i.e. p-code, language translator, operating system, editor, etc.) that was used for Pascal could be used for other languages as well. When FORTRAN was added as an alternative language to Pascal, the name of the basic system was changed from UCSD *Pascal* System to UCSD *p*-system. Depending upon whom you ask, you will hear differing stories on what the "p" stands for (e.g. *p*ortable, *p*seudocode, *p*ersonal, and even *p*ascal).

Meanwhile, the growth of microcomputer hardware contributed significantly to the spread of Pascal. Pascal takes considerably more memory than does BASIC and typically needs a minimum of two disk drives to run at all efficiently. The program (and, in the case of UCSD Pascal, the p-system) can take up to three or four disks. Once the on-board memory of microcomputers began to expand and machines were commonly sold with multiple built-in disk drives or hard disks, Pascal became far more usable. At the same time, there was a growing cadre of potential users who had first been introduced to the language on larger computers in school.

Several recent software developments continue to contribute to the spread of Pascal. One is the creation of new interpreted versions of the language, which began appearing in 1984. The most notable of these is produced by Think Technologies. The program has all the friendliness of Applesoft BASIC, but all the power and clarity of the language crafted by Wirth. A second important innovation has been versions of Pascal that run very quickly, the best known being Turbo Pascal, produced by Borland International.

Pascal and BASIC

The rising popularity of Pascal engenders the obvious question among educators of how the language compares with BASIC. Both BASIC and Pascal were originally created for teaching college-level students to program. In the case of BASIC, the main goal was to start students programming *something*, while Pascal (which postdates BASIC by almost a decade) was more directed to the *principles* behind programming than to the production of lines of code that run.

BASIC was developed shortly after the design of ALGOL but considerably before the appearance of structured programming. It is therefore unreasonable to compare the early unstructured forms of BASIC with Wirth's Pascal if we are attempting to select a "first computer language" for students today— particularly since most contemporary versions of BASIC are structured.

The issue is now less one of conceptual rigor and pedagogical appropriateness than of politics. Pascal was selected by the Educational Testing Service (in Princeton, New Jersey) as the language on which it would test high school students wishing to qualify for advanced placement in computer courses in college. John Kemeny, one of the creators of BASIC, articulately argues that the choice might well have been made for the newest structured version of BASIC, called True BASIC. Meanwhile, Kemeny and Thomas Kurtz, the other author of BASIC, are busy marketing True BASIC in hopes of catching up with and perhaps even overtaking Pascal.

THE FUTURE OF PASCAL

Debates between advocates of structured BASIC and advocates of Pascal all presuppose that the appropriate language for general computer education (or the best initial language for future computer programmers) is necessarily imperative/ algorithmic. By now it should be obvious there are other significantly distinct options. But if for the moment we even lay aside these alternative conceptual approaches to computing, there is still the question of whether Pascal (much less BASIC) is the direction of the future for imperative/algorithmic languages.

Today many of the newest and potentially most important imperative/ algorithmic languages (e.g. Modula-2, Ada) are direct descendants of Pascal. At the same time, interest in Pascal has spurred the development of structured versions of several of the older non-structured languages (especially BASIC, FORTRAN, and COBOL). To the extent that imperative/algorithmic languages are used in the foreseeable future, Pascal is likely to continue to exert a strong influence upon many of the languages we will use.

Pascal already seems to be emerging as the standard language to be learned before tackling languages growing out of Pascal. As with learning to operate a flight simulator before actually flying a plane, many students in the future will probably learn to program in Pascal in preparation for learning current and subsequent Pascal derivatives.

But what of Pascal as a language to be learned in its own right? Pascal's creator, Niklaus Wirth, long ago turned his attentions from Pascal to Modula-2. Many pundits foresee that Modula-2 will eventually replace Pascal altogether.

Given the almost ten years since its inception that it has taken for Pascal to become so popular, we may need to wait until 1990 before judging whether Modula-2 will attain comparable importance.

USING PASCAL

Buying Pascal

Pascal is ubiquitous on academic computers (both mainframes and minicomputers). The best-known implementations in the university world are UCSD Pascal, Waterloo Pascal, and perhaps Berkeley Pascal.

Pascal is also widely available for microcomputers. The early versions were generally quite slow and involved much disk swapping. However, several recent translators have revolutionized the use of Pascal on micros. Macintosh Pascal (developed by THINK Technologies but marketed by Apple) was the first interpreted version of Pascal. Even more influential has been Borland International's Turbo Pascal, a compiled language that runs extremely quickly and offers many useful extensions to the ISO Standard. Turbo Pascal is quickly becoming the dialect of choice for Pascal programmers using MS DOS and CP/M machines.

What to Read

BOOKS

The number of books available on Pascal is enormous and continuing to grow. The first two titles below represent formal definitions of the language, while the next two are excellent choices in textbooks for the beginner. The last entry is on the UCSD p-system.

Jensen, Kathleen, and Niklaus Wirth (1974). *Pascal User Manual and Report.* New York: Springer-Verlag.

The "official" definition of the Pascal language. While the manual appears quite dense to the Pascal novice, it is an invaluable guidebook for the person who already knows something of Pascal syntax or of programming more generally.

Cooper, Doug (1983). *Standard Pascal User Reference Manual.* New York: W. W. Norton.

A more "user-friendly" version of Jensen and Wirth.

Dale, Nell, and David Orshalick (1983). *Introduction to Pascal and Structured Design.* Lexington (Mass.): D. C. Heath.

This is the kind of book that should be available for all programming languages. The text is crystal-clear, makes no presuppositions about prior background, anticipates questions the reader is likely to have, and provides ample exercises and answers.

Cooper, Doug, and Michael Clancy (1982). *Oh! Pascal*. New York: W. W. Norton; 2nd ed.

The unlikely title sets the tone for a text written with humor and style.

Overgaard, Mark, and Stan Stringfellow (1983). *Personal Computing with the UCSD p-system*. Englewood Cliffs (N.J.): Prentice-Hall.

A clear introduction to the p-system underlying UCSD Pascal.

ARTICLES

Wirth, Niklaus (1985). "From Programming Language Design to Computer Construction," *Communications of the ACM* 28 (no. 2):160–164.

This is the text of Wirth's Turing Award Lecture, delivered in the fall of 1984. Wirth chronicles his own intellectual and professional history, which includes the evolution of Pascal and its successor, Modula-2.

Wirth, N., and C. A. R. Hoare (1966). "A Contribution to the Development of ALGOL," *Communications of the ACM* 9 (no. 6):413–432.

This article presents Wirth's new language that derived from ALGOL 60 and was the immediate precursor of Pascal. The new language itself was unnamed in the article, but later came to be known as ALGOL W.

Wirth, N. (1971). "The Programming Language Pascal," *Acta Informatica* 1:35–63.

The original published description of Pascal. The article articulately explains the motivation for developing Pascal and gives a concise but clear summary of its syntax.

Journal of Pascal, Ada, and Modula-2

A technical journal that carries articles on these three languages.

PILOT

PROFILE

NAME
*P*rogrammed *I*nquiry, *L*earning *or* *T*eaching

STRUCTURE

Familiar Distinctions:
  hardware: high-level
  translator: interpreted
  structural unit: sentence (unstructured)
  data: character strings, graphics

Conceptual Distinctions:
  organizing principle: imperative/algorithmic
  procedures: procedural
  extensibility: not extensible
  program/data: distinct

FUNCTIONS
computer-aided instruction (CAI)

GENEALOGY

BASIC

PILOT

Year: 1968

Author: John Starkweather (University of California Medical Center, San Francisco)

Impetus: provide easy way for computer novices to devise and run computer-aided instruction lessons

Evolution: major impact on educational world with development of microcomputers;
language may be eclipsed by more powerful languages that are also easy to learn but are additionally useful for purposes other than CAI

(Continued)

PILOT (Continued)

VERSIONS/DIALECTS
Standard: Common PILOT
Dialects: Apple PILOT
SuperPILOT

SPECIAL CHARACTERISTICS
Memory Requirements: small
Ease of Learning/Use: very easy
Availability: available for many microcomputers

WHY PILOT?

PILOT epitomizes the question of who controls computers: users themselves or professional programmers. Like COBOL, PILOT was explicitly developed with novice programmers in mind. Both languages have minimal syntax and English-like commands, and neither requires knowledge of mathematics beyond addition, subtraction, multiplication, and division.

Yet COBOL and PILOT have also been plagued by a gap between the designers' intentions and contemporary practice. In the case of COBOL, the mushrooming of "professional" data-processing departments removed office workers and managers alike from the production and use of programs. With PILOT, educators have not been distanced from the language, though the shortcomings of PILOT (and languages like it) may once again relegate educators to the role of computer consumers rather than producers.

The history of PILOT is, then, instructive not only as the story of a particular computer language but as an object lesson for planning computer languages of the future.

Computer-Aided Instruction: For Whom? By Whom?

Modern philosophies of education emphasize creation and discovery, but students must nonetheless memorize such things as the multiplication tables, the periodic chart, and conjugations of irregular verbs in foreign languages. Understandably, educators tire of repeating the same lessons, the same drills, and the same examinations. But computers don't. Educators despair of being able to tailor lessons to the individual needs of students while coping with a class of thirty or forty. But computers don't. And so computer-aided instruction was born.

Computer-aided instruction (CAI) is obviously well suited to subjects like foreign languages and arithmetic, which traditionally involve some explanation but much repetitive practice. However, an impressive number of other subjects have proved amenable to CAI as well, ranging from biology to logic to American history. In some cases, the computer plays the role of instructor, while in others its primary function is to run multiple-choice tests.

In the era of mainframe computers, CAI projects were typically engineered by people with background in computers (or mathematics or logic) who also had an interest in education. Many CAI experiments were done, for example, at Stanford University in the late 1950s and early 1960s under the direction of Patrick Suppes, a logician. The best-known project (and the one with the greatest longevity and highest price tag) came out of the University of Illinois in the 1960s and 1970s, under the direction of Donald Bitzer. Known as the PLATO system, the programs came to span the educational gamut from accounting to urban affairs. The Stanford project emphasized lower education, while the PLATO system was aimed at college-level courses. More recently, with the proliferation of microcomputers, PLATO has extended its programming to lower school levels as well.

CAI was an excellent idea—on paper. The early cost of hardware was high, and it was difficult to hook up by telephone to a mainframe computer perhaps several states away. Moreover, there were the pedagogical issues of appropriateness and power. Even CAI lessons that were well written (which frequently was not the case) were rarely keyed to the text a teacher happened to be using.

The result of prepackaged CAI programs is often a power struggle between the CAI package and the instructor for control of the classroom. Whoever wins, the student is the loser. The obvious solution is to let instructors write their own CAI materials, designing programs to dovetail with their individual syllabus and teaching style.

Teacher as Programmer: From BASIC to PILOT

This "obvious solution" makes two critical presuppositions: that teachers from kindergarten to college will learn computer programming and that they will be good at it. The history of "authoring languages" (that is, languages explicitly designed for creating CAI materials) is the history of these suppositions.

Think back to the world of computers in the mid-1960s when Stanford and the University of Illinois were embarking upon their major CAI efforts. There were no microcomputers. In fact, there were barely any minicomputers. MIT had only recently developed time sharing. Control of computer hardware resided in the hands of a very small number of people, almost none of them with professional background in education.

The situation with software was equally circumscribed. Most programming was done in FORTRAN or assembly language. COBOL was beginning to spread, but strictly as a data-processing language. BASIC had been invented at Dartmouth, though few people would hear about it for another decade. Several brave educators did stray into computer centers and remain to learn enough programming to write their own lessons. But the number remained extremely small until the spread of microcomputers in the late 1970s.

John Starkweather at the University of California Medical Center in San Francisco developed PILOT in 1968 to help overcome these problems. The language was originally designed to run on larger computers. However, only with the development and spread of microcomputers, especially in lower school education, did PILOT gain a national reputation. This growth was fostered by the fact that the syntax of PILOT grows directly out of BASIC, a language familiar to many educators who were potential writers of CAI programs.

THINKING IN PILOT

Requirements for a CAI Language

A CAI language must carry out a minimum of four functions. First, it must be able to *convey information* to its users and then *query* users about that information. (Alternatively, the CAI system may be used only for testing purposes.) Second, users must have some means of *entering responses* to questions. Third, the program needs to *compare (or match) user responses with the correct answers* embedded in the program. And fourth, there must be a way of *acting upon the results of the match.* Correct answers need to be acknowledged and users moved along to another problem. A wrong answer needs to be noted, and the user is either returned to try the problem again, given a tutorial on the subject matter, or provided the correct answer. At the same time, the program should keep track of the user's score.

Besides these four essential functions, the program may also have graphics abilities to present information (or questions) and may have basic arithmetic facilities. In general, though, CAI programming languages need very little in the way of computing power, since the goal of a CAI language is to present information and/or test whether a user's answers to questions match those provided with the program. Consequently, CAI languages tend to be very simple in structure, although the text of CAI programs tends to be disproportionately long.

The Syntax of PILOT

A PILOT program consists of a sequence of *statements* (each line of a PILOT program is a statement). The program itself has no internal structure. That is, there are no "procedures" or "functions." Like the early versions of BASIC and FORTRAN, PILOT is an unstructured language. The lack of structuring in PILOT reflects its historical roots in BASIC. In fact, as we examine the syntactic structure of PILOT, we will see constant reminders of this BASIC heritage.

(1)   Teaching and Questioning: TYPE
Suppose we are constructing a lesson and subsequent test on classical Greece. Our lesson includes the information that Socrates was the teacher of Plato, Plato

was the teacher of Aristotle, and Aristotle was the teacher of Alexander of Macedon. The beginning of our PILOT program might look like this:

> R: Teacher-student relationships among Greek philosophers and Macedonian rulers
>
> R:
>
> CH:

All statements in PILOT begin with a name—like R (for REMARK) or CH (for CLEAR SCREEN HOME), which clears the screen and sends the cursor to the upper left-hand corner. Both of these statements are reminiscent of BASIC commands. The second line in the program (R:) merely produces a blank line to make the program more readable.

The interesting part of the program begins with statements prefaced with T for TYPE. TYPE statements are ways of inputting information or requesting a response from a user, e.g.

> T: Socrates was the teacher of Plato.
>
> T: Plato was the teacher of Aristotle.
>
> T: Aristotle was the teacher of Alexander of Macedon.

We can now query users about the lesson. Queries are also entered using the TYPE statement. To be sure that this is a "closed book" test, we begin by clearing the earlier lines from the screen:

> CH:
>
> T: Who was the teacher of Aristotle?
>
> T: a.   Socrates
>
> T: b.   Plato
>
> T: c.   Alexander of Macedon

We have stated a question (using a TYPE statement) and specified three possible answers (again, using TYPE statements).

(2)   Receiving Responses: ACCEPT

The ACCEPT statement (A) provides a place for the user to respond to questions. It immediately follows a TYPE statement of the sort we just saw, i.e.

> T.   Who was the teacher of Aristotle?
>
> T: a.   Socrates
>
> T: b.   Plato
>
> T: c.   Alexander of Macedon
>
> A:

The student's response (e.g. "Plato") is then stored in a response buffer, to be compared against the correct answer that is indicated in the next program statement: the MATCH statement.

(3) Comparing Responses with Correct Answers: MATCH

The key to PILOT is the MATCH statement (M), which compares the pattern of the user response (given in A) with the pattern programmed into M. If the patterns match, the answer is judged correct, and one set of consequences follows. If the M statement and A statement do not match, the answer is deemed wrong, and another class of results ensue. If a match takes place, an internal YES flag is set that then triggers subsequent lines of programming code. A NO flag is set (again, triggering appropriate consequences) if a match does not occur.

Pattern matching in languages that emphasize character strings (that is, text) is reasonably common. The best known of the string-processing languages, SNOBOL, makes heavy use of pattern matching, as do PROLOG, Savvy, and POP-11.

(4) Consequences of Match: TY, TN, JUMP, COMPUTE

We have said that different consequences follow if a match takes place (i.e. the answe. is correct) than if the match fails (i.e. the answer is wrong). Let's consider each of these possibilities, plus some variations on the more straight-forward theme.

Assume that the questioning part of our program so far looks like this:

```
T:      Who was the teacher of Aristotle ·
T:              a.   Socrates
T:              b.   Plato
T:              c.   Alexander of Macedon
A:
M:      Plato
TY:     That's right, it was Plato.
TN:     No, you are wrong.
```

The statement TY (= TYPE if MATCH flag was set to YES) is activated if the match did take place. Typically, the program then goes on with other TYPE statements posing additional questions to be answered.

However, if the MATCH did not take place and the NO flag was set, the TN statement (= TYPE if MATCH flag was set to NO) is activated. A whole list of possibilities may then ensue. Users may be told they are wrong (as in the TN statement above) and then presented with the next question. Alternatively, they might be handed the correct answer, e.g.

```
TN:   No, you are wrong. The right answer is Plato.
```

and then sent along to the next question. A third option would be to give a hint, e.g.

> TN: No, you are wrong. Think about the relative ages of Aristotle, Plato, and Alexander.

A fourth possibility would be to return to the original lesson. And a fifth would be to let the user try again. (Of course, these possibilities can be combined.)

The last three of these possibilities requires users to be able to move about in the PILOT program. Movement can be accomplished through a branching structure known as JUMP (equivalent to GOTO statements in BASIC and many other imperative/algorithmic languages). Using JUMP statements, users can move from one point in the program to another. In assembly language, JUMP statements indicate an address in memory that the flow of control will be passed to (e.g. JMP $54F8, where $54F8 indicates in hexadecimal numbers the address in memory to go to next). In languages like BASIC with GOTO statements, the destination is typically indicated with line numbers (e.g. GOTO 660).

In PILOT, there are two ways of indicating destinations. The first is with a *label*, which names a set of program statements. For example, we might want users to be able to choose the level of difficulty of questions they will be asked. The necessary lines of programming code would look like this (the numbers on the left-hand side are added to facilitate discussion, and are *not* part of PILOT):

```
1    T:   Do you want easy questions, moderately difficult questions,
          or very difficult questions?
     T:        a.  easy
     T:        b.  moderately difficult
     T:        c.  very difficult
     A:

2    M:   easy
     JY:  EASY

3    M:   moderately difficult
     JY:  MODERATE

4    M:   very difficult
     JY:  DIFFICULT

5    *EASY
     R:   These questions are easy to answer.
     T:   Who died by drinking hemlock?
     A:
     M:   Socrates
     . . .
```

6   *MODERATE
R: These questions are moderately difficult to answer.
T: Who made two trips to Italy?
A:
M: Plato
. . .

7   *DIFFICULT
R: These questions are the hardest in the group.
T: Whose father was a physician to his student's father?
A:
M: Aristotle
. . .

The program works like this: In what we have labeled part 1 of the program, the user selects the desired level of difficulty of questions. The ACCEPT statement will match either with "easy" (part 2), "moderately difficult" (part 3), or "very difficult" (part 4). If the match occurs with "easy" (that is, the YES flag is set), control jumps down to the sequence labeled EASY (part 5). Similarly, if the match occurs with "moderately difficult," control is passed to the section labeled MODERATE (part 6), and if the match occurs with "very difficult," control moves to part 7 (DIFFICULT). (Incidentally, Aristotle's father was personal physician to Philip of Macedon, father of Alexander.)

Alternatively, the JUMP statement can be matched with a particular *type* of statement. For example, if the author of the program wants the user to keep trying until getting the answer right, a JUMP statement can be written that returns the user back to an ACCEPT statement if he or she failed to make a match with the right answer. A typical program fragment might look like this:

T: Who died by drinking hemlock?
A:
M: Socrates
      You're right, it was Socrates.
TN: No. Try again.
JN: @A

If the user answers "Socrates" in the ACCEPT statement, the conditions for TY are met, and the program responds, "You're right, it was Socrates." However, if the NO flag is set, the conditions for TN are met, and the program responds, "No. Try again." The next line of the program is then activated, and control is returned to the ACCEPT statement so that the user can indeed try again. Counters can also be added to limit the number of tries the user has.

One purpose of CAI programs is to test how well users have learned information. The simplest measure of learning is a tally of the user's right and wrong answers. PILOT has a simple COMPUTE statement that registers correct and incorrect responses by incrementing the value of a variable counter each time the YES or NO flag is set in the course of a MATCH attempt. A typical COMPUTE statement might look like this:

CY: #N = #N + 1

The statement adds 1 to the integer variable N each time a YES flag is set. In other words, each time users get an answer right, their score will be increased by 1.

(5) Graphics
Some versions of PILOT, especially those running on the Apple II series of microcomputers, have a number of features in addition to those available in Common PILOT (the standard we have been describing). The most salient additional feature is graphics. In fact, SuperPILOT (for the Apple) incorporates the same turtle graphics originally designed for Logo but now available for several other microcomputer languages used in education (e.g. micro-PROLOG).

PILOT as an Education Language

Finally, we can reflect on the workings of PILOT by casting the language in relief against BASIC and Logo, which often function alongside PILOT in lower education.

BASIC has been a jack-of-all-trades, introducing teacher and student alike to microcomputers. BASIC has provided a means of writing simple programs and has whetted the appetites of many to continue with computing. PILOT closely resembles BASIC in several obvious ways. Both languages are unstructured (i.e. they are composed of a linear sequence of statements, interrupted by JUMP or GOTO commands). PILOT directly borrows from BASIC instructions like REMARK, CLEAR SCREEN, and HOME. Neither language has very sophisticated computational power, and both are easy to learn.

Yet functionally, BASIC and PILOT are quite distinct languages. BASIC, whatever its limitations, is a general-purpose language that can (with some effort) be made to handle any sort of problem. PILOT, on the other hand, was explicitly designed for a very restricted purpose (much like word-processing programs or spreadsheets). It is extremely awkward to stretch PILOT beyond its original functions.

Logo and PILOT share an important feature that is less characteristic of BASIC. That is *control*. Logo was designed to give control to children, especially in their encounter with geometry, and PILOT was designed to give teachers control over the use of computers in their own classrooms.

THE EVOLUTION AND FUTURE OF PILOT

The Limits of CAI

The coming of the microcomputer in the late 1970s and early 1980s was forecast to revolutionize American education. Computer programs would replace textbooks, every student would have his or her own computer, and the quality of education would measurably rise.

The revolution has not materialized. Sales of computer hardware and software have slowed down from their projected growth curve, and educators are beginning to question the pedagogical soundness of existing programs. The drill-and-practice programs that ushered in the era of computer-aided instruction are unimaginative at best.

At the same time, computers in education are going in other sorts of directions. A few good educational programs are beginning to appear, in the face of which teacher-written PILOT programs seem primitive. New visually oriented technologies (e.g. videotapes, interactive video discs) easily overshadow the turtle graphics of SuperPILOT. And children themselves are developing sophisticated programming skills that outstrip the most involuted program in PILOT.

But there is another factor that may prove more important than the state of computer languages or computer technology: the state of American education itself. In the first half of the 1980s, national reviews of lower school education have declared the United States to be "A Nation at Risk" because of the blighted academic state of our pedagogy. Similar reports about the quality of higher education are being issued by the National Endowment for the Humanities, the Association of American Colleges, and the National Institute of Education. In most of these reports, the suggested solution is to increase human resources, not to augment technology.

The rationale behind these recommendations is generally that the United States needs to return to the traditional values of humanistic education. But there is another route by which we might reach the same conclusion. As the reports point out, educators are failing to teach their students in face-to-face, non-technology-aided instruction. How, then, can these same teachers be expected to design computer-based education packages that will succeed where the same educational principles used in face-to-face pedagogy have failed? For now the problems of knowing *what* to teach and *how* to teach it are compounded with the problem of how to make an instructional unit work on a computer.

Specification vs. Programming

The problems of education in general (what to teach and how to teach it) go beyond the bounds of this book. But the issue of implementation of educational materials on computers is something we can try to deal with.

PILOT was explicitly devised to help teachers come to grips with the computer implementation problem. Yet contemporary advocates of PILOT are now cautioning that good computer-aided instruction may require more powerful programming structures and more sophisticated programming skills than we can expect in working with PILOT. Tom Conlon, author of *PILOT: The Language and How to Use It*, suggests that educators learn what programs they can write productively and what programming should be left to the professionals:

> The widespread introduction of microcomputers has prompted many
> educators (sometimes under the pressure of educational administrators)

to "go it alone" regardless of the nature of the task. Many factors have led to this phenomenon: the non-availability of programming assistance; the hold which computer technology has upon some beginners; a desire for independence; and plain ignorance of what is involved all played a part. Whatever the reason, the end result has been a vast amount of wasted time and an equally huge amount of useless software. [p. 116]

Of course, Conlon is right. Yet how do we solve the problem? Conlon suggests that educators learn *when* to write their own programs and when to rely, instead, upon professionals:

There are some signs of a growing realization within education that a much more satisfactory alternative route to software development exists . . . : *if [software] can be specified, it should be.* [pp. 116–117]

By "specified," Conlon means that the educator should describe the goals and content of the software package so that a computer expert can design and implement the actual program.

Many teachers who have tried to write their own programs may breathe a sigh of relief at the suggestion "Let the experts do it." Admittedly, most teachers have neither the background nor the interest for creating educational software. However, to call in the experts is to relinquish control over what is ultimately being taught. Before giving up in defeat, we should at least consider whether other existing languages (perhaps micro-PROLOG) or languages yet to be developed (e.g. sophisticated authoring languages based on an object-oriented language like Smalltalk) would be at once easy to learn and intellectually powerful.

USING PILOT

Buying PILOT

PILOT is available for most microcomputers commonly used in lower education (including the Apple II series, the IBM PC, the Atari, and the Commodore VIC). Two different versions run on the Apple: Apple PILOT and SuperPILOT (which incorporates a number of the newer features, including turtle graphics).

What to Read

Despite the popularity of PILOT, there are few books written on the language. Here are two, the first of which was written by the creator of PILOT:

Starkweather, John A. (1985). *A User's Guide to PILOT*. Englewood Cliffs (N.J.): Prentice-Hall.
Conlon, Tom (1984). *PILOT: The Language and How to Use It*. Englewood Cliffs (N.J.): Prentice-Hall International.

PL/I

PROFILE

NAME

*P*rogramming *L*anguage One; until 1965 called NPL (*N*ew *P*rogramming *L*anguage) but renamed because NPL already used by National Physical Laboratory in England

STRUCTURE

Familiar Distinctions:
  hardware: high-level
  translator: compiled
  structural unit: procedure
  data: numerical, string

Conceptual Distinctions:
  organizing principle: imperative/algorithmic
  procedures: procedural
  extensibility: not extensible
  program/data: distinct

FUNCTIONS

science, business, and "special purpose" (including string processing and systems programming)

GENEALOGY

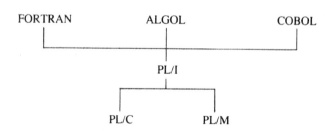

Years: 1963–64

Authors: committee (sponsored by IBM, but included non-IBM program-mers)

(Continued)

PL/I *(Continued)*

Impetus:	create single language running on single computer with single operating system (i.e. IBM 360 and OS/360) to serve needs of all users
Evolution:	language didn't become as widespread as IBM hoped (too late to compete with COBOL, too large to serve needs of individual user groups)

VERSIONS/DIALECTS

Standards:	ANSI standard of PL/I (1976)
	ANSI standard of subset of PL/I (1981)

Others: many subsets of PL/I, including PL/C

SPECIAL CHARACTERISTICS

Memory Requirements:	large
Ease of Learning / Use:	intended to be accessible to new programmers, but proved difficult
Availability.	generally available on older large IBM computers but also used on some newer machines and on micros

WHY PL/I?

In the 1950s, the Ford Motor Company decided to produce the ultimate automobile. Ford was intent upon considering the wishes of all possible consumers. In designing the car, Ford surveyed potential customers, who said they wished the next car they bought would have such and such a feature. All the "such and suches" were then pooled, and the result was called the Edsel

The car should have sold phenomenally. Instead, it was perhaps Detroit's largest fiasco. Almost no one liked the car—or bought it. Instead of Edsels taking over the roads, the name Edsel came to mean a bureaucratic white elephant.

The language PL/I can be described as the Edsel of the computer world. Created in the early 1960s, it was meant to be all things to all people. It was specifically designed to replace FORTRAN, ALGOL, and COBOL. But like the manufacturing of the Edsel, the PL/I attempt produced a very detailed (and even very good) product that nonetheless failed to attract its intended audience.

What went wrong?

The Search for a General-Purpose Language

By the early 1960s, the world of computing had polarized into three major groups: science and engineering, business, and everyone else (which generally included people working with pattern matching, list handling, and systems programming). The needs of each group were different. So were the computers (and operating systems) that each tended to use and even the users' group to which programmers belonged. The distribution went like this:

FUNCTION	LANGUAGE	CHARACTERISTICS	MACHINE	USERS' GROUP
science	FORTRAN	floating point arithmetic arrays subroutines fast computation and compilation	IBM 7090 IBM 1620	SHARE
commercial	COBOL	decimal arithmetic string-handling instructions fast and asynchronous I/O efficient object code excellent sort programs	IBM 7080 IBM 1401	GUIDE

special
purpose
	(e.g.
	JOVIAL)
		variable-length bit string
		  arithmetic
		macro libraries
		pattern-matching operators
		list handlers
		very fast response time in
		  real time
			IBM 7750
			Harvest	

Such divisions made sense as long as the three genres of programming could be kept distinct. Yet it was becoming evident in the early 1960s that applications and users were not remaining compartmentalized. Commercial users began wanting more powerful computation than COBOL provided. Science users found themselves needing more sophisticated data structures. IBM decided that as a service to its customers (and obviously to itself as well), it would create one machine, one operating system, and one programming language that would be able to do everything. The machine was to be its new System/360, running under the equally new operating system OS/360. The task now was to create an appropriate language.

Beating the Clock

Work on the new language began in October 1963. The language was to be designed by a committee of programmers from IBM and the outside. The designers initially saw the language as an extension of FORTRAN IV. However, it later became clear that if all the new features that were desired were actually incorporated, the language would no longer be compatible with earlier versions of FORTRAN. Most of these new features were to come from ALGOL and COBOL. The only reasonable conclusion was to create a new language.

IBM originally planned to release the language with its System/360, and the language committee was told to complete its work by December 1963. This was a tall order for a group of people who had to assemble every other weekend from all over the United States. The initial version of the language was finished in late February 1964, too late to be released with the first crop of 360s. This time delay may be the primary reason that PL/I failed to unseat COBOL as the standard language for business applications.

The rush to completion had other negative consequences as well. The original version of the language (and, some would argue, subsequent versions as well) was defined too quickly. It was ambiguous in many cases and sometimes incomplete. Moreover, its unwieldy size could probably have been pared down if there had been more time to sort through the pieces that had all been thrown into the brew in the attempt to create a functionally universal language. PL/I's hefty size has been one of its drawbacks for users who need only a fraction of its capabilities. (It will be instructive to see whether Ada suffers a similar fate.)

After the design committee finished initial work on the language (then named NPL for *N*ew *P*rogramming *L*anguage), the results were shipped to Hursley, England, where work began to solidify the language design and construct compilers. The language went on the market in 1965. In that same year, the name was changed from NPL to PL/I because the National Physical Laboratory in England had already laid claim to the earlier initials.

PL/I and COBOL: Design Similarities

In retrospect, both PL/I's design and its resulting problems were hardly unique. A comparison with COBOL underscores the point. Both COBOL and PL/I are largely *composites* of earlier languages rather than languages constructed afresh. COBOL is a blend of FLOW-MATIC, AIMACO, and COMTRAN, and PL/I is a compilation of FORTRAN, ALGOL, and COBOL. If both COBOL and PL/I sometimes look like patchwork quilts, it is because they are.

Furthermore, the creators of a COBOL and PL/I believed they were writing languages that would be accessible to novice programmers. The goal did not work at all for COBOL and, as we will see here, did not work much better for PL/I.

Finally, both languages were constructed under time constraints. What COBOL's designers thought would be an interim language was instead issued to the public and quickly adopted. And in the case of PL/I, the designers felt their work was too hurried.

THINKING IN PL/I

PL/I the Inheritor

While PL/I added a number of structures and expansions of its own, most of the language is directly taken from FORTRAN, ALGOL, and COBOL. The clearest way of demonstrating this genealogy is simply to note some of the features adopted from each of the three source languages:

FORTRAN:
   1. separately compiled subroutines sharing common data
   2. DO loop
   3. parameter transmission mechanisms
   4. formatted input/output

ALGOL:
   1. block structure
   2. structured statements
   3. recursion

COBOL:
   1. data structures (especially records)
   2. record-oriented input/output
   3. PICTURE type declaration
   4. report-generating facilities

Programming in PL/I

PL/I is a large and complex language. Unlike COBOL, where the entire language was intended to be accessible to novices, PL/I was designed to offer different accessibility to the seasoned programmer and to the novice. Experienced programmers have access to the entire language. Yet many programming elements have default values which the compiler will declare if less experienced programmers fail to specify them. This notion of multiple layers of users is also found in a modern language like Ada, which has the capacity to place much detail in "packages" that less experienced programmers can use without "opening."

The real powers of PL/I are not evident to the reader if we do not go into a considerable level of detail. However, rather than plunge into such detail, we will restrict our example to a short program illustrating how PL/I would handle a simple operation. The example at least gives a flavor of PL/I's origins in FORTRAN, ALGOL, and COBOL.

Our program adds two numbers together:

```
FIRST:  PROCEDURE OPTIONS (MAIN);
        DECLARE  (FIRST__NUMBER,SECOND__NUMBER,TOTAL)
             FIXED (5,0);
        FIRST__NUMBER = 4;
        SECOND__NUMBER = 4;
             TOTAL = FIRST__NUMBER + SECOND__NUMBER;
        PUT DATA (TOTAL);
        END FIRST;
```

Note the use of the word PROCEDURE in the very first line. This structuring of PL/I programs into blocks or subprograms derives from ALGOL. The general program formatting derives from the high-level language tradition begun by FORTRAN, and the use of so much ordinary English in the lines of programming code (e.g. FIRST__NUMBER,SECOND__NUMBER) is reminiscent of COBOL.

THE EVOLUTION OF PL/I

PL/I has not enjoyed the widespread adoption envisioned by its designers. It is tempting to say this is the fate of languages created by committees. Yet such an argument is obviously too simple. COBOL was created by a committee, and consider its success. The real problem with PL/I was that it tried to be too many things to too many people. Even back in 1964, when the language was first presented to members of SHARE (the science-and-engineering-oriented users' group), the participants compared the language to a Swiss Army knife with a hundred blades.

One solution over the years has been to create subsets of PL/I that contain only a portion of PL/I's capabilities. A well-known example is PL/C, created at Cornell University. PL/C has been used extensively for the teaching of PL/I.

As PL/I failed to attract users from COBOL and FORTRAN (ALGOL was never a challenge in the United States), the proponents of PL/I began shifting their prospective audience. Instead of pursuing the scientific or business market, they began exploring PL/I's usefulness in systems programming. Given all its built-in capabilities, PL/I enabled systems programmers to write in a high-level language without having to revert to assembly language.

In its day, PL/I provided a viable alternative to some uses of assembly. However, PL/I may have outrun its usefulness here. Modern languages like C were expressly designed for systems programming. Not only does C, like PL/I, have the advantages of being a high-level language, but C lacks much of the "excess baggage" of PL/I.

THE FUTURE OF PL/I

Whatever the future of PL/I as a language for systems programming, it is reasonably clear that PL/I can no longer be thought of as a general-purpose language. In the almost quarter century since PL/I was designed, our notions of what computer languages might look like and what kinds of tasks they should be expected to perform have expanded enormously. Genres like logic programming and the language FORTH didn't exist back in the 1960s, and functional/applicative and object-oriented languages were just getting started. The contemporary diversity of computer language functions and conceptual organizing principles vitiates the very idea of a single language filling everyone's needs.

USING PL/I

Buying PL/I

As an IBM language, PL/I is available on nearly all large IBM computers. There are, however, also several subsets and variations available for microcomputers. One of these is called PL/M (for "micro").

What to Read

Many of the books and articles on PL/I are several or more years old. However, a few textbook companies are now announcing new works.

BOOKS

Conway, R. W., and D. Gries (1976). *A Primer on Structured Programming Using PL/I, PL/C, and PL/CT*. Cambridge (Mass.): Winthrop Publishers. One of the standard texts on PL/I.

McCracken, Daniel D. (1978). *A Guide to PL/M Programming for Microcomputer Applications*. Reading (Mass.): Addison-Wesley.
A teach-yourself text on PL/M by one of the best-known writers of computer language textbooks.

Hunter, Bruce H. (1986). *PL/I on Micros*. Glenview, Ill.: Scott, Foresman and Co.
The book describes a general subset of PL/I (known as Subset G) that can be implemented on microcomputers running the CP/M, MP/M, or PC DOS operating systems.

ARTICLES

Radin, George (1981). "The Early History and Characteristics of PL/I," in R. L. Wexelblat, ed., *History of Programming Languages*. New York: Academic Press, pp. 551–599.
A personal account of the development of PL/I.

PROLOG

PROFILE
NAME
*PRO*gramming in *LOG*ic
STRUCTURE

Familiar Distinctions:
  hardware: high-level
  translator: usually interpreted
  structural unit: facts and rules
  data: largely symbolic
 	
Conceptual Distinctions:
  organizing principle: logic programming
  procedures: largely non-procedural (but also can be viewed procedur-
           ally)
  extensibility: extensible
  program/data: not distinct

FUNCTIONS
artificial intelligence data base management systems
GENEALOGY

First Order Predicate Calculus

             ←————— Horn Clauses

             ←————— Robinson Resolution Principle

      PROLOG

Logo		LISP	POP
SOLO	micro-PROLOG	LOGLISP	POPLOG

(Continued)

PROLOG *(Continued)*

Year: 1972

Authors: Alain Colmerauer and Philippe Roussel (University of Marseilles)

Impetus: desire to do computer-aided theorem proving

Evolution: from a theorem-proving language, PROLOG has emerged as an important language for doing AI research, as well as a general-purpose symbolic language for tasks ranging from data base management to architectural design

VERSIONS/DIALECTS

Standard: no international standard

Dialects: Edinburgh DEC 10 PROLOG
Waterloo PROLOG
PROLOG-20 (Stanford)
IC-PROLOG (Imperial College, London)

SPECIAL CHARACTERISTICS

Memory Requirements: large (programming is memory-intensive)

Ease of Learning / Use: simple but non-transparent syntax

Availability: growing availability on large computers; coming to be available on micros

WHY PROLOG?

In 1981, Japan's newly formed Institute for New Generation Technology (known as ICOT) announced a daring ten-year project intended to change the face of computing. The goal was to produce a new, "fifth" generation of computer hardware that would be able to process voluminous quantities of information. The machines were to act intelligently, accepting natural language (or nearly natural language) input. Yet the computer language selected for programming these new machines was not LISP, the mainstay of the American artificial intelligence community, but PROLOG, a relatively new language that was developed in France and whose use was largely restricted to Europe.

It took a few years for Americans to take the new language seriously. At a general session of the 1983 meetings of the American Association for Artificial Intelligence (AAAI), a question about the "PROLOG challenge" was promptly dismissed: of course the Japanese were making a mistake. In a session on LISP at the 1984 meetings of the AAAI, one LISP devotee aggressively declared that the Japanese were so uncertain about their choice of PROLOG for doing artificial intelligence programming that they were simultaneously writing all of their programs in LISP as well. But as reports of progress on the Japanese fifth-generation project have begun to spread, and as PROLOG becomes better known in the United States, the language is finally coming to be taken seriously. At a minimum, some researchers are looking to incorporate ideas from PROLOG into LISP, and at a maximum, to switch to programming in PROLOG altogether.

Unlike LISP, PROLOG didn't begin as a language for doing general work in AI. In fact, its roots are not in programming as problem solving involving natural language, but in programming as theorem proving. PROLOG is the beginning of what portends to be an increasingly important approach to computer programming, namely *logic programming*. To understand what logic has to do with programming, and what PROLOG has to do with logic, we need to step back from computers and think about language and representation.

Language into Logic: First Order Predicate Calculus

In Chapter 2 we talked about language as a means of representing something else—ideas, experiences, objects. Just as language can be used as a means of representation, other symbolic systems can be used to represent language or, more generally, the things we use language to think about. One such means of representing language (and the ideas behind language) is logic.

Logic is a formal system for talking about relationships between assumptions and conclusions. If I assume that strawberries exist and cream exists, then I can conclude that strawberries and cream can exist. If I assume that Lassie is a dog and all dogs are animals, then I can conclude that Lassie is an animal. Our statements about strawberries and cream and Lassie and animals are all linguistic statements about things in our world of experience. Logic can represent a subset of the possible expressions in natural languages.

Several kinds of logic have developed over the last several thousand years. *Propositional logic* (also known as propositional calculus) represents relationships between simple propositions. If P implies Q, and P is not the case, then Q is not the case. *First order predicate logic* (or calculus)—also known as the logic of quantification—deals with relationships between propositions that have measurable dimension such as *all* or *some* or *none*. A subset of first order predicate logic known as the logic of syllogisms was first developed in classical Greece and formalized by Aristotle. All men are mortal. All Greeks are men. Therefore all Greeks are mortal. This logic of quantification was subsequently developed by the medieval Arabs and later in medieval Europe. Today, the term *symbolic logic* is sometimes used to include both propositional logic and first order predicate logic.

Within the first order predicate logic, there are equivalence rules that allow us to write the same logical statements in more than one way. By the rules of propositional logic, it can be shown, for example, that

$$\sim(A \cdot B)$$

(read "not (A and B)") means the same thing as

$$(\sim A) \wedge (\sim B)$$

(read "not A or not B"). This equivalence can be demonstrated by way of a truth table:

A	B	A · B (A and B)	~(A · B) not (A and B)	~A (not A)	~B (not B)	(~A) ∧ (~B) (not A or not B)
T	T	T	F	F	F	F
F	T	F	T	T	F	T
T	F	F	T	F	T	T
F	F	F	T	T	T	T

where T = True
      F = False

Conversions of this sort are often useful when attempting to construct logical proofs. (They are also extremely helpful in designing electronic circuits that are based upon propositional logic.) By using one particular set of these kinds of conversion, we are said to "normalize" the propositions of predicate calculus. The possibility of "normalizing" statements in predicate calculus is, as we will see, a vital piece of the PROLOG puzzle.

Theorem Proving and Computers

Logic is a means not only of *stating* relationships between assumptions and conclusions but also of *proving* that these relationships necessarily hold. Theorem proving is a significant part of work in logic and mathematics. In order to prove theorems, it is often useful to convert logical statements into a normalized form using techniques of the sort we discussed a moment ago. One such form, developed in 1951, is known as Horn Clauses, named after the logician Alfred Horn. A clause in logic is simply a statement or sentence (e.g. If Lassie is a dog then Lassie is an animal). A Horn Clause is a particular type of logical clause, namely a clause that has at most one conclusion in it (like the conclusion that Lassie is an animal). A non-Horn Clause is obviously a clause containing more than one conclusion (e.g. If Lassie is a dog then Lassie is an animal and Lassie eats Milk Bone).

In the mid-1960s, there was a great deal of interest in using computers to aid in theorem proving. One major development was the discovery by J. Alan Robinson of what came to be called the *resolution principle*. The resolution principle was a rule of inference, that is, a rule for explaining how one proposition can follow from another. Robinson's resolution principle was designed to work with clauses that have been "normalized" in the ways we mentioned earlier.

The final preliminary step in the development of PROLOG was to combine together the restricted set of predicate calculus known as Horn Clauses with Robinson's resolution principle. Around 1970, Robert Kowalski, working first in logic and then in automatic theorem proving at the University of Edinburgh, began developing what has come to be known as logic programming. The purpose of logic programming is to use computers (and computation) as a way of making controlled logical inferences. Some of Kowalski's work in 1971 and 1972 was done with Alain Colmerauer and Philippe Roussel at the University of Marseilles. Colmerauer and Roussel are generally credited with the development of PROLOG, the first logic programming language.

From Theorem Proving to Artificial Intelligence

Given PROLOG's historical roots in the world of logic and theorem proving, it may seem strange that PROLOG is now becoming known as a language for general work in artificial intelligence. The explanation lies in the nature of logic as a means of representation. In talking about LISP, we said that programming in artificial intelligence requires a computer language that lets us represent human language, which in turn represents the things we use human language to talk about. Yet logic was itself designed for just these same purposes. Logical propositions are propositions stated in a variant of natural language and used to refer to the world of real or imagined experience. Conversely, the only way we have of referring to that experience is through symbolic representation.

And so, because of its roots in logic, PROLOG happens to have the same "symbolic" approach to representation that the developers of LISP consciously built into their language three decades ago. Though their origins are sharply distinct, the symbol-handling abilities of the two languages have much in common.

Of course LISP and PROLOG are still vastly distinct languages. LISP is a so-called list-processing language, while PROLOG is a logic programming language. In order to be able to compare the two languages—a comparison implicit in the ongoing international race for the development of fifth-generation machines—we need first to look at just how PROLOG actually works.

THINKING IN PROLOG

Since PROLOG is a computer language based on a resolution theorem prover for Horn Clauses, its syntax is constructed in clausal form. The notation used for expressing these clauses has no obvious connection with the kinds of problems that PROLOG is used for solving today. In this respect, the syntax of PROLOG is reminiscent of LISP's CARs and CDRs, terms whose meanings have become obscured over time.

PROLOG is a good example of a non-procedural language. Programming in PROLOG consists of telling the computer what is true, and then asking the computer to draw conclusions about these initial statements of truth. This is, of course, the same process used in first order predicate logic: state a number of assumptions and see what follows from them. The user doesn't have to specify *how* the conclusions are to be drawn. These instructions are already contained in the rules of first order predicate calculus or in the PROLOG language translator program.

PROLOG is also a highly extensible language. Like LISP, it comes with a number of "built-in" basic elements (functions in the case of LISP, predicates in the case of PROLOG). However, most programming requires that the user create new basic elements in order to solve the problems in which the user is interested.

Conversing with PROLOG: Facts, Rules, and Queries

Programming in PROLOG consists of three simple steps:

1. specify the *facts* you know about objects and relationships between them
2. specify the *rules* that apply to objects and their relationships
3. ask *questions* about these same objects and their relationships

To construct a program is to identify a set of facts and rules. (PROLOG makes no distinction between data and programs.) To run a program is to ask questions of this data base made up of facts and rules.

(1)   Constructing a Data Base of Facts and Rules

Constructing a PROLOG data base is much like constructing a relational data base or stipulating a knowledge base and inference engine in an expert system. Knowledge systems are vast data bases from which we can extract information and draw inferences and to which we can add new information. Expert systems are knowledge systems (plus inference rules) that emulate the behavior of human experts such as physicians, chemists, and oil prospectors. We can think about knowledge systems (and expert systems) as being highly intelligent, interactive data base management systems.

The first step is to specify the *facts*—what we know. Semantically, facts are stated as relationships between objects. An object by itself isn't a fact. Thus, facts are statements like "Michael (object) collects marbles (object)" or "John (object) sat__next__to the__girl__with__dimples (object)." *Michael* or *marbles* or *the__girl__with__dimples* is not, by itself, a fact.

Facts are expressed through the syntax of a *predicate* followed by one or more *arguments*. (Again, this is similar to LISP syntax, which is made up of function names followed by one or more arguments.) The PROLOG facts we gave above would be represented in PROLOG like this:

collects	(michael,	marbles).
predicate	$argument_1$	$argument_2$

sat_next_to	(john,	the_girl_with_dimples).
predicate	$argument_1$	$argument_2$

In the first instance, we have a predicate (*collects*) followed by two arguments (*michael* and *marbles*). In the second case, we have a predicate (*sat_next_to*) followed by two arguments (*john* and *the_girl_with_dimples*). By the syntactic rules of PROLOG, the predicate appears first, followed by the arguments enclosed in parentheses, and ended with a period. All predicates and arguments are written in lowercase letters, except that the names of variables used as arguments (like *X* or *Somebody*) begin with capital letters.

When one fact depends upon one or more other facts, there is another way to write this information. This is called a *rule*. Rules are used to describe states of affairs that the English language would express with the word *if*: "If it is raining, the ground will get wet." "Sam likes Michael if Michael collects marbles."

To form a rule in PROLOG you join together several facts by means of a syntactic convention meaning "if." The conclusion to be drawn ("Sam likes Michael") is placed on the left-hand side, and the conditions to be tested ("Michael collects marbles") are placed on the right. The left-hand side of a rule is called the *head* and the right-hand side is called the *body*. The head can have at most one fact in it ("Sam likes Michael"), while the body may have many facts (e.g. "Michael collects marbles" and "Michael was born on New Year's Day" and "Sam likes no one else"). Visually, a rule looks something like this:

PROLOG CODE:	likes(sam, michael)	:-	collects(michael, marbles).
name/meaning:	head	if	body

Facts and rules taken together are called *clauses*. A clause is any entry in the data base.

We have been talking about formulating facts and rules in PROLOG as if the "translation" between a natural language statement like "Michael collects marbles" and the PROLOG equivalent, i.e. *collects(michael, marbles)*, were obvious. Of course it isn't. The relationship between predicates (like *collects*) and arguments (like *michael* and *marbles*) is one that we the users must create. Generally speaking, the verb of a natural language sentence becomes the PROLOG predicate, and nouns are cast as arguments. However, in sentences that have linking verbs (e.g. *is*) or that have other words like prepositions in them, the translation is less literal.

Consider some examples. If I want to represent the English proposition "The grass is green," the PROLOG clause would be

green(grass).

If I want to say that "Frank is the father of Felicia," I write in PROLOG

father(frank, felicia).

Nowhere is the genitive notion "of" represented. What's more, I might choose to represent the same English sentence with

father(felicia, frank).

("The father of Felicia is Frank") so long as I am consistent in using the same order of predicates (i.e. daughter + father) whenever I use the more general fact

father(X, Y).

(2) Asking Questions and Finding Answers

After constructing a data base, it is possible to ask questions of it. A *query* is nothing more than a question being asked about objects and their relationship with one another. Queries are formed by prefacing a fact or a rule with the syntax ?-. If we want to know whether Michael collects marbles, we ask

?- collects(michael, marbles).

When you ask a question, PROLOG examines the clauses in the query and attempts to match them with clauses in the data base. The individual clauses in the query itself can be seen as *goals* to be attained in the matching process. You can think of a goal in PROLOG as being like a goal in dieting: you attain your goal if the number of pounds you are aiming for matches the number of pounds indicated when you get on the scale. A clause that is composed of a single fact constitutes a single goal, while a clause made up of a rule has one goal in the head of the rule (i.e. on the left-hand side) and one or more goals in the body (i.e. the right-hand side).

At the simplest level of matching, the query inquires about a matter of fact, e.g.

?- green(grass).

and finds a match in the data base, i.e.

green(grass).

If PROLOG finds a match, it responds "yes." If it doesn't find a match, it responds "no." The response "no," however, only means that the requisite matching fact is not in the data base, not that the clause is untrue in the real world. The response "no" doesn't mean "absolutely not" but rather "not as far as I know."

At the next level removed, the query is phrased in terms of a variable. If we ask

?- green(X).

we want to know whether there is anything green indicated in the data base. PROLOG turns to the data base and finds a predicate *green*, followed by an argument *grass*. It then assigns the value of the argument (*grass*) to the variable (X) and prints out the answer,

X = grass

PROLOG also enables you to ask whether anything else satisfies the goal *green(X)*. If the data base contains additional facts like

green(tree)
green(soup)

the user may continue the query until all possible matches have been found. PROLOG will print out first

X = tree

and then

X = soup

But PROLOG queries (and data bases) can become much more complex. A rule may have several clauses in its body (right-hand side) and the same variable may be used with different arguments. For example, we might have a rule for saying that Sam likes anyone who collects marbles and was born on Christmas Day:

likes(sam, X) :- collects(X, marbles), born(X, christmas).

Let's suppose that our data base tells us that Michael collects marbles, but that Michael was born on New Year's Day. However, Judy both collects marbles *and* was born on Christmas. When PROLOG first receives the query, it tries substituting "michael" for X. The match works for the clause

collects(michael, marbles).

but fails for

> born(michael, christmas).

Rather than quit at this point, PROLOG *backtracks* and tries the matching procedure all over again. Having already tried (and failed with) Michael as a value for X, it moves on to Judy. Again it tries for a match with the predicate

> collects(judy, marbles).

and it succeeds. It also succeeds in its attempt to match the next goal

> born(judy, christmas).

And so PROLOG responds "yes" to the query.

Programming in PROLOG

Programming in PROLOG consists of constructing a data base and asking questions of it. Because these queries are about objects and their relationships, it is not surprising that one of the easiest (and most popular) ways of illustrating how PROLOG works is to use examples based on genealogy. For a genealogical tree is quite literally a set of objects (e.g. mother, father, daughter) that are related by a set of rules (e.g. a father is a male adult who has offspring).

Consider a familiar family tree:

Abraham is married to Sarah, and they have two sons, Isaac and Ishmael. The facts about these four people (objects) are represented in the PROLOG data base as follows:

> female(sarah).
> male(abraham).
> male(isaac).
> male(ishmael).
> parents(isaac, abraham, sarah).
> parents(ishmael, abraham, sarah).

In addition, we can state a rule about the relationship between Isaac and Ishmael:

> brother(X,Y) :- male(X), parents(X, abraham, sarah),
>   parents(Y, abraham, sarah).

The rule states that for someone (X) to be a brother of someone else (Y), three conditions must obtain:

1. X must be male
2. X must have the parents Abraham and Sarah
3. Y must also have the parents Abraham and Sarah

Given the above data base, we can ask many different questions. The queries we type in are prefaced with the standard question syntax ?-. PROLOG's responses are printed just below each query. In the right-hand column are comments on what is happening in each case.

QUERY	COMMENT
?- female(sarah). yes	PROLOG checks the fact list in the data base and finds a match.
?- female(isaac). no	PROLOG checks the fact list in the data base and doesn't find a match.
?- brother(isaac, ishmael).	PROLOG first consults the goal in the head of the rule, i.e. *brother(X,Y)*, and gives X the value of *isaac*, and Y the value of *ishmael*.
	PROLOG next consults the first goal in the body of the rule, i.e. *male(X)*, and once again assigns X the value of *isaac*. The first goal is satisfied because it matches the fact *male(isaac)* in the data base.
	Finally, PROLOG consults the last two goals of the rule, i.e. *parents(X, abraham, sarah)* and *parents(Y, abraham, sarah)*, and substitutes *isaac* for X and *ishmael* for Y. The second and third goals are satisfied because the data base contains the facts *parents(isaac, abraham, sarah)* and *parents(ishmael, abraham, sarah)*.

Let's expand the family tree we first described to include the offspring of Isaac. Assume that we know that Isaac must have had a wife but we don't know her identity.

We can now add these additional facts to our data base:

```
male(jacob).
male(esau).
parents(jacob, isaac, _____).
parents(esau, isaac, _____).
```

(The use of the blank line in place of the last argument in the two clauses involving the predicate *parents* indicates that the identity of the argument is not relevant to us.) We can also reformulate our rule about brothers so that it can refer to parents other than Abraham and Sarah:

```
brother(X,Y) :- male(X), parents(X, Father, Mother),
                parents(Y, Father, Mother).
```

Again we are saying that X is the brother of Y if:

1. X is a male
2. X has two parents (represented by the variables Father and Mother)
3. Y also has two parents (again represented by the variables Father and Mother)

It is now possible to ask another series of questions of the data base. We will start with the same one we asked a moment ago about whether Isaac and Ishmael are brothers, i.e.

```
?- brother(isaac, ishmael).
```

However, now that we have changed the rule for what constitutes a brother, the query is processed somewhat differently from the way it worked the first time. The first two steps are the same: PROLOG fills in *isaac* for X and *ishmael* for Y in the goal in the head, i.e.

```
brother(X,Y).
```

and likewise fills in *isaac* for X in the first goal in the body, i.e.

```
male(X).
```

However, when PROLOG reaches the second and third goals in the body, something different happens. After substituting *isaac* for X in

```
parents(X, Father, Mother).
```

and *ishmael* for Y in

```
parents(Y, Father, Mother).
```

PROLOG must still substitute *abraham* for *Father* and *sarah* for *Mother* in both goals. These goals are now satisfied because the data base contains the facts

    parents(isaac, abraham, sarah).
    parents(ishmael, abraham, sarah).

The more generalized form of the rule permits us to make queries about whether people other than Isaac and Ishmael are brothers. We might ask

    ?- brother(jacob, esau).

As usual, we begin by consulting the goal in the head of the rule, i.e.

    brother(X,Y).

but this time substituting *jacob* for X and *esau* for Y. When we proceed to the first goal of the body, i.e.

    male(X).

we substitute our value of X, i.e. *jacob*. This first goal is satisfied because the data base contains the fact

    male(jacob).

Finally, we consult the two remaining goals in the body. Substituting *jacob* and *esau* for X and Y, i.e.

    parents(jacob, Father, Mother).
    parents(esau, Father, Mother).

we then need to substitute values for the variables *Father* and *Mother*. The values *abraham* and *sarah* won't do because they don't appear in clauses which have *jacob* and *esau* as arguments. However, looking at our additional fact list, we find the facts

    parents(jacob, isaac, _____).
    parents(esau, isaac, _____).

If we substitute *isaac* for the variable *Father* and _____ for the variable *Mother,* we are able to match both goals, and the answer to the query is "yes." The actual process by which PROLOG obtains values for variables and matches goals with facts in the data base is slightly different, but the principle is the same as illustrated here.

PROLOG vs. LISP

Now that we have some idea how PROLOG works, we can return to the question of how PROLOG differs from the other major contender in the field of artificial intelligence: LISP. The bibliography at the end of this section lists an article by Warren, Pereira, and Pereira that provides a technical comparison. We will look instead at a conceptual comparison.

On the surface of things, PROLOG and LISP have a good deal in common. Structurally, they are both high-level languages, both are designed to do symbolic rather than numerical analysis, both are highly extensible, and both make no distinction between data and programs. Like LISP, PROLOG can use lists as data structures. LISP is more procedural than PROLOG, though one can imagine LISP being less procedural, and PROLOG itself is partly procedural.

The critical distinction between LISP and PROLOG is the organizing principle that directs the construction and running of a program. LISP defines its universe in terms of functions. Everything in LISP is a pairing of functions and arguments. To run a program is to evaluate the arguments in terms of the function. To run a program is, then, to produce a *new result*. In PROLOG, programming consists of constructing a data base and asking questions about its contents. The answers are all there before you run the program. The purpose of running the program is to confirm whether the question you happen to want answered is already part of the data base. Both languages speak of functions (or predicates) and of arguments. However, LISP and PROLOG do very different things with these concatenations (s-expressions in LISP, clauses in PROLOG). LISP evaluates. PROLOG queries. LISP constructs answers. PROLOG looks to see if answers are correct.

But does this difference really matter? If computer languages are supposed to be ultimately equivalent, can't you solve the same problem in LISP as you can in PROLOG? The answer, of course, is yes. The issue is not one of equivalence but style. (You can also solve artificial intelligence problems in BASIC, but no one would think of using BASIC for serious AI work.)

Consider how LISP and PROLOG would each be used if we wanted to know whether a lion is an animal. LISP would begin by defining a function *animals* which would have as its predicate a list of items that count as animals, i.e.

    (SETQ animals '(lion tiger elephant))

If we want to know whether a lion is an animal, we need to manipulate the list of items. If we take the CAR (i.e. the first atom on the list) of the function *animals*,

    (CAR animals)

LISP returns the value

    lion

And so we can conclude that yes, a lion is an animal.

PROLOG approaches the problem in two parts. We begin by constructing a data base containing clauses about animals:

    animal(lion).
    animal(tiger).
    animal(elephant).

We can now ask

    ?- animal(lion).

Because there is a match between the goal in the query and a clause in the data base, PROLOG returns the answer

    yes

What is the difference? Without purporting to make generalizations about two languages on the basis of this very simple example, there are at least five points on which we can evaluate the use of PROLOG vs. LISP.

(1)   Habit

Non-theoretical though it may be, an important basis for preferring LISP to PROLOG is, for many people, habit. If you grew up doing AI programming in LISP, switching to PROLOG is as difficult as switching the side of the road that you drive on. No matter how hard you try (assuming that you try), the new way of doing things may remain strange.

(2)   Programming Environment

A somewhat more objective rationale for differentiating between PROLOG and LISP is the programming environments available for using each. Over the years, AI researchers have developed rich software environments for doing LISP programming, typically incorporating helpful attributes from newer languages as well (e.g. windows and mice from the Smalltalk environment). Given its newness, PROLOG lacks a comparably rich environment. However, we can expect this situation to change very shortly.

(3)   Transparency of Syntax

Advocates of both LISP and PROLOG claim that the syntax of their favorite language is very simple. At one level, they are both right. LISP is constructed only of functions, and PROLOG is made up of facts, rules, and queries. But of course such statements are oversimplifications. Defining and evaluating functions in LISP or constructing and querying data bases in PROLOG takes detailed knowledge of the functions in the languages, plus a lot of programming experience.

    Still, the languages are not equally accessible for the novice. To do any programming at all in LISP you have to know how to define functions, overcome your initial confusion about CAR and CDR (and CDDR and CAADDR), and learn at least a few of the several hundred functions built into the dialect of LISP you are using. In the case of PROLOG, you need to learn a few syntactic conventions (how to write predicates and arguments, how to formulate rules, and how to ask questions). Yet notions of information and questions about information are more intuitively obvious—at least to educated speakers of natural language—than are notions like the evaluation of functions and manipulation of lists. In short, if we compare the entry level of syntax of LISP and PROLOG, PROLOG's syntax is more transparent.

This syntactic transparency does not matter to the professional programmer (who might be just as happy if non-specialists *didn't* have any understanding of what was going on). But if the general population is to have any role in artificial intelligence programming, transparency may become a critical distinction between the two languages.

(4)   Logic, Language, and Artificial Intelligence

When LISP was first invented, the primary goal was to construct a language which could handle symbolic representation—words—with the same ease that FORTRAN handled numbers. Back in the 1950s, there was very little understanding of how natural languages themselves were constructed, and no attempt to make LISP handle symbolic representation the way that people do. Today there is a great deal of research on the structure of natural languages, and LISP is often used to program natural language models. However, no claim is made that the structure of the LISP language itself bears any conceptual relationship to the structure of natural languages. Rather LISP is merely a tool for analysis, much as a microscope is merely a tool for viewing microorganisms.

PROLOG was not designed to analyze natural language. Yet the conceptual model underlying PROLOG (i.e. the first-order predicate calculus) was itself intended to model a subset of human language. Therefore, the functional extension of PROLOG from theorem proving to artificial intelligence is a very natural shift. To the extent that logic is an appropriate model of human language, PROLOG has an advantage over LISP when it comes to doing natural language processing in that the PROLOG tool is more similar to the natural language object than is the LISP tool.

One can, of course, question whether the similarity of tool and object of manipulation is necessarily an advantage in doing artificial intelligence programming. The answer remains to be seen. In the meanwhile, however, we at least need to be aware of the fact that we are indeed dealing with two very different kinds of tools.

(5)   Data Base Models

Finally, we need to ask what kinds of artificial intelligence programs we will be writing in the future and what languages are structurally consonant with these programs. Whatever else we write, it is clear that an enormous amount of programming will be done to create expert systems or, more generally, knowledge systems.

In the United States, the development of expert systems and knowledge systems has been done almost exclusively in LISP. Yet like the use of LISP for analyzing natural language, the use of LISP in knowledge systems programming is adequate but not conceptually tailored to the task at hand. PROLOG, on the other hand, makes a perfect conceptual mesh with knowledge systems. In both cases, the data (or knowledge) base is composed of facts (knowledge) and rules on how those facts relate to one another (inference engine). In both cases, the knowledge base is queried in order to find out what is in the base, to use the base to make inferences about its contents, and to have the base acquire new information. We can expect that PROLOG will become increasingly important in developing knowledge systems, especially because comparative novices will be able to construct highly sophisticated systems without much technical background in programming.

PROLOG vs. Query Languages

Our discussion of PROLOG as a language for querying data bases raised the obvious question of how PROLOG (which we have called a logic programming language) differs from the family of languages we have called query languages (see Chapter 3). The question is a hard one to answer because the ground keeps shifting beneath us. PROLOG is indeed a logic programming language, but only the first of what promises to be many. While PROLOG began as a theorem-proving language, it has developed into a language well suited not only for sophisticated knowledge systems but for more familiar data base management as well. At the same time, query languages are only now emerging as a language type. They may look very different in five years from the way they look now.

Query languages are related to one another more by a set of user interface goals and domain of application than by linguistic organizing principle. True, query languages, like PROLOG, ask questions. But unlike PROLOG, query languages were developed to ask questions about business data bases, and up until now, business has remained the primary functional application. What's more, query languages were (and are) designed to be as user-friendly as possible. They were meant to be used in lieu of COBOL and even FORTRAN by making it possible for business personnel to write their own applications programs to access the company data base without having to ask the data-processing department (who would write a program for them in a traditional imperative/algorithmic language).

To make the languages as friendly as possible, language developers have attempted either to make the syntax very simple (as in QBE) or to construct a "natural language front end" that makes users think they can enter requests in natural language and have the computer give a response. In actual fact, computers don't yet understand natural language, and a "natural language front end" is really a stylized program that looks for a few key words and converts them into syntax the formal language translator understands (see the entries on QBE and Intellect). PROLOG programs are fairly easy to read, but not because they were designed to be used by non-programmers. In fact, the inventors of micro-PROLOG have redesigned the surface syntax of PROLOG to make the language yet more accessible to novices.

Some query languages (e.g. Intellect) work the same way that PROLOG does: construct a data base and inference rules and then query the data base. Other query languages (e.g. Clout or Themis) only function in tandem with separate commercial data base management systems. The data base management system provides the data and the inference rules, while the query language provides the natural language front end for formulating queries of the data base. Themis, for example, must be coupled with DATATRIEVE or ORACLE, while Clout can be used with a variety of popular data base management systems for personal computers.

Most query languages work on a precise matching system. As with PROLOG, a query receives a positive answer ("yes" or "53") if the form of the query matches a form in the data base. Other systems (the best known of which is Savvy) work on pattern recognition, where the query does not have to be precisely the same as an item in the data base to constitute a match.

In short, it is clear that PROLOG has much in common with many of the developing query languages. However, while one can use PROLOG in the role of a query language, PROLOG has many other functions, and query languages have many other forms.

THE EVOLUTION OF PROLOG

PROLOG has rapidly developed from a language for doing theorem proving to a language used for a vast number of functions, from relational data bases to biochemical structure analysis to architectural design to the study of natural language. Its first decade of growth was almost exclusively restricted to Europe. Much of the work was done in France and Great Britain (especially Edinburgh), but other European centers of research include Portugal, Hungary, and Czechoslovakia.

Japan's announcement that it was adopting PROLOG for its fifth-generation project catapulted PROLOG into the public eye. The initial American response of incredulity is now being followed by growing attempts to study the language and to look for ways of integrating it with LISP. Recent Japanese developments (including the building of a PROLOG machine—comparable to a LISP machine—in which the systems programming is done in PROLOG) can only raise this level of international interest.

THE FUTURE OF PROLOG

PROLOG is at once a language and an instance of a language type (i.e. logic programming). Since both PROLOG and logic programming are in their infancy, a look at the future of PROLOG reasonably entails a look at the future of logic programming.

PROLOG   337

The Language

There are two driving forces behind the future use and development of PROLOG. The first is the marketplace. Japan's race to build a fifth-generation computer is not a personal quest to climb Mount Everest. Rather it is a race to produce commercially marketable products that may earn the Japanese untold billions of dollars if they are successful. Kazuhiro Fuchi, director of ICOT, envisages a portable AI computer that will become as common as the telephone, and the market for knowledge systems extends from the Fortune 500 to the corner grocery store. Other countries (and international consortia) that are competing with the Japanese have every reason for wanting to know what their opponent is up to.

But the second driving force is the language itself. As more people involved with computers come to know about PROLOG, the audience of users who appreciate the language's simplicity, power, and functional diversity continues to grow. This audience is further bolstered by users who come first to know about micro-PROLOG and then turn to PROLOG (on larger machines) to take advantage of the language's full capabilities.

Logic Programming

Serious students of PROLOG are quick to point out that PROLOG is but the first of a family of logic programming languages. Much as FORTRAN or ALGOL was only the beginning of an approach to computer programming, PROLOG may be a crude form of what is to follow. Writers on PROLOG observe, for example, that PROLOG is partly procedural in orientation, and future logic programming languages need not be.

The best-publicized developments in logic programming have come about in Japan over the past two years. The Japanese are developing a kernel language they call KL. Its first version, known as KL0, is a logic programming language very much like PROLOG. However, it has been extended to handle some of the functions ordinarily taken care of by operating systems, and it also includes things like modular programming, concurrent processing, and data type checking.

USING PROLOG

Buying PROLOG

Like LISP, PROLOG is a very memory-intensive language to run. Therefore most of the implementations so far have been done on large computers like the DEC 10 and DEC 20. Recently, however, supermicrocomputers (with large amounts of on-board memory) have begun to run PROLOG. Tektronix has an artificial intelligence machine that runs PROLOG, LISP, and Smalltalk, and several of the dedicated LISP machines have begun to offer PROLOG as an alternative language. At the same time, the first versions of PROLOG for 16-bit microcomputers are now making their appearance, including a version called Turbo PROLOG, by Borland International.

What to Read

BOOKS

Clocksin, William F., and C. S. Mellish (1981). *Programming in Prolog.* Berlin: Springer-Verlag.
 The first—and now standard—introduction to PROLOG.
Rogers, Jean (1986). A *Prolog Primer.* Reading (Mass.): Addison-Wesley.
 An excellent introductory text which is highly accessible to novice and experienced programmer alike. Contains well-chosen exercises.
Kowalski, Robert (1979). *Logic for Problem Solving.* New York: North Holland.
 A book investigating the application of logic to problem solving and computer programming. Such use of logic in problem solving and programming conceptually underlies PROLOG.
Clark, K. L., and S.-A. Tärnlund, eds. (1982). *Logic Programming.* London: Academic Press.
 A useful collection of papers on logic programming.
Campbell, J. A., ed. (1984). *Implementations of PROLOG.* Chichester (Eng.): Ellis Horwood.
 Another good collection of articles, this time all geared to implementation issues.

ARTICLES

Clocksin, William F. (1984). "An Introduction to PROLOG," in Tim O'Shea and Marc Eisenstadt, eds., *Artificial Intelligence: Tools, Techniques, and Applications.* New York: Harper & Row, pp. 1–21.
 A brief introduction by one of the authors of the standard text.
Manuel, Tom (1984). "Cautiously Optimistic Tone Set for 5th Generation," *Electronics Week,* December 3, pp. 57–63.
 Report on progress to date on the Japanese fifth-generation project, including Japanese development in the use of PROLOG and its derivatives.
Warren, D., Pereira, L. M., and Pereira, F. (1977). "PROLOG—the Language and Its Implementation Compared with LISP," *Proc. Symp. on AI and Programming Languages.* Rochester (N.Y.): *SIGPLAN Notices* 12, no. 8, and *SIGART Newsletter* 64, pp. 109–115.
 There are very few published comparisons of PROLOG and LISP. While this one is somewhat technical, it is the standard.

QBE

PROFILE
NAME
*Q*uery-*b*y-*E*xample
STRUCTURE

Familiar Distinctions:
  hardware: high-level
  translator: n.a.
  structural unit: table
  data: entries in tables (numbers and text)
 	
Conceptual Distinctions:
  organizing principle: query language
  procedures: non-procedural
  extensibility: extensible
  program/data: not distinct

FUNCTIONS
organize and query data base of business information
GENEALOGY
no computer language precursors Year: 1975 Author: Moshé Zloof (IBM) Impetus: need for very easy-to-learn and error-proof query language for accessing large data bases Evolution: continues to be used in large businesses on large computers (little change in the language itself over time)
VERSIONS/DIALECTS
Standard: n.a.
SPECIAL CHARACTERISTICS
Memory Requirements: very large (for data base that it accesses) Ease of Learning/Use: extremely easy to learn and use Availability: for large computers

NOTE: This entry draws upon the section on "Business: COBOL and Query Languages" (under "Functional Classification") in Chapter 3, and refers to the entries on Intellect (in this chapter) and NaturalLink (in the Appendix).

WHY QUERY-BY-EXAMPLE?

Before the invention of automobiles, social analysts estimated that if urban populations continued to grow at the current rate, cities would soon be buried under mountains of horse manure. In the early days of telephones, similar analysts predicted that if telephone use continued to increase, we would all have to become telephone operators to handle the load. The growth of data bases (especially in business) has generated a similar problem: given the amount of data to be processed, early information scientists pondered whether we would all have to become computer programmers.

The automobile solved the problem of horse manure, and more sophisticated equipment drastically reduced the number of telephone operators necessary. In the world of business (and of data processing), the growth of formal query languages such as Query-by-Example (QBE) provided the first relief for the data-processing bottleneck.

The Data-Processing Bottleneck

With the increased use of ever larger business data bases in the 1960s, data-processing (or DP) departments had arisen to handle the task of computer programming. In principle, this was a reasonable division of labor for even moderate-sized companies. Over time, though, several problems began to emerge. Managers often found themselves losing touch with the methodology via which decisions were being reached in their companies. Managers knew what questions they wanted answered but were not able to ascertain whether the results provided by DP departments were skewed by the way in which the programs were asking the questions.

A more obvious problem was time lag. If a manager had a simple problem to be solved using the company data base, it could take weeks or months to get the results back from the DP department. To make even trivial changes in the program might take just as long.

And the exclusive use of DP departments to handle data was becoming increasingly expensive. Over the last twenty-five years, the cost of computer hardware has decreased dramatically. Computers selling for only a few hundred dollars today have more power than multimillion-dollar mainframes only a decade ago. Yet during the same time, the cost of software development has sharply increased. Moreover, the amount of time lost (waiting for DP to program—or reprogram—problems) can be especially costly. The move from procedural languages (like COBOL) that require professional programmers to non-procedural query languages (like QBE) was financially inevitable.

Query Languages and QBE

A large number of formal query languages were developed in the 1970s to cope with the problems we have just identified. The systems include INGRES and SQL, QUEL and SEQUEL, MARK IV and MAPPER. All the early query languages ran on large machines (mainframes or minicomputers) and most were linked to specific data base management systems (DBMSs).

QBE, a language designed by Moshé Zloof at IBM around 1975, emerged from this same genre of formal query languages. However, QBE is distinguished from other query languages in the way in which it operates.

In most query languages, users *generate* quasi-English *sentences* using a predefined lexicon (e.g. employee, city, salary) and a predefined syntax (e.g. Print all employees where employee = accountant, city = Houston, salary>200000). In QBE, users *insert* data or questions into a *visual* format. The difference is akin to the distinction between generating your own answers in an examination versus filling in numbered blanks that have been provided.

As a result, QBE is generally easier to learn than other formal query languages. You can learn most of the system in an hour or two, and tend to make very few mistakes in using the language because all the categories available for manipulation are already provided on the screen. Other formal query languages usually take a little longer to learn. Moreover, users make a few more mistakes with them than with QBE because in formulating queries, users must remember how to match the inherent vocabulary and syntax of the query language.

In beginning a query, the user is presented with a blank table. It is up to the user to fill in the table name and any of the field names and field values relevant for making the query. The user can either inquire about information already contained in the data base (e.g. how many sleds were sold last year) or modify the existing entries (e.g. updating new sales of finger paint or deleting an item from inventory when a model is discontinued).

Suppose a new secretary wants to acquaint herself with the variety of rocking horses the company sells. By entering the table name ROCKING HORSE, followed by a P (for "print"), i.e.

ROCKING HORSE P.			

the secretary will get as a response all the field names contained in the file, e.g.

ROCKING HORSE	SIZE	COLOR	PRICE

If the user now wants to know what sizes are available in green, the query

ROCKING HORSE	SIZE	COLOR	PRICE
	P.	GREEN	

will generate a list of sizes (e.g. SMALL, MEDIUM, EXTRA LARGE, EXTRA SMALL) under the SIZE column. To find out what sizes are available that cost less than $50, the query

ROCKING HORSE	SIZE	COLOR	PRICE
	P.		<50

will yield a list of sizes in the desired price range (e.g. SMALL, EXTRA SMALL).

All of these entries use *constant elements* (e.g. GREEN, <50) whose identity is known. However, the real power of QBE—and the source of the language's name—comes in using *variable elements* whose value is *not* known in advance. Say, for example, the secretary is asked to increase all prices of small rocking horses by 10%. She doesn't care what the current price of each rocking horse is. Her only concern is to raise its price appropriately.

She begins with the usual table. However, under the PRICE column she uses a variable (e.g. M for ''money'') that is multiplied by the new price ratio, i.e.

ROCKING HORSE	SIZE	COLOR	PRICE
	SMALL		M u. M 1.1

The fact that M is a variable is indicated by underlining it. ''U'' indicates ''update the entry.''

Instead of using a meaningless algebraic variable like M, the user could have entered an *example* of what a possible original price for a small rocking horse might be, say $40. She could then enter the alternative query

ROCKING HORSE	SIZE	COLOR	PRICE
	SMALL		40 u. 40 1.1

again underlining the variable ("for instance, 40") to indicate it is only a hypothetical value. The hypothetical value 40 u. 40 1.1 will generate exactly the same results as the more typical algebraic expression M u. M 1.1.

Variable elements can also be combined with constants. Suppose, for example, that our secretary wants the price of all green stuffed animals sold by the company that have names beginning with the letter A (e.g. aardvark and antelope). She could enter the following query

ROCKING HORSE	SIZE	COLOR	PRICE
	AX	GREEN	P.

and receive in return the desired list. She could also have given an "example" name like ANTEATER, where the underlining indicates the variable part of the expression. In using examples (rather than algebraic expressions) as variables, it is not even necessary for the example actually to be contained in the data base. If the store sells only green aardvarks and antelopes (but not green anteaters), only these two entries will be generated by QBE in response to the query.

Variable elements can be valuable in several ways. Most obviously, they are useful if you don't happen to know all the items (e.g. green animals with names beginning with A) that you need to manipulate. Other times you may know the names but not have any need to itemize them individually (e.g. when you are increasing all prices by 10%).

But a third and extremely important use of variables in QBE is in manipulating restricted information, that is, information whose actual value the user is not allowed to know. Let's say you are an entry-level clerk in the accounting department and are asked to calculate Christmas bonuses for the executive vice presidents. You know they will all receive 5% of their annual salary as a bonus. However, you are not privy to the actual salary figures. QBE will nonetheless let you figure the bonuses, using a variable. The query might look like this:

BONUSES	POSITION	SALARY	BONUS AMOUNT
	EXECUTIVE VICE PRES.	S	S × .05

The user could enter the algebraic variable S or make up a hypothetical figure (e.g. 1000000 or 100). The result would be the same in either case. That result would be entered directly into the data base without the clerk ever seeing it.

THE EVOLUTION OF QBE

> I'm afraid that programmers who are experienced in procedure-oriented programming are no less resistant to change than human beings seem to be in most regards. Today's methods will have to be superseded, and many of today's programmers will not be willing or able to make the transition
>
> Daniel D. McCracken, "The Changing Face of Applications Programming," *Datamation*, November 15, 1978

QBE and other formal query languages provided a critical first step in the development of "user-friendly" computing. Yet the emergence of these query languages has not been welcomed unilaterally. Much as the railroad spelled doom for the Pony Express in the American West, data-processing departments have been concerned that the widespread adoption of easily usable programming languages could spell unemployment for many programmers. Daniel Mc-Cracken's comments are as applicable today as in 1978, when query languages were just beginning to permeate the business world. *Computerworld*, a weekly newspaper directed to data processors, regularly published articles extolling the virtues of COBOL and arguing that COBOL programming will continue to dominate the business world. The proliferation of COBOL improvements, such as the development of structured COBOL, the ongoing translation of existing files of unstructured COBOL into structured COBOL, and the appearance of several versions of COBOL for microcomputers, suggests that data-processing professionals are intent upon maintaining their standing.

Many analysts argue that such a move is not in the best interests of business. As an alternative, they suggest that fourth-generation languages (in essence, formal query languages) should replace COBOL. The outcome of the battle remains to be decided. However, it may well turn out that the most important contest is not between COBOL and formal query languages like QBE, but between such query languages and *their* rival: natural language front ends.

THE FUTURE OF QBE

Formal query languages are now subject to many of the larger challenges that the computer market is facing. To begin with, businesses often find mainframes and even minicomputers more expensive to operate than microcomputers, and the traditional formal query languages all run on large machines. But even more importantly, non-professional computer users are coming to expect that software will bend to fit their needs, rather than vice versa. With the development and gradual proliferation of natural language front end systems in the early 1980s (and potential explosion in the late 1980s—see the entry on Intellect), directors of new computer installations have little motivation to introduce software that is already conceptually outdated.

This does not mean that formal query languages will be eliminated from the business world. Just as COBOL and FORTRAN will be with us for decades to come because of their vast libraries of software, we can expect QBE and its conceptual cohorts to remain in use for at least some time in installations where they are successfully entrenched. In large businesses where stand-alone micro-computers will at best remain adjuncts to larger systems, the use of such formal query languages will also likely persist.

Another reason for the projected longevity of formal query languages, especially QBE, is their reliability. If you follow the syntactic rules correctly, you are certain that your query will be understood. Natural language front end systems, at least as of now, are still extremely limited in the kind of queries they can deal with, If your ordinary language entry isn't close enough to the prototypes the system has been programmed to parse or to accept, most systems can merely respond that they don't understand. The only natural language front end system to have tackled the reliability problem is NaturalLink, which is actually quite similar to QBE in construction.

Until such natural language front ends are demonstrably superior to current query language workhorses like QBE, formal query languages will retain a significant place in the world of business computing. The only real alternative, remember, is COBOL.

USING QBE

Buying QBE

QBE is now the sort of system that large businesses rather than private individuals are likely to purchase. However, Zloof is about to release a new query system for microcomputers called DBE (*data by example*). Maintaining the principle of "picture programming" developed in QBE, DBE will be a complete applications development system including not only queries but tables, figures, reports, and so on.

What to Read

BOOKS

Martin, James (1982). *Application Development without Programmers*. Engle-wood Cliffs (N.J.): Prentice-Hall.
    Martin forcefully argues that business can (and should) free itself from the stranglehold of data-processing departments by switching from procedural languages like COBOL (for which professional programmers are needed) to (non-procedural) query languages like QBE that non-programmers can use themselves. In the book, Martin gives a brief (and highly lucid) explanation of QBE (pp. 130–143).

ARTICLES

Zloof, Moshé M. (1977). "Query-by-Example: A Data Base Language," *IBM Systems Journal*, no. 4, pp. 324–343.
    A more detailed (though still non-technical) explanation of how QBE works, written by the author of the language.

SIMULA

PROFILE
NAME
*SIM*ulation *LA*nguage
STRUCTURE

Familiar Distinctions:
   hardware: high-level
   translator: compiled
   structural unit: objects
   data: numerical plus list processing
 	
 Conceptual Distinctions:
   organizing principle: imperative/algorithmic *and* object-oriented
   procedures: procedural (ALGOL part) and non-procedural (object-oriented part)
   extensibility: extensible
   program/data: technically distinct, but both are components of classes

FUNCTIONS
discrete simulation language
GENEALOGY
ALGOL 60 | SIMULA | SIMULA 67   └─┐   Smalltalk
Years: 1965 (SIMULA); 1967 (SIMULA 67)
Authors: Ole-Johan Dahl, Bjørn Myhrhaug, and Kristen Nygaard (Norwegian Computing Centre)

(Continued)

SIMULA (Continued)

Impetus:	simulation programs were comparatively difficult to write in machine language, ALGOL, or FORTRAN
Evolution:	slow but continuing spread of SIMULA 67

VERSIONS/DIALECTS
Standards: SIMULA (I) SIMULA 67

SPECIAL CHARACTERISTICS
Memory Requirements: large
Ease of Learning/Use: average
Availability: not readily available in the U.S.

WHY SIMULA?

SIMULA was created in the mid-1960s at the Norwegian Computing Centre in Oslo. The language was designed to simulate the operation of systems composed of discrete events. A typical system to be simulated might be traffic patterns, with stoplights to be synchronized, traffic policemen to be assigned to congested intersections, and contingency plans to be offered when traffic must be diverted. Other examples include communication networks, personnel systems, or the day-to-day operation of a retail business.

The notion of simulation involves two basic elements. First, the presupposition that we are dealing with a *system* of entities that interact with one another. And second, that the course of their interaction is not predetermined. The purpose of a simulation is to try out *possible* relationships between entities without having to do real-world experiments.

Imagine a simulation of the traffic flow at rush hour on the major interstate highway passing through the center of Atlanta, Georgia. Traffic engineers may wish to know how many more vehicles you would need to add before the stream of traffic came to a dead standstill. One can hardly imagine commuters wishing to participate in the experiment—much as the results might eventually help speed their way home in the future.

The designers of SIMULA (Ole-Johan Dahl, Bjørn Myhrhaug, and Kristen Nygaard) found the languages available in the 1960s, such as machine language, ALGOL, or FORTRAN, ill suited for the task of simulation. To begin with, these languages were not good at handling list processing, complex data structures, or demands on program sequencing. Even more importantly, the conceptual framework underlying existing imperative/algorithmic languages had little relationship to the way traditional systems analysts went about constructing simulation models.

SIMULA is just one of a large number of simulation languages that have been developed over the past twenty years. Like ALGOL (from which it largely derives), SIMULA has not been widely used in the United States. Few American computer scientists know much about it, and it is rarely discussed in the popular computing press. Yet the language (however poorly understood) is generating new interest for historical reasons. For SIMULA is the direct ancestor of Smalltalk, and Smalltalk is beginning to revolutionize the way we think about human/computer interfaces. Our primary interest in SIMULA, then, is not mainly as a simulation language in its own right, but as a precursor to Smalltalk.

There are two versions of SIMULA: the original SIMULA (sometimes called SIMULA I), which was developed in 1965, and SIMULA 67, which appeared in 1967. Our discussion of SIMULA's syntax is based on SIMULA 67.

THINKING IN SIMULA

SIMULA's Dual Personality

From a 1980s perspective, SIMULA contains two distinct approaches to computer languages. At its "computing core" is the entire contents of ALGOL 60, an imperative/algorithmic language with block structure and familiar means of describing data and control structures. Yet at its "conceptual core" is an entirely new way of thinking about computing. It is a model based upon *communication*, in which the universe of discourse to be modeled is decomposed into objects and the objects communicate with one another. It is this model of communication, based on objects, that Smalltalk borrows and extends.

As you read through the rest of this section, you may find the new terminology (and concepts) initially confusing. SIMULA is not actually a difficult language. The reason for the initial confusion is that SIMULA models a problem quite differently from the way the problem would be modeled in more familiar imperative/algorithmic languages. And unlike other non-imperative/algorithmic languages (e.g. LISP or FORTH), the sheer number of new terms you need to learn for SIMULA to make any sense is comparatively large.

Our discussion will include more syntactic detail than comparable sections for other languages in this chapter. The reason is this: Once you understand the communication model as developed in SIMULA, you will find the structure of Smalltalk far more tractable.

Basic Terminology: Object, Class, Declaration List, Statement List, CLASS-Body

SIMULA's dual personality is directly reflected in the basic concepts used to structure the language. As an imperative/algorithmic language, SIMULA has a structure for handling data (the *declaration list*) and another for performing actual programming steps (the *statement list*). The declaration list plus statement list, bounded by the keywords BEGIN and END, are together referred to as a CLASS-body. The CLASS-body corresponds to the *block* in ALGOL 60.

As an object-oriented language, however, SIMULA creates a new conceptual framework for the basic elements whose activities it seeks to simulate. The smallest unit in SIMULA is the *object*. An object is a thing, a person, an event—in short, anything whose actions are part of a larger system. Note that Smalltalk is also based upon objects, but Smalltalk extends the notion of object to include far more components of the language than does SIMULA.

The SIMULA Model

To understand how SIMULA works, let's begin by looking at classes and objects (see SIMULA Figure 1). The left side of the diagram indicates the three sets of properties that apply to all objects that are members of a class. The right side of the diagram indicates how objects within a class differ from one another.

Don't let the diagram overwhelm you. We will talk about each of the components in turn, and they will soon make sense. We will first look at the theoretical structure of the model, and then work out an example showing how the components might actually be used.

The similarities between the notion of class in SIMULA and in Smalltalk are strong indeed. SIMULA's *declaration list* is much like Smalltalk's *instance variables*. The *statement list* in SIMULA is a prototype for Smalltalk's *methods*. There is also a clear family resemblance in the way SIMULA and Smalltalk distinguish among multiple objects within a class (e.g. in the assignment of actual values to variables).

Programming in SIMULA entails giving values to variables in the data sequence and controlling the flow of the action sequence. This is done by way of a communication metaphor. Looking first at the data sequence for a class, i.e. SIMULA Figure 2, we find two types of variables: a *value type variable* that refers to the items in the data sequence for a specific object and a *reference type variable* that refers to objects that are members of some other class (here called CLASS 2). During the course of a SIMULA program, value type variables are initialized and changed. Reference type variables are used to effect interaction ("communication") between the activities of different classes of objects.

The flow of action within the statement list is controlled by the *local sequence control* that allows an object to "focus its attention" upon a particular action contained in its statement list. Consider the diagram of an action sequence in SIMULA Figure 3.

At a given moment, Object 1 "wakes up" (or invokes) a particular action sequence (enumerated in the statement list). If the program simulates a sequence of actions that recur, the local sequence control may proceed from statement 1 through statement 4, and then recycle as many times as the value type variable

CLASS DECLARATION	PROPERTIES DIFFERENTIATING AMONG OBJECTS	
Properties applying to all objects in the class	Object 1	Object 2 . . .
Class Heading CLASS + name of class		

Declaration List (Data Sequence) describes data structure of objects in class:
(1) variables
  (a) value type
  (b) reference type
(2) actual data structures
	Data Structures for Object 1 lists all data structures applicable to Object 1, including values for variables	*Data Struc . . .*

Statement List (Action Sequence) describes action pattern in each object in class	*Actions for Object 1* specifies actual actions that Object 1 engages in (subset of larger statement list)	*Actions . . .*

SIMULA Figure 1   Class

in the declaration (i.e. the equivalent of a DO loop) directs it to do so. The use of local sequence control to "wake up" an action is similar to the sending of messages in Smalltalk.

Programming in SIMULA

To illustrate how this model is used to construct a program in SIMULA, we will devise a scenario that a real program might simulate. Suppose we want to

CLASS 1		
TYPE	NAME	VALUE
REFERENCE	(CLASS 2)	VALUE

SIMULA Figure 2   Data Sequence

model the operations of a daily newspaper, and in particular the writing of articles by its reporters and editors. An actual simulation of real-world events rapidly becomes very complex. There are newswriters and feature writers and sportswriters, along with analysts and editors for these categories and more. There are live events to cover, people to interview by telephone, and data banks to research. Writing a "simple" program in SIMULA can be extremely complicated *because* it is designed to handle the complex interaction of discrete events. We therefore narrow our focus to a small part of the journalism system: the activities of feature writers.

We can define a class of feature writers which, for simplicity, contains only two objects. Both objects (Feature Writer 1 and Feature Writer 2) work on the same kinds of stories but are given distinct though sometimes overlapping assignments by their editor. In gathering materials for their stories, the writers can use information that resides (in the terms of SIMULA) in other objects (e.g.

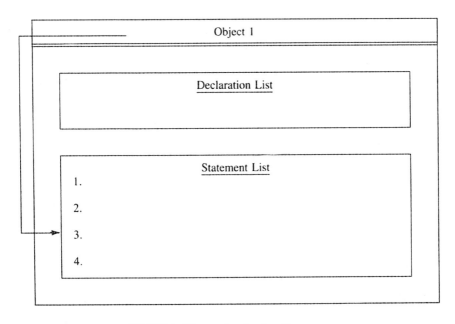

SIMULA Figure 3   Action Sequence

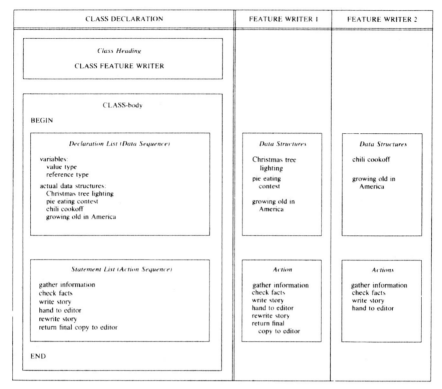

CLASS DECLARATION	FEATURE WRITER 1	FEATURE WRITER 2

Class Heading

CLASS FEATURE WRITER

CLASS-body

BEGIN

Declaration List (Data Sequence)	*Data Structures*	*Data Structures*

variables:
  value type
  reference type
actual data structures:
  Christmas tree lighting
  pie eating contest
  chili cookoff
  growing old in America
	Christmas tree
	  lighting
	pie eating
	  contest
	
	growing old in
	America
		chili cookoff
		
		growing old in
		America

Statement List (Action Sequence)	*Action*	*Actions*
gather information check facts write story hand to editor rewrite story return final copy to editor	gather information check facts write story hand to editor rewrite story return final copy to editor	gather information check facts write story hand to editor

END

SIMULA Figure 4   CLASS FEATURE WRITER

the files of medical writers). Like writers in the real world, our journalists typically approach the same story topic—and even the same data bases—with different ideas, different talents, and different degrees of interest. For example, Feature Writer 1 may always have to rewrite his stories, while Feature Writer 2 never does.

Schematically, SIMULA would structure the simulation like SIMULA Figure 4:

Look especially at the right-hand side of the figure, comparing data structures and actions for each of the two feature writers.

The differences between Feature Writer 1 and Feature Writer 2 become even clearer when we consider the way in which the data sequence is controlled for each writer (SIMULA Figure 5):

Writer 1 has been assigned three stories, while the second writer has been assigned only two. Both writers need to refer to the class MEDICAL STORIES for their assignment on growing old in America, but while the first writer is interested in heart attacks, the second is looking for information on arthritis.

In the course of their work, each writer progresses through the actions on his action list for each of the stories he is working on. Writer 1 will need to cycle

Feature Writer 1		
INTEGER	NUMBER STORIES ASSIGNED	3
REFERENCE	$\left(\begin{array}{c}\text{MEDICAL}\\\text{STORIES}\end{array}\right)$	HEART ATTACK

Feature Writer 2		
INTEGER	NUMBER STORIES ASSIGNED	2
REFERENCE	$\left(\begin{array}{c}\text{MEDICAL}\\\text{STORIES}\end{array}\right)$	ARTHRITIS

SIMULA Figure 5 DATA SEQUENCE FOR EACH OBJECT

three times through his six-item list (from "gather information" to "hand final copy to editor"), while Writer 2 will only need to cycle twice through his four-item list of actions (not having to do any rewriting, he can eliminate the last two steps from the class-defined statement list). Thus, the action sequence for the two objects (Feature Writers) might schematically look like SIMULA Figure 6 at a particular moment in time:

At any given moment, the local sequence control is at a particular point on the statement list. This point is determined by the value of the variable being acted upon at the time. Here, for example, Writer 1 is at the rewrite stage (step 5) in his story on growing old in America (story 3), while Writer 2 is writing his story (step 3) on the chili cookoff (story 1).

Our final diagram (SIMULA Figure 7) indicates the shape of a real SIMULA program that encompasses the writing of feature articles. This, of course, is only a fragment of a more complete program. Be aware that it lacks some of SIMULA's specific syntactic conventions.

THE EVOLUTION AND FUTURE OF SIMULA

Unlike many of the languages we have talked about, SIMULA has undergone comparatively little evolution since its formulation in the mid-1960s (outside of

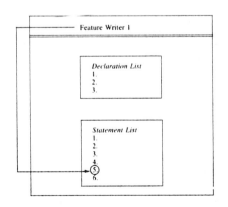
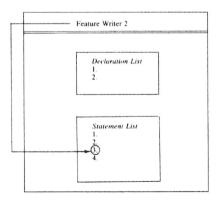

SIMULA Figure 6 ACTION SEQUENCES FOR EACH OBJECT

```
BEGIN
    COMMENT *** SIMULATION OF DAY IN THE LIFE OF A FEATUREWRITER
    CLASS FEATUREWRITER (NUMBERSTORIESASSIGNED):
    INTEGER (NUMBERSTORIESASSIGNED);

    BEGIN Data structures:
            Christmas tree lighting;
            Pie eating contest;
            Chili cookoff;
            Growing old in America;
            REF (MEDICAL STORIES) HEARTATTACK;
        REPEAT:
            Consult list of data structures and select story;
            Gather information;
            Check facts;
            Write story;
            Hand to editor;
            Rewrite story;
            Return final copy to editor;
            NUMBERSTORIESASSIGNED : = NUMBERSTORIESASSIGNED - 1;
            IF NUMBERSTORIESASSIGNED> 0 THEN GOTO REPEAT
                ELSE quit for the day;
    END;

    CLASS MEDICAL STORIES
    BEGIN
        . . .
    END;
    . . .
END;
```

SIMULA Figure 7   SAMPLE PROGRAM

the development from SIMULA to SIMULA 67). The most significant evolution has been in languages that have borrowed SIMULA's object orientation and its simulation approach to programming.

In the United States, SIMULA is little known and is unlikely to spread in its existing form. However, much of the thinking that went into SIMULA is continued (albeit in an altered form) in Smalltalk. SIMULA remains important as the progenitor of the recent explosion of object-oriented programming in the contemporary world of microcomputers.

USING SIMULA

Buying SIMULA

SIMULA is not available for microcomputers. (In fact, it is hardly available for larger machines in the United States.) The one simulation language that can be used in the United States on personal computers is a microcomputer version of the continuous simulation language DYNAMO.

What to Read

There is not much material available in print in the United States on SIMULA. What does exist has largely been written by SIMULA's inventors and is generally fairly readable.

BOOKS

Birtwistle, Graham M., Ole-Johan Dahl, Bjørn Myhrhaug, and Kristen Nygaard (1979). *SIMULA BEGIN*. Lund (Sweden): Studentlitteratur.
A textbook on SIMULA 67, complete with exercises and some answers. Part 1 ("System Description") gives a lucid introduction to both the SIMULA language and the rationales behind it. The book assumes no prior experience in programming. It is the best place to begin learning about SIMULA.

ARTICLES

Dahl, Ole-Johan, and Kristen Nygaard (1966). "SIMULA—An ALGOL-Based Simulation Language," *Communications of the ACM* 9 (no. 9):671–678.
A concise but technical overview of SIMULA.
Nygaard, Kristen, and Ole-Johan Dahl (1981). "The Development of the SIMULA Languages," in R. Wexelblat, ed., *History of Programming Languages*. New York: Academic Press, pp. 439–493.
An informal retrospective account of the development of SIMULA.

Smalltalk

PROFILE
NAME
ordinary language name indicating that the computer language is intended as a flexible system of communication
STRUCTURE

Familiar Distinctions:
   hardware: high-level
   translator: compiled
   structural unit: object
   data: handles numbers, text, graphics, and sound
 	
Conceptual distinctions:
   organizing principle: object-oriented
   procedures: non-procedural
   extensibility: extensible
   program/data: data and programs are both components of single entity
                (objects)

FUNCTIONS
education (teaching thinking) simulation
GENEALOGY
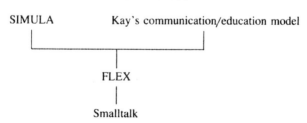
Years: 1972–80 (and continuing)
Author: Alan Kay (Learning Research Group, Xerox PARC [Palo Alto Research Center])
Impetus: Kay's conception of how computers could reshape education

(Continued)

Smalltalk *(Continued)*

Evolution:	language began at Xerox as software component of Kay's Dynabook during 1970s, used to teach programming and "thinking" in schools; recent shift from education orientation to more general information-systems orientation

VERSIONS/DIALECTS

Standards:	Smalltalk-72 Smalltalk-74 Smalltalk-76 Smalltalk-80

SPECIAL CHARACTERISTICS

Memory Requirements:	large (because contains whole integrated environment)
Ease of Learning/Use:	language itself somewhat tricky (partially because of novelty); language system intended for easy yet powerful use
Availability:	non-language parts of system widely available (icons, windows, mice), but language itself isn't

NOTE: Reading the entry on SIMULA will help considerably in making sense of all the new concepts and terminology in Smalltalk syntax.

WHY SMALLTALK?

Smalltalk is less a computer language than a philosophy of programming. The language is only one component of a system that enables computers to help users communicate information to others and, most importantly, to themselves. The language and system derive from the personal vision of Alan Kay.

While in graduate school at the University of Utah in the late 1960s, Kay designed a model for interaction between computers and people. This model conceived of a notebook-sized portable computer that would be extremely powerful. It would have a keyboard, a CRT, high-quality graphics, large memory capacity, and an external pointing device. The computer would also be productive. It would allow users not only to *manipulate* information but to *create* new constructions and learn in the process.

To appreciate how radical the hardware component of this vision was at the time, consider the state of computing in the 1960s. The personal computer had not yet been heard of. Keyboards and CRTs were still novelties in a world of punched cards, and the graphics capabilities of most mainframe computers were limited to printing pictures of Snoopy out of X's.

Kay's educational vision was equally new. At the time, the only serious educational use envisioned for computers was computer-aided instruction that either duplicated on the computer the kinds of fixed lessons a teacher might provide in subjects like foreign languages or the sciences, or created drill and practice sessions. The idea that computers could be used to help children (potentially of all ages) come up with their own new concepts was practically unheard of. The only exception was the work on Logo, just beginning in Cambridge, Massachusetts. As a derivative of LISP, Logo is an extensible language that allows children to create new concepts through the same mechanism that LISP uses to create new functions (see the entries on LISP and Logo).

Kay's earliest attempts are recorded in his master's thesis ("FLEX: A Flexible Extensible Language") and his doctoral dissertation ("The Reactive Engine"). The language FLEX allowed users to participate in an interactive dialog with the computer, creating new objects of discussion whenever needed. The language itself was but one component of what Kay then called a FLEX Machine (later called a Dynabook, since it was based upon the dynamic retrieval of information). The FLEX Machine was to be a personal computer that could react to the user's command, communicating through both text and pictures.

Kay soon joined Xerox's Palo Alto Research Center (PARC), where he organized the Learning Research Group to implement his computer/user vision. The name Smalltalk was chosen to denote the software aspects of Kay's Dynabook. To implement the software, Xerox needed to create a new set of hardware. And so a Smalltalk *system* emerged over the years that encompassed not only the formal language but a hardware and software *environment*. This environment includes high-resolution graphics (including the use of icons), a mouse as a pointing device, the use of overlapping windows, and an operating system that is not distinct from the language itself. (Use of a keyboard and a CRT were already becoming industry standards.)

THINKING IN SMALLTALK

The Smalltalk Paradox

For the new user, Smalltalk presents a paradox. From its very name to its roots in education and its current reputation as providing an environment for people who know nothing about computing, we might reasonably expect that learning Smalltalk would be very simple. Yet one look at the literature on Smalltalk abruptly dispels this illusion.

As a programming environment, Smalltalk enables users easily to create and manipulate information. As a language, Smalltalk is non-procedural in that the programmer focuses on *what* is to be carried out, leaving the details of *how* the task is to be accomplished camouflaged at a lower level of operation. Once the strangeness of the Smalltalk way of thinking wears off, the operation of the language seems natural and smooth.

At the same time, though, actually writing substantial programs in Smalltalk means learning the details of Smalltalk's grammar. And Smalltalk's grammar is unlike that of any other computer language (except, of course, SIMULA, which few students of Smalltalk know much about). Smalltalk accomplishes the same tasks as all computer languages. It organizes information, manipulates information, and produces results. As an extensible language, it also allows users to create new language components and refer to them by name. What is unique about Smalltalk is the *way* in which these tasks are carried out.

Because Smalltalk is so unlike other languages, we will look at more details of its syntax than we have for most other languages in this chapter.

Conceptual Overview

At its most basic level, Smalltalk is made up of two components: *objects* and *messages*. To program in Smalltalk is to send messages to objects. The programming notions with which many of us are familiar (such as data and algorithms, or procedures or actions) have no direct equivalents in the Smalltalk scheme. Rather, they are redefined in terms of the Smalltalk metaphor of objects and messages.

Smalltalk's roots in SIMULA are easy to detect. Both languages take the *object* as the basic linguistic unit (with *classes* being similar groups of objects). Both languages have as a primary function the *simulation* of possible events and outcomes.

Smalltalk goes beyond SIMULA in three essential ways. Smalltalk introduces the notion of *message* as a way of having objects communicate with one another. (SIMULA has the functional equivalent of messages, but they don't work quite the same way.) Smalltalk also extends SIMULA's notion of *object*. In Smalltalk, all components of the language are classified as objects. And finally, the Smalltalk environment makes it possible to implement the communication model that underlies both SIMULA and Smalltalk. In fact, in the act of creating visual icons that represent objects, Smalltalk makes literal the communication metaphor of SIMULA.

Smalltalk is both modular and extensible. By *modular* we mean that each basic unit (which in Smalltalk is an object) is self-contained. The functioning of any object doesn't depend upon the internal details of other objects. By *extensible* we are saying that users can freely create new objects at any time. In fact, the very purpose of Smalltalk is to provide the tools for creating new constructs, not to present a closed system.

Despite their differences, Smalltalk has many conceptual similarities to FORTH. Both languages are non-procedural, modular, and highy extensible. Both break down the imperative/algorithmic barrier between data and process.

And both present the language as a toolkit for the user to create things that didn't exist before out of things that did. FORTH provides a core set of *words* with which the user defines new words. Smalltalk comes with an initial set of *objects,* but the user, in the act of programming, creates new objects. PROLOG and LISP share some of these same features as well.

Basic Terminology: Object, Class, Instance, Method, Message

Smalltalk conceives of computer programming as an act of communication. When we think about communication between people, we imagine a *sender* who constructs a *message* which is conveyed to a *receiver.* When people send imperative messages (e.g. ''Be at the meeting by eight tonight'' or ''Get me a copy of Chaucer's *Canterbury Tales''*), they often don't specify *how* the request should be carried out (e.g. whether to walk to the meeting or take a cab; to buy a copy of the *Canterbury Tales* or to borrow it from the library). To communicate in Smalltalk, a sender (here, the programmer) sends a message (specifying what kind of response is required, not how to accomplish it) to a receiver (which is an object). It is up to the object to figure out how to act upon the request.

The fundamental unit of Smalltalk is the object. Formally, an object is a package of information and a description of how to manipulate it. The object might be a stove with a description of how to turn it off or on. Or it might be a number with a description of how to add or subtract other numbers to or from it.

In ordinary language, we distinguish between universals (or class terms) and particulars (or proper names). Class terms are general categories like *dog, house,* or *magazine*—the kinds of words you look up in the dictionary. Particulars are individual examples of those objects—like Lassie, the white house at the corner of Everett Avenue and Wayland Avenue, or *Infoworld.* Members of classes all have some properties in common. Yet each one is also in some way different from every other. In Smalltalk, objects that have something in common with each other (such as *Infoworld, Personal Computing, PC World*) are all *instances* of a *class* (computer magazines). All instances of a class have some features in common and some features distinguishing the instances one from another.

Instances share the name of the class of which they are part. They also share an ''outlook'' on the world that reaches beyond the class itself. Each class can receive only certain kinds of messages. A *dog* class could receive messages like ''Roll over'' or ''Eat dog biscuits,'' but not ''Be at the meeting by eight tonight.'' Each class has a list of the kind of messages that instances of that class can receive.

Classes also share two other common properties. One is a description of the kinds of variables that instances of the class can use. (This list of variables is most analogous to a declaration list in an imperative/algorithmic language.) The other common property is a description of the *methods* (that is, the actions that are to be performed) that instances actually use to act upon *messages* they receive from the outside. (These methods are similar to statement lists or algorithms in imperative/algorithmic languages.)

And so now we are led to the concept of message. A message is a request for action. (The message itself and its components also happen to be objects, but then so is everything in Smalltalk.) The message specifies *what* is to be done. Formally, a message is defined as the specification of one of any object's possible manipulations. When the message is received by the class, it is the class that specifies *how* (i.e. the method by which) the action is to be carried out by instances of that class.

The Smalltalk Model

Now that we have encountered the basic constructs in Smalltalk, we can look at how they fit into the broader Smalltalk model. We will begin by examining the structure of Smalltalk classes. The diagram in Smalltalk Figure 1 adds some new technical terms, but many of the basic components will already look familiar.

Take each of the technical terms in turn. *Public properties* are those attributes that apply to all members (instances) of a class. They are like class declarations in SIMULA. *Private properties* are the attributes distinguishing among instances. They, too, have their precise counterpart in SIMULA classes (see the diagram of a class in the entry on SIMULA). The schematic diagram above lays out the private properties for only one instance (I_1). Similar entries would have to be made for the private properties of each of the other instances in the class.

Consider the detailed specification of public properties. There are four subcomponents we have already talked about:

(1)   the *class name* (equivalent to SIMULA's class heading)
(2)   the *interface* (or *protocol*), listing the messages this class can accept
(3)   the *class variables* (or *instance variables*) describing the variables for which instances of this class may have values (similar to SIMULA's declaration list)
(4)   the list of *methods*, describing how instances in the class can act upon messages (similar to SIMULA's statement list)

The private properties serve to "customize" the class attributes (public properties) to a particular instance of that class. One way of thinking about the difference between public and private properties is to use the static metaphor of class membership: What distinguishes *Infoworld* from other computer magazines, or what distinguishes my house from yours? Another way of conceptualizing the difference is to use an active metaphor: How does *Infoworld* "act" differently from, say, *Byte* in covering the same story on the release of a new microcomputer? If we add woodburning stoves to both your house and mine, how does the same act bring about different changes in the ambiance (and heat supply) in the two houses?

Smalltalk's notion of *private memory* (or *private variables*) is roughly equivalent to the static metaphor (and to object-specific data structures in SIMULA). Private memory inserts the actual values that an instance has for a particular variable. *Infoworld* is published weekly, *Byte* is published monthly. *Infoworld* is thin, *Byte* is thick.

PUBLIC PROPERTIES	PRIVATE PROPERTIES
apply to each object (= instance) in the class	distinguish one object (= instance) from another
	Instance (= Object)₁

Class Name

Interface (Protocol)
list of messages to which instances
of the class can respond

Instance
Variables
descriptions of
variables (fields)
used by instances
of the class

Class
Variables
variables shared
by all instances
of class

Methods
description of sequences of actions
(operations) performed by instances
(specify how to do something)

Private Memory/Private Variables
pairing of instance variables with
actual values for this instance, e.g.

Field	Value
instance variable 1	value 1
instance variable 2	value 2

Set of Operations
actual execution of methods
by this instance

Class

Smalltalk Figure 1

The *set of operations* for an instance is approximately the same as the dynamic metaphor (or as object-specific actions in SIMULA). An article on Smalltalk would tend to be discursive in *Infoworld* (perhaps focusing on implementation and market possibilities) while a comparable article in *Byte* would be more technical and emphasize the details of the language. Yet both are actions upon the message "Produce an article on Smalltalk." Think of the example from the SIMULA entry of two feature writers both doing stories on growing old in America.

We've looked at the structure of objects, classes, instances, and methods. What about messages? The contents of messages look like Smalltalk Figure 2.

```
┌──────────────────────────────────────────────────────────────┐
│  ┌──────────────────────────────────────────────────────────┐ │
│  │                        Selector                           │ │
│  │  name for the manipulation whose performance is being     │ │
│  │  requested                                                │ │
│  │  (specify what should happen, not how it should happen)   │ │
│  │  e.g. MOVE                                                │ │
│  └──────────────────────────────────────────────────────────┘ │
│  ┌──────────────────────────────────────────────────────────┐ │
│  │                        Arguments                          │ │
│  │  information on specifics of desired outcome              │ │
│  │  e.g. location to which object should be moved            │ │
│  └──────────────────────────────────────────────────────────┘ │
└──────────────────────────────────────────────────────────────┘
```

Message

Smalltalk Figure 2

Messages themselves are composed of two objects. The first, the *selector*, names the kind of manipulation being requested. The second, the *arguments*, provides information on what the results should look like. Not all messages have arguments, but all messages have selectors.

Messages don't actually do anything internally. They are vessels of information. They function like an interoffice mailroom, shunting information packets from sender to receiver but not opening up the packages themselves.

We are finally ready to look at the whole communication process in Smalltalk: sending messages, receiving messages, and acting upon them. A model of the four basic components looks like Smalltalk Figure 3.

When running a Smalltalk program, you begin by sending a message. The sender might be a programmer who is sending a message to manipulate an existing object or to create a new class of objects. Alternatively, the sender could be some object sending a message to another object.

The message is a *request* for action from the receiver. Messages are not themselves actions. Instead they specify *what kind* of action is requested. However, they don't indicate how the action is to be carried out. As in all non-procedural languages, the Smalltalk compiler handles the *how* question directly.

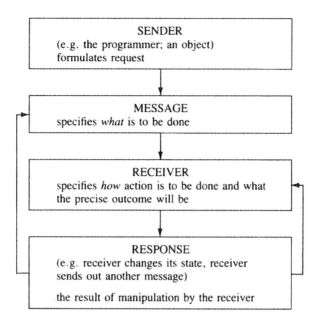

Communication Model

Smalltalk Figure 3

The receiver receives the message. At this point, several things happen. The sequence directly follows the categories we outlined in our diagram of a Smalltalk class:

First, the receiver checks with the *interface* on the public properties list of its class to be sure it can receive this kind of message. If the receiver is Lassie (an instance of the class "dog"), it is authorized to "Roll over" or to "Eat dog biscuits," but not to "Be at the meeting by eight tonight."

Second, assuming that the message is consistent with the receiver's public properties, the receiver then determines how the message is to be acted upon. This determination is done by looking at the *instance variables* and the *methods* list. At this point, the receiver can also incorporate any arguments sent by the message.

Third, moving to its private properties, the receiver then pairs variables with the values found in *private memory*. Once these variables have been assigned values, the *set of operations* can execute the methods that were described in the public properties listing.

After a message has been received, the receiver may respond in one of two ways. On the one hand, the receipt of the message may change the state of the receiver itself. (Lassie could roll over or consume a dog biscuit.) On the other hand, the receiver might send a new message, starting the communication cycle over again. (Lassie might break into a run or start barking to gain attention.)

Programming in Smalltalk

So far we have looked at the basic components of a Smalltalk program and have seen how they interact with one another when a program is running. To program in Smalltalk is to define classes and messages of the sort we have been describing. That is, the programmer describes new classes of objects, creates instances of those classes, and then sequences messages to those instances.

(1)   The Outline of Smalltalk Programs

You can think about programming in Smalltalk as filling in the blanks of the diagram we earlier used to define a class. The formatting used in Smalltalk-80 (the most current version of the language) looks like Smalltalk Figure 4 (to facilitate discussion, we have added line numbers, which do *not* exist in Smalltalk).

1	class name	identifier
2	superclass	identifier
3	instance variable names	$identifier_1$ $identifier_2$ • • • $identifier_n$
4	class variable names	$identifier_1$ $identifier_2$ • • • $identifier_n$
5	class messages and methods	
	$method_1$ $method_2$ • • • $method_n$	
6	instance messages and methods	
	$method_1$ $method_2$ • • • $method_n$	

Template for Creating Smalltalk-80 Classes, Instances, and Messages

Smalltalk Figure 4

In writing a Smalltalk 80 program, the user is first asked to give the class name of the new object being defined (line 1). The user fills in the name where we have written "identifier." Next, the user indicates (line 2) if the new class belongs, in turn, to some broader class ("superclass"), such as the class "dog" belonging to the superclass "animal." The third line calls for a listing of the names (i.e. "identifiers") of the variables that will be used in defining individual instances of the new class. And the fourth line provides room for a similar listing for the names of variables to be used in defining all instances of the new class.

The real manipulation of information takes place in the slots we have labeled lines 5 and 6. Both slots are used to spell out the messages and methods that produce communication between objects. In line 5, the program indicates those communication tools that are common to all members of the class. In line 6, the communication specific to individual instances is spelled out.

What does an actual Smalltalk-80 class template look like? Because of all the new terminology and the syntactic conventions used to implement them, even brief programs in Smalltalk can look very complex. We will look at two short interconnected examples which make use of most (though not all) of the slots in the template we have just defined.

Suppose we run a newspaper recycling plant. Every day, people come in with their newspapers, each pile weighing some amount. Some of the biggest contributors are the local Boy Scout troops. The recycling plant wants to keep track of the total amount (number of pounds) of newspapers it receives each day, and each Boy Scout troop wants to keep a record of individual contributions.

The recycling plant, the plant's collection records, and the Boy Scout troop's records can all be defined as Smalltalk objects. The troop records are a subclass of the plant records, and the plant records are, in turn, a subclass of the larger plant operations.

Consider the two smaller classes: plant records and Boy Scout troop records. The Smalltalk class (= program) for plant records might look like Smalltalk Figure 5 (again, line numbers are added for convenience of discussion).

The class PlantRecord (line 1), that is, the record of newspapers collected, is a member of the superclass RecyclingPlant (line 2). Individual instances of the class PlantRecord are governed by two variables (line 3): "date" (on which the collection was made) and "amount" (the number of pounds collected). The tallying of pounds of newspapers collected is done in the methods section (line 4). (We ignore here the syntactic details of how the tally is actually carried out.)

Turn now from the records of the recycling plant to the bookkeeping done by the contributors. Of the many donors, some are Boy Scout troops, and one group of Boy Scouts is Troop 1938. Each time Troop 1938 donates newspapers, it makes a record in its troop logbook. Each entry in the logbook is numbered. The Smalltalk class TroopRecord would look something like Smalltalk Figure 6.

1	class name	PlantRecord
2	superclass	RecyclingPlant
3	instance variable names	date amount
4	methods	

of: depositAmount on: depositDate ‖
    date ← depositDate.
    amount ← depositAmount
amount ‖
    ↑ amount
balanceChange ‖
    ↑ amount

Class PlantRecord

Smalltalk Figure 5

1	class name	TroopRecord
2	superclass	PlantRecord
3	instance variable names	number
4	methods	

number: donationNumber for: donationAmount on: donationDate ‖
    number ← donationNumber.
    date ← donationDate.
    amount ← donationAmount

of: anAmount on: aDate ‖
    self error:
      'Donation records are initialized with
      number:for:on:'
totalChange ‖ ↑ 0 - amount

Class TroopRecord

Smalltalk Figure 6

TroopRecord (line 1) is a member of the superclass PlantRecord (line 2). The instance variable specific to TroopRecord (line 3) is the number of the entry in the logbook. However, since TroopRecord is a subclass of PlantRecord, the class TroopRecord *inherits* the variables "date" and "amount" from Plant-Record. The entries for each collection are calculated by referring to the amount of papers collected each day (line 4).

(2)   Running Smalltalk Programs

In the case of almost all computer languages, programs are typed in and run in a linear order. In compiled languages like FORTRAN, C, or SIMULA, the program is typed in (using an editor), the program is compiled, and then the compiled program is run. In interpreted languages, the program as a whole doesn't need to be compiled, but the inputting and running process is still linear.

Smalltalk is very different. In the beginning of our discussion of Smalltalk, we distinguished between the Smalltalk language and the Smalltalk environment. All Smalltalk programming is done within the Smalltalk environment (though the environment can also be used with other languages).

The Smalltalk environment is *visual* and *interactive*. As a visually based system, the Smalltalk screen display enables users to see several "windows" of information simultaneously. Think of each window as one of the slots in the class templates we have been looking at. However, instead of having to look at the slots one at a time, users can choose to look at the contents of several slots together.

The system is also interactive. Users can select the order in which they want to examine (or manipulate) the contents of slots. A user may, for example, decide to define a new object but not be able to figure out what superclass it is a member of. The programmer can temporarily abandon the new object being defined and turn instead to the slot (whose contents are displayed in another window) that contains a list of all the existing classes. Having consulted the list and selected the appropriate class, the programmer can abandon the master list of classes and return to specifying the "superclass" slot for the new class being defined.

In constructing a Smalltalk program that deals with our recycling plant, the programmer might decide to open up several windows (i.e. look at several slots) at the same time. By the time the programmer had created the necessary new classes and moved back and forth between windows, the screen might schematically look something like Smalltalk Figure 7.

Windows can be opened up or closed at the will of the programmer. The size of windows can be altered, and windows can overlap one another. Programming in Smalltalk is an ongoing process. Like pictures created by turning a kaleidoscope, the program is finished when you decide to stop. (Obviously, even in Smalltalk there is some minimum set of steps you must complete before you can be said to have a program.) Unlike traditional programs, which only run when you give the "run" command, Smalltalk programs are always "running," in that any change you make in one part of the program can have immediate— and far-reaching—effects on other parts of the program (i.e. upon other objects).

THE EVOLUTION OF SMALLTALK

Smalltalk has undergone continuing evolution. Because Smalltalk has developed as an "in-house" product of Xerox, much of the story of that evolution is the

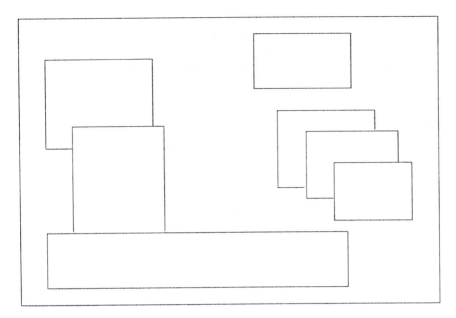

Window Example

Smalltalk Figure 7

story of work at Xerox over the years. This generalization holds true for the Smalltalk *language* and for the changing vision of appropriate *uses* for Smalltalk, but not, as we will see, for the *user interface* to the language.

Evolution in the Language

The Smalltalk language has undergone reformulation every few years at Xerox. Best known are Smalltalk-72 (the first attempt, constructed soon after Kay joined Xerox), Smalltalk-76, and Smalltalk-80 (the version upon which the recent spate of publications on Smalltalk is based). The changes have been of the nature of refinement rather than radical reconceptualization. Since the 1972 version, there has been a continuing move to extend the object-oriented perspective to more and more elements of the programming environment. In the early days (between Smalltalk-72 and Smalltalk-76), an overly flexible syntax was replaced with a stricter syntactic approach, and interpreted operation was replaced with an incremental compiler. Smalltalk-80 has been refined to make it portable to non-Xerox machines.

Evolution in Function

When he joined Xerox, Kay conceived of Smalltalk as a simulation language used for education—hence the name Learning Research Group. In 1981, the name was changed to Software Concepts Group, reflecting a shift in goals (along with the departure of Kay from Xerox).

Unlike Smalltalk-72 and Smalltalk-76, Smalltalk-80 wasn't designed with school-aged children in mind. Xerox's current goal is "to create a powerful information system, one in which the user can store, access and manipulate information so that the system can grow as the user's ideas grow" (Preface to Goldberg and Robson, *Smalltalk-80: The Language and Its Implementation*). One look at the kind of information systems the authors have in mind makes it abundantly clear that the system goes far beyond education.

Evolution in User Interface

Smalltalk is unique among languages in that a particular user interface was envisioned as necessary for the language to be implemented at all. Advances in hardware and software at Xerox made much of this user interface a reality. Icons (and graphics more generally), mice, and overlapping windows became part of the Smalltalk environment. But while you couldn't do Smalltalk without its user interface, you could use the interface without the Smalltalk language. It was this realization—plus a fateful visit by Steve Jobs (the founder of Apple) to Xerox PARC—that changed the user interface of contemporary computing.

After seeing the Smalltalk environment at work, Jobs decided to implement some of the user interface himself at Apple. The result was first the Apple Lisa, and now the Apple Macintosh. Both machines are heavily dependent upon icons, mice, and overlapping windows, yet neither is programmed in the Smalltalk language. These same user interfaces have now swept the computer industry and can be found (with varying degrees of sophistication) on most modern machines.

THE FUTURE OF SMALLTALK

The future of the Smalltalk language is still very much an unknown. A few companies are beginning to make Smalltalk available on their artificial intelligence machines. As of the writing of this book, Alan Kay is at Apple, presumably working to make a refined version of Dynabook a reality. Whether or not it will be programmed in Smalltalk remains to be seen. Meanwhile, at Xerox PARC, Smalltalk-80 is being disseminated to selected non-Xerox users. The results of these early experiments will determine whether business and industry (and perhaps eventually individual consumers) will find the Smalltalk language available on their computer dealer's shelf. The fate of the Smalltalk user interface is already clear. For the foreseeable future, graphics, mice, and windows will be as much a part of the "normal" computer interface as a keyboard and a viewing device. As computer memory becomes increasingly less expensive, we can expect the graphics to improve. Better graphics opens the possibility for sophisticated programming languages that are formulated entirely in icons instead of in strings of alphanumeric characters. While these languages probably won't

USING SMALLTALK

Buying Smalltalk

Writing and running programs in Smalltalk consumes a great deal of memory space, which is not yet commonly available in micros. However, as the memory capabilities of personal computers increase and as interest in the Smalltalk *language* grows, this situation should change considerably in the near future. Already Smalltalk-like systems are beginning to be marketed for the IBM PC, and Apple is licensing to some educational institutions a Smalltalk system for the Macintosh.

In the meanwhile, you can buy hardware and software that capitalize on the non-language-specific components of the Smalltalk environment, ranging from a mouse or windowing capabilities on up to an Apple Macintosh or a Xerox Dorado.

What to Read

Several books on Smalltalk have been published by the staff of Xerox PARC. However, they tend to presuppose a professional background in programming, as do most of the articles referred to below. Two more recent books are also included here.

BOOKS

Goldberg, Adele, and David Robson (1983). *Smalltalk-80: The Language and Its Implementation.* Reading (Mass.): Addison-Wesley.
> A textbook on the "language" aspects of Smalltalk. Clearly written, but assumes the reader "is a programmer or programming language designer who knows at least one language well."

Krasner, Glenn (1983). *Smalltalk-80: Bits of History, Words of Advice.* Reading (Mass.): Addison-Wesley.
> A set of case histories on implementations of the Smalltalk-80 system by such companies as Tektronix, Hewlett-Packard, and Digital Equipment Corporation.

Kaehler, Ted, and Dave Patterson (1986). *A Taste of Smalltalk.* New York: W. W. Norton.
> An informally written book which introduces Smalltalk to experienced programmers by illustrating how the language is used for solving the well-known "Tower of Hanoi" problem.

Timothy A. Budd (1986). *A Little Smalltalk.* Reading (Mass.): Addison-Wesley.
> A book for rank beginners based on a dialect of Smalltalk-80 developed at the University of Arizona.

ARTICLES

Byte, August 1981.

Byte devoted much of its August 1981 issue to Smalltalk. The articles provide a good cross section of the Smalltalk system, but should be read with care—and in the order suggested by the editor and by Adele Goldberg in the introductory article. David Robson's article, "Object-Oriented Software Systems," is particularly useful at the outset because it explains the major conceptual distinctions between traditional imperative/algorithmic languages on the one hand and object-oriented languages like Smalltalk on the other. Once these distinctions are clear, the formal syntax of Smalltalk begins to make some sense.

Goldberg, Adele (1979). "Educational Uses of a Dynabook," *Computers and Education* 3:247–266.

An overview of how the Smalltalk system has been used in the classroom to teach children problem-solving abilities.

Byte, May 1985.

This issue of *Byte* contains a cluster of four articles on Smalltalk. Two of them discuss implementations of Smalltalk (or Smalltalk-like languages) on microcomputers.

SNOBOL

<table>
<tr><td colspan="2" align="center">PROFILE</td></tr>
<tr><td colspan="2" align="center">NAME</td></tr>
<tr><td colspan="2">Stri*N*g *O*riented Sym*BO*lic *L*anguage</td></tr>
<tr><td colspan="2" align="center">STRUCTURE</td></tr>
<tr><td colspan="2">Familiar Distinctions:
  hardware: high-level
  translator: compiled or interpreted
  structural unit: statement, function
  data: symbolic (character strings)

Conceptual Distinctions:
  organizing principle: functional/applicative: string processing
  procedures: partly procedural, partly non-procedural
  extensibility: extensible
  program/data: distinct</td></tr>
<tr><td colspan="2" align="center">FUNCTIONS</td></tr>
<tr><td colspan="2">general-purpose language for manipulating non-numerical characters</td></tr>
<tr><td colspan="2" align="center">GENEALOGY</td></tr>
<tr><td colspan="2" align="center">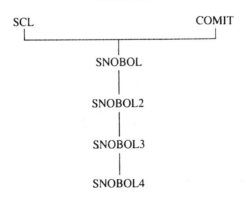</td></tr>
<tr><td colspan="2">Years: 1962–68</td></tr>
<tr><td colspan="2">Authors: Ralph Griswold, David Farber, and Ivan Polonsky (Bell Telephone Laboratories)</td></tr>
</table>

(Continued)

SNOBOL (Continued)

Impetus:	need to develop a more effective language for symbol manipulation
Evolution:	SNOBOL4 (which is quite distinct from its predecessors) was widely adopted by American colleges and universities in the late 1960s and 1970s for non-numerical programming (especially by non-scientists)

VERSIONS/DIALECTS

	SNOBOL	SNOBOL3		
Standards:	SNOBOL2	SNOBOL4		
Others: e.g.	SIL	CALSNOBOL	FASBOL	SNOBAT
	SPITBOL			

SPECIAL CHARACTERISTICS

Memory Requirements: large

Ease of Learning/Use: designed to be easy to learn and use

Availability: widely available on mainframes and some minicomputers, but not on microcomputers

WHY SNOBOL?

As a general-purpose machine, the computer can be used to manipulate many different kinds of data. Nearly all imperative/algorithmic languages were expressly designed to manipulate numerical information. It is typically as an afterthought that most handle such data as graphics or strings of characters.

Among the non-imperative/algorithmic languages, other types of data are given primary importance. Functional/applicative languages are a good example. LISP was specifically designed to manipulate lists of symbolic (meaning "non-numerical") information, and SNOBOL was created a few years later to deal with strings of characters.

SNOBOL was born in 1962 at the Programming Research Studies Department of Bell Telephone Laboratories. It resulted from the frustration that its designers, Ralph Griswold, David Farber, and Ivan Polonsky, felt in using existing computer languages in such areas as automata theory, graph analysis, and formula manipulation. The languages then available (including SCL—*Symbolic Communication Language*—and COMIT) proved cumbersome for dealing with non-numerical scientific data, such as formulas, that could be naturally represented by strings of characters. The solution was to build a better mousetrap.

As work progressed from the planning stage to the first implemented version of SNOBOL (in 1963), Griswold and his colleagues defined two objectives for the language. Functionally, they wanted a general-purpose language that could manipulate non-numerical scientific data of all sorts, including formulas, graphs, and text. And pedagogically, they sought to design a language "that would be suitable for the person who was not primarily a programmer." In this respect, SNOBOL was much in keeping with the user-oriented ideology of the inventors of COBOL and BASIC, two other languages emerging at about the same time.

During the 1960s, SNOBOL attracted considerable attention. Within just a few years, it underwent rapid evolution from SNOBOL to SNOBOL2, then SNOBOL3, and finally SNOBOL4.

While the name SNOBOL has persisted from one version to the next, the language itself has changed dramatically. SNOBOL4 in particular is a very different language from its predecessors. Most importantly, it was designed for third-generation large-scale computers that allowed users to run programs interactively. Early generations of hardware restricted users to batch processing. (See the entry on BASIC for a discussion of time sharing and its legacy, interactive computing.)

SNOBOL4 was first officially distributed in 1968. It was rapidly adopted by a number of colleges and universities to serve their non-numerical computing needs. Many institutions developed their own special implementations of SNOBOL4, and coined names for these dialects such as FASBOL, SNOBAT, and SPITBOL. SNOBOL4 is the version of the language most used today, and therefore the version we will be talking about.

THINKING IN SNOBOL

Crosscurrents: Functions and Unstructured Programming

As a functional/applicative language, SNOBOL uses the function as an important unit of analysis. Functions are the means by which SNOBOL becomes extensible.

All programming in LISP and APL (the other major functional/applicative languages) is done by writing functions. But this is not the case in SNOBOL. Not all SNOBOL programs contain functions. (In fact, for reasons of simplicity, none of the examples here contain functions.) Where functions do occur in SNOBOL, they are embedded within a programming shell that is wholly reminiscent of classical unstructured programming familiar from FORTRAN, BASIC, or COBOL. Programs are constructed in a linear sequence, with none of the subdivisions typical of structured programming languages like Pascal. The lines of a SNOBOL program may be numbered. But even more importantly, SNOBOL programs are heavily dependent upon the use of GO TO statements to control jumps from one part of the linear programming sequence to another.

Basic Components

Imperative/algorithmic languages tend to be able to handle several types of data, e.g. integers, real numbers, boolean operators, and individual characters. The functional/applicative language LISP has just one data type: the list. In much the same way, SNOBOL has one basic data type: the character string. Continuing in this vein of simplicity, there are but two major operations that SNOBOL can perform on character strings. It can *concatenate* strings (i.e. put them together), and it can attempt a *pattern match* between an exemplar string and a line of data.

Programs in SNOBOL are made up of sequences of statements. Each statement can have up to three parts (all of which are optional). The *label* in a statement is used to specify branching to that statement from somewhere else. The *rule* indicates the action to be taken in a statement. And the *GO TO* section directs the flow of control to another statement somewhere else in the program (i.e. other than the next line).

Programming in SNOBOL

Consider first a simple program fragment for concatenating two character strings. Say we are writing a program to generate new vocabulary possibilities for composing poems. We might want to start with a core vocabulary and then see what new combinations we can derive. For example, if we have the words *killer* and *bee*, we might write a program fragment like this:

```
X = 'killer'
Z = 'bee'
W = X Z
T = Z '' X
```

The variable W would assume the value 'killerbee,' and the variable T would be assigned 'bee killer.'

Consider next a short program that illustrates the three parts of statements in SNOBOL. This program reads data from a stack of punched cards. For purposes of explanation, we have indicated which parts of the statements are labels, which are actions, and which are GO TO instructions:

```
1              N = 1
2 LOOP   X = INPUT           :F(END)
3              OUTPUT = '      'X
4              N = N + 1            :(LOOP)
5 END
         ─────     ──────────────          ────────
         LABEL    ACTION                    GO TO
```

Statement 1 initializes the variable N to 1. This first statement only contains an action. The second statement opens with a label indicating that this is the beginning of a loop. The action in statement 2 is to set X equal to "input" (i.e. to check to see if there is any input). If the answer is "yes," the program continues along in linear fashion to statement 3. If not (i.e. if the attempt to find input fails), the GO TO part of the statement indicates that control of the program should be passed down to the label END (i.e. line 5), and the program is finished.

Assuming for the moment that the test for input has succeeded, we progress from statement 2 to 3. Statement 3 (composed only of an action) outputs the contents of the first card after skipping four spaces (i.e. the number of spaces between the single quotation marks). Since there is no GO TO statement, control necessarily passes to the next line in sequence, statement 4. Statement 4 increments the value of the variable N by 1, and then unconditionally follows the directions of the GO TO instruction to pass control back to the statement with the label LOOP (i.e. statement 2).

As you can see, SNOBOL programs can accomplish the same programming tasks as languages that have more formal control structures like DO loops or WHILE loops (especially familiar from the ALGOL family). However, the means that SNOBOL uses to accomplish these ends are firmly grounded in more primitive GO TO conventions of the sort found in FORTRAN or BASIC, and that ultimately derive from JUMP statements in assembly language (see the entries on BASIC and assembly language).

Finally, let's see how pattern matching works in SNOBOL. Suppose we want to write a text editor that allows us to determine when a given sequence of characters occurs in a text. We might, for example, want to italicize these characters every place they appear. To accomplish this, we need to declare what our target text is (called the *subject* in SNOBOL) and what the *pattern* is that we want to match.

Suppose we are writing an advertisement for the local Handy Dandy Supermarket chain. We might want to italicize the letters *s-u-p-e-r* every time they appear in the text (e.g. *super*market, *super* low prices). The variable A will represent the subject to be analyzed (e.g. *supermarket*) and the variable B will represent the pattern we want to match (i.e. *super*). Our program fragment might look like this:

```
A = 'SUPERMARKET'
B = 'SUPER'
A    B                          :S (END)
```

The first statement declares the value of A. The second statement compares the value of A with the value of B (i.e. SUPER). If the pattern B finds a match within A (i.e. if the character string SUPER is contained within SUPERMARKET), then a success (S) is registered, and the GO TO part of the statement (i.e. END) passes control to a subsequent statement that begins with the label END.

THE EVOLUTION OF SNOBOL

During the late 1960s and early 1970s, SNOBOL4 enjoyed considerable success among academic users who wanted a language that was symbolically rather than numerically oriented. A natural question to ask is how the use of SNOBOL compared with use of LISP, the other important language expressly designed for symbol manipulation.

SNOBOL vs. LISP

On the surface, SNOBOL and LISP have much in common. Both were developed as symbolic alternatives to number-processing languages. Both make use of functions in analyzing symbolic information, and both are capable of analyzing natural language.

But here the similarities end. LISP was devised by John McCarthy for the very specialized purpose of writing programs in the newly created field of artificial intelligence. LISP programmers were also professional AI researchers. The language was explicitly designed to manipulate *lists* of language units that typically had some meaning in natural language (e.g. adjectives, past-tense verbs, the prefix *un-*).

While SNOBOL also operates upon natural language symbols, it does so with a very different orientation from LISP. SNOBOL was designed as a general-purpose symbol-manipulating language, to be used by laymen who knew very little about computer programming. SNOBOL operates upon *strings* of characters, which may or may not have linguistic significance. While SNOBOL can pick out a word like *super*, it can just as easily do pattern matching on a string like *xmq* or *A442*. In principle, both SNOBOL and LISP can handle the same kinds of operations (much as a LISP program could, in principle, always be written in Pascal). However, the conceptual orientations and intended audiences of SNOBOL and LISP are quite distinct.

Pattern Matching Revisited: SNOBOL and Savvy

Outside of SNOBOL (and, in somewhat different ways, PROLOG and PILOT), computer languages have made very little use of the principle of pattern matching. Nearly all computer languages have some means of comparing character strings, but only SNOBOL took such comparison as a basic design feature.

Recently, the query language known as Savvy (see Appendix) has adopted a version of the pattern-matching principle for analyzing user input. However, we should not confuse the way in which pattern matching operates in these two languages. In SNOBOL, a precise target text (the *subject*) is compared character-by-character with a precise pattern. Only complete matches count as successes.

In Savvy, pattern matching is also done by comparing a target text with a precise pattern. However, since the purpose of Savvy is not symbol manipulation but natural language recognition, a target and pattern are deemed a "match" if they come *reasonably* close to one another (much as I will understand what you are saying even if you speak with a heavy accent or get some of the grammar wrong). Thus, while the pattern-matching *mechanism* is similar in the two languages, the *purposes* of the languages, as well as the criteria for what constitutes a match, are not.

THE FUTURE OF SNOBOL

In the mid-1980s, SNOBOL has been enjoying a minor renaissance in some colleges and universities in the United States. (In fact, Griswold has even created a new, more user-friendly derivative of the language, called ICON.) The only explanation would seem to be that as American higher education begins instituting computer-literacy requirements, SNOBOL remains one of the few non-numerically oriented computer languages available, and therefore is seen as appropriate for non-science students. The other options, LISP and PROLOG, are still rarely taught to general undergraduates without a background in computer science, although several new textbooks on LISP and PROLOG along with the growing popularity of artificial intelligence could alter this situation significantly within the next few years.

Yet SNOBOL has two serious drawbacks as a language for the future. Whatever its virtues as an easy-to-use language, SNOBOL remains an unstructured language. Given the intense pressure of computer science departments to teach structured programming, it is not clear how long a language like SNOBOL can survive.

Secondly, SNOBOL is, in part, outdated because of the ready availability of applications programs. Text editors and spelling checkers automatically perform many of the functions for which users once wrote SNOBOL programs. As applications programs (especially word processing) become increasingly sophisticated, the major uses of SNOBOL may become absorbed by these ready-made tools.

USING SNOBOL

Buying SNOBOL

SNOBOL is not available for microcomputers. Implementations are widely found on many mainframes and minicomputers, especially in universities.

What to Read

BOOKS

Griswold, Ralph E., and Madge T. Griswold (1973). *A SNOBOL4 Primer*. Englewood Cliffs (N.J.): Prentice-Hall.
   A text on SNOBOL4 intended for beginners.
Griswold, R., J. Poage, and I. Polonsky (1971). *The SNOBOL4 Programming Language*. 2nd edition. Englewood Cliffs (N.J.): Prentice-Hall.
   The definitive text on SNOBOL4. The book assumes some background in programming.
Peterson, W. Wesley (1974). *Introduction to Programming Languages*. Englewood Cliffs (N.J.): Prentice-Hall.

Chapter 9 of Peterson's book presents a brief but especially lucid introduction to SNOBOL.

Gaskins, Robert and Laura Gould (1972). *SNOBOL4: A Computer Programming Language for the Humanities*. Berkeley: University of California Press.
This book typifies the trend in the early 1970s of using SNOBOL for non-scientific computing.

Hockney, Susan (1986). *SNOBOL Programming for the Humanities*. New York: Oxford University Press.
As the date of the text indicates, SNOBOL is still being used by some universities for non-scientific programming.

ARTICLES

Griswold, Ralph (1981). "A History of the SNOBOL Programming Languages," in R. L. Wexelblat, ed., *History of Programming Languages*. New York: Academic Press, pp. 601–60.
A personal chronicle of the development of the SNOBOL languages by one of its creators.

PART III
CODA

CHAPTER 6

Divining the Future

Divining the future is always a risky business, and the case of computer languages is no exception. There are so many factors we can't predict—from a serious economic depression that halts technological development to a micro-computer war between the United States and the U.S.S.R. reminiscent of the science education wars resulting from the launching of Sputnik in the late 1950s. Moreover, new conceptual breakthroughs (such as automatic computer analysis of ordinary language syntax or accurate computer recognition of everyday speech) could change the computer language picture dramatically.

But predictions about computer languages differ from general forecasting (of the stock market or the outcome of a presidential election) in a crucial way. Unlike the behavior of Wall Street or of individual voters, the directions that computer languages take are potentially within our control. If we choose, we can consciously devise new languages, create educational task forces that mandate the teaching of particular languages, or use government pressure to endorse the use of one computer language or another.

Give the genial chaos that still reigns in the computer world, no unilateral dicta are likely to be issued in the next few years. However, the more we are able to understand the options available with computer languages, the better the position we will be in to make rational decisions.

Current Trends: Structure and Function

Throughout this book, we have used three basic organizing principles for looking at computer languages: structure, function, and genealogy. Since we have seen that structural distinctions have a great deal in common with genealogy, we will group together these two ways of analyzing computer languages in talking about computer language trends.

GENEALOGY/STRUCTURE

Individual Developments

Among the imperative/algorithmic languages, derivatives of the ALGOL family are continuing to grow and prosper (unlike the FORTRAN and COBOL lines).

Ada and Modula-2 represent but the latest and best known of the group of languages evolving from Pascal. The most important trend within these languages is the continuing growth of modularity (a logical extension of structured programming) and data abstraction (a logical extension of high-level programming more generally).

Functional/applicative languages appear to be undergoing a revival. The best publicized is LISP, whose success reflects mushrooming interest in artificial intelligence. However, APL is rekindling the interest of the business community, and even SNOBOL continues to attract some users, at least in academic settings.

Object-oriented languages are a revolution waiting to happen. While large components of the Smalltalk environment (e.g. the mouse, windows, pull-down menus) have pervaded recent hardware and software developments, the Smalltalk language itself is hovering on the brink of public exposure. Within the next few years we can expect to see Smalltalk commonly available on microcomputers, which should change the profile of Smalltalk considerably.

FORTH retains its status as an enigma. Its unconventional syntax (along with its lack of a user power base) has kept the language from reaching a wider audience. Should FORTH achieve even temporary popularity among the growing cadre of hobbyists and computer professionals, it could blossom into a far more widely used language.

Within the last year or two, Americans have turned from deriding logic programming as a foreign competitor to appreciating the power of logic programming languages such as PROLOG. The real breakthrough in the United States could come as applications development and expert systems designers capitalize upon the elegance and simplicity with which logic programming can be used for dealing with large data bases.

And finally, there are query languages. Query languages themselves are well entrenched in American business. The real growth here, though, is in natural language front ends used for querying large data bases. With the improvement of natural language processing techniques, we can expect the sophistication of natural language front ends to develop enormously in the next few years.

Crosscurrents

In assessing the current state of computer languages, we can also identify many structural trends that cut across conceptual language types. Here are ten such trends:

(1,2,3)   Extensibility, Procedurality, Merging of Data and Programs
Throughout this book we have commented upon the clustering of three structural trends in computer languages. A growing number of languages are extensible, allowing users to define new language components which are then indistinguishable from the language's primitives. Languages are tending to be increasingly non-procedural, requiring that users specify *what* problems are to be solved rather than *how* they are to be solved. And all of the non-imperative/algorithmic languages tend to blur the distinctions between data and programs.

(4) Size

The size of modern computer languages is a topic engendering animated discussion in the professional computing world. There is little agreement on what an appropriate size for a language might be. One faction, best exemplified by FORTH, argues that an extremely powerful language can be contained in a very small amount of space. Most computer language designers, typified by Niklaus Wirth, look to more moderately sized languages (e.g. Modula-2) that are large enough to encompass structured programming techniques but still small enough for a single individual to fathom the language in its entirety. At the other extreme are the designers of Ada, who argue that the size of a language should be judged not by the total number of lines of code in its translator, but by the conceptual design of the language. A language with even 100,000 lines of code can still be conceptually simple.

(5) Level

The early development of levels among computer languages was all undirectional: from machine code to assembly language to high-level languages to very high-level languages. In recent years, however, language designers have looked for ways of incorporating some of the advantages of low-level languages (e.g. speed, conservation of memory space, control) with the advantages of high-level languages (e.g. portability, greater conceptual match between the problem to be solved and the programming language used to solve it).

The result has been the development of several languages (including C, FORTH, and Modula-2) that combine the capabilities of both high-level and low-level programming. As the trend continues to do systems programming for new languages in the languages themselves, language designers may increasingly include some low-level programming facilities in otherwise high-level languages.

(6) Standardization

The move toward high-level languages in the late 1950s and in the 1960s was largely motivated by a desire to produce standard languages that were independent of particular machines. In the ensuing years, the American National Standards Institute has certified an increasing number of "standard" versions of computer languages. One mark of a new language's coming of age (at least among the imperative/algorithmic family) is the establishment of an ANSI standard.

Yet dialects and variants still multiply. The microcomputer revolution, fueled by the American free-enterprise system, has meant that new variants continue to appear on the market and continue to be purchased and used. We might anticipate that while standardization will become increasingly important for programs in professional programming shops where portability and maintainability are critical, variation will flourish among microcomputer programmers who are typically the sole users of their programs.

(7) Generality

Third-generation computer languages were originally designed as general-purpose systems that could be used to program any problem. The apotheosis of this movement was the appearance of PL/1 in the early 1960s.

Yet general-purpose languages have failed on two counts. On the one hand, they have tended to resemble a potpourri with little internal coherence (recall that PL/I is often compared to a Swiss Army knife). On the other hand, as the range of computer language functions has expanded, it seems increasingly less likely that any single language can be optimally suited to all users.

A single language may not even be appropriate for a general area of application. In artificial intelligence programming, for example, the creators of POPLOG (see Appendix) argue for a *cluster* of languages from which to choose for a specific programming problem. In imperative/algorithmic programming, reliability may be critical for some uses (e.g. real-time programming) but not for others (e.g. operating systems and editors). And so while Ada or Modula-2 may be an appropriate language for the first task, C may be appropriate for the second.

(8)   Concurrent Programming
As the uses of computers expand and as computer hardware designers begin breaking out of the sequential von Neumann architecture, the role of concurrent programming or multiprogramming is becoming increasingly important. Early concurrent programming languages such as Concurrent Pascal have been replaced by more sophisticated systems, including Mesa, Modula-2, and Ada. With the development of parallel processing hardware, new languages such as Occam (see Appendix) take advantage of simultaneous processing of more than one piece of information in the computer itself.

(9)   Programming Environments
One of the most important developments in programming languages over the past decade has been the creation of software environments in which the actual writing of programs can take place. This trend is exemplified by languages ranging from Ada to Smalltalk.

(10)   Production vs. Comprehension
In determining whether a computer language is difficult or easy to use, we found that we need to distinguish between the perspectives of the producer of a system and those of its user. Among the imperative/algorithmic languages, the designers of COBOL and Ada attempted to create languages that were easy to read and maintain. They placed less emphasis upon the ease with which programs could be written in the first place. Among functional/applicative languages and FORTH, the trend has been just the opposite: to devise languages that enable competent programmers to write compact and elegant code, paying less attention to whether the resulting programs are subsequently readable.

FUNCTION

In Chapter 3 we identified eight areas in which computer languages function today.

(1)   Business
The most important issue within the world of business computing is the status
of COBOL: Will COBOL (and the data-processing departments that program
in it) continue to dominate business computing, or will they be displaced by
sophisticated data base management systems and non-procedural query languages
that are increasingly supported by natural language front end systems?

The data-processing community generally maintains that COBOL is a necessary
part of the business world. Toward this end, COBOL is being "modernized,"
with structured versions, conversations of unstructured COBOL to structured
code, and use on microcomputers. At the same time, though, some DP
departments are expanding their professional domain to include the newer data
base management systems. As DBMSs become increasingly complex, they may
well pass from the hands of novices (for whom they were originally intended)
into the bailiwick of professional data processors.

(2)   Science/Engineering
While the legacy of FORTRAN remains strong in world of science and
engineering, newer imperative/algorithmic languages (all deriving from the
ALGOL family) are beginning to replace FORTRAN for many programming
problems. The major languages to watch here are Modula-2, Ada, and C.

(3)   Systems Programming
Although systems programming is traditionally the domain of professional
programmers, general-purpose languages that are well suited to systems programming have begun to enter the popular market. The best-known example is
C, although FORTH and Modula-2 are also likely candidates because they
contain low-level programming capabilities. As an increasing number of non-
professional programmers learn to use computer languages, we may also expect
more non-professionals to be doing systems programming and more user-friendly
systems programming languages to develop.

(4)   Simulation
Simulation languages, while several decades old, have enormous untapped
potential. Traditionally, their use has largely been restricted to professional
systems analysts running large computers. However, with the growing interest
in simulation in education, along with the expanding memory capabilities of
microcomputers, we can expect this situation to change in the coming years.

(5)   Applications
There is a growing trend for the learning and use of formal computer languages
to be replaced by the learning and use of applications packages. As long as
commercially available packages actually suit the needs of users, proponents of
applications software can reasonably argue that average computer users don't
need to learn the more traditional languages. However, the issue of suitability
is far from trivial. As increasingly sophisticated users purchase and become
frustrated by the limitations of existing applications software, the impetus for
writing their own may well grow.

(6) Artificial Intelligence

Artificial intelligence will be one of the largest growth areas of computer languages in the coming decade. Within the last two or three years alone, AI has gone from being an abstruse topic, of interest only to a handful of university researchers, to a field that sparks the public imagination and promises to yield practical results.

Several major software houses have announced that their next phase of commercial software will be AI programming and especially expert systems. The sudden increase of books and courses on LISP promises to yield a cadre of potential programmers for this new software.

(7) Authoring Languages

Authoring languages received moderate attention during the 1970s with the initial development of computer-aided instruction in education. However, it gradually became clear that these languages would still be time-consuming to use and that they produced software that was often tedious at best. Consequently, interest in authoring languages dropped off in the early 1980s.

Several trends seem to be altering the fate of authoring languages. One is the explosion of microcomputers in classrooms. Teachers are increasingly desiring the ability to create software directly suitable for their needs. New authoring languages are appearing that at once offer greater flexibility and make fewer programming demands upon the user than a language like PILOT. However, most of these languages are still based upon the imperative/algorithmic style, and programs written in these languages look very much like PILOT programs.

A second development is the infusion of artificial intelligence techniques into computer-aided instruction. University research centers are beginning to develop tutorial programs that use expert systems to tailor lessons to the needs of students and then identify and explain errors made in the course of running the program. The next step, now underway, is to create more general authoring languages that take advantage of these techniques but are simple enough for non-programmers to use.

Another development is the creation of ''applications toolkits'' that can be used in conjunction with sophisticated languages like Smalltalk and PROLOG. Such toolkits are analogous to common business applications programs such as Lotus 1-2-3. The toolkits, written by expert programmers, enable relative novices to construct their own programs, which could be explicit tutorials, educational data bases, or even games.

And fourth, with the development of interactive video discs that are capable of storing up to 54,000 visual images, the very uses of authoring languages are changing. Instead of merely controlling the printed information that a student can access on a CRT, authoring languages are now being used to interface video images with traditional computer functions. Authoring languages can also be extended to control other technological media useful in education such as speech analysis units, speech synthesis units, television images, and a variety of graphic input devices.

(8) Education

In Chapter 3, we identified two types of uses of computers in education: for teaching programming and for teaching thinking. In both areas, the role of computer languages is at a crossroads.

The early 1980s saw the introduction of computer literacy requirements in a large number of high schools and colleges. Often these requirements entailed teaching students to program in at least one language, typically BASIC or Pascal. However, a level of disenchantment has set in as students fail to make use of their rudimentary skills.

Part of the problem lies in the languages selected for teaching. It is not obvious that imperative/algorithmic languages are the best choice. Another part of the problem is that many teachers, especially at the college level, are only interested in training potential professional programmers, not the student body at large. In any event, a number of school systems are beginning to change their general computer education requirements. Instead of learning programming languages, students are now studying applications programs such as word processing and data base management.

The teaching of computer languages as a way of teaching thinking is an even more complex and delicate issue. We will address it in the next section.

Relevant Variables

Will the variety of computer languages we have seen up until now continue or will it cease? Will the number of computer users keep growing as it did in the 1970s and early 1980s, or will we return to the "priesthood" model of the 1950s and 1960s?

How do we go about answering these questions?

REASSESSMENT OF EXISTING LANGUAGES

An important first step will be to reassess existing computer languages. New users justifiably complain about some of the languages they are learning. Often these languages are full of terminology that makes no sense or have syntax that seems to have no logical order.

As we saw in Chapter 5, many computer languages, especially the older ones, are hardly paragons of language design. The creators of COBOL never expected their preliminary efforts to be widely distributed. The designer of FORTRAN readily admits to having made up the syntax as he went along, being far more concerned with efficiency of execution than with linguistic elegance. In other cases, languages designed for one set of needs are now being stretched to fill very different functions. BASIC, for example, was intended to introduce novices to the world of computer programming, not to solve artificial intelligence problems or do word processing.

In evaluating these languages, then, we must distinguish between languages that are well designed by contemporary standards and those which are not. We must also be careful not to assume that because languages have been poorly designed in the past, such design errors are intrinsic to the programming language enterprise.

DIVERSITY OF NEEDS

As we saw earlier in this chapter, no single general-purpose computing language is likely to evolve that will fill the needs of all programmers. However, we can identify two fundamentally distinct *styles* of programming which can both be expected to prosper in the coming years.

In Chapter 3, we developed a spectrum of six conceptual types of computer languages. On the left-hand side were imperative/algorithmic languages, which we characterized as being procedural and non-extensible and as making sharp distinctions between programs and data. As we worked to the right-hand side, we found that the other five language categories were increasingly non-procedural and extensible and blurred the distinction between programs and data.

This second group of languages has experienced considerable growth, especially in the last fifteen years. However, we have also seen that imperative/algorithmic languages continue to prosper. How can this be?

The answer is that we need to distinguish between *public* and *private* computing.

In *public* computing, programs are written to be used by many people other than the programmer and to be maintained over time. Imperative/algorithmic languages, especially the newer members of the ALGOL family, are ideally suited to public computing. They require rigorous documentation (which is built into the very structure of the languages themselves), require the programmer to spell out exactly how a problem is to be solved (through the procedural orientation of the program), and do not allow the programmer to introduce idiosyncratic elements (i.e. the languages are not extensible). The needs of public computing were recognized by the designers of Ada, who insisted that program readability and maintainability are more important considerations than efficiency in actually writing programs. More generally, the teaching of structured programming is the teaching of public computing.

Private computing involves writing programs that either are for oneself or will need to be read by only a limited audience. The non-imperative/algorithmic languages (which tend to extensible and non-procedural) are well suited to private computing. They allow programmers to focus their energies on the nature of problems themselves without becoming bogged down in implementation details. They also provide programmers with the flexibility needed to approach problems in novel ways.

Languages that are well suited to private computing encourage a great deal of ingenuity and creativity among users. It is ironic that, with the exception of

Logo, micro-PROLOG, and potentially Smalltalk, the computer languages typically used in classrooms are the public languages that are structurally least well suited to fostering independence of thought.

TEACHING THINKING

Many curricula mandate that students should be taught computer programming because it will teach them to think. But what does it mean to say that computers can be used to "teach thinking"? For most high school and college educators, the answer is not "creative" thinking. Instead, it is using the discipline of programming (typically with a structured imperative/algorithmic language) to teach students to think out problems of any sort more logically.

Even if "logical" thinking (rather than creative thought) is the goal, it is hardly likely that the teaching of computer languages can be of much help. The problem is that educators have reversed the order of cause and effect when talking about logical thinking and computer languages.

For it is not computer languages that foster logical thinking, but logical thinking that makes possible the writing of good computer programs. As any master of the *discipline* of computer programming will assure you, a good programmer must *first* understand the structure of the problem to be solved (with or without a computer) *before* attempting to code the solution into a particular language. The model of top down design that we discussed in Chapter 2 formalizes the order in which programming is to be done: first think out the problem; then reduce it to smaller and smaller subproblems; and only at the very end code it into a programming language.

The popular confusion about the relationship between thinking and programming has arisen because of the early history of computer programming itself, at least in the United States. As we said in our discussion of ALGOL, the early days of American programming were characterized by an unstructured and often brute-force approach. A programmer would look at a problem, write out lines of code, and try running it. If it didn't work the first time (and it rarely did), the programmer would tinker with the coding until it finally ran. There was often little rhyme or reason to the order in which the code was written or the procedure via which debugging was done.

At the same time, there is always an objective test of the correctness of a program: does it run and, of course, does it also yield the right answer? Because most areas of human endeavor admit of no such objective measure of correctness, some people began to look upon programming as a reasonable analogy for examining the "correctness" of one's thinking about a problem.

With the development of structured programming in the 1970s, attempts to relate thinking and programming became yet more confused. On the face of things, the structuring that goes into a Pascal program might seem to be a useful model for thinking out clearly a problem in some other domain. Yet remember that structured programming is merely a means of disciplining the programmer to organize in some rational way the lines of programming code to be composed. At best, this notion of structuring affords the programmer some hints on how to look at real-world problems: Are there several objects which are all members of the same class? Does an event occur more than one time? Is the occurrence of the event dependent upon some other event? However, for all but the most trivial problems, the programmer can't stuff reality into data structures and control structures.

Creative programming—even in imperative/algorithmic languages—is possible when the programmer is first able to see the structure inherent in the problem itself, and then goes on to determine how to translate that structure into the syntax available in a programming language. We should not forget that many of the developments among programming languages occurred when programmers saw a structure inherent in the problems they wished to solve, but found that the language they were using lacked appropriate means for encoding that structure.

COMPUTER LANGUAGES AND REPRESENTATION

Throughout this book, we have cast our discussion of computer languages in terms of a more general model of representation. In looking at the future of computer languages, two issues of representation arise. The first concerns simulation languages. We discussed simulation languages briefly in Chapter 3 and looked at SIMULA and Smalltalk in Chapter 5. Yet as we noted at the beginning of this chapter, the potential of simulation languages is only now being developed. Much of this potential derives from the way in which simulation languages handle representation.

Perhaps the most difficult problem in using computer languages comes not in learning the language's syntax or even in debugging a problem, but in figuring out how to represent a real-world problem within the artificial confines of a programming language. Unlike all of the traditional programming languages, simulation languages enable the user to create a microworld that models that part of reality for which problem solving is to be done. That is, simulation languages allow more accurate and natural representation of problems than do other programming languages.

The accuracy of problem representation has never been especially critical in scientific or business computing. Science and mathematics are themselves abstract models of reality, and algorithmic languages merely represent these already abstracted representations. In the business world, balance sheets and yearly reports (which predate computers) are also themselves representations of actual sales and actual social security numbers.

But in the world of artificial intelligence—the new horizon for simulation languages—it is the human mind that needs to be modeled, and modeled directly. It is therefore critical that the languages we use for such modeling be as flexible as possible and make only minimal presuppositions about the structure of intelligence. Despite their extensibility, the more traditional artificial intelligence languages (i.e. LISP and PROLOG) make a considerable number of assumptions about how knowledge is divided up and how components of knowledge may be related to one another. The potential of simulation languages is the greater freedom of modeling that they afford.

A second issue concerning computer languages and representation involves the use of what we might call an interrogative model of knowledge representation. Practitioners in the domains of both artificial intelligence and business are developing increasing interest in large collections of information. In the world of AI, we speak of knowledge bases. In business, we generally speak of data bases. But in both instances, we are concerned with first gathering information and then finding ways of retrieving it.

The dominant model for retrieving information from a collection (either in AI or in business) is through asking questions. In business, we have query languages that can access data base management systems. In AI, we again speak of information (or, actually, "knowledge") that is accessed by questions. In fact, in the case of logic programming, the very languages themselves are structured in terms of queries.

The query model is unproblematic in the business world. No one debates the ontological status of a year-end profit statement or of a social security number. Yet when we are talking about human knowledge, we are on shakier ontological grounds. The query representation model presupposes, first, that human knowledge can be reduced to the same kind of objective representation as profit statements and social security numbers, and second, that all knowledge we might want to deal with in a model of human intelligence can be accessed through query statements.

Both of these assumptions are dubious at best. In looking at computer languages of the future that will be used to represent what people know, we will need to be aware of what representational presuppositions the models themselves make about the nature of human knowledge.

THE MEANING OF "INTERACTIVE"

The development of time sharing in the early 1960s introduced the possibility of users working interactively with computers. Instead of having to deliver a program on stacks of punched cards to a computer operator and then wait hours or even days for the results, users could get their results within a few minutes or even seconds by inputting, compiling, and running the program via a keyboard and CRT.

In the past twenty years, the meaning of the word "interactive" has evolved through several important stages. As we saw in the entry on BASIC in Chapter 5, one significant step in the development of interactive computing was enabling users to input data while a program was actually running. Instead of having to enter all variable values as part of the original program, users could write programs that would ask questions such as "What is the value of X?" and the user would input the desired value at run time.

The option for users to manipulate programs as they were actually running opened up the possibility of an entire new approach to computing. It suggested that programmers could blur the previously strict distinction between writing and running a program.

This blurring of activity is known to many programmers as a convenient tool that, for example, lets users make corrections in programs without having formally to keep entering and exiting an editor (in compiled languages). A stronger example is a language (like LISP, APL, or FORTH) that makes no distinction between data and programs: to declare a body of data is to run a program.

But the most powerful form of this interactivity between user and program comes with the language Smalltalk, which eliminates the distinction between writing and running a program in a very powerful way. In LISP, for example, you must write a complete "program" (which may be a data specification) in order for the program to run. You can't define only half of a function and expect anything to happen. In Smalltalk, nearly every move the programmer makes has some immediate repercussions. You don't need to specify all slots in a class definition template to bring about effects (e.g. defining objects, sending messages).

A programming language that eliminates the distinction between writing and running programs has the enormous advantage of letting users interact with computers much the way they do with colleagues in everyday life. Users can try out hypotheses, see their consequences, pursue a new avenue of inquiry, and then return to the original problem without having to start from scratch each time. This give-and-take model characterizes the way in which most people think and work. To have such a model available in a programming language (be it Smalltalk or its successors) may mean that the programming of computers might actually be moving closer to the way that human beings investigate problems.

PRESSURES OF THE MARKETPLACE

Most of our discussions of computer languages have dealt with the languages themselves—their structures, their functions, and their genealogies. Yet the future of any computer language is determined not only by the language's virtues (or vices) but also by pressures of the marketplace.

These pressures come in many guises. Some come through government directives, such as the edict in the 1960s that only computers that ran COBOL would be funded by the U.S. government. Others come through organizational policy decisions (for example, that Pascal will be the language recognized by the Educational Testing Service for advanced placement in college). Still other pressures are direct results of the market. The distribution of BASIC (first as software and then as firmware) by so many microcomputer manufacturers has been directly responsible for BASIC's popularity.

IMPACT OF HARDWARE DEVELOPMENTS

At least two hardware trends bear watching. The first is the development of parallel processing machines that make it possible to avoid the sequential bottleneck of von Neumann architecture. We have already seen the beginnings of new languages (e.g. Occam) being developed to take advantage of parallel processors in hardware. We can expect this trend to continue.

The other significant trend will be the potentially explosive effects of the development of mass storage devices. The earliest computers had extremely limited memory capabilities—either of Read Only Memory (ROM) or of Read/ Write Memory (RAM). With the expansion of memory capacity over the past decade, we have seen the development of increasingly sophisticated languages (which need large amounts of memory in order to run) along with growth in the complexity of problems that computers can be used in solving.

But the real revolution is just ahead. Hard disks are now readily available for Read/Write Memory that will hold up to 20 or even 40 megabytes of information. Optical Read Only Memory disks are now appearing that will have many times that amount of storage.

What will we put on such disks, and what kinds of computer languages will we use to access their contents? These are questions we will need to begin asking over the next few years.

The Question of Control

The history of computer languages can be seen as the ebb and flow of power over computers themselves. In the earliest days, computers were strictly run by a handful of computer professionals. Even with the development of the first high-level languages such as FORTRAN and ALGOL, only a select few engaged in programming, and even then the computers themselves were not directly handled by users.

The late 1950s and early 1960s opened the doorway to programming by the naive user. First Grace Hopper's FLOW-MATIC and then COBOL and SNOBOL were attempts to make computing accessible to a broader public. At the same time, the spread of FORTRAN among broader university constituencies widened the base of programmers.

Yet despite the continued growth of programming among non-computer professionals in the universities (especially in the areas of science and engineering), business computing was soon professionalized into data-processing departments. Computer programming became a profession for which one formally trained, not an avocation one practiced on the side.

The coming of the microcomputer potentially changed all that. When hardware and software became available to anyone with a few hundred dollars and a sense of adventure, it was possible for people everywhere to experiment with computing. As the bona fides of the machine became more established, microcomputers began to move into schools, offices, and even homes. It is difficult to believe that only a decade ago few of us could have imagined the average person buying a home computer.

The 1980s are characterized by two opposing trends. On the one hand, a growing number of people are learning to use computers and learning to program them. On the other hand, as applications programs become more sophisticated, many people are questioning whether learning to program is worth the effort.

Control over computers through knowledge of computer programming could once again be returned entirely to the hands of a priesthood. Obviously we will continue to need some computer professionals who know considerably more about programming than do average laymen. But the real question is this: Will average intelligent non-computer professionals be afforded the tools necessary for programming computers to solve novel problems of their own choosing? This book has attempted to establish that such leeway is both necessary and realistic.

APPENDIX
OTHER LANGUAGES

This Appendix contains brief entries on some of the other computer languages you are likely to encounter.

CHILL

CHILL is a ALGOL-derivative language that was developed to do real-time telecommunications systems programming. It was developed under the auspices of the CCITT (Comité Consultatif International Télégraphique et Téléphonique), and its name derives from the abbreviation for CCITT *HI*gh *L*evel *L*anguage. The language, created in the second half of the 1970s, is designed to provide facilities similar to those found in Ada.

What to Read

Smedema, C. H., P. Medema, and M. Boasson (1983). *The Programming Languages: Pascal, Modula, CHILL, Ada.* Englewood Cliffs (N.J.): Prentice-Hall International.

COMAL

COMAL (*COM*mon *A*lgorithmic *L*anguage) was created in 1973 by Borge Christensen and Benedict Loefstedt in Denmark. They developed the language out of dissatisfaction with BASIC, which did not encourage structured programming skills in students.

In the early 1970s, there was no structured BASIC as an alternative to the unstructured version that was to become popular on microcomputers in the late 1970s. ALGOL, which was widely used in Europe, did have rudimentary notions of structuring (with its blocks and procedures), and Pascal (a structured language par excellence) was just being developed by Niklaus Wirth in the early 1970s. It is therefore not surprising that COMAL should be a European development, and not one that became well known in the United States, where structured programming (via Pascal) did not become fashionable until almost 1980.

COMAL retains BASIC's operating environment, including the use of an interpreter rather than a compiler, line numbers allowing the user to alter programs easily, a built-in editor, and easy means of inputting and outputting information. At the same time, COMAL uses Pascal's expanded control structures along with some of Pascal's syntactic conventions.

COMAL is widely used in Denmark, Germany, and Ireland, and runs on microcomputers. In the United States, COMAL is little known, but is available on the Commodore (the primary machine on which it runs in Europe).

What to Read

Atherton, R. (1982). *Structured Programming with COMAL*. Chichester (Eng.): Ellis Horwood.

Lindsay, Len (1984). *The COMAL Handbook*. 2nd edition. Reston (Va.): Reston Publishing Company.

DYNAMO

DYNAMO (*DYNA*mic *MO*dels) is a continuous simulation language developed in the late 1950s by the Industrial Dynamics Group at the Sloan School of Management at the Massachusetts Institute of Technology. The language evolved from an earlier program called SIMPLE, which stands for *S*imulation of *I*ndustrial *M*anagement *P*roblems with *L*ots of *E*quations.

In a continuous simulation language, the variables being analyzed change continuously. To approximate the continuous process of events, a set of first-order differential equations are used.

DYNAMO was originally developed to provide computer support for the systems-modeling technique known as *system dynamics,* which is the work of Jay Forrester and his colleagues at MIT. The DYNAMO language has typically been used on mainframe computers.

What to Read

Pugh, Alexander L., III (1970). *DYNAMO II User's Manual*. Cambridge (Mass.): MIT Press.
    The authorized handbook to the most current version of the language for large computers.

Roberts, Nancy, David F. Andersen, Ralph M. Deal, Michael S. Garet, and William A. Shaffer (1983). *Introduction to Computer Simulation: The System Dynamics Approach*. Reading (Mass.): Addison-Wesley.
    This is a version of the original language DYNAMO that was developed to be used on microcomputers with students in high school and those just

beginning college. (DYNAMO had previously been used almost exclusively on mainframe computers, and then only with advanced undergraduates and graduate students.) The result, micro-DYNAMO, is distributed for Apple II series computers by Addison-Wesley Publishing Co.

JCL

JCL (standing for *Job Control Language*) is IBM's version of a command language that runs on IBM 360 and 370 computers under its operating systems known as OS/360 and OS/370. Because so many users of mainframe computers are familiar with the IBM 360 and 370, JCL has come to be widely known and used, and therefore merits at least brief mention.

All computers need some systems programs to make the machine function. Typical systems programs include operating systems and language translators. The older mainframe computers also require a systems program known as a *command language,* which takes the programming elements that the user wants to employ in a particular program and lines them up in such a way that the computer can process them. For example, if a program employs a section of FORTRAN code, a section of assembly language code, and then several library subroutines, the command language is used to fetch all of these programming components from the appropriate storage areas and make sure they are executed at the proper time and in the proper order. That is, statements from the command language need to be added to the lines of programming code from the usual programming languages in order physically to get the desired program to run.

Command languages (which are technically part of a computer's operating system) have been in use since the late 1950s. However, it was not until IBM's development of first OS/360 and then OS/370, and the concomitant appearance of JCL, that command languages received much public attention.

What to Read

Bateman, Barry L., and Gerald N. Pitts (1981). *JCL in a System 370 Environment.* New York: Van Nostrand Reinhold.

Karel the Robot

One of the difficulties in learning computer languages (unlike learning natural foreign languages) is that the learner has no initial preconceptions of what to expect. As the teaching of computer programming languages has become more widespread over the past decade, some teachers of computer science have realized that students are often unprepared to delve immediately into the world of data structures and control structures, FOR loops and recursion. As an alternative, several have devised introductory programming languages or programming systems that make the transition smoother.

Karel the Robot is one such system. Designed by Richard Pattis at Stanford University, Karel the Robot introduces a microworld inhabited by a robot named Karel. The user/learner can program Karel to move across simulated city streets. The language used to do such programming is essentially an abstracted and simplified version of Pascal. By learning to program the moves of Karel the Robot, new students of programming can become familiar with the essential principles underlying the Pascal language before becoming distracted by syntactic detail.

In many universities, Karel the Robot is taught at the beginning of a course of Pascal. The Karel simulator can be run on both mainframes and microcomputers.

What to Read
Pattis, Richard E. (1981). *Karel the Robot.* New York: John Wiley.

KRL

KRL (*K*nowledge *R*epresentation *L*anguage) is an artificial intelligence language developed by Daniel Bobrow of Xerox Palo Alto Research Center (PARC) and Terry Winograd of Stanford University. The language is built on top of INTERLISP, one of the most fully developed dialects of LISP

KRL, as its name suggests, was designed to represent human knowledge. The language is part of a long-term project to build computer models of natural language use and understanding.

What to Read

Bobrow, Daniel G., and Terry Winograd (1977). "An Overview of KRL, a Knowledge Representation Language," *Cognitive Science* 1:3–46.
Bobrow, Daniel G., and Terry Winograd (1979). "KRL: Another Perspective," *Cognitive Science* 3.

LOGLISP

LOGLISP is an artificial intelligence language devised at Syracuse University that implements the PROLOG language within a LISP environment. The purpose of the language is to provide LISP users with the advantages of PROLOG without having to sacrifice the rich LISP programming environment that has been developed over the years.

What to Read

Robinson, J. A., and E. E. Sibert (n.d.). "LOGLISP: Motivation, Design, and Implementation," School of Computer and Information Science, Syracuse University.
Robinson, J. A., and E. E. Sibert (1982). "LOGLISP: An Alternative to PROLOG," in *Machine Intelligence* 10. Chichester (Eng.): Ellis Horwood.

MUMPS

MUMPS (*M*assachusetts General Hospital *U*tility *M*ulti-*P*rogramming *S*ystem) is a language developed in the mid-1960s as an efficient time-sharing system to be used for clinical data management. The language was designed by G. Octo Barnett at the Department of Medicine of the Harvard Medical School (Massachusetts General Hospital is one of Harvard Medical School's teaching hospitals).

The 1960s were a ripe time for developing computer languages. New interpreted languages were being designed to make use of time sharing, which had just been invented (see the entry on BASIC). COBOL had recently appeared and was already enjoying considerable success. However, COBOL had been explicitly designed for processing business data and was not directly suited to non-business data-processing needs. And finally, in the 1960s, formal data base management systems (such as DATATRIEVE or ORACLE) were only beginning to emerge, and so the only real option available for manipulating large bodies of heavily textual data was COBOL.

MUMPS was developed explicitly to serve the data-processing needs of the medical community. These generally involved manipulating large amounts of textual data and included everything from patient-record management to word processing to report generation to accounting. MUMPS is an intrepreted language that combines attributes of imperative/algorithmic languages with attributes of functional/applicative languages such as LISP.

The MUMPS language has become firmly entrenched in the medical community in the United States. It originally ran on minicomputers but now is available on both mainframes and microcomputers. MUMPS has a very active national MUMPS Users' Group (MUG), headquartered in College Park, Maryland. MUG has annual conventions, publishes books on MUMPS, and issues a quarterly magazine.

What to Read

Krieg, Arthur, and Lucille K. Shearer (1981). *Computer Programming in ANS MUMPS*. College Park (Md.): The MUMPS Users' Group.
Porter, Martin, and Duncan Pringle (1984). "MUMPS Fever," *PC Magazine*, March 20, pp. 363–367.

NaturalLink

One of the major problems with natural language front end programs is the number of cases in which the natural language front end system fails to make sense of the user's query (see the section on query languages in the discussion of "Functional Classification" in Chapter 3, and the entry on Intellect in Chapter 5). Sometimes the problem relates to the language parsing system that makes up the natural language front end: the desired answer is in the data base, but the parser isn't able to understand the user's request. Other times the problem lies in the data base: the request is interpretable to the parser, but the data base lacks the desired information. In both cases, though, the user is likely to get a response such as "I don't understand your request—try again."

Harry Tennant at Texas Instruments decided to try an alternative approach to natural language front ends. Instead of creating a system in which the user's request would need to be parsed by a language analysis program and then, if successful, passed along to the data base, Tennant decided to create a closed-menu system in which the user would make selections from a set of progressively refined menus and in which there was a zero probability of error. TI began to market the system actively in 1984.

The system, called NaturalLink, is used as a "front end" to a number of programs that are popular among computer users but normally require the user to learn sets of arbitrary commands in order to operate. Two such systems for which NaturalLink programs have been written are Dow Jones News Retrieval Service and the operating system MS DOS.

The difference between the way users access the Dow Jones service directly and the way they access it using the NaturalLink front end program is stark. A typical example might be a request for Dow Jones averages. The usual Dow Jones command for this information would be

.I/DJA

while the NaturalLink command would read

What are the Dow Jones averages?

What's more, the NaturalLink command comes not from the user's head but from successive selections from an unfolding series of menus. Each menu contains a series of options. Depending upon which option the user selects (e.g. the user wants to see closing stock prices), the program reveals a special set of appropriate menus (e.g. listing the companies for which stock prices are available). The system works very much like any procedure governed by decision trees. Consider the purchase of a new automobile. If you choose to buy a Volvo, there are certain models available. If you decide upon model X, these are the colors in which it comes. If you select blue, you may have regular or metallic paint. And so on.

The principles behind NaturalLink are quite similar to the model underlying Query-by-Example (QBE). In NaturalLink, users are given a visual display of possibilities from which to make choices. It is nearly impossible to make a mistake using NaturalLink, since only "legal" choices are offered at each step of the way. In QBE, users are presented with a labeled visual array. All users need to do is to fill in values. Users do not have to formulate queries from scratch.

The existing NaturalLink front end programs were created with a development package that Texas Instruments sells to people wanting to create their own front ends to systems whose commands are either confusing or cumbersome to learn, especially for computer novices. The real potential for NaturalLink lies not in the success of the current handful of front end programs, but in the possibilities that the development package offers to users who want to create their own interfaces.

What to Read

Tennant, Harry R., Kenneth M. Ross, Richard M. Saenz, Craig W. Thompson, and James R. Miller (1983). "Menu-Based Natural Language Understanding," *Proceedings of the 21st Annual Meeting of the Association for Computational Linguistics*, June 15–17, Cambridge (Mass.), Massachusetts Institute of Technology, pp. 151–158.

Occam

Traditional von Neumann architecture has dictated that only one piece of information can be handled at a time in a computer. However, recent hardware developments now make it possible for several microprocessors to function simultaneously. Such computers can handle several pieces of information concurrently by using multiple processors in parallel.

Nearly all computer languages have been designed on the von Neumann model—to process information sequentially. Concurrent programming or multiprogramming languages typically behave as if more than one process is occurring at a time, while in fact the processes are actually sequential (see the entry on Modula-2). With the development of parallel processing, languages will need to be able to address actual multiple processors through software.

Occam, a new language created and marketed by INMOS Limited (U.K.) and INMOS Corp. (U.S.), is explicitly designed to facilitate parallel processing. The language is named after William of Occam, a fourteenth-century English scholastic philosopher, who is popularly known for a dictum that has come to be called Occam's Razor:

> non sunt multiplicanda entia praeter necessitatem
> (never multiply entities unnecessarily)

Given the proverbial complexity of languages used for concurrent processing, Occam's designers decided to create a language in which concurrency could be expressed through comparatively simple software.

Despite its name, Occam is not a language for novices. Its use requires considerable understanding of concurrent programming, and knowledge of computer hardware is definitely helpful as well. However, the language is extremely powerful and should be of interest to people involved in parallel processing. Moreover, Occam does run on microcomputers (it is currently running on the UCSD p-system).

What to Read

Taylor, Richard, and Pete Wilson (1982). "Occam: Process-Oriented Language Meets Demands of Distributed Processing," *Electronics*, November 30.
INMOS Limited (1984). *Occam Programming Manual*. Englewood Cliffs (N.J.): Prentice-Hall.

OPS5

OPS5 (*Official Production System, Version 5*) is a language developed for use in artificial intelligence programming, offering an alternative to the other well-known AI languages—LISP, PROLOG, and Smalltalk. Each of these languages exemplifies a different style of programming. LISP is a *functional/applicative* language; PROLOG is a *logic-programming* language; and Smalltalk is an *object-oriented* language. OPS5 is a *production-system* programming language. Production systems (also sometimes called rule-based systems) offer one of several possible approaches to the representation of knowledge.

Development and use of OPS5 has been heavily concentrated at Carnegie-Mellon University. However, with publication of the first text on OPS5 (see below), use of the language may spread.

What to Read

Brownston, Lee, Robert Farrell, Elaine Kant, and Nancy Martin (1985). *Programming Expert Systems in OPS5*. Reading (Mass.): Addison-Wesley.

POP

POP is an ALGOL-based but LISP-influenced artificial intelligence language. It was developed in the late 1960s at the University of Edinburgh by R. M. Burstall, J. S. Collins, and R. J. Popplestone. Much as LISP has grown out of artificial intelligence research at MIT and has become the standard language for doing AI research in the United States, POP has emerged from work on AI at the University of Edinburgh to become something of an AI language standard in the United Kingdom.

POP has gone through several stages of evolution. The first established version was POP-2. POP-11 was later developed by Aaron Sloman at the Cognitive Studies Programme at the University of Sussex to teach humanities students about computing in general and about AI methods in particular. The most recent development is a language known as POPLOG, which is really a multilanguage AI programming environment. Based on the thesis that a single language is not necessarily best suited for all AI programming tasks, POPLOG combines the facilities of a more procedural language like POP-11 with the non-procedural power of a logic programming language like PROLOG.

POP never gained an audience in the United States, given the dominance of LISP as an AI programming language. However, the power and generality of POPLOG is such that the language could well make inroads in the United States.

What to Read

Burstall, R. M., J. S. Collins, and R. J. Popplestone (1971). *Programming in POP-2*. Department of Artificial Intelligence, University of Edinburgh.
Yazdoni, Masoud, ed. (1984). *New Horizons in Educational Computing*. Chichester (Eng.): Ellis Horwood; New York: Halsted Press (division of John Wiley).
This volume contains a series of articles on POP-11.

POPLOG

POPLOG is a multilanguage artificial intelligence programming environment, created in the spirit of LISP programming environments. It was developed at the University of Sussex. POPLOG contains two distinct programming languages: the procedural language POP-11 and the logic programming language PROLOG.

POPLOG is not actively used in the United States. However, since the language has been implemented at Sussex on a VAX minicomputer running under the standard VMS operating system, POPLOG could easily be run on hardware now available in most American universities. As interest in PROLOG continues to grow in the United States, it is possible that interest in POPLOG will grow as well.

What to Read

Sloman, A., S. Hardy, and J. Gibson (1983). "POPLOG: A Multilanguage Development Environment," *Information Technology: Research and Development* 2:109–122.
Hardy, S. (1984). "A New Software Environment for List Processing and Logic Programming," in T. O'Shea and M. Eisenstadt, eds., *Artificial Intelligence: Tools, Techniques, and Applications*. New York: Harper & Row, pp. 110–136.

Mellish, C., and S. Hardy (1984). "Integrating PROLOG in the POPLOG Environment," in J. A. Campbell, ed., *Implementations of PROLOG*. Chichester (Eng.): Ellis Horwood, pp. 147–162.

RPG

RPG (*Report Program Generator*) is a specialized language designed to allow the easy creation of reports, which businesses and comparable organizations are continually being called upon to issue. Such reports typically *present* rather than *calculate* results. RPG was originally created in 1964 to fill a gap left by the major languages then used in business (first FORTRAN and later COBOL). The language itself was formally introduced several years later.

RPG was designed to run on punched cards with a large IBM computer (either a mainframe or a minicomputer), although it will run with other manufacturers' machines as well. The system is still actively used in the business world. RPG is currently in its third version (RPG III). However, as in the case of COBOL, RPG might not survive recent developments in computer hardware and software. It could be replaced by newer fourth-generation languages that are designed for producing reports (such as FOCUS) or user-friendly applications packages whose use requires almost no training.

What to Read

Mullish, Henry, and Richard Kestenbaum (1982). *RPG and RPG II Primer: A Modern Approach.* New York: Holt, Rinehart and Winston.

Savvy

Savvy is a combination of hardware and software designed for business computing. The software includes the programming language itself, along with a program generator for data base management and a collection of business applications programs. Technically, Savvy is best classified as a query language, because the most important function of the system is to respond to commands or answer questions that draw upon an established data base. Savvy, which first appeared on the market in 1983, is designed and marketed by Excalibur Technologies Corporation of Albuquerque, New Mexico.

The program underlying Savvy is a pattern recognition system. When the user types in a comment or question, Savvy compares the digital pattern of the input with a collection of patterns that have earlier been placed in its memory. If the pattern you input exactly matches one of the patterns in the data base,

Savvy responds directly to the query or request. However, if there is a slight mismatch (e.g. because of a misspelled word or, more interestingly, because the user phrased the input somewhat differently from the way found in the data base), the Savvy program will attempt to guess what word or phrase in the data base most clearly matches your intention.

Savvy was designed to be everything from a spellling checker to a query language that accepts natural language input. Like more typical natural language front end systems such as Intellect, Themis, or Clout, the Savvy program will "understand" paraphrases of the same semantic intent (e.g. "Who are the top salesmen?" or "Give me the top salesmen" or "Who sold the most?"). However, while a language like Intellect handles paraphrase by doing an actual syntactic analysis of the input, Savvy attempts to match digital patterns with one another.

As a business system, Savvy has not enjoyed great commercial success. The explanation may have more to do with marketing strategies than with the conceptual design of the system itself. Savvy originally ran only on the Apple II series, hardly business machines. And originally, users had to purchase the entire system in order to get the Savvy language, all at a hefty price tag.

Nonetheless, the principle of pattern matching may itself prove to be quite important for computer languages of the future. Pattern matching seems to play an important role in both natural language learning and everyday language use. Often speakers don't syntactically analyze sentences, but rely instead on linear comparisons of the utterance with some "correct" model. Subsequent work on artificial intelligence may well take up this pattern-matching approach to the analysis of natural language and subsequent natural language front end programs.

What to Read

Lopiccola, Phil (1983). "AI for the Apple II?" *Popular Computing,* May, pp. 202–213.
Callamaras, Peter V. (1984). "Savvy," *Byte,* February, pp. 303–306.

SOLO

SOLO is a fairly new data base manipulation language developed at the Open University in England for use in a cognitive psychology course. The language was created to demonstrate computer models of human cognitive processes.

SOLO, which has affinities with both Logo and PROLOG, was designed to be as simple as possible from the user's perspective and to be embedded in a user-friendly environment. In Great Britain there is a growing tendency to use simple but powerful data base query languages based on LISP, PROLOG, or other artificial intelligence languages with university-level students in a multitude of disciplines (see the entry on POP).

What to Read

Eisenstadt, Marc (1983). "A User-Friendly Software Environment for the Novice Programmer," *Communications of ACM* 26 (December, no. 12):1058–1064.

Hasemer, Tony (1984). "A Very Friendly Software Environment for SOLO," in Masoud Yazdani, ed., *New Horizons in Educational Computing.* Chichester (Eng.): Ellis Horwood; New York: Halsted Press (division of John Wiley), pp. 84–100.

Turing

Turing is an imperative/algorithmic language created by Richard Holt, Jim Cordy, and J. N. P. Hume at the University of Toronto in 1982–83. The language is named after Alan Turing, the British mathematician and computer scientist who formulated the "Turing test" (for distinguishing between human beings and computers) and the notion of a Turing machine.

Turing was designed as a state-of-the-art computer language which would replace PL/1 for instructing undergraduates. The authors wanted a language that was at once more powerful and more modern than Pascal. Turing incorporates such notions as modularity and information hiding, good string-handling capabilities, and dynamic parameters and arrays. The language is also highly reliable and supports program verification. Versions of Turing run on DEC's VAX, IBM mainframe computers, and the IBM PC.

Given the newness of Turing, its use has not yet spread in the United States. Its most likely competitors are Modula-2 and Ada.

What to Read

Holt, R. C., and J. N. Hume (1984). *Introduction to Computer Science Using the Turing Programming Language.* Reston (Va.): Reston Publishing Company.

Holt, Richard (1984). "Turing: An Inside Look," *Computerworld,* May 14, In Depth, pp. 1–6.

Index

Bold type indicates major discussion

411

T